How to
Master Skills for the

TOEFL iBT

新托福考试专项进阶
——中级阅读

Reading

Intermediate

Timothy Hall | Arthur H. Milch | Denise McCormack | E2K

张洪伟，周希 译

群言出版社
Qunyan Press

图书在版编目(CIP)数据

新托福考试专项进阶. 中级阅读 / (美)哈尔(Hall, T.),(美)米尔奇(Milch, A. H.),(美)麦考马克 (McCormack, D.)编著;张洪伟,周希译. —北京:群言出版社,2009(2012.9重印)

ISBN 978-7-80080-985-9

Ⅰ. 新… Ⅱ.①哈…②米…③麦…④张…⑤周… Ⅲ.英语—阅读教学—高等教育—自学参考资料 Ⅳ. H310.41

中国版本图书馆 CIP 数据核字(2009)第 027376 号

版权登记:图字 01—2008—3945 号

新托福考试专项进阶——中级阅读

出 版 人　范　芳
责任编辑　周艳华
封面设计　大愚设计 ＋ 贾臻臻
出版发行　群言出版社(Qunyan Press)
地　　址　北京东城区东厂胡同北巷 1 号
邮政编码　100006
网　　站　www.qypublish.com
读者信箱　bj62605588@163.com
总 编 办　010—65265404　65138815
编 辑 部　010—65276609　65262436
发 行 部　010—62605588　62605019

经　　销　新华书店
读者服务　010—65220236　65265404　65263345
法律顾问　中济律师事务所
印　　刷　北京鑫丰华彩印有限公司

版　　次　2012 年 9 月第 1 版第 8 次印刷
开　　本　880mm×1230mm　1/16
印　　张　21.5
字　　数　330 千
书　　号　ISBN 978-7-80080-985-9
定　　价　38.00 元

Contents

Contents (Answer Book)

Introduction

A. Information on the TOEFL® iBT

1. The Format of the TOEFL® iBT

Section	Number of Questions	Timing	Score
Reading	• **3~5 Passages** - approximately 700 words each - 12~14 questions per passage	60~100 min.	30 points
Listening	• **2~3 Conversations** - 12~25 exchanges each (3 min.) - 5 questions per conversation • **4~6 Lectures** - 500~800 words each (3~5 min.) - 6 questions per lecture	60~90 min.	30 points
BREAK		10 min.	

Speaking	• **2 Independent Tasks**
	(preparation: 15 sec. / response: 45 sec.)
	① 1 personal experience
	② 1 personal choice/opinion
	
	• **2 Integrated Tasks:** Read-Listen-Speak
	(preparation: 30 sec. / response: 60 sec.)
	① 1 campus situation topic
	  - reading: 75~100 words (45 sec.)
	  - conversation: 150~180 words (60~80 sec.)
	② 1 academic course topic
	  - reading: 75~100 words (45 sec.)
	  - lecture: 150~220 words (60~90 sec.)
	
	• **2 Integrated Tasks:** Listen-Speak
	(preparation: 20 sec. / response: 60 sec.)
	① 1 campus situation topic
	  - conversation: 180~220 words (60~90 sec.)
	② 1 academic course topic
	  - lecture: 230~280 words (90~120 sec.)
		20 min.	30 points

Writing	• **1 Integrated Task:** Read-Listen-Write (20 min.) - reading: 230~300 words (3 min.) - lecture: 230~300 words (2 min.) - a summary of 150~225 words • **1 Independent Task** (30 min.) - a minimum 300-word essay	50 min.	30 points

2. What Is New about the TOEFL® iBT?

(1) The TOEFL® iBT is delivered through the Internet in secure test centers around the world at the same time.

(2) It tests all four language skills and is taken in the order of Reading, Listening, Speaking, and Writing, with a 10-minute break in the middle.

(3) The test is 4.0~4.5 hours long, and all of the four test sections will be completed in one day.

(4) Note-taking is allowed throughout the entire test, including the Reading section. At the end of the test, all notes are collected and destroyed at the test center.

(5) Compared with the computer-based test (CBT) and paper-based test (PBT), the TOEFL® iBT has no Structure section. Grammar is tested indirectly on questions and tasks in each section.

(6) In the Listening section, one lecture may be spoken with a British or Australian accent.

(7) There are integrated tasks requiring test takers to combine more than one language skill in the Speaking and Writing sections.

(8) In the Speaking section, test takers wear headphones and speak into a microphone when they respond. The responses are recorded and transmitted to ETS's Online Scoring Network.

(9) In the Writing section, test takers must type their responses. Handwriting is not possible.

(10) Test scores will be reported online. Test takers can see their scores online 15 business days after the test and also receive a copy of their score report by mail.

B. Information on the Reading Section

The Reading section of the TOEFL® iBT measures test takers' ability to understand university-level academic texts. This section has 3~5 passages, and the length of each passage is about 700 words. Some passages may have <u>underlined</u> words or phrases in shade. Test takers can click on them to see a definition or explanation. Test takers have to answer 12~14 questions per passage. 60~100 minutes are given to complete this section, including the time spent reading the passages and answering the questions.

1. Types of Reading Passages

(1) Exposition – Material that provides an explanation of a topic

(2) Argumentation – Material that presents a point of view about a topic and provides evidence to support it

(3) Historical narrative – An account of a past event or of a person's life, narrated or written by someone else

(1) Vocabulary (3~5 questions per set)
  _ This type of question asks you to identify the meanings of words and phrases in the reading passage.

(2) Reference (0~2 questions per set)
  _ This type of question asks you to identify the referential relationship between the words in the passage.

(3) Factual Information (3~6 questions per set)
  _ This type of question asks you to identify specific information that is explicitly stated in the passage.

(4) Negative Factual Information (0~2 questions per set)
  _ This type of question asks you to check what information is NOT mentioned in the passage.

(5) Sentence Simplification (0~1 question per set)
  _ This type of question asks you to choose the sentence that best paraphrases the essential information in the highlighted sentence.
  _ This is a new type of question introduced in the TOEFL® iBT.

Inference Questions

(6) Inference Questions (0~2 questions per set)
  _ This type of question asks you to identify an idea that is not explicitly stated in the passage.

(7) Rhetorical Purpose Questions (0~2 questions per set)
  _ This type of question asks you why the author uses particular words, phrases, or sentences.

(8) Insert Text Questions (0~1 question per set)
  _ This type of question provides an example sentence and asks you to decide where the best place for that sentence would be in the passage.

Reading to Learn Questions

(9) Prose Summary (1 question per set)
  _ This type of question asks you to complete a summary chart with major ideas from the passage.
  _ This question is worth up to 2 points, and partial credit is given.
  _ This type of question does not occur with a Fill in a Table question in a same passage.
  _ This is a new type of question introduced in the TOEFL® iBT.

(10) Fill in a Table (1 question per set)

_ This type of question asks you to identify and organize the major ideas of the passage into table categories.

_ This question is worth up to 3 points for tables with 5 correct answers and 4 points for tables with 7 correct answers. Partial credit is given.

_ This type of question does not occur with a Prose Summary question in one passage.

_ This is a new type of question introduced in the TOEFL® iBT.

2. Question Formats

There are three question formats in the Reading section:

(1) Four-choice questions with a single answer in traditional multiple-choice format

(2) Four-choice questions with a single answer that ask test takers to insert a sentence where it fits best in a passage

(3) "Reading to learn" questions with more than four choices and more than one answer

How to Use This Book

How to Master Skills for the TOEFL® iBT Reading Intermediate is designed to be used either as a textbook for a TOEFL® iBT reading preparation course or as a tool for individual learners who are preparing for the TOEFL® test on their own. With a total of 10 units, this book is organized to prepare you for the test with a comprehensive understanding of the test and thorough analysis of every question type. Each unit consists of 6 parts and provides a step-by-step program that provides question-solving strategies and the development of test-taking abilities. At the back of the book is a practice test of the Reading section of the TOEFL® iBT.

❶ Overview

This part is designed to prepare you for the type of question the unit covers. You will be given a full description of the question type and its application in the passage. You also will be given some useful tips as well as an illustrated introduction and sample.

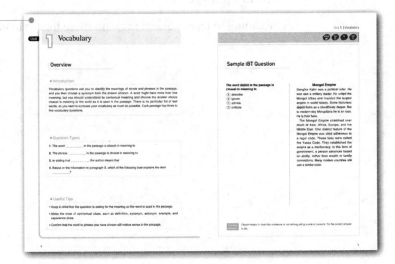

❷ Skill & Drill

The purpose of this section is to ensure that you understand the new types of questions that were described in the overview. You will be given a chance to confirm your understanding in brief texts before starting on the practice exercises. You will read some simple passages and answer the questions of a particular type. This part will help you learn how to deal with each type of question on the Reading section of the TOEFL® iBT.

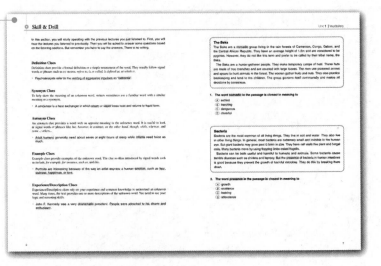

❸ Practice with Long Passages

This section is the second of the practice exercises in each unit. Six long passages are provided, and a time limit is also given for reading each passage. You first read the passage within a time limit and then solve the question or questions of the type that is mainly dealt with in the unit. Important words are also listed to help increase your understanding. Besides, a graphic organizer is provided to help you grasp the overall organization of each passage and understand important points.

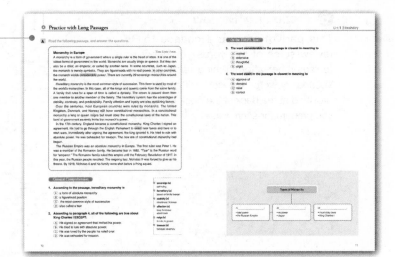

❹ Building Summary Skills

The purpose of this part is for you to understand the previous long passages thoroughly by completing the summaries of them. This will also help you enhance your ability of paraphrasing skills that are strongly recommended to those who are preparing for the TOEFL® iBT test.

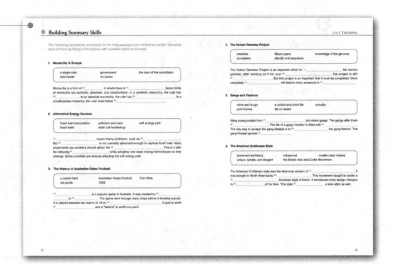

❺ Mini TOEFL iBT

This part gives you a chance to experience an actual TOEFL® iBT test in a shortened form. You will be given two passages with 6 questions each. The topics are similar to those on the actual TOEFL® test, as are the questions.

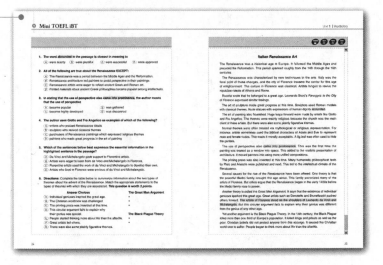

❻ Vocabulary Review

This part offers you a chance to review some of the words you need to remember after finishing each unit. Vocabulary words for each unit are also provided at the back of the book to help you prepare for each unit.

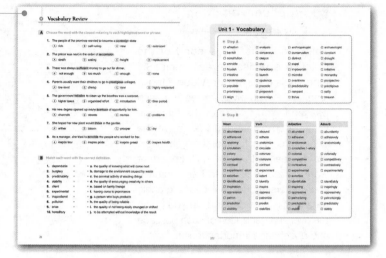

❼ Actual Test

This part offers a full practice test that is modeled on the Reading section of the TOEFL® iBT. This will familiarize you with the actual test format of the TOEFL® iBT.

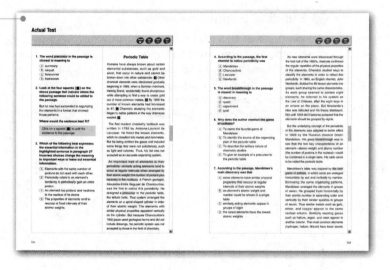

PART 1

Basic Comprehension

In this part, the reading comprehension questions include: vocabulary, reference, factual information, negative factual information, and sentence simplification. The learning objectives of these reading comprehension questions are to identify individual words, referential relations between the words in the passage, factual information, and essential sentences.

Unit 1

Vocabulary

1 Vocabulary

Overview

■ Introduction

Vocabulary questions ask you to identify the meanings of words and phrases in the passage, and you then choose a synonym from the answer choices. A word might have more than one meaning, but you should understand its contextual meaning and choose the answer choice closest in meaning to the word as it is used in the passage. There is no particular list of test words, so you need to increase your vocabulary as much as possible. Each passage has three to five vocabulary questions.

■ Question Types

1. The word _____ in the passage is closest in meaning to

2. The phrase _____ in the passage is closest in meaning to

3. In stating that _____, the author means that

4. Based on the information in paragraph X, which of the following best explains the term _____?

■ Useful Tips

• Keep in mind that the question is asking for the meaning as the word is used in the passage.

• Make the most of contextual clues, such as definition, synonym, antonym, example, and experience clues.

• Confirm that the word or phrase you have chosen still makes sense in the passage.

Sample iBT Question

The word depict in the passage is closest in meaning to

Ⓐ describe
Ⓑ ignore
Ⓒ admire
Ⓓ criticize

Mongol Empire

Genghis Kahn was a political ruler. He was also a military leader. He united the Mongol tribes and founded the largest empire in world history. Some historians depict Kahn as a bloodthirsty despot. But to modern-day Mongolians he is an icon. He is their hero.

The Mongol Empire stretched over much of Asia, Africa, Europe, and the Middle East. One distinct feature of the Mongol Empire was strict adherence to a legal code. These laws were called the Yassa Code. They established the empire as a meritocracy. In this form of government, a person advances based on ability, rather than wealth or family connections. Many modern countries still use a similar code.

 Depict means to describe someone or something using words or pictures. So the correct answer is (A).

The best way to deal with Vocabulary questions on the TOEFL® iBT is to know as much vocabulary as possible. But when you come across an unknown word while reading, it helps to use contextual clues to guess the meaning of the word.

Definition Clues

Definition clues provide a formal definition or a simple restatement of the word. They usually follow signal words or phrases such as *or, means, refers to, is, is called, is defined as,* or *which is.*

- Psychoanalysts *refer to* the venting of aggressive impulses as "catharsis."

Synonym Clues

To help show the meaning of an unknown word, writers sometimes use a familiar word with a similar meaning or a synonym.

- A condenser is a heat exchanger in which steam *or* vapor loses heat and returns to liquid form.

Antonym Clues

An antonym clue provides a word with an opposite meaning to the unknown word. It is useful to look at signal words or phrases like *but, however, in contrast, on the other hand, though, while, whereas,* and *some...; others...*

- Adult humans generally need about seven or eight hours of sleep *while* infants need twice as much.

Example Clues

Example clues provide examples of the unknown word. The clue is often introduced by signal words such as *include, for example, for instance, such as,* and *like.*

- Portraits are interesting because of the way an artist expresses a human emotion, *such as* fear, sadness, happiness, or love.

Experience/Description Clues

Experience/Description clues rely on your experience and common knowledge to understand an unknown word. Many times, the text provides one or more descriptions of the unknown word. You need to use your logic and reasoning skills.

- John F. Kennedy was a very charismatic president. People were attracted to his charm and enthusiasm.

The Baka

The Baka are a nomadic group living in the rain forests of Cameroon, Congo, Gabon, and the Central African Republic. They have an average height of 1.5m and are considered to be pygmies. However, they do not like this term and prefer to be called by their tribal name, the Baka.

The Baka are a hunter-gatherer people. They make temporary camps of huts. These huts are made of tree branches and are covered with large leaves. The men use poisoned arrows and spears to hunt animals in the forest. The women gather fruits and nuts. They also practice beekeeping and tend to the children. The group governs itself communally and makes all decisions by consensus.

1. **The word nomadic in the passage is closest in meaning to**

    (A) settled
    (B) traveling
    (C) dangerous
    (D) cheerful

Bacteria

Bacteria are the most common of all living things. They live in soil and water. They also live in other living things. In general, most bacteria are extremely small and invisible to the human eye. But giant bacteria may grow past 0.5mm in size. They have cell walls like plant and fungal cells. Many bacteria move by using flapping limbs called flagella.

Bacteria can be both useful and harmful to humans and animals. Some bacteria cause terrible diseases such as cholera and leprosy. But the presence of bacteria in human intestines is good because they prevent the growth of harmful microbes. They do this by breaking them down.

2. **The word presence in the passage is closest in meaning to**

    (A) growth
    (B) existence
    (C) bearing
    (D) attendance

Drought

A drought is an abnormally long spell of dry weather. It is a time when there is not enough water to support farming, urban, or environmental needs. It usually refers to an extended period of below-normal rainfall. But it can be caused by anything that reduces the amount of water circulation.

Humans cannot control the weather. So the causes that lead to drought cannot be stopped. The most common causes are lack of water and hot temperatures. Many scientists believe many recent droughts happened because of global warming. They claim that if we can reduce the damage done to the ozone layer, there will be fewer droughts.

3. The word spell in the passage is closest in meaning to

   Ⓐ charm
   Ⓑ zone
   Ⓒ signal
   Ⓓ period

Metaphor

A metaphor is a part of language that is a direct comparison between two unrelated things. The metaphor describes a first subject as being equal to the second subject in some way. There are many types of metaphors, such as mixed, active, and dead. A mixed metaphor combines two commonly used metaphors, to create a nonsensical image. An example of this is, "He stepped up to the plate and grabbed the bull by the horns." An active metaphor is not part of daily language, such as, "You are my sun." A dead metaphor is used to describe a metaphorical cliché, such as "to break the ice."

4. The word cliché in the passage is closest in meaning to

   Ⓐ indirect expression
   Ⓑ novel expression
   Ⓒ overused expression
   Ⓓ old-fashioned expression

Queen Elizabeth I

Queen Elizabeth I ruled England and Ireland. She sat on the throne from 1558 to 1603. She was also considered the Queen of France, but she had no power there. She was the fifth and final monarch of the Tudor Dynasty. Elizabeth was called the Virgin Queen because she never married.

The time of Elizabeth's reign is called the Elizabethan Era. Many great accomplishments took place under her reign. Shakespeare wrote his plays. Sir Francis Drake circled the globe. The English colonized North America. Shortly after her death, the American colony of Virginia was established. It was named in honor of the Virgin Queen.

5. **In stating that Sir Francis Drake circled the globe, the author means that he**

    Ⓐ drew a map

    Ⓑ measured a model globe

    Ⓒ traveled around the world

    Ⓓ ran in a circle

The Paramecium

The paramecium is an organism which is also known as a slipper because it has the shape of a slipper. Paramecia represent a group of single-celled organisms called the ciliate group. This is because their bodies are covered with cilia, which are thin tail-like limbs. Their constant motion allows the paramecium to move. The cell has a deep oral groove. This is a kind of mouth that is also filled with cilia. The mouth is used to expel water. Paramecia are commonly found in freshwater areas, especially in scum. They are attracted by acidic conditions.

6. **The word expel in the passage is closest in meaning to**

    Ⓐ push out

    Ⓑ pull in

    Ⓒ take in

    Ⓓ throw away

Practice with Long Passages

A Read the following passage, and answer the questions.

Monarchy in Europe

Time Limit: 3 min.

A monarchy is a form of government where a single ruler is the head of state. It is one of the oldest forms of government in the world. Monarchs are usually kings or queens. But they can also be a chief, an emperor, or called by another name. In some countries, such as Japan, the monarch is merely symbolic. They are figureheads with no real power. In other countries, the monarch wields considerable power. There are currently 29 sovereign monarchies around the world.

Hereditary monarchy is the most common style of succession. This form is used by most of the world's monarchies. In this case, all of the kings and queens come from the same family. A family that rules for a span of time is called a dynasty. The crown is passed down from one member to another member of the family. The hereditary system has the advantages of stability, continuity, and predictability. Family affection and loyalty are also stabilizing factors.

Over the centuries, most European countries were ruled by monarchs. The United Kingdom, Denmark, and Norway still have constitutional monarchies. In a constitutional monarchy a king or queen reigns but must obey the constitutional laws of the nation. This form of government severely limits the monarch's power.

In the 17th century, England became a constitutional monarchy. King Charles I signed an agreement. He had to go through the English Parliament to exact new taxes and laws or to start wars. Immediately after signing the agreement, the king ignored it. He tried to rule with absolute power. He was beheaded for treason. The new era of constitutional monarchy had begun.

The Russian Empire was an absolute monarchy in Europe. The first ruler was Peter I. He was a member of the Romanov family. He became tsar in 1682. "Tsar" is the Russian word for "emperor." The Romanov family ruled this empire until the February Revolution of 1917. In this year, the Russian people revolted. The reigning tsar, Nicholas II was forced to give up his throne. By 1918, Nicholas II and his family were shot before a firing squad.

General Comprehension

1. **According to the passage, hereditary monarchy is**

   (A) a form of absolute monarchy

   (B) a figurehead position

   (C) the most common style of succession

   (D) also called a tsar

2. **According to paragraph 4, all of the following are true about King Charles I EXCEPT:**

   (A) He signed an agreement that limited his power.

   (B) He tried to rule with absolute power.

   (C) He was loved by the people he ruled over.

   (D) He was beheaded for treason.

sovereign (a)
self-ruling

hereditary (a)
based on family lineage

stability (n)
steadiness; firmness

affection (n)
love; fondness; attachment

reign (v)
to rule; to govern

treason (n)
betrayal; treachery

On the TOEFL Test

3. **The word** considerable **in the passage is closest in meaning to**

   Ⓐ normal
   Ⓑ extensive
   Ⓒ thoughtful
   Ⓓ slight

4. **The word** exact **in the passage is closest in meaning to**

   Ⓐ approve of
   Ⓑ demand
   Ⓒ raise
   Ⓓ correct

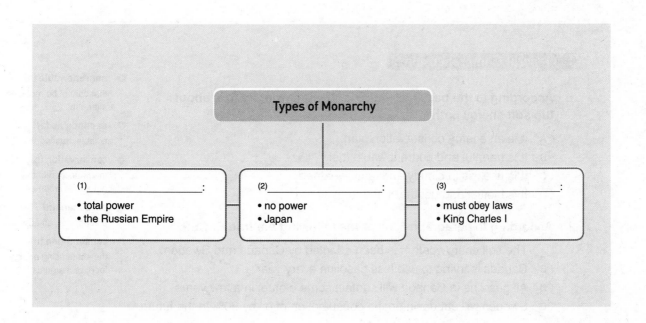

Types of Monarchy

(1)_____ :
• total power
• the Russian Empire

(2)_____ :
• no power
• Japan

(3)_____ :
• must obey laws
• King Charles I

Alternative Energy Sources

Time Limit: 2 min. 40 sec.

Fossil fuels are the cause of many problems. They create terrible pollution which leads to global warming. Many wars are fought to control oil and gas fields. Fossil fuels are also nonrenewable resources. They will be exhausted some day. Societies around the world suffer when fuel shortages occur.

Can solar power completely replace fossil fuels? Solar power is clean, safe, and inexpensive. But the idea of replacing fossil fuels with solar power alone is totally unrealistic. Current solar cell technology is not advanced enough. Solar cells are not dependable. They are useless in cloudy and rainy weather as well as at night. Also, they take up too much space. Then they fail to produce sufficient amounts of power.

The soft energy path is a good alternative to fossil fuel reliance. The soft energy path is an energy conservation plan. It is an alternative to the hard energy path. Hard energy is defined as harmful and nonrenewable. Fossil fuels and nuclear power are included. On the other hand, soft energy is defined as renewable and environmentally safe energy. Solar and wind power are soft energy. Biofuel and geothermal energy are also included.

There are many proponents of the soft energy path. They believe the solution lies in new energy production methods. The first step is to practice careful conservation in our use of hard energy technologies. Then, many new soft energy sources will be phased into use as soft energy technology improves.

Some critics claim this will damage all energy production. They feel fossil fuels are important. They want to control as much oil production as possible. They think fossil fuel consumption is good for industry.

Countries such as Canada and Sweden are taking the soft energy path. Canada is currently lessening its reliance on gasoline. In the next few years, all gasoline will contain a percentage of biofuel. Sweden has committed to decrease its reliance on oil by 40%. It says it can do this before the year 2020.

General Comprehension

1. **According to the passage, which of the following is true about the soft energy path?**
   - (A) It is an energy conservation plan.
   - (B) It is harmful and nonrenewable fuel.
   - (C) It is useless in cloudy and rainy weather.
   - (D) It is biofuel and geothermal energy.

2. **According to paragraph 6, all of the following are true EXCEPT:**
   - (A) The soft energy path has been adopted by Canada and Sweden.
   - (B) Canada is trying to use less gasoline every year.
   - (C) All gasoline in Canada will contain some biofuel in a few years.
   - (D) Sweden will cut down on the consumption of oil by 90% in the future.

nonrenewable (a)
that cannot be replaced after use

dependable (a)
reliable; trustworthy

conservation (n)
the protection of the natural environment

proponent (n)
a supporter; an advocate

consumption (n)
the act of using energy, food, or materials

On the TOEFL Test

3. **The word exhausted in the passage is closest in meaning to**

   Ⓐ wasted

   Ⓑ used up

   Ⓒ worn out

   Ⓓ burned

4. **In stating that many soft energy sources will be phased into use, the author means that they will**

   Ⓐ be an alternative to the hard energy path

   Ⓑ be used gradually

   Ⓒ be adopted by Sweden and Canada

   Ⓓ damage all energy production

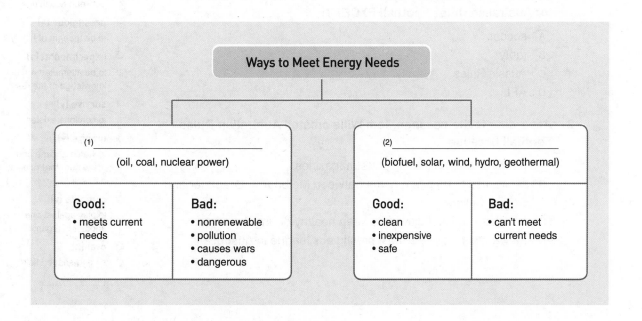

Ways to Meet Energy Needs

(1)_____
(oil, coal, nuclear power)

Good:
• meets current needs

Bad:
• nonrenewable
• pollution
• causes wars
• dangerous

(2)_____
(biofuel, solar, wind, hydro, geothermal)

Good:
• clean
• inexpensive
• safe

Bad:
• can't meet current needs

Read the following passage, and answer the questions.

The History of Australian Rules Football

Time Limit: 2 min. 40 sec.

Australian Rules Football is called by many nicknames. Lovers of the game just call it "football" or "footy." When contrasted with other forms of football, it is called "Aussie Rules" or "AFL." AFL stands for Australian Football League, which is the most prestigious league in Australia.

Australian Rules Football was created by Tom Wills in 1858. He wanted to create a sport that would keep cricket players fit through the winter. He began by writing a letter that explained his purpose to a sports magazine. It also called for the creation of a football club. In 1858, Wills and others played an experimental match that was the first game of Australian football. But few details about this match have survived.

On August 7, 1858, two important events for the game occurred. The Melbourne Football Club was founded. It was one of the world's first football clubs in any code. Also, a famous match between Melbourne Grammar School and Scotch College was played. It was umpired by Tom Wills. A second day of play took place on August 21, and then there was a third and final day on September 4. The two schools have competed every year since.

The game is played between two teams of 18 players on an oval that can also be used for cricket. These playing fields can be up to 185m long. This is almost four times the size of fields used in other forms of football.

A point called "a behind" is scored when the ball goes across the line and between a goal post and a behind post. A behind point is also scored if the ball is touched by any body part of either team's member as it passes between the goal posts. A goal is worth six points, and a behind is worth one point.

General Comprehension

1. According to paragraph 1, all of the following are nicknames for Australian Rules Football EXCEPT:

   (A) soccer
   (B) footy
   (C) Aussie Rules
   (D) AFL

2. According to the passage, Tom Wills created Australian Rules Football because

   (A) he liked contributing to sports magazines
   (B) he wanted to umpire a game between Melbourne Grammar and Scotch College
   (C) he wanted cricket players to keep healthy during the winter
   (D) he wanted to join the most prestigious league in Australia

contrast (v)
to show differences between two things

prestigious (a)
to be thought of highly

experimental (a)
to be attempted without knowledge of the result

survive (v)
to continue existence

umpire (v)
to watch a game and make sure that rules are not broken

compete (v)
to play against one another in a game

oval (n)
an egg-shaped field

On the TOEFL Test

3. **The phrase stands for in the passage is closest in meaning to**

   Ⓐ supports

   Ⓑ recalls

   Ⓒ endures

   Ⓓ represents

4. **The phrase in any code in the passage is closest in meaning to**

   Ⓐ of any style

   Ⓑ in any order

   Ⓒ in any country

   Ⓓ of any name

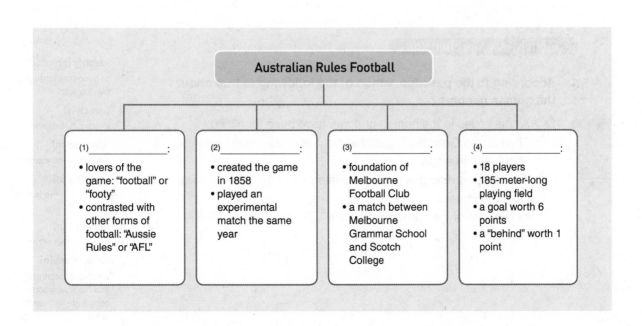

Australian Rules Football

(1)_____:
- lovers of the game: "football" or "footy"
- contrasted with other forms of football: "Aussie Rules" or "AFL"

(2)_____:
- created the game in 1858
- played an experimental match the same year

(3)_____:
- foundation of Melbourne Football Club
- a match between Melbourne Grammar School and Scotch College

(4)_____:
- 18 players
- 185-meter-long playing field
- a goal worth 6 points
- a "behind" worth 1 point

Read the following passage, and answer the questions.

The Human Genome Project

Time Limit: 2 min. 40 sec.

The Human Genome Project (HGP) is a very important effort in science. It attempts to map and sequence the genome. There are 3 billion codes in the human genome. All of these have been identified. But they still need to be sequenced. The project will also identify all the genes present.

The international HGP was launched in 1986 by Charles DeLisi. A 1987 report stated, "The ultimate goal of this initiative is to understand the human genome. Knowledge of the human genome is necessary to the continuing progress of medicine and other health sciences, as human anatomy has been for the present state of medicine."

This $3 billion project was formally founded in 1990. It was expected to take 15 years. The international consortium included geneticists from around the world.

Recently the press has made claims that the genome map is complete. But, as of 2006, it is not. The map is not expected to be finished for many more years. The central regions of each chromosome are highly repetitive DNA sequences. It is very difficult for current technology to put these in order.

The HGP has completed mapping about 92% of the genome now. Hopes are high for completion in the near future. The task is becoming easier as mapping and sequencing technologies improve.

A clear map of the genome will provide doctors with much important information. It will allow them to make many medical advances. This knowledge will lead to significant advances in the early diagnosis of breast cancer. It will also improve our ability to deal with liver and Alzheimer's disease.

Analysis of the genome promises to open new avenues in the study of human evolution. The sequence of human DNA is stored on the Internet. It is housed in a database called Genebank. This data is available for viewing by anyone.

General Comprehension

1. **According to the passage, which of the following is true about the human genome?**
   - (A) All the codes in the human genome have been identified.
   - (B) The Human Genome Project has helped people learn more about human anatomy.
   - (C) The genome map has been completed recently by the Human Genome Project.
   - (D) Knowledge of the human genome will enable doctors to cure breast cancer.

identify (v)
to become thoroughly familiar with

launch (v)
to start; to begin

progress (n)
development; advance

anatomy (n)
the parts of the human body

initiative (n)
an organized effort

consortium (n)
a group of organizations that have agreed to cooperate with each other

2. **According to the passage, all of the following people would get help from the Human Genome Project EXCEPT:**

   Ⓐ A middle-aged woman with breast cancer
   Ⓑ An old man with senile dementia
   Ⓒ A child with autism
   Ⓓ A middle-aged man with a liver problem

On the TOEFL Test

3. **In stating that the codes in the human genome still need to be sequenced, the author means that they still have to**

   Ⓐ be taken apart
   Ⓑ be put in order
   Ⓒ be discovered
   Ⓓ be processed

4. **In stating that analysis of the genome promises to open new avenues in the study of human evolution, the author means that it helps to**

   Ⓐ build new roads
   Ⓑ create new possibilities
   Ⓒ save people
   Ⓓ try new methods

The Human Genome Project

- What – a scientific effort to map and sequence (1)_____

- Why – to advance medicine and other health sciences

- When – formally founded in (2)_____

- Current state – about 92% of the human genome mapped

- Future benefits:
  – early diagnosis of breast cancer possible
  – improved treatment of (3)_____
  – progress in the study of human evolution

Read the following passage, and answer the questions.

Gangs and Violence

Time Limit: 2 min. 50 sec.

Many young people from disadvantaged social classes join gangs. Gangs are groups of individuals who share a common identity. Some anthropologists believe the gang structure is one of the most ancient forms of human organization. Gangs are often associated with criminal activities.

Street gangs tend to be populated with young people from low income or impoverished homes. In contrast, organized crime gangs such as the Italian-American Mafia usually occupy the middle or upper class stratum of society.

Gangs usually take over a territory in a city or suburb. They call this territory their "turf." One common criminal activity on their turf is "providing protection." This is a common style of extortion in which a gang provides protection from its own members for money.

Since the 1970s, many gangs have been associated with selling drugs. The most problematic substance associated with gangs is crack cocaine. They are also known to commit burglaries, car theft, and armed robberies.

Individual members of gangs are usually referred to as gangsters. These members frequently join in their teens. This is often the result of early exposure to drugs and violence. Low-income housing projects and poor neighborhoods are ideal locations for gangs to exist and thrive.

Sometimes, new recruits for a gang are "jumped in." This is when the other gang members beat up the new recruit to test their dedication and loyalty. Recruits must also sometimes commit a crime such as robbery, rape, or murder to gain entry.

Once in a gang, there are only two ways for a member to quit. One way is for the member to die. The other way is for the member to desert the gang. The deserting of a gang usually gains the deserter a death sentence from the other gang members.

Members of gangs have a very short life expectancy. Because of this lifestyle, morality is often ignored. Criminal acts of violence are not a taboo. In fact, violence is often seen as a way to gain honor and prestige within the gang.

General Comprehension

1. **According to the passage, all of the following are mentioned as illegal activities connected with gangs EXCEPT:**

   Ⓐ selling drugs
   Ⓑ lending money
   Ⓒ killing people
   Ⓓ stealing cars

be associated with (phr)
be connected with

populate (v)
to occupy; to inhabit

extortion (n)
the act of getting money by threatening someone

exposure (n)
contact

thrive (v)
to prosper; to flourish

2. **According to the passage, how can a person stop being a gang member?**
    Click on 2 answers.
    A leave the gang
    B fight against other members
    C recruit a new member
    D stop living

On the TOEFL Test

3. **The word disadvantaged in the passage is closest in meaning to**
    A disabled
    B unhappy
    C poor
    D weak

4. **In stating that new recruits for a gang are "jumped in," the author means that they are**
    A hit by other members
    B asked to build up their physical strength
    C ordered to steal money
    D forced to show their courage

Some Important Facts About Gangs

- groups of (1)_____
- controlling an area or "turf"
- (2)_____: drug dealing, car theft, burglary, extortion, murder
- gang areas: low income housing projects and poor neighborhood
- gang members usually "jumped in"
- to quit gang: (3)_____
- low life expectancy
- violence is the only way to gain prestige

Read the following passage, and answer the questions.

The American Craftsman Style

Time Limit: 2 min. 50 sec.

The American Craftsman style is a type of design. It was popular from 1900 to the 1930s. It changed the style of building in the United States.

The craftsman style originally began in Europe. The British Arts and Crafts style arose in the 1860s. The unique designs of this movement tried to ennoble the common person. Hand-made items were preferred because they were thought better than items that were mass-produced. But this British style was still Victorian. It still only served the wealthiest clients.

In 1897 a group of Boston architects brought these handcrafted styles to America. They planned a show of craft objects, which turned out to be a huge success. Here they realized the potential and established the Society of Arts and Crafts on June 28, 1897. Its slogan was "to develop and encourage higher standards in the handicrafts."

The American style began as the Victorian Era was ending. It emphasized handmade work. Originality and simplicity were highly valued. Local materials and the quality of the handicraft were very important. These traits were meant to dignify the modest homes of the middle class.

These simple designs used glass and wood that were produced locally. They were also very elegant. The metalwork was a reaction to Victorian opulence. The increase of mass-produced housing items was rejected. The American Craftsman used clean lines. It also relied on sturdy structure. Natural materials were always used in these houses if possible.

This style introduced many changes to the average American home. New designs were made for families without servants. This was a trait of the new middle class. The kitchen went from being a hidden room to a prominent one. Another development was the breakfast nook. This new area provided the family with a place to gather at any time of day.

Also, inspirational to the Craftsman style were the Shaker and Mission designs. The American Craftsman style led to the Art Deco movement of the 1930s.

General Comprehension

1. **According to the passage, the American Craftsman style is a type of**

    (A) Shaker and Mission design
    (B) house made for families with servants
    (C) design which was popular from 1900 to the 1930s
    (D) breakfast nook

2. **According to paragraph 6, all of the following are true about the American Craftsman style EXCEPT:**

    (A) The breakfast nook provided the family with a place to gather.
    (B) The kitchen became a more prominent room.
    (C) This style did not make any changes to the middle-class American home.
    (D) Houses were designed for a new middle class with no servants.

- **originally** (ad)
  at first; in the beginning
- **arise** (v)
  to happen
- **unique** (a)
  very special or unusual
- **potential** (n)
  possibility
- **sturdy** (a)
  durable; well-built
- **nook** (n)
  a small quiet place set back from the rest of a room
- **inspirational** (a)
  motivating; encouraging creativity

3. **In stating that the unique designs of this movement tried to** ennoble the common person, **the author means that the designs tried to**

   Ⓐ make ordinary people rich
   Ⓑ become very popular among common people
   Ⓒ raise ordinary people to royalty
   Ⓓ offer dignity to normal people

4. **The word** opulence **in the passage is closest in meaning to**

   Ⓐ richness
   Ⓑ greed
   Ⓒ ugliness
   Ⓓ distaste

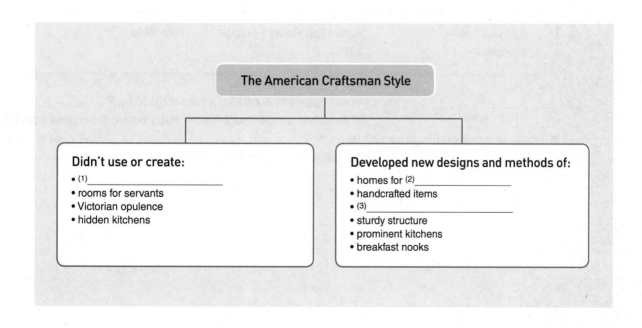

The American Craftsman Style

Didn't use or create:
- (1)_____
- rooms for servants
- Victorian opulence
- hidden kitchens

Developed new designs and methods of:
- homes for (2)_____
- handcrafted items
- (3)_____
- sturdy structure
- prominent kitchens
- breakfast nooks

Building Summary Skills

The following summaries are based on the long passages you worked on earlier. Complete each of them by filling in the blanks with suitable words or phrases.

1. Monarchy in Europe

> a single ruler   government   the laws of the constitution
>
> total power   no power

Monarchy is a form of (1)_____ in which there is (2)_____. Some forms of monarchy are symbolic, absolute, and constitutional. In a symbolic monarchy, the ruler has (3)_____. In an absolute monarchy, the ruler has (4)_____. In a constitutional monarchy, the ruler must follow (5)_____.

2. Alternative Energy Sources

> fossil fuel consumption   pollution and wars   soft energy path
>
> fossil fuels   solar cell technology

(1)_____ cause many problems, such as (2)_____.
But (3)_____ is not currently advanced enough to replace fossil fuels. Many proponents say societies should adopt the (4)_____. This is a plan for reducing (5)_____ while adopting new clean energy technologies as they emerge. Some countries are already adopting the soft energy path.

3. The History of Australian Rules Football

> a cricket field   Australian Rules Football   Tom Wills
>
> six points   1858

(1)_____ is a popular game in Australia. It was created by (2)_____
_____ in (3)_____. The game went through many steps before it became popular.
It is played between two teams of 18 on (4)_____. A goal is worth
(5)_____, and a "behind" is worth one point.

22

4. **The Human Genome Project**

> medicine   fifteen years   knowledge of the genome
> incomplete   identify and sequence

The Human Genome Project is an important effort to (1)_____ the human genome. After working on it for over (2)_____, the project is still (3)_____. But this project is so important that it must be completed. Once completed, (4)_____ will lead to many advances in (5)_____.

5. **Gangs and Violence**

> crime and drugs   a violent and short life   morality
> poor homes   die or desert

Many young people from (1)_____ join street gangs. The gangs offer them (2)_____. The life of a gang member is filled with (3)_____. The only way to escape the gang lifestyle is to (4)_____ the gang forever. The gang lifestyle ignores (5)_____.

6. **The American Craftsman Style**

> prominent architects   influenced   middle-class homes
> unique, simple, and elegant   the British Arts and Crafts Movement

The American Craftsman style was the American version of (1)_____. It was brought to North America by (2)_____. This movement sought to create a (3)_____ American style of home. It introduced many design changes to (4)_____ of the time. This style (5)_____ a later style as well.

1. **The word abounded in the passage is closest in meaning to**
   - (A) were scanty
   - (B) were plentiful
   - (C) were successful
   - (D) were approved

2. **All of the following are true about the Renaissance EXCEPT:**
   - (A) The Renaissance was a period between the Middle Ages and the Reformation.
   - (B) Renaissance architecture led painters to avoid perspective in their paintings.
   - (C) Renaissance artists were eager to reflect ancient Greek and Roman art.
   - (D) Printed materials about ancient Greek philosophies became popular among intellectuals.

3. **In stating that the use of perspective also came into prominence, the author means that the use of perspective**
   - (A) became popular
   - (B) was gathered
   - (C) became highly developed
   - (D) was discovered

4. **The author uses Giotto and Fra Angelico as examples of which of the following?**
   - (A) writers who praised Renaissance ideals
   - (B) sculptors who revived classical themes
   - (C) purchasers of Renaissance paintings which expressed religious themes
   - (D) painters who made great progress in the art of painting

5. **Which of the sentences below best expresses the essential information in the highlighted sentence in the passage?**
   - (A) Da Vinci and Michelangelo gave support to Florentine artists.
   - (B) Artists were eager to learn from da Vinci and Michelangelo in Florence.
   - (C) Florentine artists used the work of da Vinci and Michelangelo to develop their own.
   - (D) Artists who lived in Florence were envious of da Vinci and Michelangelo.

6. **Directions:** Complete the table below to summarize information about the two types of theories about the advent of the Renaissance. Match the appropriate statements to the types of theories with which they are associated. *This question is worth 3 points.*

Answer Choices	The Great Man Argument
(A) Individual geniuses inspired the great age.	•
(B) The Christian worldview was challenged.	•
(C) The printing press was invented at this time.	•
(D) This circular argument fails to explain why their genius was special.	**The Black Plague Theory**
(E) People started thinking more about life than the afterlife.	•
(F) Great artists led others.	•
(G) There were also some plainly figurative themes.	

Italian Renaissance Art

The Renaissance was a historical age in Europe. It followed the Middle Ages and preceded the Reformation. This period spanned roughly from the 14th through the 16th centuries.

The Renaissance was characterized by new techniques in the arts. Italy was the focal point of these changes, and the city of Florence became the center for this age of enlightenment. The culture in Florence was classical. Artists longed to revive the republican ideals of Athens and Rome.

Rucellai wrote that he belonged to a great age. Leonardo Bruni's *Panegyric to the City of Florence* expressed similar feelings.

The art of sculpture made great progress at this time. Sculptors used Roman models with classical themes. Nude statues with expressions of human dignity abounded.

The art of painting also flourished. Huge leaps forward were made by artists like Giotto and Fra Angelico. The themes were mainly religious because the church was the main client of these artists. But there were also some plainly figurative themes.

Normal themes were often treated via mythological or religious representation. For instance, artists sometimes used the biblical characters of Adam and Eve to represent male and female nudes. This made it morally acceptable. A fig leaf was often used to hide the genitals.

The use of perspective also came into prominence. This was the first time the painting was treated as a window into space. This added to the realistic presentation of architecture. It moved painters into using more unified compositions.

The printing press was also invented at this time. Many humanistic philosophical texts by Plato and Aristotle were published and read. This led to the intellectual climate of the Renaissance.

Several causes for the rise of the Renaissance have been offered. One theory is that the powerful Medici family brought this age about. This family patronized many of the artists of Florence. But critics argue that the Renaissance began in the early 1400s before the Medici family rose to power.

Another theory is called the Great Man Argument. It says that the existence of individual geniuses sparked this great age. Great artists such as Donatello and Brunelleschi pushed others forward. The artists of Florence stood on the shoulders of Leonardo da Vinci and Michelangelo. But this circular argument fails to explain why their genius was different from the genius of any other age.

Yet another argument is the Black Plague Theory. In the 14th century, the Black Plague killed more than one third of Europe's population. It killed kings and priests as well as the poor. Christian beliefs did not protect anyone from this scourge. It caused the Christian world view to suffer. People began to think more about life than the afterlife.

7. The word rampant in the passage is closest in meaning to

 (A) serious
 (B) widespread
 (C) uncommon
 (D) increasing

8. According to paragraph 1, all of the following are true EXCEPT:

 (A) The French Revolution was a significant event in Western history.
 (B) Absolute monarchs controlled France before the revolution.
 (C) The French people formed a new government after the revolution.
 (D) The Roman Catholic Church welcomed the revolution.

9. According to the passage, which of the following is NOT true of the factors that led to the revolution?

 (A) Old rulers were destroyed by their rigid ways.
 (B) The rising middle class joined the workers and poor people.
 (C) Napoleon started a group that began the revolution.
 (D) Enlightenment ideas influenced the people.

10. Which of the following can be inferred about the guillotine?

 (A) It was a chair for royalty to sit upon.
 (B) It was highly regarded by the king of France.
 (C) It was a device used to enact death sentences.
 (D) It was used to chop off the hands of criminals.

11. According to the passage, why did some noblemen flee the country?

 (A) Because they were in great danger
 (B) Because they did not like living a lower-class lifestyle
 (C) Because the Roman Catholic Church had too much power
 (D) Because King Louis XVI was sentenced to death

12. In stating that Queen Marie Antoinette followed him, the author means that the queen

 (A) walked behind him
 (B) was also killed
 (C) went to jail for life
 (D) became the new king

The French Revolution

The French Revolution was an important period in the history of Western Civilization. During this time, France's absolute monarchy was replaced with a republican government. The Roman Catholic Church was also forced to give up much of its power.

France would still swing between republic, empire, and monarchy for 75 years after the revolution ended. But this event is seen as a major turning point in the age of democracy.

Many political, social, and economic factors led to the revolution. The old rulers were destroyed by their own rigidity. The rising middle class allied itself with workers and the poor. They were influenced by the ideas of the Enlightenment.

In the months before the revolution, food was scarce. The price of bread was so high that workers could not afford it. Unemployment was rampant. Those who were caught stealing risked being beheaded by the guillotine. King Louis XVI failed to deal with these problems effectively.

As the revolution proceeded, the king began to fight with his officials, which led to much bloodshed. The national debt was out of control, and taxes were too high.

By this time, King Louis XVI tried to have the National Assembly closed. So, they had their meeting on a tennis court and vowed not to take a break until France had a constitution.

On July 11, 1789, King Louis tried to banish the reformist minister, Necker. Many of the citizens of Paris flew into open rebellion. On July 14th, they stormed the Bastille prison and killed its governor. They freed criminals and killed the mayor of Paris. The frightened king signed an agreement to give the people a constitution. This saved him for a while.

The slogan of the revolution was, "Liberty, equality, fraternity, or death!" This slogan is still used. It has become the rallying cry for people trying to overthrow oppressive governments.

The noblemen of France were not safe. Some tried wearing their servants' clothes while many others fled the country. Many changes took place. Towns lost their powers of heavy taxation, and the church lost most of its power and land.

By 1793, King Louis XVI was condemned to death. He was charged with conspiracy against public liberty and the general safety. On January 21, his head was chopped off by the guillotine. On October 16, Queen Marie Antoinette followed him.

By 1795, a new constitution was ratified. It installed a new legislature called the Directory. It consisted of 500 representatives. During this time, a general named Napoleon Bonaparte gained much power. By 1799, he staged a coup, and five years later, he declared himself emperor. This brought the republican phase of the French Revolution to a close.

Vocabulary Review

A Choose the word with the closest meaning to each highlighted word or phrase.

1. The people of the province wanted to become a sovereign state.
   - (A) rich
   - (B) self-ruling
   - (C) new
   - (D) colonized

2. The prince was next in the order of succession.
   - (A) death
   - (B) eating
   - (C) height
   - (D) replacement

3. There was always sufficient money to go out for dinner.
   - (A) not enough
   - (B) too much
   - (C) enough
   - (D) none

4. Parents usually want their children to go to prestigious colleges.
   - (A) low-level
   - (B) cheap
   - (C) new
   - (D) highly respected

5. The government initiative to clean up the beaches was a success.
   - (A) higher taxes
   - (B) organized effort
   - (C) introduction
   - (D) time period

6. His new degree opened up many avenues of opportunity for him.
   - (A) channels
   - (B) streets
   - (C) names
   - (D) problems

7. She hoped her new plant would thrive in the garden.
   - (A) wither
   - (B) bloom
   - (C) prosper
   - (D) dry

8. As a manager, she tried to ennoble the people who worked for her.
   - (A) inspire fear
   - (B) inspire pride
   - (C) inspire greed
   - (D) inspire health

B Match each word with the correct definition.

1. dependable   •   • **a.** the quality of knowing what will come next
2. burglary   •   • **b.** damage to the environment caused by waste
3. predictability   •   • **c.** the criminal activity of stealing things
4. stability   •   • **d.** the quality of encouraging creativity in others
5. client   •   • **e.** based on family lineage
6. experimental   •   • **f.** having come to prominence
7. inspirational   •   • **g.** a person who buys products
8. pollution   •   • **h.** the quality of being reliable
9. arise   •   • **i.** the quality of not being easily changed or shifted
10. hereditary   •   • **j.** to be attempted without knowledge of the result

Unit 2

Reference

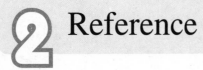

Reference

Overview

■ Introduction

Reference questions ask you to understand the relationship between a pronoun and the word which the pronoun refers to. Usually, personal pronouns such as *it, its, they, their,* and *them* are tested on the TOEFL® iBT. Sometimes other reference words such as *which, this, one, the former,* and *the latter* are also asked.

■ Question Types

1. The word _____ in the passage refers to

2. The phrase _____ in the passage refers to

■ Useful Tips

• The referent (the word to which a pronoun refers) usually appears before the pronoun in the same sentence or shows up in an earlier sentence. Sometimes, however, the referent might be found after the pronoun.

• Substitute your answer for the highlighted word or words in the passage.

• Make sure that your answer is the same number (singular or plural), gender (male or female), and case (first, second, or third person) as the highlighted pronoun.

Sample iBT Question

The word they in the passage refers to

(A) floods

(B) effects

(C) storms

(D) humans

Hurricanes

The scientific name for a hurricane is a tropical cyclone. It is fueled by the heat that is released when moist air rises and condenses. Hurricanes rotate counter-clockwise in the northern hemisphere and clockwise in the southern.

Hurricanes can produce extremely strong winds, tornadoes, heavy rain, and huge waves called storm surges. The heavy rains and huge waves create giant floods. Though the effects of these storms on humans can be catastrophic, they are also known to relieve drought conditions.

Hurricanes also carry heat away from the tropics. This is an important part of global circulation and is the way balance is maintained in the Earth's troposphere.

The highlighted word *they* is a part of the sentence which explains the effects of hurricanes on human beings. So, the pronoun *they* refers to the word *storms*, which is mentioned earlier in the same sentence. The correct answer is (C).

Skill & Drill

In order to deal with Reference questions, you need to understand the relationships between pronouns and the words which they refer to. There are four kinds of referential relationships which are asked on the TOEFL® iBT.

Personal Pronouns

Personal pronouns refer back to someone or something previously mentioned in the passage. Sometimes they can refer forward to what is mentioned later in the passage. On the TOEFL® iBT, third-person pronouns such as *it, its, they, their,* and *them* are frequently asked.

- Capuchins crack <u>walnuts</u> by repeatedly pounding them with stones.
- When it was first introduced in Europe, <u>coffee</u> was sold in pharmacies as a medicinal remedy.

Demonstratives

Demonstratives are pronouns or adjectives pointing out which item is being referred to. In English, they include *this, that, these,* and *those.* Sometimes *the former* and *the latter* are also asked on the TOEFL® iBT.

- Although the <u>initial cost</u> of a timber house is less than that of one made of brick or concrete, the long-term expense is greater.
- An organization designed to accomplish some task is called a <u>utilitarian organization</u>. Businesses are examples of this type.

Relative Pronouns

Relative pronouns such as *which, that, who, whose,* and *whom* introduce a clause that modifies the noun or noun phrase right before them. Sometimes *which* can refer to the entire previous clause.

- Penicillin kills a wide variety of <u>bacteria</u>, many of which cause disease in humans.
- In the early 1850s, many <u>daguerreotypists</u> were practicing in the United States, most of whom were in the business to make money, not art.

Indefinite Pronouns

Indefinite pronouns refer to an unknown or undetermined person, place, or thing. Indefinite pronouns include words with *some, any, every,* or *no* (e.g. *someone, anyone, everyone,* and *no one*) and *one, another, some, others, each,* and *none.*

- Diffusion is the process of introducing cultural elements from one <u>society</u> into another.
- By looking at examples of <u>atoms</u>, one discovers that each contains an equal number of electrons and protons in the nucleus.
- Lactose, a sugar present in milk, is one of the simple <u>sugars</u> used in food preparations for infants.

The Formation of Fog

The Fog is a cloud in contact with the ground. It only differs from other clouds in that it touches the Earth's surface. Most types of fog form when the relative humidity reaches 100% at ground level. Fog can form suddenly. It can dissipate just as rapidly, depending on what side of the dew point the temperature is on. Evaporation and precipitation fog are two kinds. The former is caused by water changing into gas very quickly while the other is caused by the release of water.

The foggiest place on the Earth is the Grand Banks of Newfoundland, Canada. Frequent fog in this area is caused by the meeting of the cold Labrador Current from the north and the much warmer Gulf Stream from the south.

1. **The phrase the other in the passage refers to**

   (A) evaporation fog
   (B) precipitation fog
   (C) release of water
   (D) water changing into gas

The Dragonfly

The dragonfly is an insect with large, multi-faceted eyes that allow 360 degrees of vision. It has two pairs of strong, transparent wings and a stretched-out body.

Dragonflies usually eat mosquitoes, flies, and other small insects. Many humans like them because they feed on these pests. Dragonflies live near lakes, ponds, streams, and wetlands. Their larvae, known as nymphs, are aquatic.

The life cycle of a dragonfly, from egg to the death of the adult, can last anywhere from six months to six or seven years. Most of this life cycle is spent in the larval state. During this stage, the nymph uses its gills to breathe and eats tadpoles or fish.

2. **The word them in the passage refers to**

   (A) dragonflies
   (B) mosquitoes
   (C) flies
   (D) insects

Ecology

Ecology is the study of living things in their habitats. It studies why they live in a certain area and how many of a species can survive in one place. It also looks at a species' interactions with other living things.

The environment of a living thing includes various physical factors. Some such factors are sunlight and climate. Geology is another factor. The other living things that share a habitat make up yet another factor.

Ecology is a broad science. One branch is behavior ecology. It looks at the way a single living thing adapts to its habitat. Population ecology studies a single species. There are many more branches of this science.

3. **The phrase this science in the passage refers to**

   Ⓐ geology
   Ⓑ ecology
   Ⓒ behavior ecology
   Ⓓ population ecology

Hypothesis

A hypothesis is a suggested explanation of an event that is not already understood by science. It suggests a possible connection between two or more phenomena in a reasoned way. Scientists base hypotheses on their observations or on theories.

The scientific method requires that one can test a hypothesis. Many members of the scientific community demand that a hypothesis be falsifiable. This means that it can possibly be proven false.

A famous example posits a man who goes to a new country and sees only white sheep. He forms a hypothesis that all the sheep in this country are white. But if one black sheep is observed, the hypothesis would be proven false.

4. **The word it in the passage refers to**

   Ⓐ scientific method
   Ⓑ scientific community
   Ⓒ hypothesis
   Ⓓ example

Newton's Laws of Motion

Newton's Laws of Motion are three physical laws. To understand the first law, imagine an apple resting on a table. It remains at rest until and unless it is pushed.

For the second law, imagine a hand pushing the same apple softly, causing it to move just a little. If the hand hits it with increased force, the force will make it hit a wall in the direction and with the momentum with which it was hit.

An example of Newton's third law is the reaction of the apple hitting the wall. There must be an opposite and equal reaction for every action. In this case, the reaction could be a dent in the wall or the apple exploding into bits.

5. **The word it in the passage refers to**

   (A) hand
   (B) apple
   (C) force
   (D) momentum

Biological Kingdoms

In 1735, Carolus Linnaeus published a book about kingdoms. In his book, he distinguished two kingdoms of living things: the animal kingdom and the vegetable kingdom. Everything on Earth fell into one or the other. He later created a third kingdom for minerals.

Years later, bacteria were discovered. Biologists realized that they did not fit into any of the three kingdoms. Another kingdom was named for them. This was called the kingdom Monera.

As science progressed and learned more about living things, new kingdoms were needed. In 1969, Robert Whittaker recognized a fifth kingdom. This kingdom was named for Fungi. By 1980, yet another kingdom was named. It was named to separate further microscopic organisms.

6. **The word them in the passage refers to**

   (A) minerals
   (B) bacteria
   (C) biologists
   (D) kingdoms

Practice with Long Passages

A Read the following passage, and answer the questions.

El Nino and La Nina

Time Limit: 3 min.

El Nino and La Nina are phenomena that take place between the ocean and the atmosphere on a global scale. These are major temperature changes in the surface waters of the tropical Pacific Ocean. El Nino indicates a rise of 0.5℃ or more. La Nina indicates a drop of the same degree. These changes must be sustained for a period longer than five months to be called El Nino or La Nina.

Many of the countries affected by these climatic changes are third-world nations in South America and Africa. Their economies are largely dependent on the farming and fishing sectors. These industries are a major source of food supply, employment, and foreign exchange. So, new methods for predicting these climatic changes can have a great socio-economic impact for these countries.

El Nino/La Nina episodes usually occur irregularly. In recent years, they have happened every 2 to 7 years. They usually last for one or two years. The effects of El Nino are very wide ranging. Many places experience weather that is the reverse of their normal climate. Some areas even experience terrible flooding due to heavy rainfall. There are also many forest fires because of heavy drought. On the other hand, the effects of La Nino begin to develop worldwide. During a La Nina, trade winds can become very strong, and an abnormal accumulation of colder than normal water can occur in the Central and Eastern Pacific.

In the normal Pacific pattern of ocean atmosphere system, equatorial winds gather, and then warm water pools towards the west. Cold water upswells along the South American coast. This brings fish up the coast, where they support the local fishing industry, because they follow the cool, nutrient-rich water.

When El Nino takes effect, the warm water flows toward the South American coast. The absence of cold upswelling increases warming. This sends the fish population out to sea instead of swimming along the coast. These conditions severely damage the local fishing industries.

The causes of El Nino and La Nina are still undiscovered. But many scientists are dedicating their careers to understanding these global weather phenomena better.

General Comprehension

1. **According to the passage, the causes of El Nino and La Nina are**

   (A) not yet discovered
   (B) normal ocean atmosphere patterns
   (C) cold water that upswells along the South American coast
   (D) heavy drought and flooding

○ **phenomenon (n)**
a natural occurrence that requires scientific explanation

○ **impact (n)**
a strong effect

○ **drought (n)**
a period of abnormally dry weather

○ **upswell (v)**
(water) to rush up towards the surface

2. **According to paragraph 4, all of the following about the normal Pacific pattern of ocean atmosphere system are true EXCEPT:**

   Ⓐ Equatorial winds gather.
   Ⓑ Fish do not swim in the cool, nutrient-rich water.
   Ⓒ Cold water upswells along the South American coast.
   Ⓓ Warm water pools towards the west.

On the TOEFL Test

3. **The word their in the passage refers to**

   Ⓐ the countries
   Ⓑ climatic changes
   Ⓒ third-world nations
   Ⓓ South America and Africa

4. **The word this in the passage refers to**

   Ⓐ El Nino
   Ⓑ South American coast
   Ⓒ cold upswelling
   Ⓓ warming

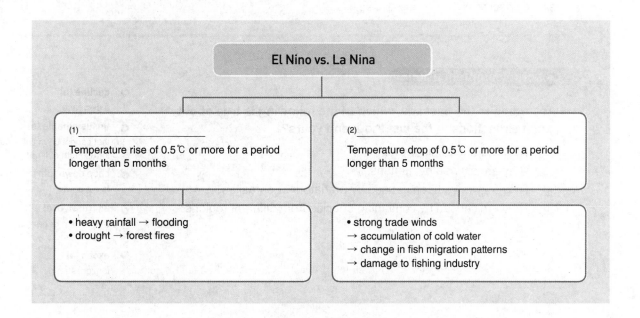

El Nino vs. La Nina

(1) _____
Temperature rise of 0.5℃ or more for a period longer than 5 months

(2) _____
Temperature drop of 0.5℃ or more for a period longer than 5 months

• heavy rainfall → flooding
• drought → forest fires

• strong trade winds
  → accumulation of cold water
  → change in fish migration patterns
  → damage to fishing industry

Read the following passage, and answer the questions.

The Decline of Biodiversity

Time Limit: 2 min. 50 sec.

Biodiversity is the range of living things in an area. During the last 100 years, scientists have seen a great decline in biodiversity. This means a great loss for humans as the stewards of the planet Earth.

Some studies show that one in eight plant species is threatened with extinction. It is estimated that 140,000 species of plants are lost each year. Many of these lost plants could have been very useful in creating new drugs to combat disease. This is due to the use of unsustainable ecological practices.

Most of the extinctions in the last thousand years are due to humans. The main cause is the chopping down of tropical rain forests. These habitats are being turned into pasture, cropland, and orchards. Most of this destruction is done to create pasture for beef cattle. It is also done to make wheat for bread as well as fruit for human consumption.

The introduction of exotic species is another threat. When exotic species are introduced to a habitat, they try to establish a self-sustaining population. Then they threaten the local species. These foreign species may be predators or parasites. Or they may simply be aggressive. They deprive the local species of nutrients. Because the local species haven't had a chance to evolve, they often lack defenses. They cannot compete against the exotic species.

The rich diversity across the world exists only because of barriers. The main barriers are seas and oceans. These barriers could never be crossed by natural means. But since humans invented ships and airplanes, it is now possible for species to meet. There is no time for them to adapt, but humans continue to combine species from different regions. The world's ecosystems will soon be dominated by very few, aggressive super-species.

In order to reverse these problems, people need to minimize their consumption. They need to consume less beef and other products that require damage to the natural environment. Also, governments need to impose strict rules against destroying natural land and introducing exotic species.

General Comprehension

1. **According to the passage, which of the following is true about most extinctions in the last thousand years?**

   Ⓐ They are due to biodiversity.

   Ⓑ They are caused by humans.

   Ⓒ They may have been caused by predators or parasites.

   Ⓓ They are caused by combining species from different regions.

○ **decline (n)**
a decrease

○ **unsustainable (a)**
that cannot be maintained
for a length of time

○ **chop down (phr)**
to cut down

○ **aggressive (a)**
threatening or dangerous
towards others

○ **exotic (a)**
foreign; strange

2. **According to paragraph 4, all of the following about exotic species are true EXCEPT:**

(A) They try to established a self-sustaining population when introduced to a new area.

(B) They are a threat to biodiversity.

(C) They assist the local species in finding nutrients.

(D) They may be predators or parasites.

On the TOEFL Test

3. **The word this in the passage refers to**

(A) biodiversity

(B) decline

(C) loss

(D) Earth

4. **The word many in the passage refers to**

(A) studies

(B) plant species

(C) lost plants

(D) new drugs

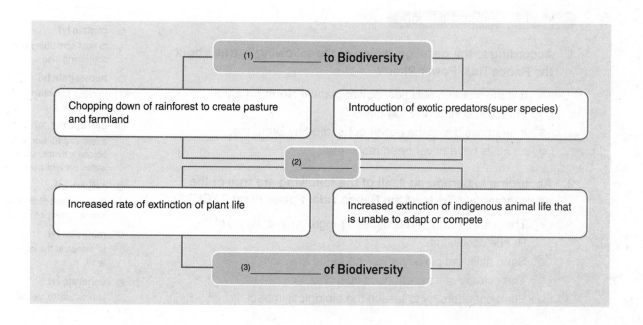

Tidal Power Plants

Time Limit: 2 min. 50 sec.

Tidal power is a way of creating electricity. Tidal power systems capture the energy contained in masses of water as the tide moves them. The ecological effects of this method are still being studied, and there are only a few of these power plants in use around the world. But many governments are making plans to build more. Right now, there are eight tidal power plants proposed for America, Mexico, and Canada.

The Rance Tidal Power Plant was the world's first electrical generating station powered by tidal energy. It is located on the Rance River in Bretagne, France. The construction of this plant necessitated draining the surrounding area. Two dams were built over two years.

Construction of the actual plant took place on July 20, 1963. At this time, the Rance was entirely blocked by the two dams. The plant was completed in 1966. On December 4, 1967, it was connected to the French national power grid. The plant cost about 524 million Euros to build. It produces 3% of the power consumed by Bretagne. The project had very high costs, but these costs have been recovered. The power from this plant is cheaper than the cost of nuclear power.

The plant's barrage has caused progressive silting of the Rance ecosystem. Sand-eels and plaice have disappeared. But sea bass and cuttlefish have returned to the river. Tides still flow in the estuary. The operators of the plant are still trying to minimize the biological impact.

The first and only tidal power plant in North America is the Annapolis Royal Generating Station. It is located in Annapolis Royal in Canada. It was originally constructed in 1984 to look at alternative methods for generating electricity. However, it has also created changes to the local environment. The water and air temperature in the area have changed. Moreover, the siltation patterns of the river have shifted, and the riverbanks on both sides of the dam have increased.

General Comprehension

1. **According to the passage, which of the following is true about the Rance Tidal Power Plant?**

   (A) It is the first and only tidal power plant in North America.
   (B) This project had very low costs.
   (C) It produces 3% of the power consumed by Bretagne.
   (D) Its costs have never been recovered.

2. **According to paragraph 4, all of the following are true of the environmental effects of the Rance Tidal Power Plant EXCEPT:**

   (A) The plant's barrage has caused progressive draining of the Rance ecosystem.
   (B) Sand eels and plaice cannot be found anymore.
   (C) The estuary still experiences tidal flow.
   (D) Plant operators try to lessen the biological impact.

contain (v)
to hold something within something else

necessitate (v)
to make something necessary

barrage (n)
a wall or a barrier built across a river to store water, prevent a flood, etc.

estuary (n)
the wide part of the river where it flows into the sea

minimize (v)
to reduce to the lowest level

generate (v)
to produce; to create

On the TOEFL Test

3. **The word them in the passage refers to**

    Ⓐ tidal power systems

    Ⓑ masses of water

    Ⓒ ecological effects

    Ⓓ governments

4. **The word it in the passage refers to**

    Ⓐ North America

    Ⓑ Annapolis Royal Generating Station

    Ⓒ electricity

    Ⓓ local environment

Tidal Power Plants

- create (1)_____

- cheaper/safer/cleaner than (2)_____

- (3)_____ (the world's first power plant)

- only 1 tidal power plant in North America
  (Annapolis Royal Generating Station in Annapolis, Royal, Canada)

Read the following passage, and answer the questions.

The Komodo Dragon

Time Limit: 3 min.

The Komodo dragon is the largest living lizard in the world. It grows to an average length of 2 to 3 meters. In the wild, adults tend to weigh about 70 kilograms. It is a member of the monitor lizard family.

Komodo dragons inhabit various islands in Indonesia. Sightings of them were first reported to Europeans in 1910. Widespread knowledge came after 1912 in which Peter Ouwens, the director of the zoological museum at Bogor, Java, published a paper on the topic. In 1980, Komodo National Park was funded to help protect their population.

Komodo dragons are carnivorous. Although they like the flesh of dead animals, they hunt live prey. They begin with a stealthy approach. Then they launch into a short, sudden charge. During this time, they can run briefly at speeds of up to 20 kilometers per hour.

The Komodo dragon is not considered venomous, but its teeth are home to over 50 strains of bacteria. If the initial bite does not kill its prey, deadly infections will kill the creature in a week. Then the Komodo dragon finds its victim. It follows the smell and feeds upon the dead flesh.

The dragon also has large claws that are used when it is younger. It uses these to climb trees to escape from the jaws of older dragons. But when they get older, these claws are used mainly as weapons.

The Komodo dragon's prey is wide-ranging. They include wild pigs, goats, deer, and water buffaloes. In the wild, it has also been observed to eat smaller dragons. Occasionally, it has eaten humans and human corpses. Over a dozen human deaths have been attributed to dragon bites in the last 100 years.

The Komodo dragon is a vulnerable species. There are approximately 6,000 living Komodo dragons. Mating occurs between May and August, with the eggs laid in September. The female lays her eggs in the ground or in tree hollows. This gives some protection. Clutches usually contain an average of 20 eggs. Once born, they take about five years to mature. They can live for up to 30 years.

General Comprehension

1. According to the paragraph, which of the following is true about Komodo Dragons?

Ⓐ They tend to weigh 12 kilograms.
Ⓑ They only eat humans.
Ⓒ They are members of the monitor lizard family.
Ⓓ They can live for up to 100 years.

inhabit (v)
to live somewhere

carnivorous (a)
meat-eating

prey (n)
a living thing that is killed to feed another living thing

stealthy (a)
secretive

charge (n)
attack

2. **According to paragraph 4, all of the following are true of the Komodo Dragon EXCEPT:**

    Ⓐ Over 50 strains of bacteria live in its teeth.
    Ⓑ It will not eat rotten flesh.
    Ⓒ It follows the scent of rotting flesh to find its victim.
    Ⓓ A victim of its bite will die from infections within a week.

On the TOEFL Test

3. **The word them in the passage refers to**

    Ⓐ Komodo dragons
    Ⓑ islands
    Ⓒ Europeans
    Ⓓ Komodo National Park

4. **The word these in the passage refers to**

    Ⓐ claws
    Ⓑ trees
    Ⓒ jaws
    Ⓓ weapons

| The Komodo Dragon |

- (1)_____ in the world – 2 to 3 meters long
- A member of the monitor lizard family
- Inhabits (2)_____
- First sighted by Europeans in 1910
- Teeth hold over 50 strains of bacteria
- Eats wild pigs, goats, deer, water buffaloes, and humans
- (3)_____ Komodo dragons currently living

Read the following passage, and answer the questions.

Nanotechnology

Time Limit: 2 min. 40 sec.

Nanotechnology is a new field of applied science. It is an effort to create very tiny machines on a nano scale. A nano is a unit of measurement which stands for ten to the negative power of nine. It is used to describe very small things.

One example of nanotechnology in modern use is the making of polymers. These are based on molecular structure. Another is the design of computer chip layouts. These are based on surface science.

At the nano-size level, the properties of many materials change. For example, copper changes from opaque to clear. Solid gold becomes liquid at room temperature. Insulators like silicon become conductors. All of these activities open up many potential risks.

Due to their altered states, nano particles become more mobile. They are also more likely to react with other things. There are four ways for nano particles to enter the human body. They can be inhaled, swallowed, absorbed through the skin, or injected. Once these particles are in the body, they are highly mobile.

In fact, the way these particles react inside living things is still not fully understood. But scientists guess that these tiny objects could easily overload defensive cells. This would weaken a body's defenses against diseases. Humans could easily lose control of particles this size. This would lead to mass epidemics that would cause widespread disease and death.

Another concern about nanotechnology is of the environmental risks. One report details the possible disaster of the Earth being covered in a gray, sticky substance. This terrible event is attributed to the unrestrained self-replication of microscopic robots. These robots are called nanobots and are able to control themselves.

Therefore, scientists need to collect much more data before they are allowed to create and release nanobots. They should be highly regulated by laws that only allow licensed scientists to do safe experiments.

General Comprehension

1. **According to the passage, a modern use of nanotechnology is**

    (A) for the construction of microscopic robots
    (B) for creating gray, sticky substances
    (C) in the making of polymers
    (D) to create environmental weapons

2. **According to paragraph 1 which of the following is NOT true about nanotechnology?**

    (A) Its name describes things that are very small.
    (B) It describes the effort to make machines on a tiny scale.
    (C) Its name describes the measurement of ten to the negative power of nine.
    (D) It is an old field of theoretical science.

apply (v)
to use something

regulate (v)
to control something using laws or rules

opaque (a)
that cannot be seen through

inhale (v)
to breathe in

epidemic (n)
a wave of sickness that sweeps over a group of people

On the TOEFL Test

3. **The word another in the passage refers to**

   Ⓐ example
   Ⓑ nanotech
   Ⓒ molecular structure
   Ⓓ surface structure

4. **The word they in the passage refers to**

   Ⓐ scientists
   Ⓑ data
   Ⓒ nanobots
   Ⓓ experiments

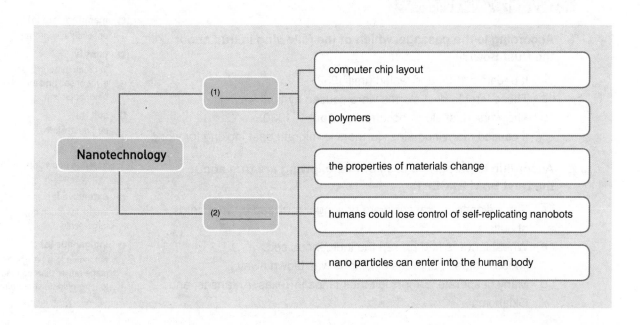

The Dust Bowl

Time Limit: 2 min. 30 sec.

The Dust Bowl was a series of dust storms in the central United States and Canada. These took place in the mid to late 1930s. They were caused by massive droughts and decades of inappropriate farming techniques. The fertile soil of the Great Plains was exposed through the removal of grass during plowing.

During the droughts the soil dried out, became dust, and blew away. The wind blew the dust east in very large black clouds. The clouds made the sky appear black all the way to Chicago. Eventually the soil was lost when it blew out to the Atlantic Ocean.

The Dust Bowl began in 1934 and lasted until 1939. On November 11, 1933, a very strong dust storm stripped topsoil from parched South Dakota farmlands. It was just one of a series of terrible dust storms that year.

Then, on May 11, 1934, a strong, two-day storm removed massive amounts of Great Plains topsoil in one of the worst storms of the Dust Bowl. Once again, the dust clouds blew all the way to Chicago, where the filth fell like snow.

April 14, 1935, is known as Black Sunday. One of the worst "black blizzards" occurred throughout the Dust Bowl. It caused extensive damage and turned the day to night. Witnesses reported that they could not see five feet in front of them at certain points.

Topsoil across millions of acres was blown away because the indigenous sod had been broken for wheat farming. Vast herds of buffalo were no longer fertilizing the rest of the indigenous grasses. This ecological disaster caused an exodus from Texas, Arkansas, Oklahoma, and the surrounding Great Plains. Over 500,000 Americans became homeless. Many of these homeless people migrated west looking for work. These people were called "Okies" even when they were not from Oklahoma.

General Comprehension

1. **According to the passage, which of the following is true about the Dust Bowl?**

   (A) It began in 1934 and lasted until 1939.
   (B) These terrible dust storms were caused by tidal waves.
   (C) The worst dust storm occurred on April 1, 1930.
   (D) It caused many homeless farmers to migrate east looking for work.

2. **According to paragraph 6, all of the following are true about the Dust Bowl EXCEPT:**

   (A) The indigenous grasses were no longer fertilized by vast herds of buffalo.
   (B) Wheat farmers had broken the indigenous sod.
   (C) Topsoil across hundreds of islands was blown away.
   (D) Many desperate farmers left their lands in Texas, Arkansas, and Oklahoma.

inappropriate (a)
unsuitable; improper

plow (v)
to break through the top layer of soil and mix it before planting

soil (n)
dirt; dust; earth

blizzard (n)
a terrible snowstorm with strong winds

extensive (a)
broad; far-reaching; large-scale

indigenous (a)
belonging to a particular place rather than coming to it from somewhere else

On the TOEFL Test

3. The word it in the passage refers to

- Ⓐ drought
- Ⓑ dust
- Ⓒ wind
- Ⓓ soil

4. The phrase that year in the passage refers to

- Ⓐ 1933
- Ⓑ 1934
- Ⓒ 1935
- Ⓓ 1939

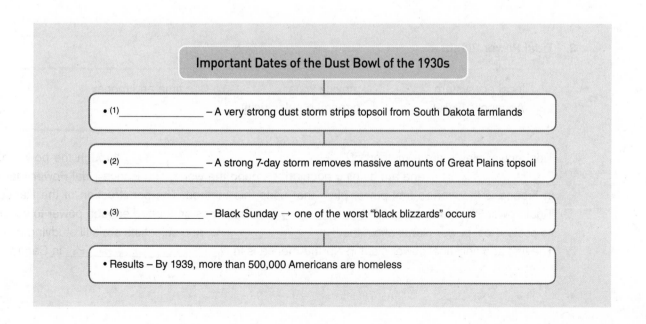

Important Dates of the Dust Bowl of the 1930s

- (1)_____ – A very strong dust storm strips topsoil from South Dakota farmlands

- (2)_____ – A strong 7-day storm removes massive amounts of Great Plains topsoil

- (3)_____ – Black Sunday → one of the worst "black blizzards" occurs

- Results – By 1939, more than 500,000 Americans are homeless

Building Summary Skills

The following summaries are based on the long passages you worked on earlier. Complete each of them by filling in the blanks with suitable words or phrases.

1. El Nino and La Nina

> South America and Africa   drought, flooding, and forest fires   irregularly
> migratory patterns   temperature changes

El Nino and La Nina are major (1)_____ that affect a large portion of the world's climate. The economies of many nations in (2)_____ are strongly affected by these climate changes. El Nino and La Nina occur (3)_____ and can cause some damaging effects such as (4)_____. These changes also affect the (5)_____ of fish, which affects the fishing industry. Scientists do not fully understand El Nino and La Nina yet, but they are studying them very closely.

2. The Decline of Biodiversity

> living things   unsustainable environmental practices   biodiversity
> rain forests   foreign species

(1)_____, which describes the range of (2)_____, has been declining rapidly over the past century. Many species of plants are becoming extinct because of (3)_____ _____. Humans are the biggest cause of these environmental problems, mainly because they chop down so much of the (4)_____. Another threat to biodiversity is the introduction of (5)_____, which overtake local species. Humans need to take strong steps to stop the decline of biodiversity.

3. Tidal Power Plants

> local ecosystem   moving water   time and money
> Annapolis Royal   generating electricity

Tidal power plants are a method of (1)_____ through the power of (2)_____ and are gaining popularity around the world. The Rance Tidal Power Plant in France is the world's first power plant that uses this method. The construction of the Rance Tidal Power Plant took a lot of (3)_____, but it has generated enough power to cover its costs. Tidal power plants affect the (4)_____, and scientists are still studying how. The first and only tidal power plant in North America is in (5)_____ in Canada.

4. **The Komodo Dragon**

> their own species
> population
>
> infects the prey
> the islands of Indonesia
>
> largest living lizards

Komodo dragons are the (1)_____ in the world today. They live on
(2)_____. They eat meat, which they kill by a bite that
(3)_____ and kills it over a period of days. Komodo dragons eat a wide range of
other animals, including (4)_____. Today, the (5)_____ of Komodo dragons
is not very large.

5. **Nanotechnology**

> human bodies
> unpredictable
>
> microscopic machines
> self-replicating nanobots
>
> nanotechnology

(1)_____ is the risky science of building (2)_____. This technology could
be very useful, but it is (3)_____ since the properties of many materials change
at the microscopic level. Some scientists worry that machines this small could easily enter
(4)_____ and cause effects that nobody can predict. Another concern is that
(5)_____ could damage the environment on a very large and unexpected
scale. Experiments with nanotechnology should be done in a very cautious fashion as regulated
by the government.

6. **The Dust Bowl**

> blown away
> dusty, infertile ground
>
> a series of terrible storms
> America and Canada
>
> natural disaster

The Dust Bowl was (1)_____ in the 1930s that damaged the farming
industries in (2)_____. Farming was damaged because the fertile layer of topsoil
was (3)_____ by powerful winds, leaving only (4)_____.
Some of these storms were so bad that the sky was turned black and no one could see the sun.
Many farmers were made homeless by this (5)_____ and were forced to travel
west looking for work.

1. **The word deduced in the passage is closest in meaning to**

   - (A) reduced
   - (B) inferred
   - (C) told
   - (D) eliminated

2. **The word them in the passage refers to**

   - (A) climate models
   - (B) weather data
   - (C) current conditions
   - (D) supercomputers

3. **According to paragraph 1, which of the following is true of meteorology?**

   - (A) It explains the science of outer space bodies such as meteors.
   - (B) It explains biological phenomena.
   - (C) It explains events that occur in the weather.
   - (D) It explains the science of things that fall to Earth such as rain and snow.

4. **According to paragraph 2, all of the following are true EXCEPT:**

   - (A) Aristotle was the first to use the term meteorology.
   - (B) Aristotle was the first to examine the evaporation process.
   - (C) Aristotle could predict the weather up to a week in advance.
   - (D) Aristotle saw how the hot sun turned water into mist.

5. **According to the passage, what can be inferred about satellites and weather forecasting?**

   - (A) Global weather information was not available before the launch of satellites.
   - (B) Satellites enabled scientists to identify the cause of El Nino.
   - (C) Satellites are responsible for influencing weather patterns.
   - (D) Human methods of weather forecasting have become useless because of satellites.

6. **Why does the author mention a Norwegian scientist in paragraph 6?**

   - (A) To explain why the purposes of weather forecasting changed
   - (B) To show how modern methods of weather forecasting began
   - (C) To describe when scientific concepts began to be used in forecasting
   - (D) To claim that weather forecasting should be based on natural laws

Meteorology

Meteorology is the study of the Earth's atmosphere. It focuses on weather processes and forecasting and explaining weather events. These events are bound by the factors that exist in the atmosphere, such as temperature, air pressure, and water vapor. These factors interact to create climate patterns.

The term *meteorology* was first coined by Aristotle in 350 B.C. He was the first to observe and record the process by which water evaporates. He noticed how the hot sun turned it into mist and then the cool air returned it to Earth on the following day.

In 1607, Galileo made the first tool to measure temperature. A few years later, his assistant made the first barometer. By 1648, Pascal saw that air pressure falls with height. He also guessed that there is a vacuum above the atmosphere.

In 1667, Robert Hooke built a tool to measure the speed of wind. Later, Edmund Haley mapped the trade winds for sailors. He also deduced that changes in the atmosphere are driven by solar heat.

By the 20th century, science began to understand many important weather events. Perhaps the most important concept was how the rotation of the Earth affects the flow of air. This large-scale force was named the Coriolis Effect.

In 1904, a Norwegian scientist said that it was possible to predict the weather by means of calculations based on natural laws. This led to the field of modern weather forecasting.

By the 1950s, forecasters began using computers. These early machines helped them to do experiments. The first forecasts were produced using models of low and high temperatures.

After about a decade, the first weather satellite was launched. This event led to the age of global weather information. Satellites became important tools for studying everything from forest fires to El Nino. They gave scientists a large-scale view of the planet.

These days, climate models are used to compare weather data from past years. The historical data is cross-referenced with current conditions. This gives scientists data to study long-term climate shifts. Effects such as global warming are now better understood. Currently, powerful new supercomputers are being used. With them it is possible to create working models of the atmosphere.

Many human methods of weather forecasting are also employed. These methods rely on the skill and judgment of the forecasters who used them. Many of the methods allow us an accuracy rate of more than 50%.

In this age of weather forecasting, many people depend on information about the weather. It increases the successful production of food. It also saves lives when natural disasters strike. Mankind's ability to predict the weather has reached new levels of unprecedented accuracy.

7. **The phrase fend for in the passage is closest in meaning to**
   - (A) take care of
   - (B) move
   - (C) feed
   - (D) look for

8. **According to the passage, which of the following is NOT true of chipmunks?**
   - (A) The chipmunk breeds during two seasons every year.
   - (B) The average number of offspring is six.
   - (C) Chipmunk mothers hide their young underground.
   - (D) Chipmunks have various kinds of natural predators.

9. **Which of the following can be inferred about chipmunks?**
   - (A) They cannot fight against their predators.
   - (B) They grow their own food.
   - (C) They use the homes of other animals.
   - (D) They cannot climb trees.

10. **Why does the author mention the chipmunk's cheeks?**
    - (A) To show that the chipmunk uses them to defend itself.
    - (B) To explain that they help the chipmunk carry and store food.
    - (C) To show that they are extremely large.
    - (D) To describe the chipmunk's ability to fly.

11. **In stating that chipmunks are traditionally hoarders, the author means that chipmunks**
    - (A) can run extremely fast to escape predators
    - (B) can fly using their cheek muscles
    - (C) have twelve breeding sessions per year
    - (D) store food in order to survive during the long winter months

12. **The word they in the passage refers to**
    - (A) seeds
    - (B) animals
    - (C) chipmunks
    - (D) habitat

Chipmunks

The Earth is covered with millions of species of animals, and each is responsible for filling an important niche in the delicate ecosystem of the planet. The chipmunk, although small in size, is no less vital to the health of a habitat. Chipmunks are small rodents that inhabit the forests of North America and Asia. There are twenty-five different species of chipmunks. Many of them are marked by their reddish-brown fur with white and black stripes that cover the length of their bodies.

Unlike many of its rodent relatives, the chipmunk has two breeding seasons a year. The first spans from February to April, and the second from June to August. The average number of offspring for a chipmunk is four, but there have been litters as small as one and as big as nine. Mothers keep their young hidden underground in their homes for up to six weeks until they are old enough to fend for themselves. Some of their natural predators include cats, dogs, eagles, hawks, foxes, coyotes, and wolves. In the wild, a chipmunk's lifespan is typically only a year, but some have been known to live up to five years.

Although mating season is an exception, chipmunks spend most of their time alone building their homes, looking for food, and hiding from predators. They are often found climbing in trees looking for food.

Chipmunks are traditionally hoarders. They spend the spring and summer stocking their burrows with nuts, seeds, insects, berries, and other foods in order to hibernate during the long winter without starving. Other sources of food include fungi, bird's eggs, grain, and worms.

One of the most remarkable features of chipmunks is their cheeks. Chipmunks have special pouches on both sides of their head that can be stretched and filled with food. Once completely filled, each cheek can become as large as the chipmunk's head. This ability allows chipmunks to carry a large amount of food to and from their burrow with ease.

Chipmunks, like other small rodents, are known as "spreaders." They are responsible for the spreading of seed, fungi, and other types of vegetation. Often times, a few pieces of food that the chipmunk brings to the burrow get left behind or dropped along their way. This seed begins to grow, in turn providing more food and shelter for other animals in the habitat.

Whether they are spreading seeds or they become the prey of other animals, chipmunks are an important part of any habitat. They are very much a part of the ever-evolving cycle present in nature.

Vocabulary Review

A Choose the word with the closest meaning to each highlighted word or phrase.

1. The sign indicates the correct direction to the store.
   - Ⓐ looks
   - Ⓑ shows
   - Ⓒ says
   - Ⓓ needs

2. The impact of the tidal wave on the coastal people was terrible.
   - Ⓐ time
   - Ⓑ cost
   - Ⓒ effect
   - Ⓓ use

3. The decline of the African elephant can be linked to poaching.
   - Ⓐ decrease
   - Ⓑ change
   - Ⓒ growth
   - Ⓓ limitation

4. Because of his hard work, he was able to recover his losses from the accident.
   - Ⓐ find
   - Ⓑ sell
   - Ⓒ take back
   - Ⓓ escape

5. This dinosaur was known to be carnivorous.
   - Ⓐ vegetative
   - Ⓑ nocturnal
   - Ⓒ tardy
   - Ⓓ flesh-eating

6. His approach was so stealthy that no one noticed him coming.
   - Ⓐ fast
   - Ⓑ secretive
   - Ⓒ expected
   - Ⓓ noisy

7. He is applying everything he learned in photography class at his new job.
   - Ⓐ using
   - Ⓑ needing
   - Ⓒ saying
   - Ⓓ wanting

8. If you look at the watch, you can tell it is exotic.
   - Ⓐ sharp
   - Ⓑ normal
   - Ⓒ original
   - Ⓓ unusual

B Match each word with the correct definition.

1. upswell •
2. soil •
3. phenomenon •
4. plow •
5. chop down •
6. epidemic •
7. barrage •
8. regulate •
9. necessitate •
10. prey •

- • **a.** to cut down
- • **b.** to break through the top layer of soil and mix it before planting
- • **c.** a wave of sickness that sweeps over a group of people
- • **d.** (water) to rush up towards the surface
- • **e.** a natural occurrence that requires a scientific explanation
- • **f.** to control something using laws or rules
- • **g.** a living thing that is killed to feed another living thing
- • **h.** to make something necessary
- • **i.** a nutrient-rich layer of dirt for planting
- • **j.** a wall or a barrier built across a river to store water, prevent a flood, etc.

Unit 3

Factual Information

3 Factual Information

Overview

■ Introduction

Factual Information questions ask you to identify facts, details, or other information that is explicitly mentioned in the passage. The information is often found in just one or two paragraphs of the passage. So you can find the correct answer without even reading the whole passage. You just need to quickly find the right spot in the passage that has the information about which the question asks. This is one of the most frequent question types on the TOEFL® iBT.

■ Question Types

1. According to the passage, which of the following is true of _____?

2. According to paragraph X, who [when/ where/ what/ how/ why] _____?

3. According to the passage, X did Y because _____?

4. The author's description of X mentions which of the following?

■ Useful Tips

• Read the questions first to know what exactly is being asked.

• Scan the passage to find out where the relevant information is in the passage.

• Remove the choices that are not relevant to the passage.

• Do not choose an answer just because it is mentioned in the passage.

Sample iBT Question

According to the passage, what are ballet dancers famous for?

(A) Their dancing, miming acting, and music

(B) Their clothes and shoes

(C) Their elegant movements

(D) Their balancing skills

Ballet

Ballet is an art form that makes use of dancing, miming, acting, and music. It can be performed alone or with an opera. Ballet dancers are famous for their gracefulness. They are also known for amazing feats of physical strength. Many ballet techniques resemble positions and footwork used in fencing. Both ballet and fencing have similar requirements of balance and movement. Also, both of these forms developed during the same historical period. Ballet became popular in the royal courts of Italy and France during the Renaissance. For the past four hundred years, this dance form has been refined, most notably by Russian dance companies that travel and perform. Today, ballet is one of the most well-preserved dances in the world.

Correct Answer The question asks what is famous about ballet dancers. The third sentence of the passage says that they are famous for their gracefulness. So the correct answer is (C) because 'elegant movement' is a paraphrase of 'gracefulness.'

The key to success in Factual Information questions is the ability to scan for correct information in the passage. You need to practice reading the questions first and spot the relevant information in the passage quickly. You do not have to read every part of the passage.

Read the questions first. Use the key words highlighted in each question to scan for the answer in the passage.

> ## Opinions
> An opinion is a thought or idea held about something that is important to the holder. It is not a fact, so it cannot be proven correct or incorrect. But in the case of the United States Supreme Court, the word "opinion" has a different meaning. For the court, an opinion is a decision. It establishes the way a law will be followed in the future. The court gave an opinion in the 1971 case of *Roe vs. Wade*. It was in favor of abortion being legal. This made it possible for pregnant women in the United States to have an abortion. It is an example of an opinion that has caused controversy. This has continued for many years after it was issued.

1. **According to the passage, what does a court's opinion establish?**
    - (A) Thoughts or ideas about a particular event
    - (B) Controversy over important issues
    - (C) Future interpretations of the law
    - (D) Facts about legal matters

> ## Quilting
> Quilts were traditionally used to cover beds as warm, top blankets. But these days, many quilts are treated as works of art and are hung on walls to be displayed. In colonial times, most women spent their time weaving and making clothing. But wealthy women were able to spend their time making fine quilts. These women formed groups called quilting bees. Quilts are often sewn to commemorate important events such as a wedding or a birth. Quilters sew important dates or names into a quilt using a needlepoint technique. They also incorporate pieces of a person's clothing or an important flag in the quilt to create a historical document.

2. **According to the passage, why do people often sew quilts?**
    - (A) To remind people of historic events
    - (B) To make flags that people can enjoy and use to represent them
    - (C) To make lots of money for use by the federal government in wars
    - (D) To make them displayed in cultural exhibits

The History of Medicine

In 1960, the earliest proof of medicine was found buried with a prehistoric man. With him were eight kinds of plants. All of these are still used for their healing benefits today. In cultures around the world, medicine has developed differently. In traditional Chinese medicine, doctors heal by changing the flow of energy through the body. In India, doctors heal by trying to restore harmony between the mind, the body, and the soul. Western medicine first developed in Europe. Doctors focus mainly on diet and hygiene as a way to restore health. Now, as technology grows and the world becomes smaller, doctors are using the best parts of medicine from all over the world.

3. **According to the passage, what are doctors doing with medicine from all over the world?**

   Ⓐ They bury it with prehistoric men in order to create historical records.
   Ⓑ They develop it in European clinics.
   Ⓒ They use it to heal the mind, body, and soul of wounded people.
   Ⓓ They combine and use the most effective parts.

Print Journalism

Print journalism can be split into several categories. They are newspapers, news magazines, and general interest magazines. There are also trade and hobby magazines. Finally, there are newsletters, private publications, online news pages, and blogs.

   Newspaper journalists use the inverted pyramid style. This style is used for straight or hard news reports rather than features. Written hard news reports are expected to be spare in the use of words, and to list all of the important information first. The story can be cut from the bottom when there is not enough space for it. Feature stories are written in a looser style.

4. **According to the passage, what is the characteristic of written hard news reports?**

   Ⓐ They are long and wordy.
   Ⓑ They do not use many words.
   Ⓒ They deal with as few facts as possible.
   Ⓓ They are printed in a magazine.

A Read the following passage, and answer the questions.

Optical Fiber

Time Limit: 2 min. 30 sec.

Optical fibers are thin and transparent fibers made of glass or plastic. They are used for sending light signals. The signals can carry information or light. Optical fibers are commonly used in communication systems.

The study of optical fibers and their uses is called fiber optics. Optical fibers transmit light because of a scientific principle called total internal reflection. According to the principle, light continues to bounce through an optical fiber when the outer layer of the fiber is thicker than in the center.

The history of fiber optics began in England during the Victorian period. At that time, scientists used the total internal reflection principle to light streams of water in public fountains. In the middle of the 20th century, fiber optics was used by doctors. They created a tool called the gastroscope. This tool allowed doctors to see into a patient's stomach and intestines. By 1977, telephone companies began to use fiber optic cables. They used them to send telephone signals very long distances.

In the past, copper cable was used to send electric signals. But the optical fiber has become more popular because it offers several advantages over copper cable. Optical fibers can send signals very long distances with low loss. It is also much lighter than copper. Just 7 kilograms of optical fibers can replace 20 tons of copper cable. This is very useful for aircraft.

The only disadvantages of optical fibers are in short distances. In small amounts, optical fibers can be more expensive than copper cable. It is also harder to splice and cannot send power along with a signal.

In this age of computers, there is an increased need for bandwidth. Optical fibers can send huge amounts of data over long distances. The science of fiber optics is more useful than ever.

General Comprehension

1. **The word transmit in the passage is closest in meaning to**

   (A) send
   (B) control
   (C) trap
   (D) save

2. **The word them in the passage refers to**

   (A) telephone companies
   (B) fiber optic cables
   (C) telephone signals
   (D) very long distances

- **transparent (a)**
  clear and easy to see through
- **internal (a)**
  inside
- **bounce (v)**
  to rebound from something
- **intestine (n)**
  the tubes in a human body that process food and carry waste out of body
- **splice (v)**
  to connect two cables

On the TOEFL Test

3. **The author's description of total internal reflection mentions which of the following?**
   - (A) the explosion of light
   - (B) a vacuum of light
   - (C) the continuous bouncing of light
   - (D) the absence of light

4. **According to the passage, copper cable was used in the past to**
   - (A) make optical fibers
   - (B) send light through streams of water
   - (C) see into patients' stomachs
   - (D) send electric signals

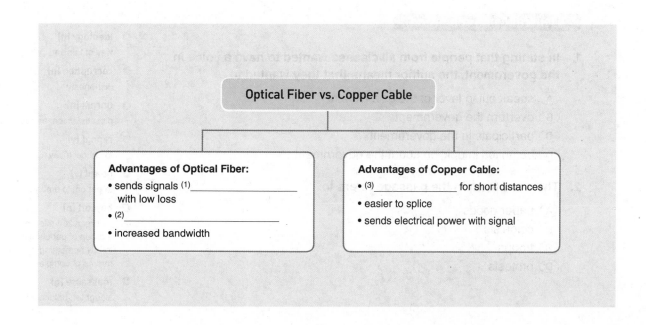

Optical Fiber vs. Copper Cable

Advantages of Optical Fiber:
- sends signals (1)_____ with low loss
- (2)_____
- increased bandwidth

Advantages of Copper Cable:
- (3)_____ for short distances
- easier to splice
- sends electrical power with signal

Read the following passage, and answer the questions.

The American Revolution

Time Limit: 2 min. 30 sec.

The American Revolution ended British rule over America. The result was the formation of the United States in 1776.

The American Revolution began with a shift in ideology. The Americans were unhappy with the British monarchy. Founding fathers such as Thomas Jefferson and Samuel Adams led the new way of thinking. People from all classes wanted to have a voice in the government. Corruption was seen as the greatest evil. Civic virtue was seen as the greatest good. Family status no longer decided a person's place in society.

The unrest that led to the Revolutionary War can be linked to three events. First, in 1765, the British Parliament passed the Stamp Act. This tax on all paper goods was passed to pay for more British troops in America. The colonists complained because they were already being taxed to pay for troops to put them down. This led to more protests and disobedience. The Stamp Act was repealed.

The second wave came in 1767. Parliament passed the Townshend Acts. These acts taxed goods such as glass, paint, and paper. Colonists organized boycotts of these products. More British troops arrived in Boston, and violence broke out. British soldiers fired their guns into an angry mob. They killed five colonists. This was called the Boston Massacre.

The third event leading to the revolution took place in 1773. Although the British government repealed the Townshend Acts, it left behind one tax on tea. A group of angry Bostonians boarded a British ship. They dumped all of its tea into the harbor. This event was called the Boston Tea Party.

The British government and the American colonists could not repair their relationship. By 1775, fighting broke out in Lexington. In 1776, the American Declaration of Independence was passed. By 1781, the fighting ended. The British withdrew from America.

General Comprehension

1. In stating that people from all classes wanted to have a voice in the government, the author means that they wanted to
   - (A) speak out in favor of the government
   - (B) overturn the government
   - (C) participate in the government
   - (D) be united in opinion about the government

2. The word them in the passage refers to
   - (A) paper goods
   - (B) colonists
   - (C) troops
   - (D) protests

ideology (n)
way of thinking

corruption (n)
dishonesty

unrest (n)
dissatisfaction; protest

repeal (v)
to cancel a law

board (v)
to get on; to embark

boycott (n)
an organized effort by a group of people not to buy something as a means of complaining

massacre (n)
slaughter; holocaust

On the TOEFL Test

3. **According to the passage, which of the following is true of the American Revolution?**

   (A) It helped the British gain more land.

   (B) It freed America from British rule.

   (C) It was a minor war.

   (D) It was triggered by the British government's corruption.

4. **According to paragraph 5, why did the American colonists bring about the Boston Tea Party?**

   (A) They were angry about the British tax on tea.

   (B) They did not want the Townshend Acts.

   (C) They wanted to fight the British.

   (D) They wanted to go back to Britain.

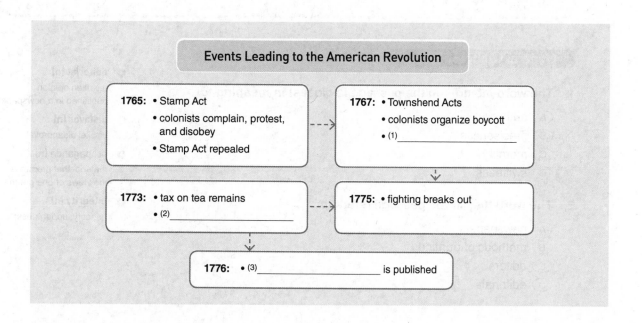

Events Leading to the American Revolution

1765: • Stamp Act
• colonists complain, protest, and disobey
• Stamp Act repealed

1767: • Townshend Acts
• colonists organize boycott
• (1)_____

1773: • tax on tea remains
• (2)_____

1775: • fighting breaks out

1776: • (3)_____ is published

Read the following passage, and answer the questions.

American Newspapers in the 19th Century

Time Limit: 2 min. 50 sec.

In 1844, the telegraph became widely used. Now newspapers could get reports from far away. A wire service called the Associated Press (AP) was started to gather news. With fresh daily news reports, local newspapers began all around the country. But New York City was the center of the newspaper industry.

Newspapers around the nation entered an age of growth. This lasted until the Civil War broke out in 1861. During this time, newspapers improved. Methods of printing and delivery were perfected, and writing and reporting became clearer and fresher. Editors such as Samuel Bowles and Horace Greeley made editorials popular again. At that time, editorials had fallen into disfavor. Most people felt they were just tools for the propaganda of political parties. Through his editorials, Greeley became a leading voice against slavery.

In 1851, Henry J. Raymond began the *New York Times*. This paper greatly improved upon the other newspapers. People thought that Greeley's *New York Tribune* was too political. On the opposite end, James G. Bennett's *New York Herald* was only concerned with looking nice and selling more copies. But the *New York Times* had both journalistic integrity and visual appeal. It reached a new height of excellence. The *New York Times* became the most respected newspaper in the country. It still is today.

By 1895, two men ruled media empires. Both Joseph Pulitzer and William Randolph Hearst owned newspapers in cities around the country. In New York, Pulitzer's *New York World* and Hearst's *New York Journal* battled to win readers. They were both accused of focusing on crime stories and deaths. People felt they were exaggerating headlines. They only wanted to attract the curiosity of readers. This practice was termed "yellow journalism." It was called "yellow" for two reasons. One reason was that both papers published a cartoon about the same popular character named the Yellow Kid. The other reason is that yellow was the color used to describe anything cowardly and dishonest. Many people think this problem still takes place in journalism today.

General Comprehension

1. The word integrity in the passage is closest in meaning to

- (A) authority
- (B) preciseness
- (C) morality
- (D) swiftness

2. The word they in the passage refers to

- (A) newspapers
- (B) methods of printing
- (C) editors
- (D) editorials

editorial (n)
a written opinion published in a newspaper

disfavor (n)
dislike; disapproval

propaganda (n)
material that promotes the views of one group

integrity (n)
honesty; uprightness

On the TOEFL Test

3. **According to paragraph 1, newspapers were able to get reports from far away because**

   (A) they had long-distance reporters

   (B) the telegraph was used to send information

   (C) New York City started a wire service

   (D) lots of local newspapers began throughout the country

4. **According to paragraph 4, why was the practice of exaggerating headlines to win readers called "yellow journalism"?**

   (A) The color yellow described actions thought to be cowardly.

   (B) Yellow was the color that stood for both the *New York World* and *New York Journal*.

   (C) People liked a cartoon character called the Yellow Kid.

   (D) The newspapers were printed on yellow paper.

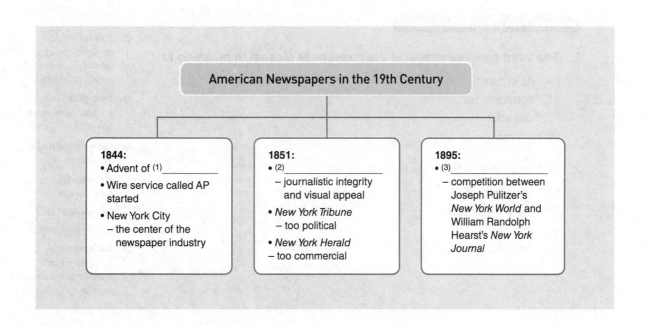

| American Newspapers in the 19th Century |

1844:	**1851:**	**1895:**
• Advent of (1)_____	• (2)_____	• (3)_____
• Wire service called AP started	– journalistic integrity and visual appeal	– competition between Joseph Pulitzer's *New York World* and William Randolph Hearst's *New York Journal*

• New York City
  – the center of the newspaper industry
	• *New York Tribune*
	  – too political
	• *New York Herald*
	  – too commercial	

The Statue of Liberty and the Liberty Bell

Time Limit: 2 min. 50 sec.

In America, two monuments symbolize the ideal of freedom that the country holds dear. The Statue of Liberty and the Liberty Bell represent freedom in different ways. The Statue of Liberty brings about feelings of hope for freedom to immigrants who enter the USA. The Liberty Bell commemorates the struggle for freedom that marks America's past.

In the past, the Statue of Liberty was the first thing people saw when their boats approached America. The statue stands over 45 meters tall. It was given as a gift to the United States in 1885 by France. The date was chosen to mark the centennial of the establishment of the United States.

The sculpture is made of copper. The internal structure was designed by Gustave Eiffel, who also designed the famous tower bearing his name in Paris. The statue is located on Liberty Island in New York Harbor. In her right hand Lady Liberty holds a torch. It is meant to light the way of freedom across the land. In her left hand she holds a tablet with the date 1776 inscribed on it. This is to commemorate the year America declared its independence from Great Britain. It is possible to go inside the statue. Many people enjoy climbing the stairs to enter her head and torch.

The Liberty Bell is located in Philadelphia, Pennsylvania, and is most famous for being rung on July 8, 1776. It was rung to summon citizens for the first public reading of the Declaration of Independence. It was also rung in 1774 to announce the opening of the First Continental Congress. Inside the bell is cast an inscription from the Bible's Leviticus 25:10. This passage states, "Proclaim liberty throughout all the land unto all the inhabitants thereof." The Liberty Bell was originally cast in 1752. It got its famous crack in 1753 the first time it was rung.

In 1965, the FBI uncovered a plot by terrorists to destroy the Statue of Liberty and the Liberty Bell. But these attacks on the symbols of freedom were quickly stopped.

General Comprehension

1. **The word commemorates in the passage is closest in meaning to**
   - (A) celebrates
   - (B) commences
   - (C) destroys
   - (D) claims

2. **The word her in the passage refers to**
   - (A) the Liberty Bell
   - (B) the famous tower
   - (C) the statue
   - (D) America

monument (n)
an object meant to symbolize an important event or concept

immigrant (n)
a person who moves from one country to another

commemorate (v)
to celebrate

struggle (n)
fight; conflict

centennial (n)
a 100-year birthday

sculpture (n)
a structure that represents the image of something

3. **According to the passage, why did France give the Statue of Liberty to the United States?**

    Ⓐ To pay off a debt
    Ⓑ To build up the friendship between both countries
    Ⓒ To make New York Harbor look nicer
    Ⓓ To celebrate the hundred-year birthday of America

4. **According to paragraph 4, the Liberty Bell is most famous for being rung when?**

    Ⓐ On July 4, 1776
    Ⓑ On July 8, 1776
    Ⓒ On December 25, 1776
    Ⓓ On January 1, 1776

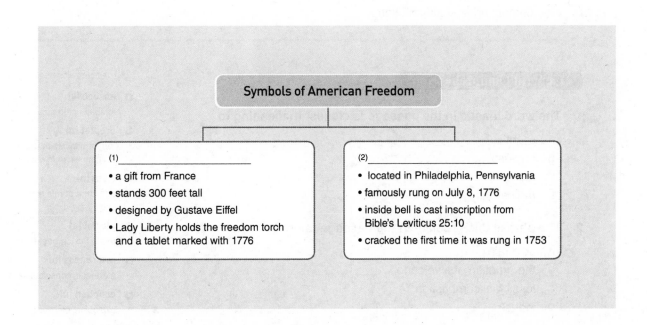

Symbols of American Freedom

(1)_____
- a gift from France
- stands 300 feet tall
- designed by Gustave Eiffel
- Lady Liberty holds the freedom torch and a tablet marked with 1776

(2)_____
- located in Philadelphia, Pennsylvania
- famously rung on July 8, 1776
- inside bell is cast inscription from Bible's Leviticus 25:10
- cracked the first time it was rung in 1753

Read the following passage, and answer the questions.

Acid Rain

Time Limit: 2 min. 50 sec.

Acid rain occurs when sulfur and nitrogen gases are released into the air. Once in the air, the chemicals are absorbed by rain clouds. The polluted water droplets fall to Earth as rain, snow, or sleet. This increases the acidity of the soil. It also affects the chemical balance of lakes and streams.

The United States Environmental Protection Agency says that acid rain is a serious problem which affects large parts of the U.S. and Canada. It damages rivers, streams, lakes, and forests.

The best way to show the increase in acid rain is to check glacial ice. Scientists can see the drastic increase of acid levels. These changes have been occurring since the Industrial Revolution.

This industrial acid rain is also a large problem in China, Eastern Europe, and Russia. Areas downwind from these places, such as Korea and Japan, suffer the negative effects.

Acid rain was first reported in Manchester, England. This was an important city during the British Industrial Revolution. But the acid rain problem was not studied closely until the late 1960s. A Canadian scientist named Harold Harvey was the first to research a "dead" lake. In the 1990s the *New York Times* published reports about acid rain effects. This brought the problem into public awareness.

Acid rain can be caused by natural occurrences such as the eruption of a volcano. But the main causes of acid rain are from fossil fuel combustion and industry. Factories, motor vehicles, and electricity generation are the leading causes of this problem.

Acid rain kills many forms of animal life, such as birds, fish, and insects. It also damages buildings. It is even suspected to have negative health effects on humans. In addition, acid rain damages soil. This makes it difficult for farmers to grow food.

Scientists are searching for ways to reverse the effects of acid rain. There are some international treaties that hope to reduce this global problem. One such treaty is the Convention on Long Range Transboundary Air Pollution, which is to protect human environment against air pollution.

General Comprehension

1. **The word drastic in the passage is closest in meaning to**

   (A) slight
   (B) endless
   (C) moderate
   (D) radical

2. **The phrase this problem in the passage refers to**

   (A) acid rain
   (B) the eruption of a volcano
   (C) fossil fuel combustion
   (D) industry

absorb (v)
to soak up; to take in

droplet (n)
the form in which water collects when in motion

sleet (n)
a mixture of rain and snow

glacial (a)
related to ice or glaciers

awareness (n)
alertness; consciousness

eruption (n)
explosion; ejection

On the TOEFL Test

3. **According to paragraph 1, when does acid rain occur?**
   - Ⓐ When the sun is too hot and burns the atmosphere.
   - Ⓑ When sulfur and nitrogen gases escape into the air.
   - Ⓒ When airplanes pollute the atmosphere.
   - Ⓓ When greenhouses release gas into the atmosphere.

4. **According to the passage, what is the best way to show the increase in acid rain?**
   - Ⓐ Check the floor of the ocean.
   - Ⓑ Test many small animals.
   - Ⓒ Check the ice on a glacier.
   - Ⓓ Check with many scientists.

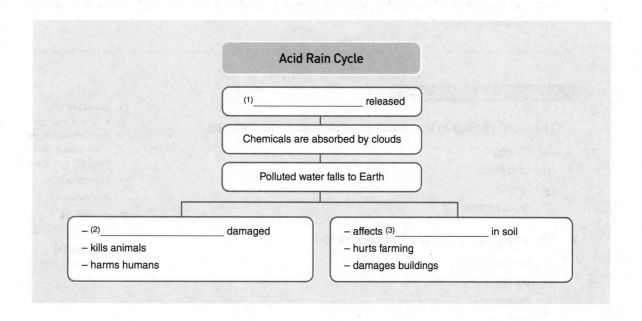

Vaudeville

Time Limit: 3 min.

Before the age of radio, movies, and television, many people enjoyed variety theater. In America this entertainment theater was called vaudeville. The term *vaudeville* comes from the French "voix de ville." It means "voice of the city." For just five cents, people could be entertained. Popular acts included music, comics, magic, animal acts, acrobatics, and even lectures.

A routine vaudeville show usually began with a silly act, such as acrobats or trick bicyclists. This allowed audience members to arrive late and find their seats. The show peaked in the middle with the "headliner." This act was usually the best in the show. The show would conclude with a "chaser" act. This act was considered good enough to feature but dull enough to make audiences leave the theater.

Between the years 1880 and 1920, vaudeville enjoyed great popularity. Industry was growing in the U.S. People had more money to spend on entertainment. Many theaters tried very hard to appear polite and family-oriented. They wanted to draw in middle-class customers. Performers were not allowed to use bad language. They could not even say the word "hell." But the performers often disobeyed the rules, and this delighted the audiences.

Successful theater owners insisted their theaters appear rich and majestic. The curtains and seats were covered in the finest red velvet. The beautiful woodwork was gilded with gold trim. They made the theaters look like palaces. Still, they housed silly acts such as juggling dogs. By the 1890s, vaudeville peaked. It became equal to churches and public schools in popularity. It was a great place for people to gather.

There was no exact end to vaudeville. But in 1910, movie theaters opened. They offered entertaining films at a lower price. This shrank vaudeville's audience continually. Ironically, movies were first shown in vaudeville theaters. By the 1930s, the Great Depression hit the U.S. Vaudeville disappeared.

Many famous American film and television stars began on the vaudeville stage. Performers such as the Three Stooges, the Marx Brothers, Buster Keaton, and Judy Garland all began their careers in vaudeville.

General Comprehension

1. **The word peaked in the passage is closest in meaning to**

   (A) thrived
   (B) climaxed
   (C) began
   (D) disappeared

2. **The word they in the passage refers to**

   (A) theater owners
   (B) curtains and seats
   (C) theaters
   (D) palaces

acrobatics (n)
a form of entertainment in which people perform great feats of balance, strength, and bravery

conclude (v)
to finish

delight (v)
to please immensely

majestic (a)
dignified; grand

On the TOEFL Test

3. **According to paragraph 2, why did a vaudeville show usually start off with a silly act?**

Ⓐ Because the audience needed time to arrive and find their seats.

Ⓑ Because the audience preferred to begin with silly acts.

Ⓒ Because silly acts got the audience ready for serious ones.

Ⓓ Because that was the only type of act the theater owner could find.

4. **According to the passage, what led to the disappearance of vaudeville?**

Ⓐ the invention of radio and television

Ⓑ the decline of the middle class

Ⓒ politicians and religious figures

Ⓓ movie theaters and the Great Depression

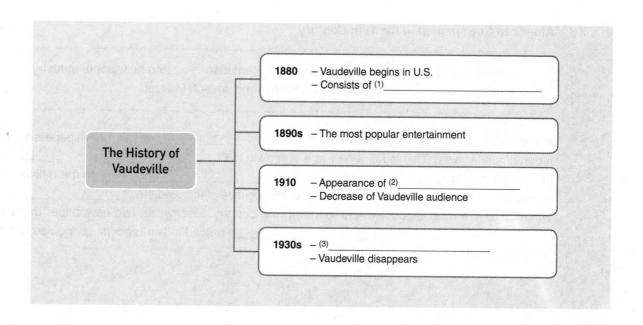

The History of Vaudeville

1880 – Vaudeville begins in U.S.
– Consists of (1)_____

1890s – The most popular entertainment

1910 – Appearance of (2)_____
– Decrease of Vaudeville audience

1930s – (3)_____
– Vaudeville disappears

Building Summary Skills

The following summaries are based on the long passages you worked on earlier. Complete each of them by filling in the blanks with suitable words or phrases.

1. **Optical Fiber**

> in England   copper cable   glass or plastic
> medical equipment   light and information

Optical fibers are made of (1)_____ and are very useful for sending (2)_____
_____. The study of fiber optics has shown that light can be bounced continuously down an
optical fiber. The concept behind optical fibers was discovered (3)_____ and later adapted
into (4)_____. An optical fiber has many advantages over (5)_____.
In this age of information, an optical fiber is very useful.

2. **The American Revolution**

> Thomas Jefferson   the Boston Tea Party   British rule
> the United States   the Revolutionary War

The American Revolution was the war that ended (1)_____ over the colonies of North
America and established (2)_____ as a country. The revolution began with a shift
in ideology that was led by great men such as (3)_____ and Samuel Adams.
Three main events led up to (4)_____. These events were the Stamp Act of
1765, the Townshend Acts of 1767, and (5)_____ in 1773. By 1781 the fighting
ended, and the British withdrew from North America.

3. **American Newspapers in the 19th Century**

> *New York Times*   the writing and visual presentation   the newspaper industry
> the telegraph   William Randolph Hearst and Joseph Pulitzer

In the middle of the 1800s, the wide use of (1)_____ enabled newspapers to get
reports from far away. This led to a new age of growth in (2)_____. During
this time, everything from (3)_____ to the delivery of
newspapers improved. New York was the most competitive place, and the (4)_____
emerged as the most respected newspaper in the country. Meanwhile, two newspaper owners,
(5)_____, battled to win readers, giving rise to the
unethical practice of yellow journalism.

4. The Statue of Liberty and the Liberty Bell

> Philadelphia, Pennsylvania   America's ideal of freedom   Gustave Eiffel
> the Declaration of Independence   the 100-year birthday

Two monuments are the best symbols of (1)_____: the Statue of Liberty and the Liberty Bell. The Statue of Liberty was given to the United States by France as a gift in 1885 to mark (2)_____ of the United States. It was designed by (3)_____, and stands 45 meters tall in New York Harbor. The Liberty Bell is located in (4)_____, and was most famously rung on July 8, 1776, to announce the first public reading of (5)_____. It has a crack which was made when it was rung for the first time.

5. Acid Rain

> sulfur and nitrogen gases   the health of humans   acid rain
> industrialized countries   the poisoning of bodies of water

(1)_____ is a pollution problem caused by the release of (2)_____ into the air. This problem has been observed in many (3)_____. Acid rain causes many problems such as (4)_____, killing animals, damaging soil, and harming (5)_____. Scientists are searching for ways to reduce this problem.

6. Vaudeville

> a variety of acts   inexpensive live entertainment   the Great Depression
> a headliner   the late 1800s and early 1900s

Vaudeville was a form of (1)_____ that was very popular in the United States in (2)_____. Vaudeville entertained the audience with (3)_____, including trained animals, acrobats, magic, comedy, musical performances, and lecturers. A typical vaudeville show began with an opener, peaked with (4)_____, and closed with a chaser. At the height of its popularity, vaudeville theaters were among the most popular places for people to gather. By the early 1900s, movie theaters and (5)_____ _____ caused vaudeville to disappear.

1. **The word assassinate in the passage is closest in meaning to**

   Ⓐ help
   Ⓑ kill
   Ⓒ elect
   Ⓓ hurt

2. **The word his in the passage refers to**

   Ⓐ her first husband
   Ⓑ one man
   Ⓒ Charles Dickenson
   Ⓓ Andrew Jackson

3. **According to paragraph 1, the meaning of Andrew Jackson's nickname was**

   Ⓐ sharp steel
   Ⓑ hard wood
   Ⓒ strong wind
   Ⓓ tough leather

4. **According to paragraph 2, which is NOT true about Andrew Jackson?**

   Ⓐ He joined the army in his late teens.
   Ⓑ He and his brother were captured by the British.
   Ⓒ He got wounded by a British soldier.
   Ⓓ He found all his family dead when he got free and returned home.

5. **Which of the following can be inferred from paragraph 4 about Andrew Jackson?**

   Ⓐ He liked to swim in Florida.
   Ⓑ He did not like Seminole culture.
   Ⓒ He was a strong military leader.
   Ⓓ He wanted to be president of the United States.

6. **The author discusses Andrew Jackson's treatment of the Native Americans in paragraph 6 in order to**

   Ⓐ show the negative side of Andrew Jackson's presidency
   Ⓑ show that Andrew Jackson was a ruthless leader
   Ⓒ show that Andrew Jackson helped his country
   Ⓓ show how patriotic Andrew Jackson was

President Andrew Jackson

Andrew Jackson was the seventh president of the United States. He was also the first governor of Florida. Jackson was known to be a very tough soldier. His nickname was "Old Hickory," after the hard wood.

At age 13, Jackson joined the army to fight against the British in the Revolutionary War. He and his brother were captured. He was cut in the face and hand by a British soldier because he refused to clean the soldier's boots. Afterwards, he always hated the British. After being released, his brother died. He returned home and found his mother and the rest of his family dead.

In the Battle of New Orleans in 1815, Jackson led 6,000 soldiers against 12,000 British soldiers. America was victorious. The British army lost 2,000 soldiers while only 8 of Jackson's men died.

In 1817, Jackson led his men against the Spanish and the Seminole Indians in Florida. He crushed the Seminoles. Then he forced the Spanish to cede power of Florida to the U.S. He was made the first U.S. governor of Florida.

Andrew Jackson ran for president in the election of 1824. Many people, like Thomas Jefferson, thought he was too lawless to be president. Jackson lost the election to John Quincy Adams. By the election of 1828, Jackson was able to come back. He defeated Adams and became president.

The most controversial part of Jackson's presidency was his treatment of American Indians. In 1830, his Indian Removal Act became a law. At this time, 45,000 Cherokee Indians were forced to give up their land and move west. Thousands died on a march called "the trail of tears." One historian called this period "one of the unhappiest chapters in American history."

On January 30, 1835, Richard Lawrence tried to assassinate President Jackson. The mentally ill man approached Jackson and fired two pistols at him. The bullets missed Jackson. Then the president attacked Lawrence with his cane.

Andrew Jackson married his wife Rachel after she divorced her first husband. Afterwards, many people attacked her honor. Jackson fought in 103 duels to defend his wife's honor. In all of those duels, Jackson only killed one man, named Charles Dickenson. He insulted Jackson's wife, so they had a duel. Dickenson shot first. His bullet hit Andrew Jackson in his ribs. Then Jackson shot and killed Dickenson. Jackson had many wounds from his numerous duels. They hurt him for the rest of his life. He often coughed up blood. He died at the age of 78 of tuberculosis and heart failure.

7. The word infallible in the passage is closest in meaning to

(A) correct

(B) valuable

(C) logical

(D) doubtful

8. The word it in the passage refers to

(A) knowledge

(B) truth

(C) dialectic

(D) logic

9. The author's description of Aristotle mentions which of the following?

(A) Hercules

(B) Julius Caesar

(C) Aristophenes

(D) King Philip of Macedon

10. The author's description of Aristotle's life mentions all of the following EXCEPT:

(A) He became the leader of ancient Greece.

(B) He was a student of Plato.

(C) He spent time on islands studying biology.

(D) He opened an academy called the Lyceum.

11. Which of the following can be inferred from paragraph 3 about Aristotle?

(A) He did not like to think about science.

(B) He was most interested in drama.

(C) He was primarily a poet.

(D) He was of very high intelligence.

12. Why does the author mention Aristotle's system of logic?

(A) To show how smart he was.

(B) To prove that he was the greatest thinker of all time.

(C) To show his influence on the formation of the scientific method.

(D) To prove that Plato was a greater thinker than Aristotle.

Aristotle and the Development of Science in Ancient Greece

Western science comes from ancient Greece. Aristotle was a great thinker of this era. Although he was not the first scientist or philosopher, he was the most influential. He was a student of Plato and the teacher of Alexander the Great.

From the ages of 18 to 37, Aristotle was a student. He attended Plato's school, called the Academy. Then he traveled for a few years. He studied biology on various islands. Then King Philip of Macedon called for Aristotle. He wanted him to teach his son Alexander. The boy was then 13. Years later, Alexander left Aristotle and went on to conquer Asia. Aristotle returned to Athens. He opened an academy called the Lyceum, where he trained scientists.

Aristotle wrote books on many subjects. His works covered every topic. He was aware of everything from science to art. None of his books have survived in their entirety. However, Aristotle's studies became the foundation of western philosophy and science.

Aristotle valued knowledge gained from the five senses. He used his senses and the dialectic to seek truth. This dialectic originated with Plato, but Aristotle refined it. Aristotle's dialectic relied on logic. It was a way of answering a question with another question. The answers could be used to find truth. These methods are called inductive and deductive logic.

Based on Aristotle's logic, the scientific method was formed. The scientific method is a process used by scientists. First, they make a hypothesis. Then they test it with an experiment. The scientific method is the most important method in modern western science. Aristotle did not do many experiments himself. But his system of logic led others to discover many things. Sir Isaac Newton and Galileo used the scientific method. Their discoveries are an example of Aristotle's influence.

Aristotle also created the idea of categories. He studied every branch of science possible. Then he separated them into different groups. He was familiar with every subject from zoology to geology. His written works make up a huge body of Greek knowledge.

Aristotle has many critics as well. Some scholars think he did not have respect for women. Some think his work is too confusing. He often seems not to obey his own logical rules. And in the Middle Ages, his work, which was treated as infallible, was used to oppress people. But Aristotle's work has been referenced for thousands of years. His studies are a pillar that holds up our modern society.

Vocabulary Review

A Choose the word with the closest meaning to each highlighted word or phrase.

1. The computer was experiencing an internal problem.
   - (A) international
   - (B) inner
   - (C) outside
   - (D) lasting forever

2. His job was to splice electrical wires inside houses.
   - (A) destroy
   - (B) remove
   - (C) connect
   - (D) buy

3. The group had an ideology that many other people found offensive.
   - (A) vehicle
   - (B) smell
   - (C) haircut
   - (D) way of thinking

4. The citizens protested until the unfair law was repealed.
   - (A) canceled
   - (B) noticed
   - (C) joined
   - (D) doubled

5. The actress fell into disfavor when she changed her style.
   - (A) fame
   - (B) unpopularity
   - (C) wealth
   - (D) debt

6. The park was unveiled to commemorate the veterans of World War I.
   - (A) remember
   - (B) scold
   - (C) thank
   - (D) show

7. The worker's struggle to receive fair pay was finally successful.
   - (A) long question
   - (B) long time
   - (C) long fight
   - (D) long speech

8. Their new house looks very majestic with its huge columns and beautiful entryway.
   - (A) splendid
   - (B) enormous
   - (C) expensive
   - (D) attractive

B Match each word with the correct definition.

1. propaganda •
2. unrest •
3. corruption •
4. integrity •
5. glacial •
6. massacre •
7. eruption •
8. monument •
9. intestine •
10. droplet •

- **a.** the quality of coming from a large ice mass
- **b.** an internal explosion that causes outward movement
- **c.** the tubes in a human body that process food and carry waste out of the body
- **d.** an event in which three or more innocent people are killed
- **e.** material that promotes the views of one group
- **f.** the form in which water collects when in motion
- **g.** an object meant to symbolize an important event or concept
- **h.** dishonesty in a publicly held office
- **i.** dissatisfaction; protest
- **j.** the quality of being honest and upright

Unit 4

Negative Factual Information

Negative Factual Information

Overview

■ Introduction

Negative Factual Information questions ask you to find wrong information that is not mentioned in the passage. You should decide which of the answer choices is not discussed in the passage or does not agree with one or more statements in the passage. Like Factual Information questions, scanning is the key skill for this question type. However, you need to scan more of the passage to make sure that your answer is correct.

■ Question Types

1. According to the passage, which of the following is NOT true of _____?

2. All of the following are mentioned in paragraph X as _____ EXCEPT:

3. The author's description of _____ mentions all of the following EXCEPT:

4. Which of the following is NOT mentioned in the passage?

■ Useful Tips

• Make use of the key words in the question and answer choices to spot relevant information in the passage.

• Don't forget that the necessary information may be spread out over an entire paragraph or several paragraphs.

• Make sure that your answer is NOT mentioned in the passage or contradicts the passage.

Sample iBT Question

According to the passage, all of the following are true EXCEPT:

Ⓐ Ladybugs are helpful for gardening.

Ⓑ Ladybugs are poisonous to other insects.

Ⓒ Ladybugs are insectivores.

Ⓓ Ladybugs are sold at many garden supply shops.

Ladybugs

Many people do not like insects. They scream or attempt to squash a bug when they see it. One exception is the ladybug. Most people see this colorful little beetle as a friend.

The ladybug is an especially useful friend to gardeners. Many garden supply shops sell these beetles. Gardeners buy them and put the ladybugs in their garden. This is because ladybugs eat other harmful insects.

Once in the garden, the ladybug will eat all sorts of pests. Aphids and fruit flies become meals for this insectivore. These pests would otherwise threaten the plants in the garden. Some gardeners even install special rows of grass called beetle-bunkers to give the ladybugs a place to thrive.

 Check and make sure which choice is not mentioned in the passage. Ladybugs help with gardening because they eat harmful insects. For that reason, they are sold at garden supply shops and even raised by gardeners. So the correct answer is (B).

Skill & Drill

Scanning is the key skill to deal with Negative Factual Information questions. But unlike Factual Information questions, you should scan more of the passage because relevant information may be spread out over more than one part of the passage. You need to decide which of the answer choices is not true or not mentioned in the passage.

Read the questions and answer choices first. Then scan for the information you need to answer the questions. Try to eliminate obviously wrong answer choices.

Caterpillars

A caterpillar is the larval form of a butterfly or a moth. It has a long, segmented body. The body is soft. This allows it to grow quickly as it consumes much food, like a balloon. Caterpillars are eating machines as they prepare to enter the pupa stage.

Like all insects, caterpillars do not breathe through their mouths. They pull in air through tubes along the sides of their body. Their eyesight is very poor, so they use antennae to locate food.

Caterpillars have various defenses to protect them from birds and other animals. Their bodies are capable of adapting camouflage. Some caterpillars look like snakes or leaves. Some caterpillars eat poison leaves and become toxic.

1. **According to the passage, which of the following is NOT true of the caterpillar?**

    (A) It locates food with feelers and eats a lot.
    (B) It protects itself from enemies in various ways.
    (C) It is the larval form of all insects.
    (D) It breathes through the sides of its body.

The Refrigerator

One invention that changed the daily lives of humans is the refrigerator. In the time before its invention, people had to spend a lot of time gathering fresh food every day. The only way to keep food cold was to have a large block of ice delivered to the home. This was costly and very inconvenient.

The first home refrigerators came onto the market in 1911. At that time, a refrigerator cost almost twice as much as a new car. The early models took up a lot of space in the home. Sometimes two rooms were needed.

By 1927 General Electric introduced the Monitor-Top refrigerator. This was the first model to be widely used and is still functional today.

2. **The author's description of the refrigerator mentions all of the following EXCEPT:**

    (A) the effect of refrigerators as an invention
    (B) the convenience of using ice to keep food fresh
    (C) the size of early refrigerators
    (D) the popularization of refrigerators

Kinds of Wind

Wind is the movement of air over the Earth's surface. It is caused by uneven heating of the atmosphere. The two major influences on wind are the heating between the equator and the poles and the Earth's rotation.

One way to classify different kinds of wind is by the forces that cause it. Prevailing winds, such as the trade winds, the westerlies, and the jet streams, are caused by global circulation. Synoptic winds are caused by warm and cold fronts clashing. Mesoscale winds are produced by thunderstorms. Microscale winds are very short bursts that happen suddenly.

Winds are some of the most common yet powerful forces shaping our lives and our planet every day.

3. **According to the passage, which of the following is NOT true about wind?**

   Ⓐ The clash of cold fronts causes synoptic winds.
   Ⓑ Very short, sudden bursts of wind are called microscale.
   Ⓒ The trade winds are caused by global rotation.
   Ⓓ Thunderstorms produce mesoscale winds.

Hummingbirds

Hummingbirds are known for their ability to hover in mid-air by rapidly flapping their wings. A hummingbird flaps 15 to 80 times per second. This action enables them to maintain position while drinking from flower blossoms. They get their name from the humming sound made by their wings.

The Bee hummingbird is the smallest bird in the world, weighing 1.8 grams. The Rufous hummingbird is more typical, weighing 3 grams. The Giant hummingbird weighs as much as 24 grams.

Hummingbirds have the highest metabolism of any animal beside insects. Their hearts can beat as many as 1,260 beats per minute. In order to sustain this, they must consume more than their own body weight in food each day.

4. **According to the passage, which of the following is NOT true about hummingbirds?**

   Ⓐ Their name comes from the humming noise their wings make.
   Ⓑ Their wings can beat from 15 to 80 times every second.
   Ⓒ The Rufous hummingbird is about twice as heavy as the Bee hummingbird.
   Ⓓ They have a higher metabolism than insects do.

Practice with Long Passages

Read the following passage, and answer the questions.

Coral Reefs

Time Limit: 2 min. 50 sec .

Coral reefs grow in photic zones of tropical seas, where sufficient light penetrates into the water. In order to survive, the reef must be in an area with mild wave action. Mild wave action is not so strong that it tears the reef. But it is strong enough to stir the water and deliver food and oxygen.

Coral reefs are made of millions of skeletons from small animals called polyps. After polyps die, waves and fish break down their skeletons. Then the fragments settle into the reef and cause it to grow. Algae feed on the skeletons and convert the material to limestone. The limestone is deposited over the reef and forms a protective crust. These algae grow best in clear, shallow water.

Most of the world's reefs are located in the tropical waters of the Pacific or Indian Oceans. There are few reefs on the western coasts of North and South America and Africa. This is due to the strong, cold coastal currents in these areas.

Coral reefs support a vast array of biodiversity. They create a habitat for many species of fish and plant life to thrive. Without the reefs, many of these species would face extinction.

Currently, there are several threats to the reefs of the world. Much pollution that runs off from factories and farms kills coral reef life. The water quality in these areas often becomes poisonous, killing off the coral reefs and the creatures that live on and around them.

Another threat to coral reefs is over-fishing and destructive fishing by humans. Many fishermen who trap exotic fish for pet shops use cyanide gas to stun fish. This process decreases the lifespan of the captured fish and poisons the reef. Dynamite fishing is another method that damages reef ecosystems. It kills the corals which are the habitat for a healthy reef. Many conservation groups are actively trying to protect the coral reefs of the world.

General Comprehension

1. The word convert in the passage is closest in meaning to

  Ⓐ destroy
  Ⓑ change
  Ⓒ condense
  Ⓓ eliminate

2. The word them in the passage refers to

  Ⓐ factories
  Ⓑ farms
  Ⓒ these areas
  Ⓓ coral reefs

○ **photic (a)**
penetrated by light, especially sunlight

○ **stir (v)**
to mix; to shake

○ **fragment (n)**
a small piece

○ **shallow (a)**
not deep

○ **current (n)**
a force of waves that do not break the surface of a body of water

○ **habitat (n)**
a place where one or more species of living organisms thrives

On the TOEFL Test

3. **According to paragraph 2, all of the following are true EXCEPT:**

    Ⓐ Thousands of polyp skeletons settle into the reef and cause it to grow.
    Ⓑ The skeletons of reefs are decomposed by waves and fish.
    Ⓒ Clear, shallow water is the best place for algae to grow.
    Ⓓ Algae eat skeletons, turning them into limestone.

4. **According to paragraph 6, which of the following is NOT true about coral reefs?**

    Ⓐ Many fishermen catch exotic fish for profit by using helium gas.
    Ⓑ Coral reefs can be damaged by over-fishing.
    Ⓒ A lot of conservation groups work hard to protect coral reefs.
    Ⓓ The process of cyanide fishing poisons coral reefs.

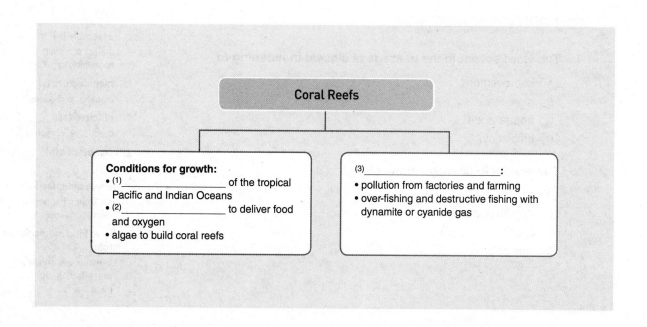

Coral Reefs

Conditions for growth:
• (1)_____ of the tropical Pacific and Indian Oceans
• (2)_____ to deliver food and oxygen
• algae to build coral reefs

(3)_____:
• pollution from factories and farming
• over-fishing and destructive fishing with dynamite or cyanide gas

Mass Production and the Ford Model-T

Time Limit: 2 min. 50 sec.

The production of large amounts of products on an assembly line is called mass production. The advent of the production line changed the way people worked and lived in the 20th century. This method did not become popular until Henry Ford's Ford Motor Company began manufacturing the Model-T car in 1908.

Henry Ford was the inventor of the car and president of the company. He was always searching for a more efficient method of production. In 1913 he introduced moving assembly lines to his production plants. By 1914, the Ford assembly line was so efficient that it took 93 minutes to produce one Model-T. They came off the assembly line every 3 minutes. Ford produced more cars than all of its competitors combined.

In addition, Ford's assembly line introduced a new level of worker safety. This method of having workers stay in an assigned position led to fewer accidents. Ford also shocked the nation with an unprecedented $5 per day pay scale. This effort on the part of Ford to attract talented workers more than doubled the worker's minimum wage.

In 1908, the price for a Model-T was $825, and it fell every year after. By 1916, the price of the Model-T had dropped to $360. There were more Model-Ts than any other car on the road. The only color available in this model was black. This was because black paint was cheaper and dried faster, keeping production costs down. Henry Ford was heard to have joked, "Any customer can have a car painted any color he wants, so long as it is black."

By the 1920s, 15 million Model-Ts had been produced. This record held for 30 years. Many people learned to drive in a Model-T. They had very fond memories of the car.

The Model-T revolution changed the way people around the world work and travel. Now, assembly lines employ people in every industrial nation. Also, people use cars in their everyday lives.

General Comprehension

1. **The word advent in the passage is closest in meaning to**

   A improvement

   B increase

   C appearance

   D efficiency

2. **The word it in passage refers to**

   A this model

   B any customer

   C a car

   D any color

assembly (n)
the act of putting something together

manufacture (v)
to make; to produce

efficient (a)
productive; competent

competitor (n)
rival

unprecedented (a)
not having happened before; unusual

have fond memories of (phr)
to remember something with affection and pleasure

3. According to the passage, which of the following is NOT true of Henry Ford?

   Ⓐ He surprised the nation with a $5 per day pay cut.

   Ⓑ He was president of the Ford Motor Company.

   Ⓒ He tried to find new and better ways to produce cars cheaply.

   Ⓓ He brought automated assembly lines into the Ford production plants in 1913.

4. The author's description of the Model-T revolution mentions all of the following EXCEPT:

   Ⓐ It changed the lives of people around the world.

   Ⓑ It changed the way people went on vacation.

   Ⓒ It made every industrial nation employ people on assembly lines.

   Ⓓ It made cars a part of people's everyday lives.

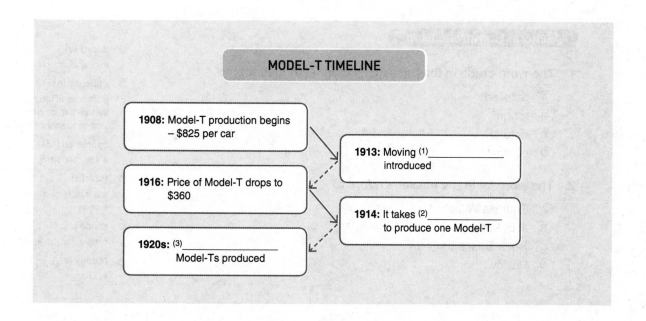

MODEL-T TIMELINE

1908: Model-T production begins – $825 per car

1913: Moving (1)_____ introduced

1916: Price of Model-T drops to $360

1914: It takes (2)_____ to produce one Model-T

1920s: (3)_____ Model-Ts produced

Read the following passage, and answer the questions.

Pioneers in Neurology

Time Limit: 2 min. 30 sec.

The history of neurology goes back to ancient Egypt. Scrolls depict disorders of the brain. They had a basic understanding of the nervous system. Egyptians even performed simple brain surgery.

In ancient Greece, the famous physician Hippocrates was convinced epilepsy had a physical cause. Before him, it was considered a punishment by the gods. Another Greek physician, Galen, looked at the nervous system in specimens. He cut a certain nerve in the brain of an ape. Then he noticed the ape lost its voice.

In 1664, Thomas Willis published *Anatomy of the Brain*. In it he described the circle of Willis, which enables the flow of blood through the brain. He was also the first to use the word *neurology*. In the 1700s, Bailie and Cruvielher published the first illustrations of the brain. This helped doctors and scientists. They began to understand diseases such as brain damage in stroke.

In 1837, J. E. Purkinje was the first to look at a neuron. He saw it through a microscope. This led to an understanding that progressed past crude drawings. The famous philosopher Rene Descartes thought about the brain. He had a theory about behavior. He thought every activity of an animal was a necessary reaction to an external stimulus. Some doctors experimented on patients. They were able to understand more about the nervous system.

A new understanding of neurological behavior was reached by Pavlov, a Russian physiologist. He trained his dogs to salivate at the ring of a bell. This established that a simple reflex could be modified by higher brain functions.

By 1878, William McEwen removed a brain tumor from a patient. The patient lived for many years after. When he performed his surgeries, he used tools such as the tendon hammer. X-rays and the CT scan were not far behind. These developments led to the field of neurology that helps people today.

General Comprehension

1. **The word crude in the passage is closest in meaning to**

   (A) detailed
   (B) rough
   (C) natural
   (D) original

2. **The word he in the passage refers to**

   (A) Thomas Willis
   (B) J. E. Purkinje
   (C) Rene Descates
   (D) Pavlov

depict (v)
to describe; to show

epilepsy (n)
a disease of the nervous system that causes victims to shake violently

specimen (n)
a scientific sample

flow (n)
the quality of continuous motion

crude (a)
simple; not advanced

modify (v)
to change

3. The author's description of the ancient Egyptians mentions all of the following EXCEPT:

Ⓐ Disorders of the brain are shown in their scrolls.

Ⓑ They successfully completed brain transplants.

Ⓒ The nervous system was understood on a basic level.

Ⓓ Simple brain surgery was completed.

4. According to paragraph 4, all of the following are true EXCEPT:

Ⓐ A working model of a human brain was built by scientists.

Ⓑ Rene Descartes theorized about the brain and behavior.

Ⓒ More about the nervous system could be explained by experimenting on patients.

Ⓓ The first to look at a neuron through a microscope was J.E. Purkinje.

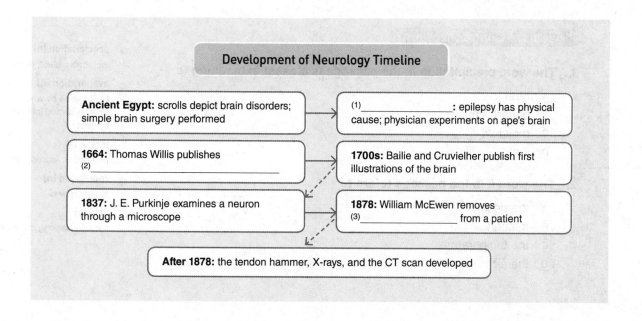

Development of Neurology Timeline

Ancient Egypt: scrolls depict brain disorders; simple brain surgery performed

(1)_____ : epilepsy has physical cause; physician experiments on ape's brain

1664: Thomas Willis publishes (2)_____

1700s: Bailie and Cruvielher publish first illustrations of the brain

1837: J. E. Purkinje examines a neuron through a microscope

1878: William McEwen removes (3)_____ from a patient

After 1878: the tendon hammer, X-rays, and the CT scan developed

The Effects of Desert Weather

Time Limit: 2 min. 40 sec.

A desert is a type of landscape that receives little precipitation. Deserts are normally defined as areas that receive annual precipitation of less than 250mm. But some places such as Tucson, Arizona receive more but are still called deserts. That is because they have a much higher rate of evaporation.

Many environmentalists argue that desert regions are increasing. This process is called desertification. It happens when useful soil is blown away by wind. Then the temperature rises, and an area that was once fertile becomes desert. They say that this is due to global warming. It is also due to overdevelopment. Both of these problems are major threats to humanity.

True deserts have very sparse vegetation. These deserts exist in the most arid regions of Earth. In these places, rainfall is rare and infrequent.

Deserts have a reputation for supporting little life. But this is not true. Deserts have many animals that hide during daylight. About one fifth of the Earth is covered in desert.

Desert landscapes are often composed of sand and rocky surfaces. Sand dunes and stony surfaces called regs are often found in deserts. Cold deserts have similar features but receive snow instead of rain. Antarctica is the largest cold desert. The largest hot desert is the Sahara.

Most deserts have an extreme temperature range. The temperature is very low at night. This is because the air is so dry that it holds little heat. The desert cools as soon as the sun sets. Cloudless skies also increase the release of heat at night.

Sand covers only about 20% of Earth's deserts. There are six forms of deserts. One of the forms is a mountain or a basin desert. Hamada deserts are comprised of plateau landforms. Regs consist of rock pavements. Ergs are formed by sand seas. Intermontane basins occur at high elevations. Finally, badlands are arid regions comprised of clay-rich soil.

General Comprehension

1. **The word precipitation in the passage is closest in meaning to**

   (A) heat
   (B) desertification
   (C) moisture
   (D) sand

2. **The word it in the passage refers to**

   (A) the desert
   (B) the sun
   (C) the temperature
   (D) the air

precipitation (n)
rain, snow, sleet, or hail

evaporation (n)
the process by which water is turned into gas by heat

fertile (a)
productive; fecund; rich

reputation (n)
fame; renown

arid (a)
very dry; lacking moisture

On the TOEFL Test

3. **According to the author's description of deserts, all of the following are true EXCEPT:**

   Ⓐ They receive much precipitation during the nighttime.
   Ⓑ There is a small amount of vegetation in them.
   Ⓒ They are often covered in sand and rocky surfaces.
   Ⓓ There are six forms of them.

4. **According to the passage, which of the following is NOT true?**

   Ⓐ Desert regions are on the rise, according to many environmentalists.
   Ⓑ Deserts are found only in hot regions on the earth.
   Ⓒ As soon as the sun sets, the desert becomes cooler.
   Ⓓ Global warming is said to be a cause of desertification.

Deserts

- have little precipitation, normally less than 250mm
- are increasing through desertification
- (1)_____ – the largest cold desert
- the Sahara – the largest hot desert

| **Mountain or basin desert** | **Hamada:** plateau landforms | (2)_____: rock pavements |

| (3)_____: sand seas | **Intermontane basins:** at high elevations | **Badlands:** arid regions of clay-rich soil |

Read the following passage, and answer the questions.

The Migration of the Monarch Butterfly

Time Limit: 2 min. 30 sec.

The Monarch butterfly is found in North America. Since the 19th century, it has also appeared in New Zealand, Australia, and the Canary Islands. It can also be found as a migrant in the Azores, Portugal, and Spain. In some places, the Monarch is also known as the wandering butterfly.

Monarchs are known for migrating long distances. They migrate every year. They fly southward in large numbers from August through October. Then in the spring they migrate northward.

During the migration, females deposit eggs for the next generation. North American Monarchs are separated into two populations. One group lives east of the Rocky Mountains. This group spends winters in Michoacan, Mexico. The group that lives in the west spends winter in central California, mainly in Pacific Grove and Santa Cruz.

The length of the Monarch's migration journey is longer than a single butterfly's lifespan. Butterflies born in early summer live less than two months. The final generation of the summer lives about seven months. During this time they fly to their winter home. This generation does not reproduce until it leaves the winter location in the spring.

Scientists still do not understand how the species can return to the same winter location over a gap in generations. This is the subject of much research. It is assumed that the flight patterns are inherited. Studies suggest that they are based on a combination of circadian rhythm and the position of the sun in the sky. A new study suggests that the Monarchs have special ultraviolet photoreceptors that give them a sense of direction.

A few Monarchs appear in Great Britain in years with favorable conditions. Some Monarchs also live on the island of Hawaii. These butterflies do not migrate. They live for six to eight weeks if the gardens have enough nectar-producing flowers to support them.

General Comprehension

1. The word migrate in the passage is closest in meaning to

- (A) travel seasonally
- (B) escape from danger
- (C) search for food
- (D) prepare for winter

2. The word they in the passage refers to

- (A) scientists
- (B) the species
- (C) generations
- (D) the flight patterns

generation (n)
a group of the same species all born at the same time

reproduce (v)
to have babies

inherit (v)
for parents to pass down traits to offspring

circadian rhythm (phr)
biological behavior based on day and night cycles

nectar (n)
the sweet, nutritious fluid within the blossom of a flower

On the TOEFL Test

3. **The author's description of the Monarch butterfly in paragraphs 1 and 2 mentions all of the following EXCEPT:**

    Ⓐ the locations where it lives
    Ⓑ its migration route
    Ⓒ its nickname
    Ⓓ the time and direction of its migration

4. **According to the passage, which of the following is NOT true?**

    Ⓐ Hawaiian butterflies do not migrate.
    Ⓑ Early summer butterflies do not live to be two months old.
    Ⓒ A few Monarchs appear in Russia with the proper conditions.
    Ⓓ Monarch butterflies migrate each year.

Facts about Monarch Butterflies

- (1)_____ every year
- Fly southward during August to October and northward in the spring
- (2)_____
  - One group living east of the Rocky Mountains winters in Michoacan, Mexico.
  - Western group winters in central California.
- Scientists don't fully understand their migration patterns.
- Some Monarchs live in (3)_____ and don't migrate.

The Development of the Typewriter

Time Limit: 2 min. 30 sec.

No single person invented the typewriter. A number of people have contributed to its creation. In 1714, Henry Mill received a patent. It was for a machine similar to the typewriter. But nothing else is known about it. Another early innovator was a man named Turri. His machine allowed the blind to write. Turri also invented carbon paper.

In 1829, William Austin Burt patented a machine called the Typographer. Some consider it the first typewriter. This machine was slower than handwriting.

In 1865, Reverend Hansen created the Writing Ball. This was the first typewriter to go into production. But it was still too slow. The first machine to type faster than a human hand could write was built in 1867 by Sholes and Glidden. They sold the patent to Remington. He began producing this machine in 1873.

One problem with the early typewriters was visibility. The position of the typebar blocked the page. So, the typist could not see what they had just typed. In 1895 this problem was solved. "Visible" typewriters were produced. The older models stayed on the market as late as 1915.

IBM began producing the electric Selectric typewriter in the 20th century. It featured a spherical type ball. It immediately dominated the market. The type ball was an important improvement. It eliminated jams when two keys were struck at once. Many of these machines are still used today.

In the 1980s came the final major development. The type ball was replaced with the daisy wheel. The daisy wheel is simpler and cheaper than the type ball. But it wears out more quickly.

Today, typewriters are still sometimes used. They are useful when a computer is impractical or inconvenient. Companies such as Smith Corona, Olivetti, and Brother still make them. Generally, however, typewriters have been replaced by computers.

General Comprehension

1. The word innovator in the passage is closest in meaning to

(A) inventor
(B) owner
(C) philosopher
(D) typist

2. The word it in the passage refers to

(A) IBM
(B) the electric Selectric typewriter
(C) the market
(D) the type ball

invent (v)
to discover or create something for the first time

carbon (n)
an element present in all living things

visible (a)
able to be seen by the naked eye

dominate (v)
to control with power

replace (v)
to take the place of something; to substitute

3. According to the passage, all of the following are true EXCEPT:

    Ⓐ There were many contributors to the development of the typewriter.

    Ⓑ It can be said that the first typewriter was developed by William Austin Burt.

    Ⓒ Sholes and Glidden created a typewriter that was faster than handwriting.

    Ⓓ Visible typewriters went on the market starting in 1915.

4. According to the passage, which of the following is NOT true?

    Ⓐ Remington produced Sholes and Glidden's typewriter in 1873.

    Ⓑ The IBM Selectric typewriter solved the jamming problem of older models.

    Ⓒ The daisy wheel replaced the type ball since it cost less and was more durable.

    Ⓓ Some companies still produce typewriters because they are still in use.

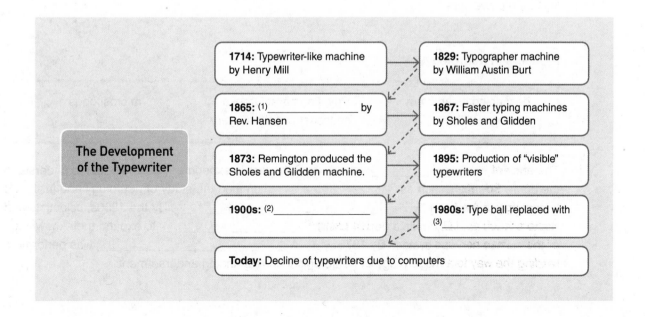

The Development of the Typewriter

1714: Typewriter-like machine by Henry Mill

1829: Typographer machine by William Austin Burt

1865: (1)_____ by Rev. Hansen

1867: Faster typing machines by Sholes and Glidden

1873: Remington produced the Sholes and Glidden machine.

1895: Production of "visible" typewriters

1900s: (2)_____

1980s: Type ball replaced with (3)_____

Today: Decline of typewriters due to computers

Building Summary Skills

The following summaries are based on the long passages you worked on earlier. Complete each of them by filling in the blanks with suitable words or phrases.

1. Coral Reefs

> become extinct   the tropical Indian and Pacific Ocean regions   tiny polyps
> mild wave action   pollution, over-fishing, and destructive fishing

Coral reefs grow best in photic tropical zones with (1)_____. Reefs are made of the skeletons of millions of (2)_____ that have been turned into limestone by algae. These reefs are most common in (3)_____. Reefs are important because they support a wide range of species that would otherwise (4)_____. There are many threats to reefs, such as (5)_____ that conservation groups are fighting against.

2. Mass Production and the Ford Model-T

> by the 1920s   moving assembly lines   the Model-T car
> became lower   Henry Ford

(1)_____ changed the way people worked and lived in the 20th century with his Ford Model-T and the mass assembly line it was produced on. After beginning Ford Motor Company and inventing (2)_____, Ford introduced (3)_____ in his production plants. These were so effective that the Model-T car became common around the world and the price (4)_____ every year. (5)_____, there were more Model-Ts on the road than any other car, and people around the world worked on assembly lines and drove cars.

3. Pioneers in Neurology

> describing its anatomy   Egyptians and Greeks   microscopes
> Thomas Willis   successful brain surgery

The ancient (1)_____ were the first to experiment on and begin to understand the brain. Scientists such as (2)_____ created the study of neurology and furthered knowledge of the brain by (3)_____. By the 1800s, scientists and doctors, such as J.E. Purkinje began using (4)_____ to expand their knowledge of the human nervous system. By 1878, (5)_____ was performed, leading the way to a modern age of neurological understanding and treatment.

4. The Effects of Desert Weather

> global warming   receive little precipitation   desertification
> intermontane basins, and badlands   supporting life forms

Deserts are regions that (1)_____. (2)_____ is the process by which fertile land becomes desert. Many environmentalists argue that temperature increases due to (3)_____ are accelerating the rate of desertification around the world. Deserts are capable of (4)_____ that have adapted to their harsh environments. There are six kinds of deserts, including mountain or basin deserts, hamada deserts, regs, ergs, (5)_____.

5. The Migration of the Monarch Butterfly

> migrate so far   alive   the same winter location
> very different life spans   North America

The Monarch butterfly is found in some parts of the world, including (1)_____. Scientists wonder how the Monarch is able to (2)_____ every year. New generations of the Monarch return to (3)_____ every year even though they were not (4)_____ at the time of the last migration. Scientists are curious about the fact that Monarchs have (5)_____ based on their place in the seasonal migration cycle.

6. The Development of the Typewriter

> typewriters   full of small improvements   the computer
> no single person   over the years

(1)_____ invented the typewriter, but many people have contributed to its creation (2)_____. The history of the typewriter is (3)_____ made over the years. When problems such as the type bar blocking the typist's view arose, new improvements corrected them. These days the typewriter has been replaced by (4)_____. But some people still use (5)_____, and some companies still make them.

1. **The word fatal in the passage is closest in meaning to**

   (A) harmful
   (B) deadly
   (C) surprising
   (D) dangerous

2. **According to paragraph 1, which of the following is true of chimpanzees?**

   (A) West and Central Africa are home to the common chimp.
   (B) The bonobo chimp lives in Madagascar.
   (C) There are five kinds of chimps.
   (D) The three species of chimp are separated by the Congo River boundary.

3. **According to the passage, all of the following are true EXCEPT:**

   (A) Wild chimps rarely live past the age of 40.
   (B) Chimps can make and use simple tools.
   (C) Chimps sometimes attack children.
   (D) Adult male chimps can be up to 3m tall.

4. **Which of the following can be inferred about chimpanzees?**

   (A) They are as intelligent as humans.
   (B) They can be very dangerous.
   (C) They can do factory work if trained properly.
   (D) They are not genetically related to humans.

5. **In paragraph 5, why does the author mention that plans were made to create a workforce of chimps?**

   (A) To show that chimps can use simple tools
   (B) To show that chimps like helping humans
   (C) To show that the intelligence of chimps is sometimes exaggerated
   (D) To show that chimps make excellent menial workers

6. **The word their in the passage refers to**

   (A) chimps
   (B) humans
   (C) observers
   (D) plans

Chimpanzees

There are two types of chimpanzees. The common chimp lives in West and Central Africa. Its cousin is the bonobo or pygmy chimp, which comes from the forests of the Democratic Republic of Congo. The Congo River forms a boundary between the two species.

Adult male chimps can weigh between 35 to 70kg. They usually stand 0.9 to 1.2m tall. Females usually weigh 26 to 50kg and stand 0.66 to 1m tall. Chimps rarely live past 40 years old in the wild. But in captivity they have been known to reach the age of 60.

African people have been in contact with chimps for thousands of years. The first recorded encounter between a European and a chimp occurred in the 1600s. The diary of Portuguese explorer Duarte Pacheco Pereira documented chimps. He noted their simple use of tools.

Chimps were brought from Angola to Europe in the 1600s. The first was given as a gift to the Prince of Orange in 1640. Scientists were fascinated at the similarities between the chimps and humans. Over the next 20 years, many chimps were exported to Europe.

In 1859, Darwin's *Theory of Evolution* was published. This spurred interest in chimps as a link to humans. Observers at the time were interested in the chimp's behavior. They were searching for similarities to human behavior. Their main goal was to discover whether chimps were inherently "good." Their interest was not grounded in practical science, however. The tendency of the time was to greatly exaggerate the chimp's intelligence. At one point, plans were made to create a workforce of chimps. The idea was make chimps fill menial labor positions such as factory work.

Chimps were treated with much more serious scientific interest in the 20th century. Before 1960, almost nothing was known about chimps' behavior in their natural habitat. Then Jane Goodall went to live in Tanzania's Gombe Forest. There she lived among the chimps and observed their habits. Her discovery of chimps making tools was groundbreaking. It was previously believed that only humans did this.

Common chimps sometimes attack humans. In Uganda, many children have been attacked by chimps. These attacks are usually fatal for the children. One reason for these attacks is that the chimps mistake the children for a species of monkey. This monkey is called the Western Red Colobus. It is one of the common chimp's favorite foods.

Humans must be very careful around chimps. They view humans as their rivals. Also, the average chimp has five times the upper body strength of an adult human male. This was proven when former NASCAR (National Association for Stock Car Automobile Racing) driver Saint James Davis was attacked and almost killed by a chimp.

7. **The word it in the passage refers to**

   Ⓐ glass

   Ⓑ sand

   Ⓒ silicon

   Ⓓ iron

8. **Which of the following is the author's definition of glass?**

   Ⓐ uniform, amorphous, solid material

   Ⓑ silicon dioxide formed into a shape

   Ⓒ solid material with iron content

   Ⓓ tin oxide mixed with sulfur and carbon

9. **According to paragraph 3, which of the following is NOT true about glass?**

   Ⓐ Obsidian is a naturally occurring form of glass.

   Ⓑ Stone Age people made weapons and tools from glass.

   Ⓒ It is believed that the Phoenicians produced glass for the first time in history.

   Ⓓ The Phoenicians coated their pottery with glass 3000 years ago.

10. **The author of the passage implies that**

   Ⓐ the Romans were the first to produce soda glass using a new technique

   Ⓑ Mediterranean people did not use potash in their glassworks

   Ⓒ hand-blown glassworks are now considered antique items due to their scarcity

   Ⓓ delicate crystal works are created by many diamond artisans

11. **The author discusses glass jars and beads in paragraph 4 in order to show that**

   Ⓐ glass comes from natural sources in ancient Egypt

   Ⓑ glass was once a rare and prized object in ancient Egypt

   Ⓒ glass was used as a currency in ancient Egypt

   Ⓓ glass was invented by the ancient Egyptians

12. **The word polish in the passage is closest in meaning to**

   Ⓐ rub

   Ⓑ break

   Ⓒ bond

   Ⓓ sell

Glassmaking

Glass is a uniform, amorphous, solid material. It is composed mainly of silicon dioxide. This is the major raw material of sand. If raw materials contain as much as 1% iron, the glass will come out colored. So fine glass factories enrich their silicon to make it more pure.

When glass is made naturally, it tends to be colored green. This is due to the iron content. But glassblowers add powdered metals to change the color of the glass. By adding sulfur and carbon, glass will become colored yellowish to black. Tin oxide can be used to create white glass. Also, a little cobalt will color glass a deep blue. And small concentrations of selenium can yield a brilliant color known as "selenium ruby."

Obsidian is glass that occurs naturally from hot magma flows. This glass has been used to create sharp knives, arrowheads, and tools since the Stone Age. According to history, the first glassmakers were the Phoenicians. They used glass to coat their pottery as early as 3000 B.C.

Around 1500 B.C., the ancient Egyptians made glass jars and beads. The beads they created consisted of metal rods with melted glass wrapped around them. The beads were prized possessions. They were thought to have magic powers.

The Romans developed many new glassmaking techniques. They also spread the use of glass as far as China and the British Isles.

In Northern Europe, around 1000 A.D., a new method of glasswork was discovered. The use of soda glass was replaced with some other glass contained potash. This was important because potash was much more plentiful. Potash is obtained from wood ashes. From this point on, Northern European and Mediterranean glassworks were distinguishable from each other.

In 11th-century Germany, the techniques for making sheet glass were invented. This led to the modern methods of making the windows we use in all houses and buildings. By the 14th century, Venice was the center for fine glassworks. In that city, all sorts of luxury items, such as mirrors, dinnerware, and vases, were made.

Hand-blown glass is still considered a commodity to this day. Some of the most famous fine glass artists are Dale Chihuly, Rene Lalique, and Louis Comfort Tiffany. Their works are in museums such as the Smithsonian. Some of their works sell for many thousands of dollars.

Cold work techniques are used for turning glass into fine crystal. Crystal manufacturers such as Edinburgh Crystal and Waterford Crystal used diamond saws to cut and polish glass into beautiful designs.

Vocabulary Review

A Choose the word with the closest meaning to each highlighted word or phrase.

1. Many people enrich themselves by taking educational classes.
   - (A) damage
   - (B) improve
   - (C) help
   - (D) research

2. His business specialized in manufacturing vacuum cleaners.
   - (A) selling
   - (B) buying
   - (C) making
   - (D) fixing

3. The filmmaker tried to depict the lives of the early colonists in his movie.
   - (A) laugh at
   - (B) destroy
   - (C) name
   - (D) show

4. He spent many months working on his car to modify its fuel injection system.
   - (A) change
   - (B) remove
   - (C) transfer
   - (D) resell

5. She was disappointed that her garden couldn't grow vegetables because it was so arid.
   - (A) dry
   - (B) flooded
   - (C) fertile
   - (D) ugly

6. He hoped to inherit his father's successful business.
   - (A) buy
   - (B) receive
   - (C) find
   - (D) take

7. Anybody who has seen him play the game chess has seen him dominate the board.
   - (A) lose
   - (B) win
   - (C) control
   - (D) tie

8. Their first encounter was at the birthday party of a mutual friend.
   - (A) meeting
   - (B) argument
   - (C) disagreement
   - (D) formal introduction

B Match each word with the correct definition.

1. evaporation •
2. migrant •
3. scroll •
4. epilepsy •
5. lifespan •
6. advent •
7. habitat •
8. fragment •
9. innovator •
10. skeleton •

- **a.** a disease of the nervous system that causes victims to shake violently
- **b.** a place where one or more species of living organisms thrives
- **c.** a small piece
- **d.** one who improves pre-existing objects or solves problems practically
- **e.** the process by which water is turned into gas by heat
- **f.** one who goes to a new country for an extended period of time
- **g.** an old form of paper that writings were kept on
- **h.** the bone structure within an organism
- **i.** the arrival of an important person or thing
- **j.** the expected length of life for a living organism

Sentence Simplification

Unit 5

Sentence Simplification

Sentence Simplification

Overview

■ Introduction

Sentence Simplification questions ask you to choose a sentence that best paraphrases the original sentence in the passage. The correct answer uses different vocabulary and different grammar to restate the essential meaning of the original sentence in a simpler way. This type of question does not appear in every reading passage. Also, there is never more than one Sentence Simplification question in a passage.

■ Question Type

Which of the following best expresses the essential information in the highlighted sentence?
Incorrect answer choices change the meaning in important ways or leave out essential information.

■ Useful Tips

- Figure out what essential information is in the original sentence.

- Don't focus on minor information such as details and examples.

- Keep in mind that incorrect answers contradict something in the original sentence or leave out important information from the original sentence.

- Make sure that your answer agrees with the main argument of the paragraph or the passage as a whole.

Sample iBT Question

Which of the following best expresses the essential information in the highlighted sentence? *Incorrect* **answer choices change the meaning in important ways or leave out essential information.**

(A) Blue mussels use special bodily structures to stay on objects.

(B) Blue mussels have strong thread-like appendages growing out of their bodies.

(C) Blue mussels live on rocks and other things that grow strong thread-like strings.

(D) Blue mussels eat thread-like substances on rocks and other objects to survive.

The Blue Mussel

The blue mussel is an edible bivalve. It is commonly farmed and harvested for food around the world. They attach themselves to rocks and other objects by strong, thread-like structures called byssal threads. The shell of the blue mussel is smooth, with a sculpting of concentric lines but no radiating ribs. They are purple, blue, or sometimes brown in color. Blue mussels are preyed upon by starfish. They are also eaten by the Dogwhelk, a carnivorous, rocky-shore mollusk. Blue mussels are part of a long-term environmental monitoring program in Prince William Sound, Alaska. The study examines how the blue mussel's hydrocarbon signature helps with ecosystem recovery.

 The essential information in the original sentence is that the blue mussel has special bodily structures and uses them to cling to objects. So the correct answer is (A).

In order to answer Sentence Simplification questions, you should choose the sentence that best paraphrases the essential information in the highlighted sentence. A good paraphrase has different words and sentence structure from the original sentence. It does not focus on minor information such as details and examples.

Folk Medicine

Folk medicine refers to traditional methods of healing. It is used to deal with illness and injury. It is also used to aid with childbirth and to maintain wellness. It is a body of knowledge distinct from scientific medicine. But both types of medicine may coexist in the same culture. It is usually unwritten and transmitted orally until someone collects it. Within a culture, elements of folk medicine may be known by many adults. It is gathered and applied by healers and shamans. Midwives, witches, and dealers in herbs also use it. This medicine is not always collected into a system. Many treatments may seem to contradict each other.

1. **Which of the following best expresses the essential information in the highlighted sentence?**

   Ⓐ Many people in cultural groups think folk medicine is good.
   Ⓑ Folk medicine is part of a culture known to many grown-ups.
   Ⓒ Within some cultures, only adults can practice folk medicine.
   Ⓓ Adults treat themselves with folk medicine in some cultures.

Jury Selection

In the United States, the criminal justice system and some civil cases require a jury. These people are selected at random from the adult population in the same district served by the court concerned. A person who is serving on a jury is known as a juror. The number of jurors is usually six or twelve. They are chosen based on their ability to consider the trial fairly. There is always the possibility of jurors not completing the trial for health or other reasons. So, some alternate jurors are often nominated. They also follow the trial but do not take part in deciding the verdict.

2. **Which of the following best expresses the essential information in the highlighted sentence?**

   Ⓐ The people on a jury are randomly chosen from the same jurisdiction.
   Ⓑ The adult population in the same area randomly selects the people on the court.
   Ⓒ The jury is made up of the entire adult population in the same jurisdiction.
   Ⓓ There is a random selection of courts by the adult population.

Oaks

The term *oak* can be used to name hundreds of species of trees and shrubs. Oaks are native to the northern hemisphere. They include deciduous and evergreen species, extending from cold latitudes to tropical Asia and the Americas.

Oaks have spirally arranged leaves with a lobbed margin in many species. Some have serrated leaves or entire leaves with a smooth margin. The flowers are catkins, produced in spring. The fruit is a nut called an acorn, borne in a cup-like structure. Each acorn contains one seed and takes 6~18 months to mature. The length depends on the species. Oaks with evergreen leaves are called "live oaks," but they are not a distinct group. Their members are scattered among other sections.

3. **Which of the following best expresses the essential information in the highlighted sentence?**

   (A) All the deciduous and evergreen trees in Asia and the Americas are oaks.
   (B) Deciduous and evergreen oaks are found in cold and hot Asia and the Americas.
   (C) Oaks are deciduous or evergreen trees found in both cold and hot regions.
   (D) Deciduous and evergreen species of oaks survive best at cold or hot latitudes.

The Lumber Industry

Trees felled to make wood are called timber, and wood cut into boards is called lumber. Lumber is supplied either rough or finished. Rough lumber is the raw material for furniture making. It is available in many species, but usually hardwoods. Finished lumber is supplied in standard sizes and is used mostly by the construction industry. Lumber was one of the first industries in the United States. Maine and New York were early leaders in production. Later expansion led to Michigan, Oregon, Washington, and California. The men who cut the trees down to make lumber are known as lumberjacks. These men are often characters in early American folklore.

4. **Which of the following best expresses the essential information in the highlighted sentence?**

   (A) The construction industry accounts for most of the use of standardized lumber.
   (B) Lumber comes in standard sizes provided by the construction industry.
   (C) The construction industry provides most of the lumber in standard sizes.
   (D) Standard sizes in the construction industry are important for finished lumber.

Practice with Long Passages

A Read the following passage, and answer the questions.

Wheat Production

Time Limit: 2 min. 50 sec.

Wheat is cultivated worldwide. Globally it is the most important human food grain. It ranks second in total production as a cereal crop behind maize. The third is rice. Wheat is a staple food used to make flour for leavened, flat, and steamed breads. It is also used for cookies, cakes, pasta, noodles, and couscous. In addition, it is used to make forms of alcohol such as beer and vodka. These days it is even being used in biofuel. The husk of the grain, separated when milling white flour, is bran. Wheat is planted to a limited extent as a forage crop for livestock. The straw can be used as fodder for livestock or as a construction material for roofing hatch.

Harvested wheat grain is classified according to grain properties for the purposes of the commodities market. Wheat buyers use the classifications to help decide which wheat to purchase. Each class has special uses. Wheat producers determine which classes of wheat are most profitable to cultivate with this system.

Wheat is widely cultivated as a cash crop because it produces a good yield per unit area. It also grows well in a temperate climate, even with a moderately short growing season. It yields high-quality flour that is widely used in baking. Most bread is made with wheat flour, including many breads named for the other grains they contain, like rye and oat breads. Many other popular foods are made from wheat flour as well. This results in a large demand for the grain, even in economies with a significant food surplus.

There are six classes of wheat grown in the United States. Durum wheat is very hard with light colored grain. Hard Red Spring wheat is brownish and contains a lot of protein. Hard Red Winter wheat is similar and is primarily grown in Kansas. Soft Red Winter wheat is soft and low in protein. Hard White wheat is light colored and chalky. Soft White wheat has very little protein and is grown in temperate, moist areas.

General Comprehension

1. **According to the passage, which of the following is true about wheat?**

   (A) It has a low yield per unit area.
   (B) It has a long growing season.
   (C) It is the most important cereal crop to humans.
   (D) It is primarily grown in Kansas.

2. **According to paragraph 4, the six classes of wheat include all of the following EXCEPT:**

   (A) Durum
   (B) Soft Red Winter
   (C) Hard White
   (D) Blue Sweet

---

cultivate (v)
to grow; to farm

rank (v)
to achieve a level or place on a list

maize (n)
corn

staple (n)
something that is used every day

profitable (a)
able to be sold for money

yield (n)
the amount of something that is produced

On the TOEFL Test

3. **Which of the following best expresses the essential information in the highlighted sentence?** *Incorrect* **answer choices change the meaning in important ways or leave out essential information.**

Wheat is planted to a limited extent as a forage crop for livestock.

Ⓐ Wheat is planted to increase crops and livestock.
Ⓑ Some wheat is planted for farm animals to eat.
Ⓒ Wheat can be found planted on farms with animals.
Ⓓ Many farms plant less wheat if they have animals.

4. **Which of the following best expresses the essential information in the highlighted sentence?** *Incorrect* **answer choices change the meaning in important ways or leave out essential information.**

Wheat is widely cultivated as a cash crop because it produces a good yield per unit area.

Ⓐ High productivity of wheat makes people grow a lot of it for profit.
Ⓑ Wheat is widely grown in places where people need lots of cash.
Ⓒ Wheat must be grown over a wide space, which costs a lot.
Ⓓ Wheat is the most abundant cash crop in the world.

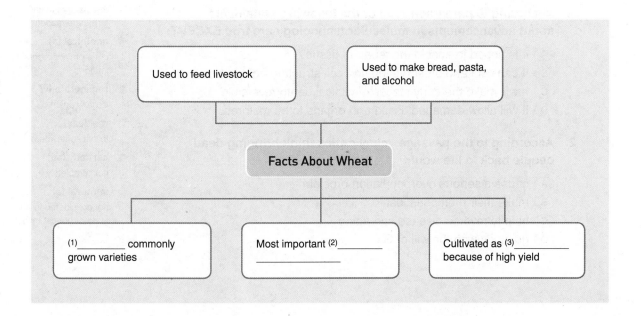

Used to feed livestock

Used to make bread, pasta, and alcohol

Facts About Wheat

(1)_____ commonly grown varieties

Most important (2)_____
_____

Cultivated as (3)_____ because of high yield

Read the following passage, and answer the questions.

Cryonics

Time Limit: 2 min. 40 sec.

Cryonics is the practice of cooling dead organic tissue. This is used on humans or animals that have recently died. The hope is to bring them back to life in the near future. By law, it can only be performed on humans after they are legally dead. Many scientists and doctors think cryonics is totally unethical. However, there are also many who support cryonics.

Supporters of cryonics hope that future technology will improve. Molecular technology is especially hoped to reverse the early stages of clinical death. It is hoped that this will enable the repair of tissue on a very tiny level. It could also allow damaged tissues and organs to be regenerated. They also assume that disease and aging will one day be reversible.

These supporters want to store the memory and identity from the brain of people who have recently died. Cryonics attempts to do this by using fluid that preserves the brain. If this is done before cooling, it will prevent injury. This cooling fluid saves the fine cell structures of the brain where memory and identity reside.

Critics of cryonics think this process is a waste of time and money. They base their opinions on the current level of science. It is true that cells, tissues, blood vessels, and some small animal organs can be reversibly preserved. Some frogs can even survive for a few months in a partially frozen state if they are kept a few degrees above freezing. But this is not true cryo-preservation. There is no proof that the identity and memory of a person can be restored after death has occurred.

Critics also think that if it were possible to bring dead people back to life, it would cause many social problems. Critics worry it would cause a huge overpopulation problem. Many also think trying to reverse death is immoral because it goes against the will of their God.

General Comprehension

1. **According to paragraph 2, all of the following statements about advancements in molecular technology are true EXCEPT:**

    (A) It is hoped to enable the repair of tissue.
    (B) It can cool and preserve the fine cell structures of the brain.
    (C) It will make the early stages of clinical death reversible.
    (D) It will allow damaged tissue and organs to be restored.

2. **According to the passage, many critics think bringing dead people back to life would**

    (A) cause a serious overpopulation problem
    (B) make their memories lost
    (C) help to reverse disease and aging
    (D) go along with the will of God

tissue (n)
the material that life forms are made of

unethical (a)
not morally acceptable; immoral

regenerate (v)
to grow again

reside (v)
to live somewhere

partially (ad)
not completely

immoral (a)
not considered to be good or honest by most people

3. **Which of the following best expresses the essential information in the highlighted sentence?** *Incorrect* **answer choices change the meaning in important ways or leave out essential information.**

    By law, it can only be performed on humans after they are legally dead.

    (A) Laws forbid the use of cryonics on dead people.
    (B) Cryonics is legally used to bring dead people back to life.
    (C) By law, cryonics should be used prior to people's death.
    (D) Laws limit the use of cryonics to legally dead people.

4. **Which of the following best expresses the essential information in the highlighted sentence?** *Incorrect* **answer choices change the meaning in important ways or leave out essential information.**

    There is no proof that the identity and memory of a person can be restored after death has occurred.

    (A) Human memory and identity can be saved by the process of cryonics.
    (B) A person should prove that his identity and memory can be restored after death.
    (C) Nobody knows if a person's memory and identity can be brought back after death.
    (D) Death is the first stage of proving that memory and identity can be restored.

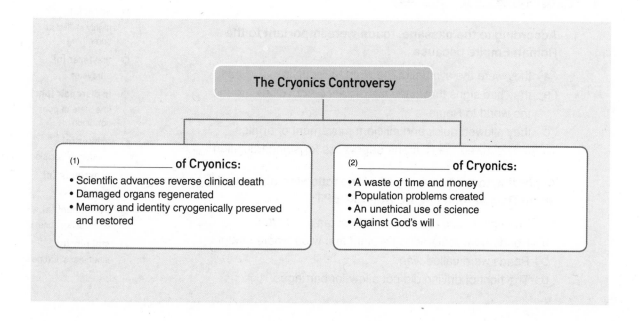

The Cryonics Controversy

(1)_____ of Cryonics:
• Scientific advances reverse clinical death
• Damaged organs regenerated
• Memory and identity cryogenically preserved and restored

(2)_____ of Cryonics:
• A waste of time and money
• Population problems created
• An unethical use of science
• Against God's will

Read the following passage, and answer the questions.

Road Law in Rome

Time Limit: 2 min. 50 sec.

Roads were essential for the growth of the Roman Empire. These roads enabled them to move armies quickly and efficiently. There is even a proverb that says, "All roads lead to Rome." At its peak, the Roman road system spanned 53,000 miles and contained about 372 links. The Romans were adept at constructing these roads, which were called *viae*.

Prepared *viae* began in history as the streets of Rome. The laws of the Twelve Tables, dated to approximately 450 B.C., specify that a road shall be 8 feet wide where straight and 16 where curved. The tables command Romans to build roads and give wayfarers the right to pass over private land where the road is in disrepair. Therefore, building roads that would not need frequent repair became an ideological objective.

Roman law defined the right to use a road as a *servitus*, or claim. The right of going established a claim to use a footpath across private land. The right of driving allowed for a carriage. A road combined both types of claims as long as it was of the proper width, which was determined by an arbiter. The default width was 8 feet. In these rather dry laws, the prevalence of public domain over private can be seen, which characterized the republic.

The Romans had a preference for standardization whenever they could. After being made permanent commissioner of roads in 20 B.C., Augustus set up a golden milestone near the temple of Saturn. On this were listed all of the cities in the empire and the distance to them. This was later called the navel of Rome.

Roman roads were very important in maintaining both the stability and the expansion of the empire. The legions made good time on them. These roads are still used a thousand years later. During the fall of the Roman Empire, the same roads offered avenues of invasion to the barbarians. This contributed to Roman military reverses.

General Comprehension

1. **According to the passage, roads were important to the Roman Empire because**

   Ⓐ they were the symbol of the Roman republic

   Ⓑ they had signs that listed the distance from cities around the world to Rome

   Ⓒ they allowed quick and efficient movement of armies

   Ⓓ they showed the Romans' eagerness for standardization

2. **According to the passage, all of the following statements about Roman road law are true EXCEPT:**

   Ⓐ The right to use roads was defined as a *servitus*.

   Ⓑ Roads were required to be eight feet wide where straight.

   Ⓒ Roads were called *viae*.

   Ⓓ The right of driving did not allow for carriages.

---

adept (a)
highly skilled at something

wayfarer (n)
a traveler

in disrepair (phr)
in a state of poor condition

arbiter (n)
a judge or decision maker

prevalence (n)
commonness

permanent (a)
everlasting; constant

stability (n)
steadiness; firmness

On the TOEFL Test

3. **Which of the following best expresses the essential information in the highlighted sentence?** *Incorrect* **answer choices change the meaning in important ways or leave out essential information.**

    In these rather dry laws, the prevalence of public domain over private can be seen, which characterized the republic.

    (A) Roman republicans believed privacy was more important than public life.
    (B) The Romans separated public life from private life by law.
    (C) One characteristic of the Roman republic was the strict enactment of public law.
    (D) The laws of the Roman republic tended to put public life before private.

4. **Which of the following best expresses the essential information in the highlighted sentence?** *Incorrect* **answer choices change the meaning in important ways or leave out essential information.**

    During the fall of the Roman Empire, the same roads offered avenues of invasion to the barbarians.

    (A) The Roman Empire built roads to allow the barbarians to invade.
    (B) The barbarians invaded Rome on those roads, leading to its downfall.
    (C) The barbarians preferred to invade the Roman Empire on roads and avenues.
    (D) The Roman Empire offered the barbarians a chance to invade on different avenues.

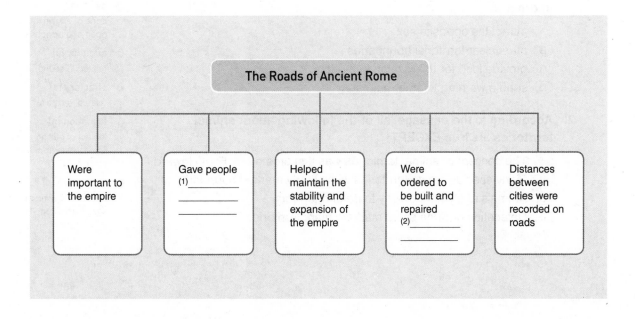

Animal Territoriality

Time Limit: 2 min. 40 sec.

The term *territory* refers to any area that an animal defends. Animals that defend territories are territorial. The idea of animal territories was first introduced by Eliot Howard. He wrote of this concept in a book published in 1920. In the 1930s the concept was developed further by Margaret Morse Nice, who elaborated on it through her studies on the song sparrow. Later, it was widely popularized by Robert Ardrey in his book *The Territorial Imperative*. The popularity of the book led to an exaggerated idea of the importance of territory. This concept was thought to be part of the field of social ecology. In fact, however, only a small number of species have territories with clear boundaries. Within these boundaries, they live and find all the resources they need.

The most obvious examples of territory are with birds and fish. These animals often develop bright colors to warn others away from their territories. The European robin and the Siamese fighting fish adopt these kinds of colors to defend their territories. These areas usually contain their nest sites and offer sufficient food for them and their young.

Defense rarely takes the form of overt fights. More frequently there is a highly noticeable display. This display may be visual. An example of this is the red breast of the robin. Or it may be auditory. Many bird songs or the calls of gibbons are made for this reason. Or it can be olfactory. This is carried out through the deposit of scent marks. These marks may be deposited by urination or by defecation. Dogs mark their scent in these ways. Or scent marks can be placed by rubbing parts of the bodies that bear specialized scent glands against the objects in a territory. Cats mark their scent by rubbing their faces and flanks against objects.

General Comprehension

1. **According to paragraph 2, animals often develop bright colors in order to**

    (A) attract the opposite sex
    (B) mark clear territorial boundaries
    (C) provide food for their young in the nest
    (D) send a warning to other animals

2. **According to the passage, all of the following about animal territories are true EXCEPT:**

    (A) The concept of animal territories was first created by Eliot Howard.
    (B) Many species create territories with clearly marked boundaries.
    (C) Animals rarely fight overtly to defend territory.
    (D) Defecation or urine scent markers mark territories.

○ **exaggerate (v)**
to overstate

○ **overt (a)**
done or shown in an open and obvious way

○ **auditory (a)**
related to sound

○ **olfactory (a)**
related to smell

○ **urination (n)**
the act of getting rid of liquid waste from the body

○ **defecation (n)**
the act of getting rid of solid waste from the body

3. **Which of the following best expresses the essential information in the highlighted sentence?** *Incorrect* **answer choices change the meaning in important ways or leave out essential information.**

In the 1930s the concept was developed further by Margaret Morse Nice, who elaborated on it through her studies on the song sparrow.

  Ⓐ In the 1930s, Margaret Morse Nice began to study the song sparrow.
  Ⓑ The concept of the song sparrow territories was suggested by Margaret Morse Nice in the 1930s.
  Ⓒ Margaret Morse Nice furthered the concept of animal territories by studying song sparrows in the 1930s.
  Ⓓ Studies on the song sparrow were popularized by Margaret Morse Nice in the 1930s.

4. **Which of the following best expresses the essential information in the highlighted sentence?** *Incorrect* **answer choices change the meaning in important ways or leave out essential information.**

Or scent marks can be placed by rubbing parts of the bodies that bear specialized scent glands against the objects in a territory.

  Ⓐ Rubbing particular body parts against the objects in a territory is a way of leaving scent marks.
  Ⓑ Some animals have scent glands that are marked by different objects in their territories.
  Ⓒ The objects in a territory contain specialized scent marks from different body parts of different animals.
  Ⓓ With scent marks left by rubbing, animals claim different objects in their territories.

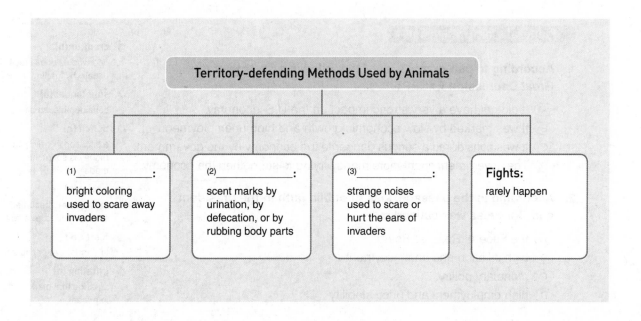

Territory-defending Methods Used by Animals

(1)_____:
bright coloring used to scare away invaders

(2)_____:
scent marks by urination, by defecation, or by rubbing body parts

(3)_____:
strange noises used to scare or hurt the ears of invaders

Fights:
rarely happen

Read the following passage, and answer the questions.

The Flow of Activity in the U.S. Economy

Time Limit: 2 min. 50 sec.

The United States has the largest economy in the world. But since the early 1980s, the United States has changed. It once was the world's largest creditor, but now it has a substantial current account deficit. It has also taken on a large national debt. The national debt is now about 64% of the current GDP and is the highest since the 1950s.

The federal government guides the economic pace to maintain steady growth. Not only does it attempt to maintain steady growth, but it also works for high employment and price stability. Adjusting spending and taxes can slow down or speed up economic growth. Managing the money supply and controlling credit can also affect this rate. This process also affects the level of prices and employment.

In the past, the Great Depression of the 1930s had a great effect on the U.S. economy. Periods of slow economic growth and high unemployment were seen as the greatest economic threats. The danger of recession was serious. The government tried to make the economy stronger by spending more money. It also cut taxes so that consumers would spend more. It fostered rapid growth in the money supply.

Also, in the 1970s there were major price increases, particularly for energy. This created a strong fear of inflation, which led to an overall increase in the level of prices. As a result, government leaders began to focus more on holding back inflation.

Many changes took place between the 1960s and the 1990s. In the 1960s, the government had faith in fiscal policy. The president and the U.S. Congress played a large role in directing the economy. But periods of high inflation and joblessness weakened the public's faith in them. The overall slow pace also damaged their image. Now, monetary policy is used to control the flow of economic activity. This policy is directed by the nation's central bank, known as the Federal Reserve Board (FRB). It has much independence from the president and Congress.

General Comprehension

1. **According to paragraph 3, all of the following are true of the Great Depression EXCEPT:**

   (A) It did not have a very strong impact on the U.S. economy.
   (B) It was marked by slow economic growth and high unemployment.
   (C) It was considered a serious danger to the economy by the government.
   (D) The government spent more money trying to strengthen the economy.

2. **According to the passage, loss of public faith in the president and Congress was caused by**

   (A) the Federal Reserve Board
   (B) high inflation and unemployment
   (C) monetary policy
   (D) high employment and price stability

creditor (n)
one who extends credit, usually by loaning money

substantial (a)
considerable; ample

deficit (n)
a situation in which more money is spent than made

adjust (v)
to change; to become accustomed to; to adapt

foster (v)
to promote; to encourage

inflation (n)
a period that marks a rise in prices

On the TOEFL Test

3. **Which of the following best expresses the essential information in the highlighted sentence?** *Incorrect* **answer choices change the meaning in important ways or leave out essential information.**

    Not only does it attempt to maintain steady growth, but it also works for high employment and price stability.

    Ⓐ The federal government keeps growth steady but cannot maintain high employment and stable prices.
    Ⓑ Because it needs high employment and stable prices, the federal government needs steady growth.
    Ⓒ Without constant growth, the federal government cannot have high employment and stable prices.
    Ⓓ The federal government tries to achieve growth, high employment, and unchanging prices.

4. **Which of the following best expresses the essential information in the highlighted sentence?** *Incorrect* **answer choices change the meaning in important ways or leave out essential information.**

    This created a strong fear of inflation, which led to an overall increase in the level of prices.

    Ⓐ Worries about inflation caused by increasing energy prices raised overall prices.
    Ⓑ The high increase in prices caused a strong fear of inflation of energy prices.
    Ⓒ People were afraid of inflation and also worried about increasing prices of energy.
    Ⓓ The overall increase in prices caused inflation in fuel and energy prices.

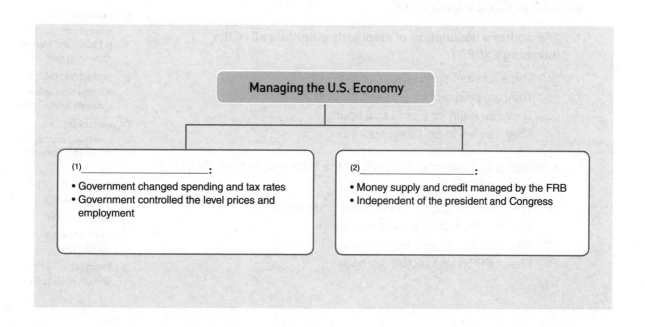

Managing the U.S. Economy

(1)_____:
• Government changed spending and tax rates
• Government controlled the level prices and employment

(2)_____:
• Money supply and credit managed by the FRB
• Independent of the president and Congress

F Read the following passage, and answer the questions.

Evolution of the Elephant

Time Limit: 2 min. 50 sec.

Elephants are the only remaining family in their biological order. There are three living species of elephants. These are the African bush and forest elephants and the Asian. Other species have been extinct since the last ice age.

Elephants are the largest land mammals alive today. Their pregnancy period is 22 months. It is the longest of any land animal. At birth, it is common for an elephant calf to weigh 120kg. An elephant may live as long as 70 years, and some even live longer. The largest elephant ever recorded was shot in Angola in 1956. It was male and weighed about 12,000kg. The smallest elephants were about the size of a calf or a large pig. They were a prehistoric variant that lived on the island of Crete. They existed until between 3,000 and 5,000 B.C.

Elephants are increasingly threatened by humans. Human-elephant conflicts are often deadly. They kill 150 elephants and up to 100 people per year in Asia. The African elephant population has gone from 3 million in 1970 to about 600,000 in 1989. The numbers of this beast then dropped even further. By 2,000 the number was down to 272,000. In recent years, efforts to save these animals have helped it rise. The elephant is now protected around the world. Many restrictions have been enacted for their benefit, strictly limiting their capture and domestic use. Trade in products such as ivory is also controlled.

Some scientists believe the elephant family is distantly related to sea cows. They also think there is a link between elephants and hyraxes. The fossil evidence does not offer certain proof while many believe the genetic evidence shows this. One theory suggests that these animals spent most of their time underwater. They would have used their trunks like snorkels for breathing. Modern elephants still have this ability, and they are known to swim like that. They can swim for up to 6 hours and 50km.

General Comprehension

1. **The author's description of elephants mentions all of the following EXCEPT:**

   (A) Three different species exist today.
   (B) They are pregnant for a period of 22 months.
   (C) They can swim for less than 6 hours.
   (D) They can live to be 120 years or longer.

2. **According to paragraph 4, which of the following is true about modern elephants?**

   (A) They can spend most of their time underwater.
   (B) They are the size of a calf or large pig.
   (C) They use their trunks like snorkels.
   (D) They can run up to 50km per hour.

mammal (n)
animals that give birth to babies and feed their young with milk

prehistoric (a)
from the time before recorded human history

variant (n)
something that slightly differs from something else

conflict (n)
disagreement; argument

restriction (n)
a rule that limits something

enact (v)
to make or pass a law

On the TOEFL Test

3. **Which of the following best expresses the essential information in the highlighted sentence?** *Incorrect* **answer choices change the meaning in important ways or leave out essential information.**

Many restrictions have been enacted for their benefit, strictly limiting their capture and domestic use.

(A) Laws have been passed to help protect elephants from people.
(B) Laws allowing elephants to be captured and raised domestically have been passed.
(C) Without laws, elephants would be captured and put in zoos.
(D) The laws benefit people by allowing elephants to be captured.

4. **Which of the following best expresses the essential information in the highlighted sentence?** *Incorrect* **answer choices change the meaning in important ways or leave out essential information.**

The fossil evidence does not offer certain proof while many believe the genetic evidence shows this.

(A) People believe what the fossil and genetic evidence shows about the link between elephants and hyraxes.
(B) The fossil and genetic evidence clearly shows the link between elephants and hydraxes.
(C) The genetic evidence is believed to show the link between elephants and hydraxes by supporters of the fossil evidence.
(D) Unlike the fossil evidence, the genetic evidence seems to show a clear link between elephants and hydraxes.

The Elephant

- Three species in existence – (1)_____ & one Asian type
- The largest land mammals
- Pregnancy period – 22 months
- Life span – up to 70 years
- Weight – (2)_____
- The largest elephant ever weighed – 12,000 kg
- A long nose – breathing underwater for up to (3)_____

Building Summary Skills

The following summaries are based on the long passages you worked on earlier. Complete each of them by filling in the blanks with suitable words or phrases.

1. Wheat Production

classification system	the quality and price	six classes
profitable crop	widely grown	

Wheat is one of the most (1)_____ and important crops in the world. It has many important uses by humans. Wheat grain is harvested according to a (2)_____ that determines (3)_____. Wheat is a very (4)_____ because it is used so widely in products that are consumed daily. There are (5)_____ of wheat grown in the United States.

2. Cryonics

not possible	preserve the memory	unethical
cryonics	freezing animals or humans	

(1)_____ is the controversial process of (2)_____ immediately after death in hopes of reviving them at a later date. Although reversing death is (3)_____ _____ through current scientific methods, practitioners of cryonics hope future advances will make it possible. Their current goal is to (4)_____ and identity of those who die. Critics of cryonics think it is (5)_____ as well as a waste of time.

3. Road Law in Rome

invade and conquer	building and administering laws	Roman roads
the golden milestone	in disrepair	

Roads were a very important part of the Roman Empire, and the Romans were very advanced at (1)_____ to control them. (2)_____ were built to very strict measurements, and laws protected travelers when roads were not available or (3)_____ _____. There was even a point from which all roads to Rome led, called (4)_____ _____. Roman roads eventually enabled barbarians to (5)_____ Rome, but its roads still exist today.

4. Animal Territoriality

> | territories | bright colors or strong smells | mark their territory |
> | few animals | in the early 20th century | |

Animals defend areas called (1)_____, which are important to them. This concept was introduced (2)_____ although it was greatly exaggerated. Many animals develop (3)_____ to protect their territories. (4)_____ fight over territory. Many common animals (5)_____ with their own smell.

5. The Flow of Activity in the U.S. Economy

> | the direction of the economy | the U.S. economy | the nation's central bank |
> | the president and Congress's role | the Great Depression | |

(1)_____ was once the most powerful in the world, but it is now the most indebted. The federal government controls many factors that change (2)_____.
During (3)_____, the federal government shifted its economic philosophy from creating growth to holding back prices. Because of these changes, the public has lost faith in (4)_____ in influencing the economy. (5)_____ now independently attempts to guide the economy.

6. The Evolution of the Elephant

> | by humans | the longest pregnancy period | increase their numbers |
> | three species | sea cows and possibly hyraxes | |

There are only (1)_____ of elephants still living today. They are the largest of all land mammals and have (2)_____. These days, elephants have been endangered (3)_____, but efforts are being made to (4)_____.
Scientists think elephants are genetically related to (5)_____ although there is not enough evidence to prove this.

1. **The word it in the passage refers to**

   (A) John Deere
   (B) steel plow
   (C) farming
   (D) soil

2. **According to paragraph 1, the U.S. economy became the largest and most modern in the world because**

   (A) the U.S. won the American Revolution
   (B) there were many new inventions
   (C) America imported many European products
   (D) the economy grew steadily for more than 150 years

3. **Which of the following best expresses the essential information in the highlighted sentence?** *Incorrect* **answer choices change the meaning in important ways or leave out essential information.**

   (A) New England grew more rapidly than European countries.
   (B) There was rapid growth everywhere in the United States, including New England.
   (C) Only one area besides New England in America experienced fast growth.
   (D) Fast growth occurred in New England first in America.

4. **Which of the following can be inferred about Pennsylvania's industry?**

   (A) It had a textile industry similar to Massachusetts'.
   (B) It often competed against Massachusetts and other states.
   (C) Its iron industry was stronger than in other states.
   (D) It was the richest state in the country.

5. **Why does the author mention practical inventions in paragraph 4?**

   (A) To exemplify the reasons for the development of industry in America
   (B) To show how America became so rich by selling new products
   (C) To illustrate how intelligent American inventors were
   (D) To prove that most useful inventions came from America

6. **The word boomed in the passage is closest in meaning to**

   (A) imploded
   (B) increased
   (C) shrank
   (D) continued

The Development of Industry in America

After the American Revolution, industry in the U.S. was behind Europe. But it was not very far behind. Several waves of inventions and growth soon hit. This happened over a period of 150 years. These advances made the U.S. economy the largest and most modern in the world.

During the American Revolution, America had not yet entered its industrial age. Most manufacturing was done in people's homes. Whereas Britain was industrialized, America had not caught on yet. Then Francis Cabot Lowell went to Britain in 1811. He memorized the secrets to constructing a power loom. After he and his associates returned to America, they founded some textile plants in Boston. The most famous was in Lowell, Massachusetts. It was built in 1822. The Lowell system employed many "mill girls." They lived in dormitories in order to run the factory.

New England was the home of a growing textile industry. It was the first area of the United States to experience such rapid growth. This growth also occurred in Pennsylvania. The iron industry pushed that state along and helped it to grow even faster.

Then the direction of progress began to change. This new period took place between 1810 and the 1860s. Factories continued to expand. But greater strides were being taken in inventing. American manufacturing and agriculture was greatly improved. These improvements came from practical inventions. Richard Chenaworth invented the cast-iron plow. It was useful because it had replaceable parts. John Deere created the steel plow, which made farming faster because the soil did not stick to it. Eli Whitney invented the cotton gin and the jig. This began a huge cotton industry in the south. Samuel Morse invented the telegraph, which began the age of long-range communication. Elisha Otis invented the passenger elevator. This led to modern-day skyscrapers. Finally, George Pullman created the sleeping car for trains. This allowed for long-distance travel.

From the 1850s on, industry in the United States boomed. The Civil War was over. With the victory of the North, Northern business entrepreneurs flourished. Government was eager to see business expand. The innovations listed above caused swift and dramatic changes. Railroads were now needed to carry goods across the country. People in the south traded cotton. They sold their product to the north and to Britain.

By the early 1900s, cars were needed by many people. The auto industry introduced a new dimension of growth to America. By the 1920s, Henry Ford introduced his Model-T. With it came the modern assembly line.

7. The word **specialize** in the passage is closest in meaning to

    Ⓐ focus

    Ⓑ prefer

    Ⓒ examine

    Ⓓ discuss

8. Which of the following best expresses the essential information in the highlighted sentence in paragraph 1? *Incorrect* answer choices change the meaning in important ways or leave out essential information.

    Ⓐ Small living creatures that people cannot see are always in food.

    Ⓑ No one realized that our foods consisted of small, living organisms.

    Ⓒ People did not realize that our foods held invisible, tiny, living creatures.

    Ⓓ Nobody thought organisms living in food were too tiny to see.

9. The word **reproduce** in the passage is closest in meaning to

    Ⓐ become pregnant

    Ⓑ fertilize

    Ⓒ duplicate

    Ⓓ combine

10. Why does the author mention **the first single-celled microbes formed around 4 billion years ago**?

    Ⓐ To show how basic they are

    Ⓑ To indicate how long they have been on Earth

    Ⓒ To show how much they have mutated over the years

    Ⓓ To explain why they are still in existence

11. The author mentions all of the following as places where extremophiles have been found EXCEPT:

    Ⓐ the Arctic area

    Ⓑ oceans

    Ⓒ volcanoes

    Ⓓ deserts

12. Which of the following can be inferred about extremophiles?

    Ⓐ Scientists have discovered simple ways to kill them.

    Ⓑ They are less resistant to influences than microbes.

    Ⓒ There are more of them in existence than microbes.

    Ⓓ Scientists will possibly find them in outer space in the future.

Microbes

Before the discovery of microbes, the changes that took place in foods as they aged were a mystery. Nobody knew why grapes turned into wine and milk turned into cheese. No one even thought that there were living organisms too small to be seen by the naked eye at work on our foods. Then, in 1676, a Dutch scientist discovered these microscopic creatures.

We now know much more about microbes. Scientists who specialize in their study look at the various forms of these tiny creatures. These microbes can take the forms of bacteria, fungi, archaea, or eukaryotes. Viruses are not considered to be microbes since they are not alive. Microbes can be single or have multiple cells. A few single-celled microbes, known as protists, are visible to the naked eye.

Microbes are usually found in water or other liquids that are below the boiling point. Scientists have taken samples of microbes from hot springs, on the ocean floor, and even from deep within the Earth's crust. These microbes are important parts of the Earth's many ecosystems. They are responsible for recycling nutrients and are also an important part of the nitrogen cycle.

Scientists believe the first single-celled microbes formed around 4 billion years ago. These were the first life forms on Earth and were the only ones for 3 billion years. Microbes reproduce quickly and vastly. They are able freely to exchange genes between different species. They also mutate at an accelerated rate, which allows them to evolve swiftly in order to adapt to new environments. A problem associated with the ability of microbes to evolve so rapidly is the development of 'super bugs' that are able to resist modern antibiotic drugs.

The simplest microbes are bacteria. They are also among the most common group of living things on Earth. They can be found in all environments where the temperature is below 140 degrees Celsius. They are present in sea water, soil, and even within the human stomach and intestines. The genome of bacteria is a single strand of DNA. Bacteria are surrounded by a cell wall. They are known to reproduce by a process called binary fission. By this process they split again and again. Some bacteria are able to double every ten minutes under prime conditions.

Another variety of microbes is archaea. These are single-celled creatures with no nuclei. These microbes are common in all types of habitats, including extreme environments. Eukaryotes are different from bacteria and archaea. They have multi-celled structures called organelles within them. The eukaryote DNA is housed within the nucleus organelle.

One of the most interesting kinds of microbes is the extremophile. These are microbes that have adapted to highly hostile environments. These robust creatures can be found at the North and South Poles, in deserts, and in the deep sea. These microbes have even been found as far as 7km below the Earth's surface. Some extremophiles have survived in a vacuum and are resistant to radiation. This leads scientists to believe that it is possible for them to survive in space.

Vocabulary Review

A Choose the word with the closest meaning to each highlighted word or phrase.

1. They wanted to cultivate tomatoes in their backyard.
   - (A) eat
   - (B) find
   - (C) use
   - (D) grow

2. She hoped to prevent an accident by checking the brakes on her car.
   - (A) help
   - (B) encourage
   - (C) stop
   - (D) need

3. The scientists were experts at tissue and organ regeneration.
   - (A) removal
   - (B) repair
   - (C) damage
   - (D) replacement

4. He wanted to increase the pace of our walking.
   - (A) difficulty
   - (B) ease
   - (C) style
   - (D) speed

5. He was known to help wayfarers in need.
   - (A) people
   - (B) travelers
   - (C) stray animals
   - (D) vegetables

6. The popular new product was based on the designer's concept.
   - (A) idea
   - (B) work
   - (C) promise
   - (D) design

7. A mother moose will always defend her young children.
   - (A) hurt
   - (B) help
   - (C) protect
   - (D) enjoy

8. We were fascinated to view so many exotic creatures at the nature park.
   - (A) people
   - (B) scenes
   - (C) plants
   - (D) animals

B Match each word with the correct definition.

1. prevalence •   • **a.** not morally acceptable; immoral
2. creditor •   • **b.** a line that marks an area
3. staple •   • **c.** from the time before recorded human history
4. olfactory •   • **d.** a period that marks a rise in prices
5. unethical •   • **e.** the amount of something that is produced
6. inflation •   • **f.** one who extends credit, usually by loaning money
7. prehistoric •   • **g.** a situation in which more money is spent than made
8. deficit •   • **h.** something that is used every day
9. yield •   • **i.** commonness
10. boundary •   • **j.** related to smell

PART 2

Making Inferences

In this part, the reading comprehension questions include: rhetorical purpose, inference, and insert text. The learning objectives of these comprehension questions are to understand the rhetorical function of a statement or paragraph, the logic of the passage, and strongly implied ideas in the text.

Unit 6

Rhetorical Purpose

Rhetorical Purpose

Overview

■ Introduction

Rhetorical Purpose questions ask you to understand why and how the author uses a particular piece of information in the passage. This information can be used to argue, define, explain, or compare ideas. Because this type of question usually focuses on the logical development of the passage, you need to figure out how one sentence or paragraph relates to another.

■ Question Types

1. The author discusses X in paragraph _____ in order to ~

2. Why does the author mention X?

3. The author uses X as an example of ~

4. Why does the author quote X in the passage?

5. In paragraph _____, why does the author give details about X?

6. In paragraph _____, the author explains X by ~

7. How does the author explain the idea of X in paragraph _____?

■ Useful Tips

• Read the question first, and then recognize the author's purpose immediately by scanning the specific phrases or paragraphs.

• Focus on the logical links between sentences and paragraphs, not on the overall organization of the passage.

• Familiarize yourself with the words or phrases for rhetorical functions like *to illustrate, to criticize, to explain, to contrast, to compare, to note,* etc.

Sample iBT Question

Why does the author mention it is much different from the physical activity of observing the stars?

(A) To support why astrophysics is difficult to study

(B) To explain why astrophysicists study objects in space

(C) To show how different astrophysics is from other sciences

(D) To explain how astrophysicists solve theoretical problems

Astrophysics

Astrophysics looks at the makeup of outer space as a branch of astronomy. Scientists in this field consider the brightness and density of objects in space. They examine the fabric of all celestial objects. This is a difficult science because it is purely theoretical. It is much different from the physical activity of observing the stars. None of the events that astrophysicists study can be created on Earth. These scientists must create theoretical models from real observations. Then, they solve the problems that arise. Astrophysics is said to be the only branch of science that has never been able to obtain a single specimen.

The highlighted sentence elaborates on the fact that astrophysics is purely theoretical by contrasting it with the visible activity of stargazing. This is to provide a supporting detail as to why astrophysics is difficult to study. So the correct answer is (A).

Skill & Drill

Rhetorical Purpose questions ask you why the author uses particular words, phrases, or sentences in particular paragraphs. These expressions can be used to define, argue, explain, illustrate, or contrast ideas. So you need to look at the logical links between ideas rather than focusing on the overall organization of the whole passage.

Comb Jelly

The comb jelly is a sea creature but not a true jellyfish. This is because it lacks poison stingers. There are more than 100 kinds of comb jelly living in the world's oceans. They make up a large amount of plankton biomass. One species is the sea gooseberry, which is native to the North Sea. It has reached a very high population. Its numbers are so high that it often clogs fishermen's nets. Few other species are known to do this. The fragile makeup of comb jelly makes it very difficult to research, so data on its lifespan is not available. But it is known that comb jelly reproduces even before adulthood. So it is assumed that their generational cycle is short.

1. **Why does the author mention that it lacks poison stingers?**
   - (A) To explain how comb jelly is not fully understood by scientists
   - (B) To note that comb jelly often clogs the nets of fishermen
   - (C) To contrast comb jelly with species of true jellyfish
   - (D) To discuss how comb jelly make up a large amount of plankton biomass

---

White and Brown Dwarfs

A low or medium mass star goes into the white dwarf stage when it dies. They reach this stage after entering the red giant stage and shedding their outer material. A white dwarf is the size of the Earth but has the density of the sun. It is the densest mass in the universe except for black holes and neutron or quark stars. On the other hand, the brown dwarf is different from the white dwarf because it has a very low density. It is made mostly of gas and is often difficult to tell apart from a large planet.

2. **Why does the author mention that a white dwarf is the size of the Earth but has the density of the sun?**
   - (A) To show that white dwarfs are made mostly of gas
   - (B) To illustrate that white dwarfs have very high density
   - (C) To explain that white dwarfs were once red giants
   - (D) To highlight that a white dwarf is often hard to tell apart from a large planet

Spider Sociality

Spiders are predatory animals. In many cases, the female will eat the male after mating. Some types of female spiders are also known to eat their own babies. Most spiders are solitary creatures, but a few species of spiders that build webs live together in large colonies. Although they show social behavior, they are not as well evolved as social insects such as bees and ants. The most social species are probably Anelosimus eximius. They can form colonies of up to fifty thousand individuals. Many spiders only live one or two years. But it is common for tarantulas to live around twenty years.

3. **The author uses tarantulas as an example of**

    (A) spiders that eat their young
    (B) solitary spiders
    (C) socially evolved spiders
    (D) spiders that live relatively long

Handicrafts

Handicrafts are useful and attractive devices. They are usually made by hand, but sometimes simple tools are used. The term is usually applied to traditional ways of making goods. The unique style of the items is important. Such items often have cultural and religious meanings. Items made by mass production or machines are not handicrafts. Handicraft items are intended to be used and worn. This is what makes them different from decorative arts and crafts. They have a purpose beyond simple decoration. Handicrafts are usually thought of as more traditional works. They are created as a part of daily life.

4. **Why does the author mention that Items made by mass production or machines are not handicrafts.?**

    (A) To highlight that the author does not like these types of items
    (B) To explain that handicrafts cannot be produced in large quantities
    (C) To show that handicrafts must be produced by hand
    (D) To demonstrate that handicrafts are better than machine-produced items

Practice with Long Passages

A Read the following passage, and answer the questions.

Neptune

Time Limit: 2 min. 50 sec.

Neptune is the solar system's eighth and outermost planet. It has the fourth largest diameter of the planets, and its mass is the third largest. In fact, it is 17 times the mass of Earth. Although Uranus is the near twin of Neptune, Neptune is slightly more massive. Neptune is named after the Roman god of the sea.

Neptune's atmosphere is mostly made up of hydrogen and helium. There are also traces of methane. These cause the planet's blue appearance. It is more vivid than that of Uranus, which has similar amounts of methane. Therefore, it is assumed that an unknown component causes Neptune's intense color.

This planet has many strange aspects that make it interesting to scientists. One such aspect is that Neptune has the strongest winds of any planet in the solar system. They blow as fast as 2,500km per hour. Also, there are thirteen confirmed moons orbiting Neptune. Notable for its retrograde orbit is Triton. This moon has a nitrogen/methane atmosphere and is very cold.

The temperature at the top of Neptune's clouds stays around −210 degrees Celsius. This makes it one of the coldest planets in the solar system. This coldness is caused by Neptune's great distance from the sun. The temperature at the center of the planet is about 7,000 degrees Celsius due to extremely hot gases and rock in the center. This is hotter than the surface of the sun. But the planet's outermost layers are extremely cold.

The Voyager 2 probe flew by Neptune in 1989 and discovered a region called the Great Dark Spot. This spot was viewed on its southern hemisphere. This is comparable to the Great Red Spot on Jupiter. Also, faint rings have been detected around the planet. These are much smaller than Saturn's rings. These rings were discovered by Edward Guinan's research team. They were at first thought to be incomplete, fading out before they rounded the planet. But Voyager 2 disproved this belief with photos of complete rings.

General Comprehension

1. **According to the author's description of Neptune, which of the following is true?**

   (A) It has the fifth largest diameter of the planets in the solar system.
   (B) It was discovered by Edward Guinan and his team.
   (C) It is about 9,000 degrees Celsius at its center.
   (D) It has a very cold atmosphere containing hydrogen, helium, and methane.

2. **According to paragraph 3, all of the following about Neptune are true EXCEPT:**

   (A) No other planet in the solar system has stronger winds than Neptune.
   (B) Triton has a very cold, oxygen/methane atmosphere.
   (C) The moon Triton has a retrograde orbit.
   (D) Neptune has 13 moons orbiting it.

outermost (a)
furthest from the center

component (n)
a part of a whole of something

vivid (a)
very bright

notable (a)
important, noteworthy

retrograde (a)
moving backwards

region (n)
an area

detect (v)
to discover; to notice

3. **Why does the author mention that Neptune is 17 times the mass of Earth?**

   Ⓐ To give an idea of Neptune's massive size
   Ⓑ To show that we could have much more space if we lived on Neptune
   Ⓒ To show that Neptune is a better planet than Earth
   Ⓓ To give an idea of how tiny and insignificant Earth is

4. **Why does the author say that an unknown component causes Neptune's intense color?**

   Ⓐ To show that Neptune is much larger than Earth
   Ⓑ To tell that Neptune is named after the Roman god of the sea
   Ⓒ To explain that Neptune is more vivid than Uranus
   Ⓓ To indicate that Neptune's atmosphere has some amounts of methane

NEPTUNE

- Core temperature: (1)_____
- Eighth and outermost planet in solar system
- Fourth largest diameter of all planets in solar system
- Atmosphere of (2)_____
- Strongest winds of any planet in solar system
- Orbited by (3)_____

The Metaphysics of Aristotle

Time Limit: 2 min. 50 sec.

Aristotle was one of the most influential thinkers of all time. In an age before science and technology existed, he created many fields of study. One of these was metaphysics. He argued that the causes of all things could be understood by studying their beginnings. He claimed that we have scientific knowledge when we know the cause of something. To know a thing's existence is to know the reason for its existence. He was the first to set the guidelines for all later causal theories. According to Aristotle's theory, all the causes may fall into several groups.

He defined causes by placing them in four major divisions. The Material Cause is the way a thing comes into existence from the combination of its parts. An example of this is a cheeseburger. It is assembled from meat, bread, and cheese. Alone, these do not make a cheeseburger, but together they are the cause of its existence. The Formal Cause tells us what a thing is. The Formal Cause of a flood is an overabundance of water. The Efficient Cause describes the reason for a change. An example of this is that a fire was burning, but it was put out by rain, which caused it to end. The Final Cause is the reason that something is done. For instance, a country may go to war to protect its borders, which is the cause for the war.

The concept of substance is also examined in the metaphysics of Aristotle. He concludes that a particular substance is a combination of both matter and form. He went on to define the five major elements. He named Fire, which is hot and dry. Earth, he said, is cold and dry. Air he claimed to be hot and wet. Water was cold and wet to him. Finally, he named Aether, the divine substance that makes up the heavenly spheres and bodies.

These classifications recorded by Aristotle paved the way for the modern physical sciences. One can imagine his work as the concrete foundation upon which the building of modern physics is built.

General Comprehension

1. **According to the passage, which of the following is true of Aristotle?**

   (A) He determined the parameters for later causal theories.
   (B) His classifications were rejected by modern science.
   (C) He claimed that the element Fire was hot and wet.
   (D) He said the Final Cause describes the reason for a change.

2. **According to paragraph 3, all of the following are true about the concept of substance EXCEPT:**

   (A) Matter and form combine to make something.
   (B) Aristotle classified the elements of substance into five categories.
   (C) The elements Earth and Air were defined as having opposite characteristics.
   (D) Aether is the divine substance that makes clouds.

influential (a)
important; authoritative

metaphysics (n)
the theoretical philosophy of being and knowing

causal (a)
relating to the cause of something

overabundance (n)
an excess

border (n)
a line that separates two distinct areas

On the TOEFL Test

3. Why does the author mention a cheeseburger?

- Ⓐ To explain the Formal Cause
- Ⓑ To exemplify the Material Cause
- Ⓒ To illustrate the Efficient Cause
- Ⓓ To introduce the Final Cause

4. Why does the author mention Aether?

- Ⓐ To prove it was used to make up the heavenly spheres and bodies
- Ⓑ To exemplify an element that is hot and wet
- Ⓒ To show that Aristotle thought it was a useful substance
- Ⓓ To list a major element named by Aristotle

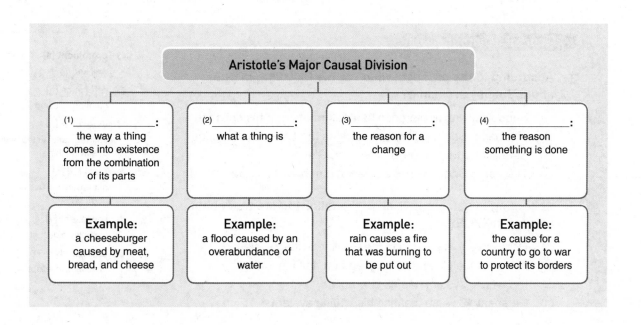

Aristotle's Major Causal Division

(1)_____: the way a thing comes into existence from the combination of its parts

(2)_____: what a thing is

(3)_____: the reason for a change

(4)_____: the reason something is done

Example: a cheeseburger caused by meat, bread, and cheese

Example: a flood caused by an overabundance of water

Example: rain causes a fire that was burning to be put out

Example: the cause for a country to go to war to protect its borders

Read the following passage, and answer the questions.

Sequoyah

Time Limit: 2 min. 40 sec.

Sequoyah was a Cherokee Native American. He was also known as George Gist. His main skill was as a silversmith. But he is famous for inventing the Cherokee written language. This earned him a place of honor on the list of those who invented writing systems.

Sequoyah's place and exact date of birth are unknown. This is because no written records exist. Guesswork by historians places his birth somewhere between 1760 and 1776. Places in Tennessee, Georgia, North Carolina, Alabama, or South Carolina are suspected to be the location. James Mooney, a prominent historian of the Cherokee people, quotes a cousin who said that Sequoyah and his mother spent his early years in the village of Tuskegee, Tennessee.

The name Sequoyah comes from the Cherokee word meaning "hog." This nickname may be a reference to a childhood deformity. Or it could refer to later injury that left him disabled.

Sequoyah's father was either white or part-white and part Native American. But Sequoyah could not speak English. This may be proof that he and his mother were abandoned by his white father. Sequoyah moved to Willstown, Alabama, at some point in 1809. He established his trade as a silversmith there.

The white settler's writing often impressed Sequoyah. He called papers with English written on them "talking leaves." Sequoyah began work on creating a system of writing for the Cherokee language around 1809. He created 85 characters to represent various syllables. It took Sequoyah 12 years to complete this work.

Sequoyah then taught his daughter to read and write in the new system he had created. The locals were amazed by this. But the medicine men of the tribe said he was being controlled by evil spirits. So Sequoyah taught his system to a group of warriors. Then the other people of the tribe accepted it. The Cherokee nation fully embraced the new system by 1823. It gave them a way to record their history for future generations.

General Comprehension

1. According to the passage, which of the following is true about Sequoyah's name?

(A) Sequoyah was a reference to a deformity from his childhood.
(B) The name Sequoyah means "tree" in the Cherokee language.
(C) Sequoyah's real name was George Gist.
(D) The name Sequoyah was given to him by his mother.

2. According to paragraph 5, all of the following are true about Sequoyah EXCEPT:

(A) He was very interested in the English writing system.
(B) He wrote the Cherokee language on "talking leaves."
(C) His writing system has 85 characters.
(D) He spent 12 years creating his writing system.

prominent (a)
well-known

reference (n)
mention; allusion

deformity (n)
an irregularity in the body of a living thing

disabled (a)
not having full use of one's body

represent (v)
to show; to describe

embrace (v)
to accept; to adopt

3. Why does the author mention no written records exist?

Ⓐ To state the fact that Sequoyah was also known as George Gist
Ⓑ To illustrate the reason Sequoyah was famous
Ⓒ To preface the fact that Sequoyah's main skill was as a silversmith
Ⓓ To explain why Sequoyah's exact date and place of birth are unknown

4. Why does the author mention that Sequoyah taught his system to a group of warriors?

Ⓐ To show how Sequoyah got his tribe to accept his writing system
Ⓑ To illustrate Sequoyah's intelligence
Ⓒ To show that even warriors could become literate
Ⓓ To define this as the event that made Sequoyah famous

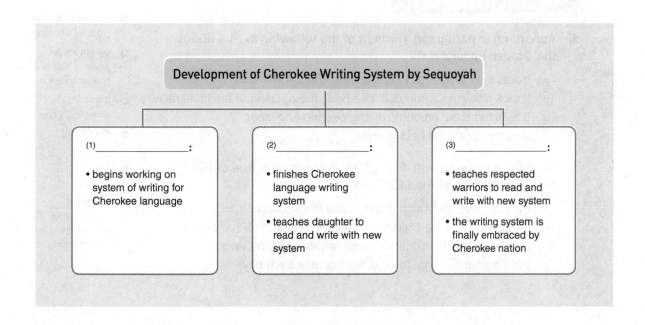

Development of Cherokee Writing System by Sequoyah

(1)_____ :

• begins working on system of writing for Cherokee language

(2)_____ :

• finishes Cherokee language writing system
• teaches daughter to read and write with new system

(3)_____ :

• teaches respected warriors to read and write with new system
• the writing system is finally embraced by Cherokee nation

The First Transcontinental Railroad

Time Limit: 2 min. 40 sec.

The first transcontinental railroad was built in the United States. It ran across North America. It was begun and completed in the 1860s. This linked the railway network of the eastern United States with California. The famous Golden Spike event was held on May 9, 1869. It was a ceremony to open the railway. This railway created a nationwide mode of travel. It changed the population and economy of the American West. It also completed the move away from wagon trains.

This railroad was agreed to be built by the Pacific Railway Act of 1862. It was heavily backed by the federal government. It was the victory of a decades-long effort to build such a line. It was one of the great achievements by Abraham Lincoln. It was completed four years after his death. Building the railway took huge feats of engineering and labor. The tracks run across the plains and high mountains. The railway is comprised of the Union Pacific Railroad and the Central Pacific Railroad. The two were privately built, but both were backed by the federal government. They lead westward and eastward.

The building of the railroad was meant to bind the Union together during the strife of the American Civil War. It filled the West with white settlers. This contributed to the decline of the Native Americans in these areas.

Most of the Union Pacific track was built by Irish laborers. Veterans of the Union and Confederate armies and Mormons also helped build the tracks. Most of the Central Pacific was built by Chinese laborers. At first, Chinese people were thought to be too fragile to do this type of work. But later, more people were brought over from China. Most workers were paid between one and three dollars per day. But the Chinese workers received much less. Eventually, they went on strike. This gained them a small increase in salary.

General Comprehension

1. **According to paragraph 1, which of the following is true about the Golden Spike event?**

   (A) It was the name of the first transcontinental railroad.
   (B) It took place in California to celebrate the opening of the local railway.
   (C) It required great amounts of engineering and labor.
   (D) It was a ceremony held in 1869.

2. **According to paragraph 4, all of the following are true of the transcontinental railroad EXCEPT:**

   (A) Irish laborers laid much of the Union Pacific track.
   (B) People thought the Chinese lacked the strength for hard work.
   (C) Soldiers in the Confederate army helped build the track.
   (D) Workers typically got three dollars or less each day.

transcontinental (a)
crossing a continent

ceremony (n)
an event held to mark a special occasion

mode (n)
a method or type

decade (n)
ten years

feat (n)
an effort

strike (n)
an event in which workers do not work to express their dissatisfaction

3. **How does the author explain the idea that the railroad contributed to the decline of the Native Americans in paragraph 3?**

     Ⓐ By saying the railroad increased the number of whites in the West
     Ⓑ By saying the railroad brought guns to the settlers
     Ⓒ By saying the railroad bound the Union together
     Ⓓ By saying the railroad carried troops to fight the Native Americans from the Atlantic to Pacific

4. **Why does the author mention Chinese people?**

     Ⓐ To explain that they were not paid as much as other laborers
     Ⓑ To show that they were too weak to build the railroad
     Ⓒ To describe their actions while they were striking
     Ⓓ To mention that they were the most responsible for the Central Pacific line

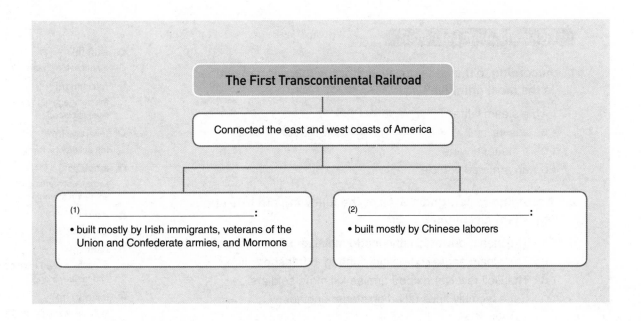

The First Transcontinental Railroad

Connected the east and west coasts of America

(1)_____ :
• built mostly by Irish immigrants, veterans of the Union and Confederate armies, and Mormons

(2)_____ :
• built mostly by Chinese laborers

Mechanization

Time Limit: 2 min. 50 sec.

The shift from human labor to machines is called mechanization. It has changed human history forever. Machines enable people to do much more work while using much less strength. Humans have been making machines in simple and complex forms since before the time of recorded history.

The simplest kind of machine is a lever. This can be a stick that is placed under an object and over a stone or other object. The object underneath the stick acts as a fulcrum. This gives the stick leverage. When the person presses down on the stick with force, it pushes off the fulcrum and lifts the object on top of the stick. In this act, the person's strength is amplified by the lever. They can use less force to lift more weight. This is one of the guiding principles for the development of all machines. The machine does the work for the human, who exerts a minimal amount of force.

One important machine was the steam-powered lathe. This device increased the speed and accuracy at which metal and woodwork could be done. Another helpful machine was the steam engine, which made steamboats and steam-powered trains possible. This led to a revolution in transportation. The Colt revolver was the first machine pistol that was able to fire repeated shots. This device made warfare more deadly. The early 20th century saw the mechanization of car assembly lines with the Ford system. This changed the way people worked and traveled.

The term *mechanization* is also used by military forces. This term refers to the use of tracked armored vehicles. The armored personnel carrier is one of these vehicles. It is used to move large amounts of troops around a battlefield very quickly. It also protects them so that as few soldiers as possible are killed on the way into battle. In the past, many soldiers died before even reaching a battle. The mobility and fighting capability is greatly increased by mechanization. In modern countries, all armed forces are supported by mechanized infantry.

General Comprehension

1. **According to the passage, which of the following machines is the most primitive?**

   Ⓐ a steam lathe
   Ⓑ a lever
   Ⓒ a steam engine
   Ⓓ an armored vehicle

2. **According to paragraph 3, all of the following are true about important machines EXCEPT:**

   Ⓐ The steam-powered lathe made metal and woodwork much faster.
   Ⓑ The steam engine completely changed transportation.
   Ⓒ The Colt revolver helped armies kill more soldiers.
   Ⓓ Car assembly lines relied on steam engines.

shift (n)
a noticeable change

fulcrum (n)
the point against which a lever is placed

leverage (n)
the action of a lever

amplify (v)
to make something or someone stronger

exert (v)
to use force

lathe (n)
a machine used in wood and metalworking

infantry (n)
soldiers who fight on the ground

3. **Why does the author mention the shift from human labor to machines?**

    Ⓐ To explain how humans discovered mechanization

    Ⓑ To explain what mechanization is

    Ⓒ To show that machines replaced human labor

    Ⓓ To prove machines are more efficient than human labor

4. **The author mentions that in the past, many soldiers died before even reaching a battle in paragraph 4 in order to**

    Ⓐ explain the usefulness of the Colt revolver

    Ⓑ show that the steam powered lathe was useful

    Ⓒ emphasize the value of the armored personnel carrier

    Ⓓ describe mechanized infantry

Mechanization

- the shift from human labor to machines → more work with less strength
- (1)_____ → the simplest machine
- steam-powered lathe → speedier and more accurate metal and woodwork
- steam engine → steamboats and steam-powered trains
- (2)_____ → deadlier warfare
- (3)_____ → changed the way people work and live

The Mammoth

Time Limit: 2 min. 50 sec.

The most commonly found prehistoric fossil is that of the mammoth. It was a variety of elephant that is now extinct. Mammoths had long, curved teeth called tusks. The northern species were covered in thick, woolly hair. They roamed the earth during the Pleistocene epoch. This time period spanned from 1.6 million to around 10,000 years ago.

The mammoth blood line is related most closely to the modern Asian elephant. The genes of the two African elephant varieties do not resemble those of the mammoth as closely. The Asian elephant and mammoth's common ancestor split off from the African elephant's line. This divergence took place about 6 to 7.3 million years ago. Asian elephants and mammoths diverged from one another a half million years later.

Scientists believe that the mammoth originally evolved in North Africa. Its origins stretch back some 4.8 million years ago. Bones that date back this far have been found in Chad, Libya, Morocco, and Tunisia. Sites in South Africa and Kenya have also revealed the ancient remains that are thought to be the oldest of the species.

The African mammoth then migrated. The fossil record shows that it eventually reached north to Europe. A new species, which is termed the southern mammoth, soon came about. This was the species that lived throughout Asia and Europe. Studies deduce that it then crossed the now-sunken Bering Strait Land Bridge. This was the frozen land structure that linked Asia and North America through present-day Siberia and Alaska. This brought the mammoth onto the North American continent.

Then around 700,000 years ago, the warm climate began to change. In Europe, Asia, and North America, the savannah plains became steppes that were colder and less fertile. The southern mammoths were the first variety of the species to die off. A new variety, the woolly mammoth, evolved 300,000 years ago. This beast was covered in a thick coat of woolly hair. It was able to cope with the extreme cold of the ice ages.

General Comprehension

1. **According to the passage, which of the following is true of the mammoth?**
   - (A) Its bones have been found in New York City.
   - (B) Scientists find its fossils more than any other animal.
   - (C) It became extinct 10,000 years ago.
   - (D) Its blood line is not related to the modern Asian elephant.

2. **According to paragraph 4, all of the following about the mammoth are true EXCEPT:**
   - (A) The southern mammoth wandered the lands of Europe.
   - (B) The southern mammoth evolved from the African mammoth.
   - (C) The southern mammoth came to North America over a land bridge.
   - (D) The fossil record shows the African mammoth was related to the dinosaurs.

epoch (n)
a period of history marked by notable events

diverge (v)
to separate; to split

reveal (v)
to uncover; to disclose

deduce (v)
to infer

cope with (phr)
to deal with; to survive

3.   Why does the author mention the modern Asian elephant?

ⓐ To support the belief that it became extinct at the same time as the mammoth

ⓑ To compare its physical features to the woolly mammoth

ⓒ To define it as the closest genetic relative of the mammoth

ⓓ To portray it as a common enemy of the mammoth

4.   The author uses Chad, Libya, Morocco, and Tunisia as examples of

ⓐ places where the mammoth never existed

ⓑ places where remains of mammoths have been found

ⓒ places that were too hot for the woolly mammoth

ⓓ places where the oldest mammoths were lived

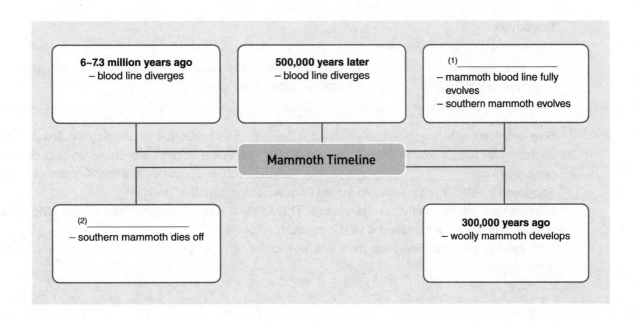

6~7.3 million years ago
– blood line diverges

500,000 years later
– blood line diverges

(1)_____
– mammoth blood line fully evolves
– southern mammoth evolves

Mammoth Timeline

(2)_____
– southern mammoth dies off

300,000 years ago
– woolly mammoth develops

Building Summary Skills

The following summaries are based on the long passages you worked on earlier. Complete each of them by filling in the blanks with suitable words or phrases.

1. Neptune

> a vivid blue appearance   Voyager 2   hot core temperature
> the fourth largest   the outermost planet

Neptune is (1)_____ of the solar system and is (2)_____ in diameter and the third largest in mass. Its atmosphere is composed mostly of gas, and it has (3)_____. There are many strange facts about the planet, such as its high winds, 13 moons, and (4)_____ that make it interesting to scientists. The only human probe ever to visit and collect information on Neptune was (5)_____.

2. The Metaphysics of Aristotle

> the causes of things   the substance of matter and form   modern science
> metaphysics   four major categories

Aristotle was one of the most important thinkers of all time because he created many fields of study, one of which is (1)_____. He created the guidelines for understanding (2)_____, of which there are (3)_____. He made many conclusions about (4)_____ as well as defining five major elements. His classifications laid important foundations for (5)_____ that are used today.

3. Sequoyah

> 85 characters   a group of respected warriors   a system of writing
> record their history   Cherokee Native American

Sequoyah was a (1)_____ who is famous for creating the first system of writing for the Cherokee people. His exact place and date of birth are unknown because his people lacked (2)_____ for recording historical data. After 12 years of work, Sequoyah created a writing system for the Cherokee language that used (3)_____ to represent the sounds of the language. This system was at first rejected by the Cherokee people, but they later accepted it after Sequoyah taught it to (4)_____. This system gave the Cherokee people a way to (5)_____ for future generations.

4. **The First Transcontinental Railroad**

> the federal government   Ireland and China   Native Americans
> President Abraham Lincoln   run across North America

The first transcontinental railroad to (1)_____ was completed in 1869 and commemorated with the famous Golden Spike event. The railroad was heavily backed by (2)_____ and stands as one of the great achievements of (3)_____ _____. The building had many effects, such as bringing the Union states together during the Civil War as well as leading to the decline of (4)_____ in the West by populating it with white settlers. Much of the railroad was built by immigrant laborers from (5)_____ as well as by veterans of the Union and Confederate armies and Mormons.

5. **Mechanization**

> the steam-powered lathe   warfare   mechanization
> human history   the lever

(1)_____ has been changed by the shift from human labor to (2)_____. A good example of a simple machine that relieves a human of labor is (3)_____. Some very important machines were (4)_____, steam-powered trains, the Colt revolver, and the mechanization of car assembly lines. Military forces have also mechanized their forces, which results in many advantages in (5)_____.

6. **The Mammoth**

> North Africa   over 7 million years ago   climate changes
> a prehistoric variety   the Asian variety of elephant

The mammoth was (1)_____ that is now extinct and whose fossil remains are the most commonly found. Mammoths are most closely related to (2)_____ _____, having genetically split off from the African varieties of elephant (3)_____ _____. Due to fossil evidence, scientists believe the mammoth originally evolved in (4)_____ and then migrated around the world, ending up in North America. Mammoths began to die off due to (5)_____ that began 700,000 years ago.

1. **The word inhibited in the passage is closest in meaning to**

   (A) strengthened
   (B) weakened
   (C) destroyed
   (D) increased

2. **The word it in the passage refers to**

   (A) Central Asia
   (B) the West
   (C) a large sunspot
   (D) the mystery

3. **According to paragraph 1, which of the following is true of sunspots?**

   (A) Galileo saw them through filtered dust.
   (B) Astronomers have puzzled over them for a long time.
   (C) They were first observed during the Middle Ages.
   (D) They are regions of the sun that have stopped burning.

4. **According to the passage, which of the following is NOT true?**

   (A) Dark spots on the surface of the sun are called sunspots.
   (B) Scientists have succeeded in estimating how often sunspots appeared as far back as 11,000.
   (C) Starspots are sunspots that appear on other stars.
   (D) Sunspot activity was at its lowest 8,000 years ago.

5. **Which of the following can be inferred about the normal convection of the sun?**

   (A) It is not inhibited by areas with low levels of magnetism.
   (B) It is more inhibited by areas with low levels of magnetism.
   (C) It is not affected by the level of magnetism at all.
   (D) It makes sunspots larger due to low levels of magnetism.

6. **The author discusses magnetic flux tubes in paragraph 4 in order to**

   (A) show that scientists do not fully understand sunspots
   (B) support the theory that sunspots are areas of low magnetism
   (C) explain that they are closely connected with sunspots
   (D) prove that scientists fully understand sunspots

Sunspots

Sunspots are dark regions on the surface of the sun. They have been a mystery to astronomers for thousands of years. Chinese astronomers made references to them in 28 B.C. They could see the largest spot groups. These were visible to them when the sun's glare was filtered by dust blown by the wind from the deserts of Central Asia. In the West, a large sunspot was viewed during the Middle Ages. But the mystery of this observation was not clearly understood until 1612 when Galileo explained it.

Sunspots have been recorded by astronomers since the year 1700 A.D. Current scientists have been able to estimate the cycle of appearance of these sunspots back to 11,000 B.C. The most recent trend of sunspots rises upward from 1900 to the 1960s. The sun was similarly active over 8,000 years ago.

The sunspot areas have lower temperatures than the areas around them. They also show heightened magnetic activity. The normal convection of the sun is inhibited by this high level of magnetism. The result is formation of low surface temperature areas. But these areas are still too bright to look at directly. These sunspots burn at temperatures as low as 4,000 degrees Kelvin. Meanwhile, the rest of the sun burns at 5,700 degrees Kelvin. This difference is the cause of the clearly visible dark spots. Similar spots observed on stars other than the sun are called starspots.

It is not fully understood how sunspots come into being. But quite clear is the fact that they are the visible counterparts of magnetic flux tubes in the convective zone of the sun. The magnetic flux tubes get "wound up" by differential rotation. When the stress on the flux tubes reaches a certain limit, they curl up like a rubber band and puncture the sun's surface. At the puncture points, convection is inhibited. Then energy flux from the sun's interior decreases, which drops the surface temperature.

The number of spots is connected to the intensity of solar radiation. This connection has been recorded since 1979, when satellite measurements of radiation became available. Since sunspots are dark, it would be natural to assume that more spots means less solar radiation. However, the areas surrounding sunspots are brighter. The overall effect is that more spots cause the sun to burn brighter. But this variation is too small to notice with the naked eye. A period called the Maunder Minimum marked a time when there were hardly any sunspots on the sun. At this time, the Earth was believed to have cooled by up to 1 degree Celsius.

7. The word **severity** in the passage is closest in meaning to

   Ⓐ electricity
   Ⓑ intensity
   Ⓒ frequency
   Ⓓ danger

8. According to paragraph 1, which of the following is true of thunderstorms?

   Ⓐ They are created by thundersnow.
   Ⓑ They are produced by heavy rain and hail.
   Ⓒ They often cause snow to fall.
   Ⓓ A cumulonimbus cloud causes them.

9. According to paragraph 2, the author's description of the formation of thunderstorms mentions all of the following EXCEPT:

   Ⓐ They form only when the atmosphere is unstable.
   Ⓑ They produce a large amount of condensation.
   Ⓒ It is characterized by moisture in the lower atmosphere.
   Ⓓ The temperature of the air often rises.

10. According to paragraph 3, which of the following can be inferred about thunderstorms?

   Ⓐ Thunderstorms occur in Europe.
   Ⓑ Thunderstorms never occur in Australia.
   Ⓒ Thunderstorms mostly occur in Uganda.
   Ⓓ Florida has more thunderstorms than Bogor.

11. Why does the author mention **Florida**?

   Ⓐ To show that it is in a temperate region
   Ⓑ To describe a place that receives few thunderstorms
   Ⓒ To say it gets more thunderstorms than most places
   Ⓓ To prove that there are daily thunderstorms there all year long

12. Which of the following best expresses the essential information in the highlighted sentence? *Incorrect* answer choices change the meaning in important ways or leave out essential information.

   Ⓐ The Romans thought Jupiter and Vulcan were fighting each other with lightning bolts.
   Ⓑ The Romans thought thunderstorms were caused by Jupiter throwing lightning bolts.
   Ⓒ The Romans wanted to fight against gods such as Jupiter and Vulcan.
   Ⓓ The Romans thought Vulcan created thunderstorms with which to battle Jupiter.

The Frequency of Thunderstorms

Thunderstorms are called electrical storms due to the presence of lightning and thunder. These violent storms are produced by a cumulonimbus cloud, which can make heavy rain or hail. On rare occasions the cloud can bring snow. This snow usually happens during the winter months and is called thundersnow.

When heavy condensation occurs in an unstable atmosphere, thunderstorms form. This event produces a wide range of water droplets and ice crystals. A deep, upward motion supports it. It is often marked by the presence of three conditions. Sufficient moisture in the lower atmosphere is the first. This is reflected by high dewpoint temperatures. A large drop in air temperature and increasing height are the second. This is termed adiabatic lapse rate. A force such as mechanical convergence is the third. This force occurs along the cold front and focuses its lift.

Thunderstorms happen all over the world. They even hit the polar regions. The areas with the most storms are tropical rainforest areas. Here they may occur on a daily basis. Kampala and Tororo in Uganda are said to have more thunderstorms than any other region on Earth. Bogor on the Indonesian island of Java is also said to be very thunderous. In temperate regions, thunderstorms happen mostly in spring. However, they can hit along with cold fronts at any time of year. Florida is the most thunderous region outside the tropics. The violent storms hit over the south and central regions of this state. They often happen daily in the summer.

The USA gets the most powerful and dangerous storms. The most severe storms touch down in the Midwest and the southern states. These storms yield very large hail. They also turn out powerful tornadoes. Thunderstorms are uncommon on the West Coast of the United States. But they do hit inland areas. Sacramento and the San Joaquin Valley of California get hit with thunderstorms. Storms in the Northwest take on similar patterns as those in the Midwest. But their frequency and severity are much less.

Early human civilizations were powerfully influenced by the frequency of thunderstorms. The Romans thought they were battles waged by Jupiter, who hurled lightning bolts forged by Vulcan. Increased frequency of thunderstorms made the Romans anxious to the point that they would sacrifice many animals to appease this angry god. Native Americans believed these thunderstorms to be linked to servants of the Great Spirit. They also felt the frequency was linked to the spirit's anger. Nowadays, storm chasers head to the Great Plains of the United States and Canadian prairies every spring. They explore storms and tornadoes visually and scientifically in the summer. For these thrill seekers, more frequent storms satisfy their desire for adventure.

Vocabulary Review

A Choose the word with the closest meaning to each highlighted word or phrase.

1. He gave a very vivid description of the accident.
   - (A) graphic
   - (B) dim
   - (C) beautiful
   - (D) ugly

2. They were unable to detect the problem with the airplane's engine.
   - (A) fix
   - (B) hear
   - (C) find
   - (D) cause

3. He was a very prominent politician in the town.
   - (A) beloved
   - (B) famous
   - (C) disliked
   - (D) problematic

4. The teacher thought that it was an extraordinary feat for the student to come to class on time.
   - (A) action
   - (B) foot
   - (C) trick
   - (D) hope

5. There was a shift in the mood of everybody in the room once the baby began to cry.
   - (A) change
   - (B) emergency
   - (C) break
   - (D) trouble

6. After running the marathon, he was unable to exert any strength.
   - (A) make
   - (B) find
   - (C) use
   - (D) have

7. From the available evidence, the detective was able to deduce that he had committed the crime.
   - (A) know
   - (B) infer
   - (C) imply
   - (D) decide

8. She was unable to cope with the cold weather and had to go inside.
   - (A) enjoy
   - (B) deal with
   - (C) accept
   - (D) block

B Match each word with the correct definition.

1. spike •   • **a.** an amount that is too much of something
2. retrograde •   • **b.** to make something or someone stronger
3. deformity •   • **c.** a period of history marked by notable events
4. epoch •   • **d.** a large, metal nail that is driven through something to fasten or hold it down
5. amplify •   • **e.** furthest from the center
6. infantry •   • **f.** a grassy plain in a tropical or sub-tropical region
7. savannah •   • **g.** soldiers who fight on the ground
8. metaphysics •   • **h.** moving backwards
9. outermost •   • **i.** the theoretical philosophy of being and knowing
10. overabundance • • **j.** an irregularity in the body of a living thing

Unit 7

Inference

7 Inference

Overview

■ Introduction

Inference questions ask you to understand an argument or an idea that is strongly suggested but not clearly mentioned in the passage. So you should use logical thinking in order to make an inference based on some information in the passage. You need to figure out the logical implications of the author's words as well as the surface meaning of those words.

■ Question Types

1. Which of the following can be inferred about X?

2. Which of the following can be inferred from paragraph _____ about X?

3. According to the passage, it can be inferred that ~

4. The author of the passage implies that ~

5. It can be inferred from the passage that the author most likely believes which of the following about X?

6. Which of the following statements most accurately reflects the author's opinion about X?

■ Useful Tips

• Think logically to draw a reasonable conclusion from what is implied in the passage.

• Remember that the correct answer doesn't contradict the main idea of the passage.

• Don't choose an answer just because it is mentioned in the passage.

Sample iBT Question

Which of the following can be inferred about the American women's suffrage movement?

(A) Alice Paul led all of the major groups.

(B) Its leading groups did not agree with each other's methods.

(C) Most of the women in it used nonviolent methods.

(D) Suffragists were unsuccessful at achieving most of their goals.

The American Women's Suffrage Movement

Suffrage is the civil right to vote. It was the goal of many women's groups. In many western democracies, suffrage was a major movement of the late 19th and early 20th century. Suffragists protested strongly for many years, demanding equality with men and the right to vote. Alice Paul was a well-known suffragist. She was also the leader of the American National Women's Party. There were two suffrage parties in America around this time. One was largely peaceful. They tried to advance their cause in a peaceful manner. But the other was willing to commit acts of violence. This party once released 100 rats at a polling station in New Hampshire.

 Correct Answer The passage mentions two leading suffrage parties in America. One of them was peaceful while the other group was aggressive. Each group adopted different methods to gain women's voting right. Therefore, the correct answer is (B).

Inference questions ask you to understand an idea that is not explicitly stated in the passage. You need to use logical thinking to draw a correct conclusion from the author's words in the passage. Your conclusion must agree with the main idea of the passage.

Sponges

Sponges are animals. They are members of the phylum Porifera. They are primitive filter feeders that dwell underwater. They are able to pump water through their bodies to filter out particles of food matter. Sponges are among the simplest of animals. They have no true tissue. They also lack muscles, nerves, and internal organs. There are over 5,000 known species of sponges. They can be found attached to surfaces of rocks and live in intertidal zones. They can be found at depths of 8,500 meters and deeper. The fossil record of sponges dates back to the Precambrian Era. But new species are still commonly discovered.

1. **The author of the passage implies that**

   (A) most sponges live in the deep sea
   (B) sponges are more complicated than people think
   (C) sponges have been evolving since the Precambrian Era
   (D) more species of sponges will be discovered in the future

Tenochtitlan

Tenochtitlan was the capital city of the ancient Aztec Empire. This is now the site of modern-day Mexico City. This ancient city was constructed over a series of islets in Lake Texcoco. The city plan was based on a symmetrical layout. Four sections divide the city into areas called campans. Canals interlaced the city and were useful for transportation. The city was built according to a fixed plan that centered on the ritual precinct. Here the Great Pyramid of Tenochtitlan rose 60 meters above the city. Houses were made of wood and loam. Their roofs were made of reed. But pyramids, temples, and palaces were generally made of stone.

2. **According to the passage, it can be inferred that**

   (A) Tenochtitlan had an important role in the Aztec's religion
   (B) the Aztecs constructed many large pyramids
   (C) Tenochtitlan was built completely on the water
   (D) many buildings from Tenochtitlan still exist today

Electronic Music

Electronic music is created through the use of devices. All of these run on electricity. They are systems that use low levels of power. Before electronic music, many composers wanted to use new technology. They tried to use this technology to make music. Several instruments were created that employed new electronic and mechanical designs. The Moog keyboard was one such instrument. It was used to record the music of Beethoven for the film *A Clockwork Orange* in the 1970s. This was one of the first electronic music recordings. In the late 1990s, electronic music split off into many genres. Its styles and sub-styles are too many to list. There are no strict rules for this kind of music.

3. **It can be inferred from the passage that the author most likely believes which of the following about electronic music?**

    (A) It is not as good as music created by real instruments.
    (B) It has greatly increased in popularity.
    (C) It should be used more often in movie soundtracks.
    (D) It needs to have strict rules.

Ocean Current

The constant motion of water flowing into Earth's oceans creates ocean currents. Ocean currents can flow for thousands of kilometers. This happens more often in regions bordering an ocean. The Gulf Stream is the best example. This current makes northwest Europe much more temperate than other regions at the same latitude. The Hawaiian Islands are another example. The climate there is somewhat cooler than on other islands that occupy the same tropical latitudes. This is because of the California Current. Knowledge of surface ocean currents is important. The costs of shipping can be greatly reduced with such information. This is because the current motion carries ships along. Fuel costs can be greatly reduced this way.

4. **Which of the following can be inferred about ocean currents?**

    (A) They are typically found in the middle of the ocean.
    (B) They always make places cooler when they pass through.
    (C) They tend to move slower than other parts of the ocean.
    (D) They can change the temperature of areas they flow through.

Practice with Long Passages

A Read the following passage, and answer the questions.

Bats and Echolocation

Time Limit: 2 min. 40 sec.

Bats are mammals whose forelimbs have developed as wings. This makes them the only mammal in the world that is capable of flight. There are about 1,100 species of bats around the world.

Bats can be separated into two suborders: megabats and microbats. Not all megabats are larger than microbats. There are two major differences between the two kinds of bats. Microbats use echolocation to direct themselves. They also use this ability to find food. Megabats do not have this ability. Instead, they have a claw on their second toe and forelimb. Microbats do not have this claw.

Megabats are known to eat fruit, nectar, and pollen. Microbats eat insects, blood from larger animals, small mammals, and fish. The echolocation used by microbats is a form of biological sonar. It is also used by dolphins and whales.

Echolocation is a process by which animals emit calls out to the area around them. They listen to the echoes that return from various objects in the area. They use these echoes to locate, range, and identify objects. Ranging is done by measuring the time delay between the animal's vocals and the echo's return. Microbats use their ears to perform this task.

In 1794, a scientist conducted a series of experiments on bats. He concluded that they navigated through their sense of hearing. But the scientific community rejected his findings. In 1938, another scientist described the ultrasound echolocation used by bats.

Microbats use echolocation to navigate and forage in total darkness. They emerge from their caves or roosts as the sun sets. They forage for insects during the night. Their ability allows them to occupy a special niche. This is the time where there are often many insects. These insects come out at night since there are often fewer predators. There is much less competition for food at this time and fewer species that may prey on the bats themselves.

General Comprehension

1. **According to the passage, which of the following is true about bats?**

   (A) Scientists know that bats navigate with their eyes.
   (B) There are more than 1,200 kinds of bats around the world.
   (C) Bats are the only mammal in the world that can fly.
   (D) All species of bats use biological sonar to locate objects.

2. **According to the passage, all of the following are true about microbats EXCEPT:**

   (A) They use their ears to perform echolocation.
   (B) They feed on fruit, nectar, and pollen.
   (C) Their ability to live in the dark is advantageous for them.
   (D) They hunt at night because there is more prey then.

- **separated (a)**
  divided
- **emit (v)**
  to send out
- **range (v)**
  to determine how far away something is
- **forage (v)**
  to search for food
- **predator (n)**
  an animal that hunts another animal

On the TOEFL Test

3. Which of the following can be inferred from paragraph 2 about bats?

  (A) There are a number of kinds of bats.
  (B) The wings of microbats and megabats look the same.
  (C) They all rely upon echolocation to find their food.
  (D) Some microbats are larger than megabats.

4. Which of the following can be inferred about research on bats?

  (A) It has gone on for a long time.
  (B) It must always be done at night.
  (C) Scientists need to conduct more experiments.
  (D) It is mostly incorrect.

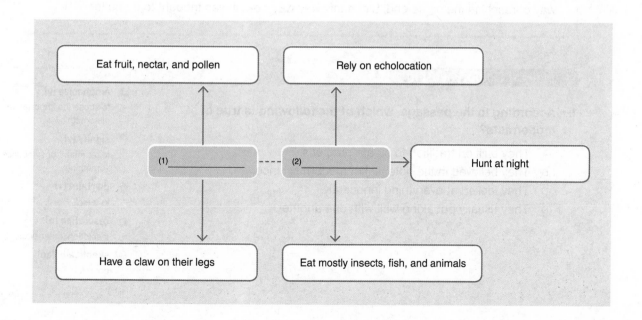

Read the following passage, and answer the questions.

Modernism

Time Limit: 3 min.

Modernism was a movement that strove for progress. It swept through every aspect of culture in the 20th century. It emphasized the power of human beings. It also encouraged the overthrow of traditional ways. Modernists believed they could make, improve, and reshape their own lives and the world. They thought they could do this through the use of science and technology.

Modernism was very important because it signified a change in thought. It expressed the effects of the Industrial Revolution on the human mind. It also served as a meeting point between art, philosophy, and technology.

The history of modernism consists of a series of movements. The members of these groups wanted to create progress. This began with painters in France in the mid-1800s. Some of the first were Impressionist painters such as Eduard Manet and Claude Monet. These painters showed that humans do not see the subject of a painting but rather the light and shading that carries the image to their eyes. Another early modernist was Gustave Eiffel. His Eiffel Tower changed people's ideas of architecture and its possibilities.

However, one major problem of modernists is that they often disclaimed the authenticity of other modernists. These conflicts often occurred over very relative issues. They would argue over who used a style first or whose style was more derivative of another popular modernist. These arguments often had no resolution. They only served to waste time and energy.

Some historians divide the 20th century into modern and post-modern periods. They claim that the post-modernists used modernist styles and principles in consumer products. These styles showed up in many commercial products. Modern styles were used on record album cover art, postcards, and even the graphic design of the signs for the London Underground.

But others see the modernists and post-modernists as parts of the same group. They looked at everything skeptically. The goal is always to find anything that was "holding back" progress. Whatever was found to be the cause was then replaced. It was replaced with a new way of reaching the same end. Since this way was new, it was thought to be better.

General Comprehension

1. **According to the passage, which of the following is true of modernists?**

   (A) They built on tradition to create progress.
   (B) They believed in the potential of modern science.
   (C) They looked at everything innocently.
   (D) They usually got along well with one another.

---

emphasize (v)
to stress the importance of something

signify (v)
to represent or symbolize something

disclaim (v)
to reject

resolution (n)
a solution; an answer

skeptically (ad)
doubtfully

2. **According to paragraph 5, all of the following are true about post-modernists EXCEPT:**

Ⓐ They created commercial products with modernist styles and principles.

Ⓑ Record cover art is a common post-modernist product.

Ⓒ The signs for the London Underground are post-modern designs.

Ⓓ The 20th century is divided into pre-modern and post-modern periods.

On the TOEFL Test

3. **In paragraph 2, the author of the passage implies that**

Ⓐ modernism was independent of other disciplines

Ⓑ modernism was not particularly important

Ⓒ modernism was a reaction to the Industrial Revolution

Ⓓ modernism relied heavily upon philosophy

4. **According to paragraph 3, what can be inferred about Eduard Manet?**

Ⓐ He preferred architecture to painting.

Ⓑ He recognized the importance of light in painting.

Ⓒ He tried to paint humans as they are seen.

Ⓓ He was friends with Gustave Eiffel.

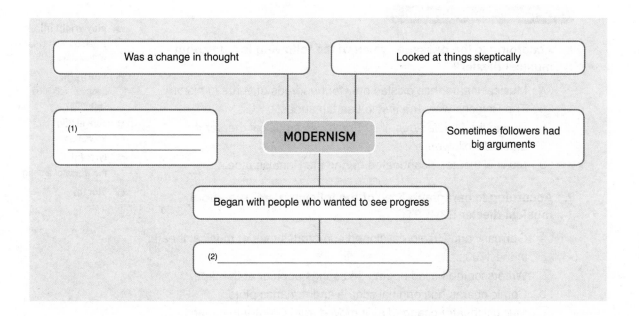

Read the following passage, and answer the questions.

Musical Theater

Time Limit: 2 min. 50 sec.

Musical theater is a form of entertainment that tells stories through songs, words, and dancing. The history of this form goes back several thousand years. Some of the first musicals were developed in ancient India and Greece. The Greeks added music and dances to their popular stage plays. Some of the great Greek playwrights were even known to compose their own music to accompany their plays.

Hundreds of years later, in 3 B.C., this form reemerged. The Roman comic writer Plautus added songs, dances, and orchestrations to his plays. In order to make their dance steps loud enough to be heard by audiences in large open theaters, the actors put metal chips on their shoes. These were the earliest form of tap shoes.

During the Middle Ages, plays became a method for the Church to spread its teachings. The liturgy was taught through religious dramas set to chants. These plays were so popular that they became a form of entertainment separate from the Church. In them, prose dialogs and liturgical chants alternated to keep audiences interested.

These forms developed into the time of the Renaissance, forming an Italian tradition. Silly clowns acted their way through stories known by all of the common people. This comic entertainment form was known as Opera Buffa. This new tradition carried over to France in the 1600s. There, the great writer Moliere was able to convert some of his comedies into musicals. These were accompanied by music written by Jean Baptiste Lully.

This form of entertainment spread between countries in Europe and kept changing. In Germany and Britain, the 1700s saw the rise of two different forms of musical theater. The first was the ballad opera. The writers of this dramatic form of theater borrowed popular songs of the day and rewrote the lyrics to fit their needs. But comic operas were different in that they had original scores and plot lines that were full of romance.

General Comprehension

1. **According to the passage, which of the following is true about musical theater?**

   (A) Musical theater has existed only for hundreds of years in history.
   (B) The Romans were the first to use tap shoes.
   (C) During the Middle Ages, the church used musical theater to entertain followers.
   (D) Musical theater disappeared during the Renaissance.

2. **According to paragraph 5, all of the following are true about musical theater EXCEPT:**

   (A) Germany and Britain developed numerous types of musical theater in the 1700s.
   (B) Writers for the ballad opera used songs popular at the time.
   (C) Comic operas had original scores and romantic plots.
   (D) Musical theater changed as it moved from country to country.

playwright (n)
a person who creates or writes plays

liturgy (n)
a kind of religious ceremony

convert (v)
to change

lyric (n)
the words of a song

plot (n)
a story

On the TOEFL Test

3. **According to paragraphs 1 and 2, which of the following can be inferred about musical theater?**

   (A) People were enthusiastic about musical theater in ancient India.
   (B) Roman theater had tap dancing as its main component.
   (C) People did not perform musical theater for a long time in history.
   (D) There were typically small audiences for Roman theater performances.

4. **The author of the passage implies that**

   (A) every written story was changed into a musical
   (B) Opera Buffa was enjoyed by ordinary people
   (C) Germany and Britain were the last countries to develop musical theater
   (D) comic operas were first played in India

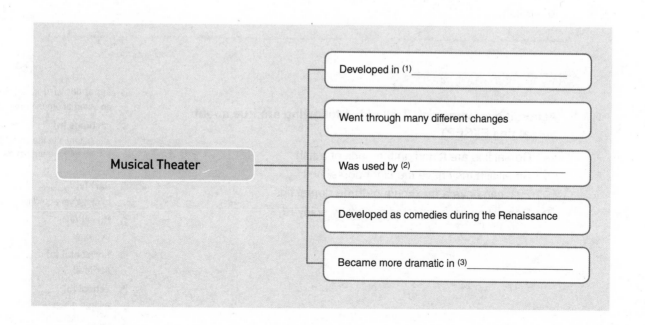

Read the following passage, and answer the questions.

The Fins of Fish

Time Limit: 3 min.

All fish have streamlined bodies that allow them to pass through water with ease. Part of their evolutionary design are fins, which are flat appendages made of cartilage and covered in scales. All fish have several different types of fins on their bodies that give them control as they pass through the water. Fins allow them to turn, to slow down and speed up, and to stop and hold a single position in the water.

The dorsal fins are located in the center of the back of a fish and can be pointed or blunt. A pointed dorsal fin increases the fish's speed while the blunt-shaped fin offers more control to small fish in strong waters. Fish can have up to three of these fins on their backs. They are supported by two kinds of cartilage rays, spiny and soft. A fin can contain either or both types of rays. The spiny rays sometimes also act as defensive weapons, having sharp points or even poison tips.

The anal, pectoral, and pelvic fins of fish are also supported by rays. These small fins give a fish control over fine movements, allowing it to dart quickly with flashes of motion. By using these, fish can position themselves for feeding or in a school formation with other fish. The anal fin is located on the bottom part of the fish behind its anus.

The pectoral fins are located on the sides of the fish, like wings on a bird. Their cartilage structure is parallel in design with the forelimbs of land creatures. The paired pelvic fins are located below and behind the pectoral fins. These are parallel to the hindlimbs of land creatures. By flapping these fins, a fish gains momentum to move itself through the water.

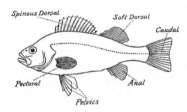

The tail fins are also referred to as caudal fins. These allow for turning and thrusting through the water. Some fish that are able to swim very swiftly have a horizontal caudal keel fin just in front of the tail fin. This forms a kind of ridge on the tail. It adds speed and stability to the fish.

General Comprehension

1. **According to paragraph 2, all of the following are true about dorsal fins EXCEPT:**

   Ⓐ Dorsal fins are found on the back of a fish.
   Ⓑ Small fish may have the blunt dorsal fins.
   Ⓒ Fish can have a maximum of three dorsal fins.
   Ⓓ Dorsal fins are supported mainly by spiny rays.

- **appendage (n)**
  an external organ or part
- **cartilage (n)**
  a substance in the body similar to bone but not as hard
- **dart (v)**
  to move very quickly
- **thrust (v)**
  to propel
- **horizontal (a)**
  flat; level
- **school (n)**
  a large group of fish

2. **According to the passage, which of the following is true about fish fins?**

    (A) Fins are made of bones and covered in scales.

    (B) Pelvic fins are to a fish as forelimbs are to a land animal.

    (C) Pectoral fins add speed and stability to the fish.

    (D) Caudal fins enable a fish to turn while swimming.

On the TOEFL Test

3. **Which of the following can be inferred from paragraph 1 about fish?**

    (A) They have at least ten fins on their bodies.

    (B) They would drown without fins.

    (C) They are not constantly moving.

    (D) Every part of their bodies has fins.

4. **The author of the passage implies that fish**

    (A) need all of their fins for different roles

    (B) can do without their dorsal fins

    (C) used to walk on land

    (D) have too many fins in some cases

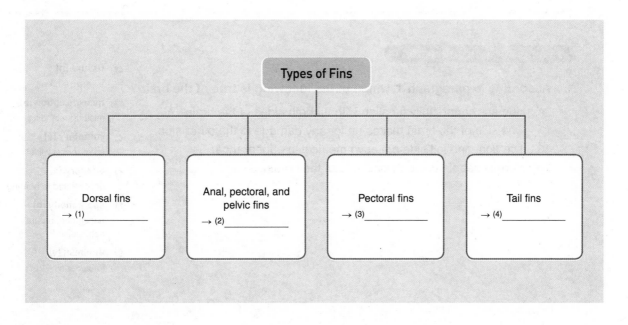

Read the following passage, and answer the questions.

The Functions of the Human Brain

Time Limit: 3 min.

The human brain is separated into two distinct sides by a fissure. Every structure in each side of the brain is mirrored on the other side. But each side takes on different main functions. This has led to the myth that people only use the right or left side of their brain. But this is a misconception since a fully functioning human must use both sides of his or her brain to perform the full range of skills and functions.

The human brain consists of five sections. These are the parietal, frontal, occipital, and temporal lobes, as well as the cerebellum. The parietal lobe is the part of the brain that combines sensory information from all of the body parts. It is also used to judge space through vision. This is the least understood region of the brain.

The brain's frontal lobe contains the body's gyrus and motor cortex tissue. This is the material through which the brain can control the body's voluntary movements. The frontal lobe has also been found to govern impulse control, judgment, memory, language, motor functions, problem solving, sexual behavior, socialization, and spontaneity. A large number of the body's activities are managed through this lobe.

The occipital lobe is the part of the brain that processes vision. It is the smallest of the four lobes, located in the rear area of the brain. Regions of this lobe process color, aspects of space, and motion perception. If this lobe is damaged, the ability of sight can be diminished or lost.

The temporal lobes rest low on either sides of the brain. This lobe contains the auditory cortex. This controls the body's ability to hear and process sound. It also controls high-level processing such as speech. It manages such functions as comprehension, verbal memory, naming, and language.

The cerebellum lies at the base of the brain at the point where it connects to the spinal cord. This region functions as the meeting point of sensory perception and muscle control through the nervous system.

General Comprehension

1. **According to paragraph 1, which of the following is true of the brain?**

   Ⓐ Humans cannot fully function without both sides of the brain.
   Ⓑ One side of the brain makes up for any damage to the other side.
   Ⓒ The right and left side are asymmetrical in appearance.
   Ⓓ Normal people use only one side of their brain.

fissure (n)
a crack; a break

misconception (n)
misunderstanding

voluntary (a)
on purpose; willful

auditory (a)
of or related to hearing

spontaneity (n)
unplanned, natural behavior

diminish (v)
to decrease

2. **According to the passage, all of the following are true about the lobes of the brain EXCEPT:**

   (A) The parietal lobe processes sensory information from other body parts.
   (B) The frontal lobe controls impulse and problem solving skills.
   (C) The occipital lobe is the largest part of the brain.
   (D) The temporal lobe is connected to sound processing ability.

On the TOEFL Test

3. **The author of the passage implies that**

   (A) scientists should learn more about the parietal lobe
   (B) the parietal lobe is not particularly important
   (C) the brain is the largest organ in the body
   (D) the cerebellum is the least interesting part

4. **According to the passage, it can be inferred that**

   (A) people with good judgment have large frontal lobes
   (B) people can function properly without their frontal lobes
   (C) a blind person may have damaged his or her occipital lobe
   (D) the occipital lobe has many different colors

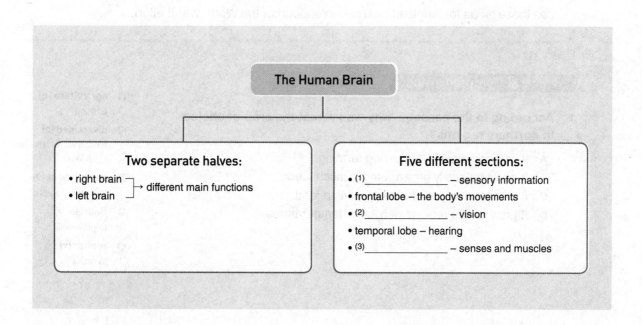

The Human Brain

Two separate halves:
- right brain ⎤
- left brain ⎦→ different main functions

Five different sections:
- (1)_____ – sensory information
- frontal lobe – the body's movements
- (2)_____ – vision
- temporal lobe – hearing
- (3)_____ – senses and muscles

Agriculture in America

Time Limit: 3 min.

America's foundation rests on its agriculture industry. This industry feeds all of the citizens of the country. It also exports food to other countries around the world. However, this industry did not develop instantly. It took centuries of refinement to create an agricultural base that is capable of sustaining the entire population.

The westward movement of colonies spread farms across the U.S. Settlers traveled to new areas and built their farms. Their efforts created new towns and cities. The supply chains that led to these new areas became the roads that run throughout the nation.

Wheat was often the crop of choice in northern regions. The reason for this is that wheat crops are easily grown in cool regions. This crop was usually planted in newly settled lands. These new areas were known as the "wheat frontier." This zone of newly settled wheat farms moved west over the years. After these wheat farms moved on, more diversified farms took their place.

In the Midwest, the farming of corn and raising of hogs was a common agricultural combination. Hogs and corn complement each other. This is because in the time before canals and railroads, it was difficult to get grain to market. So the grain could be fed to the hogs, which were much easier to transport.

In the warm southern regions, cotton and herds of beef cattle were the most popular products. The reason behind this was that both flourish in the heat. Tobacco farming was also common in the South. Until the Civil War, this was done through the use of slave labor. Slaves were also used in agriculture in the Northeast. They were used there up to the early 1800s. But slavery was prohibited in the Midwest. The Freedom Ordinance of 1787 outlawed it.

During the time of the Great Depression, huge areas of the Midwest were abandoned. This was due to the Dust Bowl storms that swept through the region and rendered the soil useless for farming. These regions were then made into national forests. But in the 1940s, efforts to use these areas for farmland resumed in support of the World War II effort.

General Comprehension

1. **According to the passage, why was wheat the crop of choice in northern regions?**

   (A) It was complementary to hog farming.
   (B) It could be easily grown without much labor.
   (C) It was an ideal crop for newly settled land.
   (D) It grew well in regions with lower temperatures.

agriculture (n)
farming

diversified (a)
having many different qualities

complement (v)
to go well together

flourish (v)
to grow well

render (v)
to make

2. **According to the passage, which of the following is NOT true about American agriculture?**

Ⓐ Corn and hogs were often grown together in the Midwest.

Ⓑ The farming of beef cattle was widely performed in the South.

Ⓒ Tobacco farming was done through the use of slave labor in the Northeast.

Ⓓ Many Midwestern people had to give up farming due to the Dust Bowl.

On the TOEFL Test

3. **The author of the passage implies that**

Ⓐ it takes a long time to build up a country's agricultural base

Ⓑ agriculture is the most important industry in a country

Ⓒ American agriculture cannot yet support the entire country

Ⓓ America's economy is based on agriculture

4. **Which of the following can be inferred about the Midwest?**

Ⓐ Hogs were the only animals raised there.

Ⓑ It did not have good transportation systems.

Ⓒ Many people grew wheat instead of corn.

Ⓓ Trains were built there to transport the hogs.

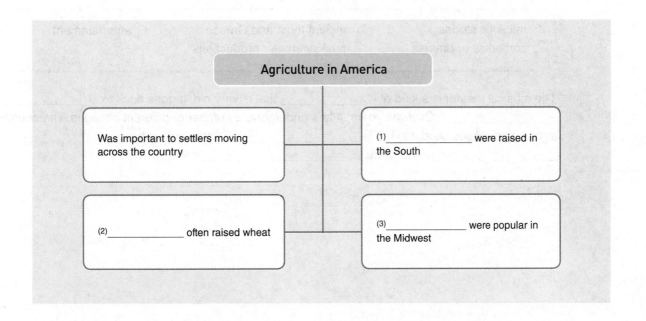

Agriculture in America

Was important to settlers moving across the country

(1)_____ were raised in the South

(2)_____ often raised wheat

(3)_____ were popular in the Midwest

Building Summary Skills

The following summaries are based on the long passages you worked on earlier. Complete each of them by filling in the blanks with suitable words or phrases.

1. Bats and Echolocation

> herbivorous   megabats and microbats   hunt at night
> the only mammals   ultrasound echolocation

Bats are (1)_____ that can fly. There are two suborders of bats: (2)_____
_____. These bats are different from each other. Megabats have a claw on their legs
and are typically (3)_____. Microbats use (4)_____ to get
around and hunt insects, small animals, and fish. They usually (5)_____ when there
are a lot of insects, much less competition for food, and fewer enemies.

2. Modernism

> improve their lives   Eduard Manet and Gustave Eiffel   modernism
> useless arguments   the twentieth century

(1)_____ was an important movement in (2)_____. It encouraged
people to forget about traditional ways and to try to (3)_____. Its members,
like (4)_____, wanted to create progress. But sometimes they got
into (5)_____. Still, the effects of modernism can be seen everywhere today.

3. Musical Theater

> religious stories   ancient India and Greece   entertainment
> comedies or dramas   musical theater productions

The musical theater is a kind of (1)_____ that is very old. It goes back to (2)_____
_____. Over the years, it has undergone a number of different changes. The church
in the Middle Ages used it to tell (3)_____. Other cultures created (4)_____
_____ that were (5)_____.

4. The Fins of Fish

> dart quickly through the water   dorsal fins   control its speed
> on the side of fish   turn in the water

An important evolutionary development in fish is their fins. (1)_____ are located on the back and help the fish (2)_____. The anal, pectoral, and pelvic fins let the fish (3)_____. The pectoral fins (4)_____ help give them momentum. And the tail fins let the fish (5)_____.

5. The Functions of the Human Brain

> the body's movements   the occipital lobe   the left and right
> the senses and muscles   the parietal lobe

The human brain is divided into two separate halves, (1)_____. There are five different sections: the parietal, frontal, occipital, and temporal lobes and the cerebellum. (2)_____ controls sensory information, while the frontal lobe controls (3)_____. (4)_____ controls vision, and the temporal lobe controls hearing. The cerebellum controls (5)_____.

6. Agriculture in America

> moved west   crops and animals   farmed and unfarmed
> agriculture   farming the land

(1)_____ has long been important in America for a number of reasons. As people (2)_____ across the country, they lived by (3)_____. Various regions in the country raised different (4)_____, including cotton, wheat, corn, hogs, and cattle. Some parts of the country have gone back and forth between being (5)_____.

1. **The word confirmed is closest in meaning to**

    (A) verified   (B) requested   (C) assumed   (D) denied

2. **The author of the passage implies that**

    (A) parasites can prosper while living alone
    (B) all parasitic relationships involve one form harming another
    (C) many hunters have parasites
    (D) mosquitoes and hunters are advanced parasites

3. **The word they in the passage refers to**

    (A) ectoparasites   (B) hosts   (C) leeches   (D) chemical cues

4. **The phrase fend for is closest in meaning to**

    (A) hatch   (B) live amongst   (C) suffer   (D) take care of

5. **According to the passage, all of the following are parasites EXCEPT:**

    (A) hookworms
    (B) termites
    (C) human fetuses
    (D) Cuckoo birds

6. **Directions:** Complete the table below to summarize information about parasites. Match the appropriate statements to the characteristics of the parasites with which they are associated. *This question is worth 3 points.*

Answer Choices	Endoparasites
(A) They find new hosts in complex ways.	•
(B) They find their host by passive means.	•
(C) They feed off their host until it dies.	•
(D) They live in the intestines of their host.	**Ectoparasites**
(E) Leeches are one example of them.	•
(F) The hookworm is a member of this group.	•
(G) All free-living animals are this kind of parasite.	

Parasitism

Parasitism describes a relationship between two life forms of different species. It occurs when one life form harms another. In order to be described as parasitism, the two life forms must live together for long periods of time. This does not include animals that hunt and eat their prey or the times when a mosquito feeds off its host.

There are two major kinds of parasites: endo- and ecto-parasites. Endoparasites live inside the body of a host. An example is the hookworm, which lives in the stomach of a human or animal. Many of these parasites find their hosts by passive means. They live in the intestines. There they lay eggs, which are passed through waste products into the outer environment. Once outside the host, they are picked up by other people or animals in unclean areas.

Ectoparasites develop complex ways of finding new hosts. Some aquatic leeches locate their hosts through their motion sensors. They learn their host's identity through the temperature of the skin and chemical cues. Once they have confirmed that it is a desirable host, they use hook-like teeth to attach themselves. After they are attached, they dig through the skin and begin to suck blood.

The way a parasite feeds off its host is also separated into two major distinctions, that of necrotrophs and biotrophs. Necrotrophs are parasites that consume their host's tissue until the host dies. In this relationship, the host usually dies from loss of tissue or nutrients. Biotrophic parasites cannot survive on a host once it has died. They must keep their hosts alive to survive themselves. Many viruses are biotrophic. They use their host's genetic and cellular processes to multiply.

Biotrophic parasitism is a very common way for life forms to survive. At least half of all animals go through a phase of their life where they are parasitic. This includes human fetuses during the time they live inside their mother's womb. This behavior is also common amongst plants and fungi. All free-living animals are host to one or more types of parasites.

Some parasites are social. They learn how to take advantage of the behavior of a social host species. Some parasitic insects like nematodes join ant or termite colonies. They are able to feed on colony members until the group is so weak that it ceases to exist. Many species of Cuckoo bird steal food caught by their host. They even use other birds as babysitters by depositing their eggs in the nests of other birds. The Cuckoo young are raised by the adults of the other bird species while the adult Cuckoos fend for themselves.

7. **The word controversy is closest in meaning to**

   (A) debate   (B) anger   (C) research   (D) interest

8. **According to the passage, what did Pangaea look like?**

   (A) It looked like a sphere.
   (B) It resembled Africa.
   (C) It was shaped like Panthalassa.
   (D) It was shaped like a C.

9. **According to the passage, what can be inferred about continental drift?**

   (A) It was caused by Alfred Wegener.
   (B) It happened recently.
   (C) It was unknown before the 1900s.
   (D) It is named after a Greek phrase.

10. **The word this in the passage refers to**

   (A) the Tethys Ocean   (B) Pangaea   (C) a rift   (D) the east

11. **The word proponents is closest in meaning to**

   (A) creators   (B) opponents   (C) disputers   (D) supporters

12. **Directions:** An introductory sentence for a brief summary of the passage is provided below. Complete the summary by selecting the THREE answer choices that express the most important ideas in the passage. Some answer choices do not belong in the summary because they express ideas that are not in the passage or are minor ideas in the passage. *This question is worth 2 points.*

There are various theories about the history of the Pangaea supercontinent.

   •
   •
   •

Answer Choices

(A) Some people believe the Earth was created by God.

(B) Pangaea was an enormous continent that spread out over the equator.

(C) One breakup of Pangaea occurred during the Jurassic Period.

(D) Alfred Wegener was the first to call the giant continent Pangaea.

(E) Pangaea is believed to have split into two smaller continents.

(F) Scientists disagree over when Pangaea was split up.

Pangaea

Scientists in the early 1900s thought of the continental drift theory. They said that a great number of years ago, the seven continents we know today were a single, giant continent. A scientist named Alfred Wegener named it Pangaea. The name Pangaea comes from the Greek phrase for "all Earth."

This theory stirred up great controversy. The theory's timeline went against popular belief that Earth was only a few thousand years old. People wanted to believe that God had created Earth rather than the forces of nature. Wegener argued in favor of the continental drift theory in 1920.

Pangaea was a C-shaped landform that was spread across the equator. The large body of water within the crescent was called the Tethys Sea. The vast ocean that flowed around the continent was called Panthalassa.

The area of Pangaea would have been very vast. Inland regions would have been extremely dry from a lack of water. Animals could migrate freely from the North to the South Poles.

There were three major phases in the breakup of Pangaea. It is believed to have begun breaking up about 180 million years ago (mya). This happened in the Jurassic Period. Over many millions of years, it broke into the seven continents as we know them today.

The first phase of the breakup began about 180 mya. This change started when a large fault line ruptured. Activity would have been initiated through earthquakes and volcanic eruptions. A rift was created through Pangaea that stretched from the Tethys Ocean to the east. This took place between what is now North America and Africa. The first split created two smaller continents. The southern one is known as Gondwana and the northern one Laurasia.

The second major phase in the breakup began about 150 to 140 mya. At this time, the minor continent of Gondwana broke into four continents. These became Africa, South America, India, and Australia.

The third major and final phase of the breakup was about 60 to 55 mya. North America broke free from Eurasia. This opened up the Norwegian Sea.

But the proponents of this theory also say that Pangaea was not the first giant continent. They have reconstructed several other continental phases by tracing back the Earth's geological history. The most recent continent before Pangea is named Pannotia. Scientists think it would have formed about 600 mya. They believe it divided again about 50 million years later. An even earlier continent has been named Rodinia. Scientists think it would have formed about 1,100 mya and then divided 750 million years later. The earliest possible giant continent is Columbia. Scientists think it existed between 1.8 and 1.5 billion years ago.

Vocabulary Review

A Choose the word with the closest meaning to each highlighted word or phrase.

1. The small community began to flourish and became bigger.
   - (A) thrive
   - (B) build
   - (C) improve
   - (D) shrink

2. The workers abandoned the factory because it was too old and dangerous.
   - (A) repaired
   - (B) sold
   - (C) left
   - (D) fixed

3. The two parties came to a resolution on the contract.
   - (A) disagreement
   - (B) solution
   - (C) promise
   - (D) problem

4. The earthquake caused a fissure to appear in the earth.
   - (A) hole
   - (B) crack
   - (C) weakness
   - (D) ditch

5. The politician tried to convert people to think the same way as he.
   - (A) change
   - (B) direct
   - (C) frighten
   - (D) encourage

6. Mary looked at John skeptically when he told her about the news.
   - (A) happily
   - (B) angrily
   - (C) sadly
   - (D) doubtfully

7. Lions are some of the top predators in Africa.
   - (A) animals
   - (B) hunters
   - (C) insects
   - (D) killers

8. The professor's explanation was beyond our comprehension.
   - (A) ability
   - (B) experience
   - (C) memories
   - (D) understanding

B Match each word with the correct definition.

1. mammal •   • **a.** person who creates or writes plays
2. cartilage •   • **b.** of or related to hearing
3. school •   • **c.** to stress the importance of something
4. emphasize •   • **d.** a warm-blooded species of animal
5. conclude •   • **e.** to move very quickly or suddenly
6. diversified •   • **f.** a substance in the body similar to bone but not as hard
7. dart •   • **g.** a kind of religious ceremony
8. auditory •   • **h.** having many different qualities
9. playwright •   • **i.** a large group of fish
10. liturgy •   • **j.** to determine; to reach an opinion about something

Unit 8

Insert Text

8 Insert Text

Overview

■ Introduction

Insert Text questions ask you to determine where the best place for a given sentence would be in the passage. In this type of question, you will see four black squares appearing in one paragraph or spreading across the end of one paragraph and the beginning of the next. In either case, you need to understand the logical stream of the passage and focus on any grammatical connections between sentences, such as conjunctions, pronouns, demonstratives, and repeated words or phrases.

■ Question Type

Look at the four squares [■] that indicate where the following sentence could be added to the passage.

[a sentence to be inserted into the passage]

Where would the sentence best fit?

Click on a square [■] to add the sentence to the passage.

■ Useful Tips

• Put the sentence in each place next to the squares.

• Try to pay attention to the logical connection between sentences.

• Be familiar with connecting words such as *on the other hand, for example, on the contrary, similarly, in contrast, furthermore, therefore, in other words, as a result, finally,* etc.

Sample iBT Question

Look at the four squares [■] that indicate where the following sentence could be added to the passage.

The only spacecraft to have visited the planet is NASA's Voyager 2.

Where would the sentence best fit?

Click on a square [■] to add the sentence to the passage.

Uranus

Uranus is the seventh farthest planet from the sun. Its orbit is between that of Saturn and Neptune. It is the third largest planet by diameter. It has the fourth largest mass of any planet in the solar system. Uranus is named after the Greek god of the sky. This god also created all of the other gods. **A** Currently, no other visits are planned. **B** Voyager 2 was launched in 1977. **C** This unmanned probe made its closest approach to Uranus on January 24, 1986. **D** It then continued to Neptune. Uranus is the first planet discovered in modern times. It is also the first planet to be found using the technology of a telescope. Before this, all of the other planets were discovered by the naked eye.

 The new sentence is about Voyager 2's visit to Uranus. And the sentence after the first square mentions 'no other visits,' which means that there was already a visit to Uranus. So the new sentence should go in the place where **A** is.

Skill & Drill

Insert Text questions ask you where the best place for a given sentence would be in the passage. You should understand the logical flow of the information in the passage. It is helpful to check out pronouns, linking words, demonstratives, and repeated words or phrases.

Molecules

A molecule is a group of two or more atoms. This group is held together by bonds. These substances are not always divisible into smaller fractions of the same substance. A molecule is considered the smallest particle of a substance. **A** In this state it still holds its composition and chemical properties. **B** It is better to consider that many substances are composed of networks of atoms or ions. **C** Scientists think of them this way instead of as molecular units. **D** A molecule is a stable entity which consists of two or more atoms. The idea of molecules was first stated in 1811. It was thought up by a scientist named Avogadro.

1. **Look at the four squares [■] that indicate where the following sentence could be added to the passage.**

   This makes the concept easier to understand.

   Where would the sentence best fit?

Eclipse

The word *eclipse* comes from the Greek phrase "to vanish." It is an astronomical event. It takes place when one celestial object enters the shadow of another. **A** The term is most often used to describe a solar eclipse, which is when the moon's shadow passes over Earth's surface. **B** There is also a lunar eclipse, which is when the moon enters Earth's shadow. **C** It also refers to events outside of the Earth-moon system and can be used to describe a planet passing through the shadow cast by one of its moons. **D** It could be a moon passing into the shadow cast by the planet it orbits, or it could even be a moon going into the shadow of another moon.

2. **Look at the four squares [■] that indicate where the following sentence could be added to the passage.**

   However, there are eclipses throughout the solar system.

   Where would the sentence best fit?

Jazz

Jazz is a musical art form that comes from America. It was first played in New Orleans around the start of the 20th century. Its roots come from African American music. **A** It was later combined with Western music technique and theory. **B** Jazz employs blue notes, swing, call and response, and improvisation. **C** After beginning in African-American communities, these styles spread in the 1920s. **D** They influenced many other musical styles. The instruments used in marching and dance bands at the turn of the century became the basic instruments of jazz. Bass, reeds, and drums were used with the Western 12-tone scale. Where or who the word *jazz* came from is uncertain.

3. **Look at the four squares [■] that indicate where the following sentence could be added to the passage.**

   But it has many other influences.

   Where would the sentence best fit?

Sophocles

Sophocles was one of the three great tragic playwrights in ancient Greece. One document recorded that he wrote 123 plays. He won more first prizes in dramatic competitions than any other playwright. Submissions to dramatic festivals included four plays. **A** Three were tragedies. The final one was called a satyr play. **B** He also placed second in all the other competitions he entered. **C** He won his first victory in 468 B.C. although scholars now think this may not have been the first time he competed. **D** Only seven of Sophocles' tragedies have survived in their complete form. The most famous of these are the three plays concerning Oedipus and Antigone. These are well known as the *Oedipus Cycle*.

4. **Look at the four squares [■] that indicate where the following sentence could be added to the passage.**

   It was a more comical entry and not a drama.

   Where would the sentence best fit?

Practice with Long Passages

The Observatories at Mauna Kea

Time Limit: 3 min. 10 sec.

Eleven research stations sit atop Mauna Kea. This is the best place to look at stars in the world. *Mauna Kea* means "white mountain" in Hawaiian. This mountain is a dormant volcano on the island of Hawaii. It is the highest point in the Pacific Basin. It is also the highest island-mountain in the world. Mauna Kea rises 9,750m from the ocean floor. It reaches an altitude of 4,205m above sea level. Its summit is above 40% of the Earth's atmosphere.

The atmosphere above Mauna Kea is extremely dry and clear. This is due to a cloud layer that floats below the summit. These clouds isolate the upper atmosphere from the lower moist maritime air. This ensures that the summit skies are pure and dry. The clouds keep the air around the summit free from pollutants.

This clarity makes Mauna Kea an ideal place for studying the stars. The number of clear nights is the highest in the world. The seeing factor is also very high here. Another factor that makes the stars so clear is the mountain's distance from city lights. A strong island-wide lighting law ensures an extremely dark sky.

The Astronomy Precinct on Mauna Kea was established in 1967. **1A** The Astronomy Precinct is located on protected land. **1B** This land is protected because of its sacred place in Hawaiian culture. **1C** This precinct was built to be an international center for astronomers to come and study stars. **1D**

The dorms for scientists are located below the summit. They are at about 3,000m above sea level. A visitor information station is located a hundred meters further below. Scientists and other visitors are told to stay at the lower level for 30 minutes. They do this to acclimate themselves before reaching the summit. This prevents altitude sickness.

Twelve telescopes are located at the summit. They are funded by companies and agencies of various nations. The University of Hawaii controls two telescopes. Two twin telescopes are run by the Keck Observatory. Subaru owns and administers another telescope. **2A** The United Kingdom has an infrared telescope while Canada and France have a joint-effort telescope. **2B** Another is owned and operated by California Technical University. **2C** The groups that make up this effort help mankind better understand outer space. **2D**

General Comprehension

1. **According to the passage, which of the following is true of Mauna Kea?**

   (A) It is the highest point in the Atlantic Basin.
   (B) The moist sea air makes it a good place for studying the stars.
   (C) There are 15 telescopes located at the summit.
   (D) Its summit skies are dry and pollutant-free.

dormant (a)
not active

isolate (v)
to be alone

seeing factor (phr)
the ability to see something in a certain place

sacred (a)
holy

acclimate (v)
to become used to something

2. **According to paragraph 6, all of the following are true of the telescopes at Mauna Kea EXCEPT:**

   (A) Two telescopes are run by the University of Hawaii.
   (B) There is a telescope that is owned jointly by Canada and France.
   (C) An infrared telescope is owned and administrated by Subaru.
   (D) The Keck Observatory controls a couple of twin telescopes.

On the TOEFL Test

3. **Look at the four squares [■] that indicate where the following sentence could be added to the passage.**

   It has been in existence for almost forty years.

   Where would the sentence best fit?

4. **Look at the four squares [■] that indicate where the following sentence could be added to the passage.**

   The rest are operated by other various entities.

   Where would the sentence best fit?

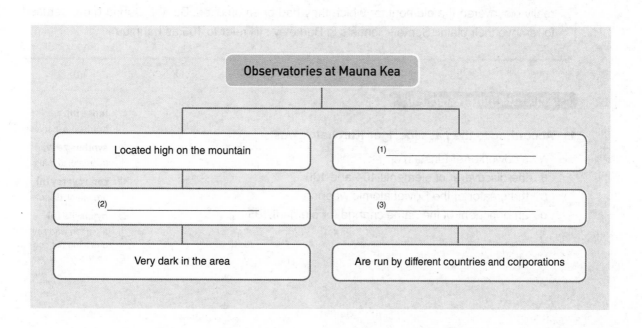

Observatories at Mauna Kea

- Located high on the mountain
- (1)_____
- (2)_____
- (3)_____
- Very dark in the area
- Are run by different countries and corporations

Read the following passage, and answer the questions.

The Element Naming Controversy

Time Limit: 3 min. 20 sec.

The 1960s was a very tense time between the USA and the Soviet Union. **1A** Even the scientists from these countries were arguing. **1B** Around this time, many scientists were in a race to be the first to synthesize elements. **1C** They wanted to be the first in order to earn the naming rights. **1D** A major controversy arose and was not resolved until 1997. This problem came about when a few groups of scientists claimed to have made the same elements at the same time. The main research labs involved in this crisis were the American lab in Berkeley and the Soviet lab in Dubna.

When Soviet scientists synthesized element 104, they named it after Igor Kurchatov. He was the father of the Soviet atomic bomb. The Americans strongly objected to this. They did not want to refer to an element named after an enemy who invented a weapon to destroy their country. But they were called hypocrites since they had named an element after Einstein, who also worked on atomic weapons.

Then, members of the international element naming board objected to the American name for 106, seaborgium. This was because the scientist Glenn T. Seaborg was still alive. **2A** He was handing out periodic tables signed with his name. **2B** This went against the board's rules. **2C** In 1994, the commission proposed a new set of names. **2D** They attempted to resolve the dispute. They tried to do this by replacing the name for 104 with a name after the Soviet Dubna Research Center. They proposed not to name 106 after Seaborg.

This solution was objected to by the American Chemical Society. They felt they should have the right to propose the name for 106. It should be whatever they wanted. The international board decided that credit for element 106 should be shared between Berkeley and Dubna. But the Dubna group had not yet offered a name. In addition, many American books already used the earlier names.

Finally in 1997, the names were agreed on. But in 1999, Seaborg was still disputing the name change for 105. It had been changed from hahnium to dubnium. He said they had not really discovered the element for which they had been credited. But the Dubna group refused to remove their claim. Some scientists in Berkeley still refer to 105 as hahnium.

General Comprehension

1. **According to the passage, Igor Kurchatov was**

   (A) a coworker of Einstein
   (B) the discoverer of elements 104 and 106
   (C) the creator of the Soviet atomic weapon
   (D) an opponent of the name change for element 105

tense (a)
worrisome; nervous

synthesize (v)
to create; to make

controversy (n)
argument; dispute

hypocrite (n)
a person who says one thing but does the opposite

2. **According to the passage, all of the following are true of the element naming controversy between the USA and the Soviet Union EXCEPT:**

Ⓐ The Americans did not want element 106 named after the Dubna Research Center.

Ⓑ Soviet scientists objected to the American name for element 106.

Ⓒ The American and Soviet labs were recommended to share credit for element 106.

Ⓓ The Soviet group from Dubna offered many alternative names to elements 104 and 106.

On the TOEFL Test

3. **Look at the four squares [■] that indicate where the following sentence could be added to the passage.**

This was in the middle of the Cold War.

Where would the sentence best fit?

4. **Look at the four squares [■] that indicate where the following sentence could be added to the passage.**

So they refused to allow this to be the element's name.

Where would the sentence best fit?

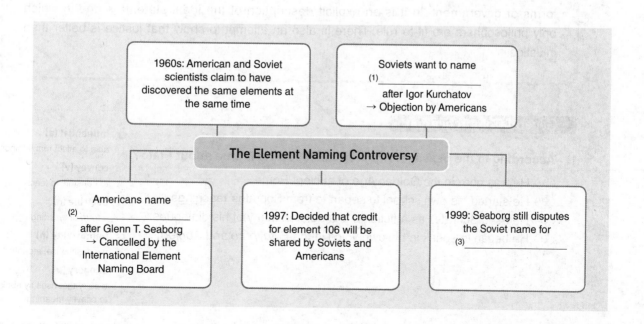

Read the following passage, and answer the questions.

Plato

Time Limit: 3 min. 20 sec.

Plato was born in the golden age of ancient Greece. His real name was Aristocles. But historians think he was given the nickname Plato because of his broad stature. In Greek, *plato* means "broad." It is also said that Plato had a wide, broad forehead. His parents were influential citizens in Athens. **1A** Plato began his career as a student of Socrates. **1B** When his master died, Plato studied in Egypt and Italy. **1C** He then returned to Athens and started his own school. **1D** There Plato tried to pass on the Socratic style of thinking. He guided his students towards the discovery of truth.

Plato tried to convey Socrates' teachings. He did this by writing down his master's conversations. These dialogues are the primary source of historical information about Socrates. Early dialogues look at a single issue. But they rarely come to conclusions about these issues. The *Euthyphro*, one of Plato's dialogues, points out a dilemma about any appeal to authority in defense of moral judgments. The *Apology* offers a description of the philosophical life. This description is presented as Socrates presents his own in defense before an Athenian jury.

The dialogues of Plato use Socrates as a fictional character. But the middle dialogues express Plato's own views about philosophical issues. **2A** In the *Meno*, Plato reports the Socratic notion that no one knowingly does wrong. **2B** He also introduces the doctrine of recollection. **2C** This is done in an attempt to discover whether or not virtue can be taught. **2D** The *Phaedo* continues the development of Platonic notions. It presents the doctrine of the forms. These arguments claim to show the immortality of the human soul.

The masterpiece among the middle dialogues is the *Republic*. It begins with a conversation about the nature of justice. It then proceeds directly to an extended discussion of justice, wisdom, courage, and moderation. He looks at the ways in which these appear to individual human beings and in society as a whole. The allegory of the cave captures the powerful image of the possibilities for human life. The dialogue concludes with a review of various forms of government. In it is an explicit description of the ideal state. It is one in which only philosophers are fit to rule. There is also an attempt to show that justice is better than injustice.

General Comprehension

1. **According to the passage, which of the following is true about Plato?**

   (A) He was born in the Golden Age of ancient Rome.
   (B) He started his own school to separate from Socrates' teachings.
   (C) He used Socrates as a fictional character in many of his dialogues.
   (D) He began to speak in his own voice in the *Euthyphro* and *Apology*.

○ **influential (a)**
able to affect many things

○ **convey (v)**
to transmit; to teach

○ **doctrine (n)**
a form of teaching

○ **immortality (n)**
everlasting life; eternity

○ **allegory (n)**
a story that uses symbols
to convey meaning

2. **The word one in the passage refers to**

    (A) human life
    (B) dialogue
    (C) government
    (D) ideal state

On the TOEFL Test

3. **Look at the four squares [■] that indicate where the following sentence could be added to the passage.**

    He was greatly influenced by his master's thoughts and ideas.

    Where would the sentence best fit?

4. **Look at the four squares [■] that indicate where the following sentence could be added to the passage.**

    They do not depict Socrates as a main character.

    Where would the sentence best fit?

PLATO

- real name – (1)_____
- a student of Socrates'
- founded his own school
- wrote many works of philosophy
- used Socrates as a character in (2)_____
  – the *Euthyphro & Apology*
- middle dialogues didn't use Socrates
  – the *Meno & Phaedo*
- (3)_____ – the greatest middle dialogue

Read the following passage, and answer the questions.

Loie Fuller

Time Limit: 2 min. 40 sec.

Loie Fuller pioneered the field of modern dance. She was also an innovator in the field of lighting techniques. She was born in Chicago, and she began her career as a child actress. She later performed dances in burlesque, vaudeville, and circus shows. She was an early practitioner of the free dance method. She danced with natural movements that she developed herself. She also created improvisation techniques, combining her dance moves with flowing silk costumes. These were lit up by colored lighting that she designed.

Fuller became famous in America. She was known for works such as "Serpentine Dance." **1A** But she felt unhappy that she was not taken seriously by the public. **1B** She felt they still saw her as an actress. **1C** The people of Paris received her warmly. **1D** She remained in France to continue her work. She was a regular performer at the Folies Bergere. There she performed such works as the Fire Dance. She became the embodiment of the Art Nouveau movement.

Many French artists and scientists were attracted to Fuller's groundbreaking work. Her fans included greats such as Jules Cheret, Henri de Toulouse-Lautrec, and Marie Curie. **2A** Fuller also filed many patents related to stage lighting. **2B** This included chemical compounds for creating color gel. **2C** She was even a member of the French Astronomical Society. **2D**

Fuller arranged many tours of Europe for early modern dancers. She was known as the first American modern dancer to perform in Europe. She also introduced Isadora Duncan to the audiences of Paris. She is famous for causing modern dance to be accepted as a serious art form.

Fuller returned to America once in a while. She came back to stage performances by her students. They were called the "Fullerets" or Muses. But she was in Paris at the end of her life. Breast cancer took her in 1928. She was cremated, and her ashes were buried in Paris.

General Comprehension

1. **According to paragraph 1, all of the following about Loie Fuller are true EXCEPT:**

   A She created many techniques for stage lighting.
   B She danced with unnatural movements.
   C She used to dance wearing silk outfits.
   D She started out as a child actress.

2. **According to the passage, Loie Fuller was not happy because**

   A she felt unappreciated as a dancer in America
   B not so many French people were attracted to her work
   C she had to perform dances in vaudeville
   D her "Serpentine Dance" was severely criticized

pioneer (v)
to be the leader in something

improvisation (n)
creativeness; the act of creating new things

embodiment (n)
the ideal; the perfect model

groundbreaking (a)
new; innovative

cremate (v)
to burn a dead body to turn it into ashes

On the TOEFL Test

3. **Look at the four squares [■] that indicate where the following sentence could be added to the passage.**

   However, she felt different in Europe.

   Where would the sentence best fit?

4. **Look at the four squares [■] that indicate where the following sentence could be added to the passage.**

   But she also had many fans who were just regular people.

   Where would the sentence best fit?

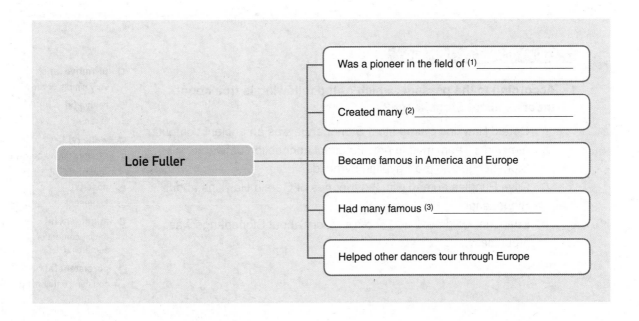

Read the following passage, and answer the questions.

Ancient Astronomy

Time Limit: 2 min. 50 sec.

Many ancient societies studied the stars. Now, many scientists study the stargazing practices of those societies. They also look at the tools these early societies made to look at stars. This form of archaeology and astronomy is currently studied as a serious branch of science. But in the beginning, it was very controversial. Many people were not willing to believe that primitive humans could understand the science of astronomy.

At the end of the 19th century, the astronomer Norman Lockyer was active in this field. **1A** His studies covered Stonehenge and the pyramids of Egypt. **1B** He tried to bring this field into wide acceptance as a serious branch of science. **1C** But on the British Isles, interest in this field waned. **1D** Then in the 1960s, there was new interest. It was revived by astronomer Gerald Hawkins. He proposed that Stonehenge was a Stone Age computer. This interesting concept made people interested again.

Around the same time, an engineer named Alexander Thom published the results of a study. His article stated that there was a widespread practice of accurate astronomy in ancient cultures. He said Stonehenge was used on the British Isles during ancient times. **2A** Hawkins's claims were widely dismissed. **2B** But Thom's analysis posed a problem. **2C** This challenged the historical academic beliefs at that time. **2D** A re-evaluation of Thom's fieldwork by Clive Ruggles tried to show that his claims were not supportable. But there was evidence of widespread interest in astronomy at these Stone Age sites.

Only one scientist, Euan Mackie, agreed that Thom's theories needed to be tested. This man went to the Kintraw standing stone site in Argyllshire in 1970 and 1971. Here he checked whether Thom's prediction about the accuracy of the observation platform above the stone was correct. He checked the alignment of the platform with the stone. He found that it was correct. Thom's conclusions were accepted. These were published in new prehistoric accounts of Britain. These persistent scientists proved that people from long ago did study the stars with accurate results. History was changed forever.

General Comprehension

1. **According to the passage, which of the following is true about theories about Stonehenge?**

   (A) Gerald Hawkins claimed that Stonehenge was an ancient computer.
   (B) Alexander Thom tried to prove a direct connection between Stonehenge and the Egyptian pyramids.
   (C) Clive Ruggles agreed with the theories of Gerald Hawkins about Stonehenge.
   (D) Euan Mackie proved that Thom's theory about Stonehenge was groundless.

primitive (a)
very simple or basic

revive (v)
to renew

wane (v)
to decrease; to become less

pose (v)
to present

alignment (n)
the placement of something

persistent (a)
constant; unrelenting

2. According to paragraph 4, all of the following are true about Euan Mackie EXCEPT:

   Ⓐ In 1970 and 1971 he went to the Kintraw standing stone site.
   Ⓑ He checked on the accuracy of the observation platform above the stone.
   Ⓒ He found that the alignment of the platform was not correct.
   Ⓓ The results of his test helped rewrite early history.

On the TOEFL Test

3. Look at the four squares [■] that indicate where the following sentence could be added to the passage.

   People simply were not interested in studying it.

   Where would the sentence best fit?

4. Look at the four squares [■] that indicate where the following sentence could be added to the passage.

   His conclusions startled many people.

   Where would the sentence best fit?

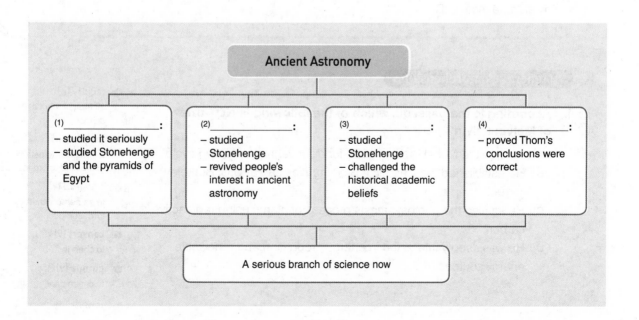

Melvin Calvin

Time Limit: 3 min. 10 sec.

Melvin Calvin will forever be remembered as a great chemist. He spent his whole life working towards discovery. He and his team discovered the Calvin cycle. This cycle is the route that carbon travels through plants. This discovery is world-famous for "unlocking the secrets of photosynthesis" in plants. For this he was awarded the 1961 Nobel Prize in Chemistry.

Calvin joined the faculty at the University of California at Berkeley in 1937. **1A** By 1963, he was named Professor of Molecular Biology. **1B** He was the founder and director of the Chemical Biodynamics Lab. **1C** He was also the associate director of the Berkeley Radiation Lab at the same time. **1D**

According to legend, on the day of the Japanese surrender in World War II, the head of the laboratory came to Calvin. He said, "Now is the time to do something useful with radioactive carbon." He was referring to the isotope of carbon that had been discovered in 1940. This isotope had been used in the atomic bombs that were dropped on Japan. In response, Calvin organized a team of Rad Lab researchers. They began to study the photosynthetic process. This is the process by which green plants convert energy from the sun into chemical energy.

Calvin and his team used the carbon-14 isotope as a tracer. They mapped the complete route that carbon travels through a plant. The path starts from its intake as carbon dioxide from the air to the point where it changes into carbohydrates. **2A** In doing so, the Calvin group showed that sunlight acts on the chlorophyll in a plant. **2B** It fuels the creation of organic compounds. **2C** Before this discovery, sunlight was believed to act only on the carbon dioxide within a plant. **2D**

Calvin's work led to a lifelong interest in energy production. He also spent many years testing the chemical evolution of life. He wrote a book on the subject that was published in 1969. Calvin actively pursued scientific research into his old age. He studied the use of oil-producing plants. He looked at them as renewable sources of energy. Calvin even analyzed moon rocks. He was a man who loved science. It was more important to him than the many awards he received.

General Comprehension

1. **According to the passage, which of the following is NOT true of Melvin Calvin?**

   (A) He won the Nobel Prize in 1961 for discovering the Calvin cycle.

   (B) He established the Chemical Biodynamics Lab at U.C. Berkeley in 1963.

   (C) He studied the photosynthesis process of plants using radioactive carbon.

   (D) He was deeply interested in energy production and renewable energy sources.

faculty (n)
all the teachers at a school

founder (n)
a person who establishes some kind of organization

organize (v)
to gather together; to form something

convert (v)
to change

pursue (v)
to chase after

2. **The word** pursued **in the passage is closest in meaning to**

   (A) widened

   (B) accomplished

   (C) continued

   (D) followed

On the TOEFL Test

3. **Look at the four squares [■] that indicate where the following sentence could be added to the passage.**

   He quickly became an important professor there.

   Where would the sentence best fit?

4. **Look at the four squares [■] that indicate where the following sentence could be added to the passage.**

   But now scientists understand this process much better.

   Where would the sentence best fit?

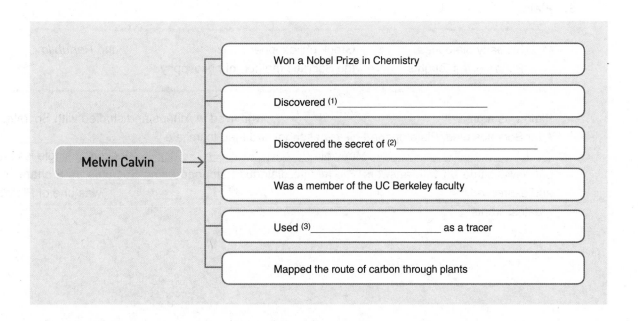

Building Summary Skills

The following summaries are based on the long passages you worked on earlier. Complete each of them by filling in the blanks with suitable words or phrases.

1. The Observatories at Mauna Kea

> Mauna Kea in Hawaii   twelve telescopes   the air quality
> very dark and clear   1967

There are many research stations located on (1)_____. These observatories are located there because of (2)_____ and the fact that the night skies are (3)_____. The Astronomy Precinct there was established in (4)_____. There are (5)_____ located there that are run by different countries or corporations.

2. The Element Naming Controversy

> American scientists   in the 1960s   the USA and Soviet Union
> naming controversies   the Soviet name

(1)_____, tensions between (2)_____ even caused problems between scientists. There were (3)_____ over various elements that different laboratories created. The Americans objected to (4)_____, and the Soviets objected to the American name. Finally, an agreement on the name was arrived at, but some (5)_____ still use the old name.

3. Plato

> his early dialogues   Greek philosopher   the *Republic*
> Plato's own thoughts   the Socratic method of philosophy

Plato was a great (1)_____ who lived in Athens and studied with Socrates. After Socrates died, Plato opened his own school and tried to imitate (2)_____. Many of (3)_____ looked at single issues but never came up with answers. His middle dialogues stopped using Socrates as a character and expressed (4)_____. (5)_____ was one of Plato's greatest works.

4. Loie Fuller

> modern dance   helped other artists   important French fans
> improvisation   felt unappreciated

Loie Fuller was a pioneer in the field of (1)_____. She created many new dance movements through (2)_____. She became famous in America, but she (3)_____, so she moved to France, where she had many fans. She had many (4)_____, including Jules Cheret, Henri de Toulouse-Lautrec, and Marie Curie. She toured Europe and also (5)_____ to do so.

5. Ancient Astronomy

> Alexander Thom   Stonehenge   the stargazing practices
> Thom's conclusions   Norman Lockyer

Nowadays, many scientists study (1)_____ of ancient societies. (2)_____ was an early scholar who looked into these practices. Gerald Hawkins also looked at (3)_____ and noticed how it was connected to astronomy. Most people discounted Hawkins's work, but (4)_____ produced new evidence to support it. Euan Mackie went to Stonehenge and proved that (5)_____ were correct.

6. Melvin Calvin

> the secrets of photosynthesis   the Calvin cycle   a great chemist
> the carbon-14 isotope   UC Berkeley

Melvin Calvin was (1)_____ who won a Nobel Prize. He discovered (2)_____, which helped to unlock (3)_____.
He worked at (4)_____, where he was a professor. He used (5)_____ to trace the route of carbon through the plant. He studied many different things through the course of his life.

1. **The word it in the passage refers to**

    (A) the Chinook language

    (B) every group

    (C) potlatch

    (D) a different way

2. **Which of the following Indian tribes is NOT mentioned as practicing the potlatch in the passage?**

    (A) Haida

    (B) Cherokee

    (C) Salish

    (D) Tlingit

3. **The word witnessed is closest in meaning to**

    (A) studied

    (B) practiced

    (C) enjoyed

    (D) viewed

4. **Look at the four squares [■] that indicate where the following sentence could be added to the passage.**

    But there were also many other special foods.

    Where would the sentence best fit?

5. **The word influx is closest in meaning to**

    (A) arrival

    (B) export

    (C) possibility

    (D) interest

6. **The author of the passage implies that**

    (A) the potlatch was always a friendly occasion

    (B) missionaries wanted the potlatch to continue

    (C) the potlatch is a tradition that continues today

    (D) potlatching stopped in Canada after 1885

The Potlatch Ceremony

A potlatch was a religious ceremony held by some American Indian tribes. This ceremony was extremely important to their social structure. These tribes were from regions along the Pacific Northwest coast. These regions ranged from the United States to British Columbia, Canada. Some of the tribes were the Haida, Nuxalk, Salish, and Tlingit.

The name *potlatch* is derived from the Chinook language. Every group that participated in the ceremony has a different way of saying it. The Chinook_word sounds like the English words "pot" and "latch." But it has nothing to do with these things.

Originally, the potlatch was held to commemorate important events. It could be the death of a highly respected person or a new child being born. Social ranks in American Indian societies were limited. So when a person changed his rank to a higher one, it had to be witnessed in order for people to accept it.

The potlatch took the form of a ceremonial feast. **A** It traditionally featured seal meat or salmon. **B** During the feast, relationships of hierarchy between groups were created and strengthened through the exchange of gifts, dance performances, and other ceremonies. **C** The host family made great efforts to demonstrate their wealth by giving away their possessions. **D** This prompted prominent guests to return the favor by holding their own potlatch ceremonies.

Before the arrival of the Europeans, potlatch gifts might be preserved food, boats, or human slaves. The influx of new sorts of goods such as blankets and copper caused a negative change in the potlatch in the late 18th and 19th centuries. Some groups used the potlatch as an arena for battle. At this arena, highly competitive contests of status took place. In some cases, gifts were destroyed after being received.

Potlatching was made illegal in Canada in 1885 and outlawed in the United States in the late 19th century because missionaries and government agents desired this. They thought it was a foolish custom. In their view, it was wasteful, unproductive, and bad for the people who did it. Despite the ban, potlatching continued secretly for many years.

Years later, numerous tribes begged the government to repeal the ban. They compared the potlatch to Christmas. They said the potlatch was a feast where friends exchanged gifts, like Christmas. Potlatching became less of an issue in the 20th century. So the ban was dropped.

Today, many ethnographers study the potlatch. They are fascinated by this festive event. The sponsors of a potlatch hand out many valuable items. They earn prestige in return. This prestige increases with the richness of the potlatch.

7. The word **ironically** in the passage is closest in meaning to

    Ⓐ amusingly
    Ⓑ groundlessly
    Ⓒ hypocritically
    Ⓓ scarily

8. According to the passage, what format does literary criticism commonly come in?

    Ⓐ television
    Ⓑ book
    Ⓒ magazine
    Ⓓ newspaper

9. Look at the four squares [■] that indicate where the following sentence could be added to the passage.

    So these people were taking a big risk by engaging in criticism.

    Where would the sentence best fit?

10. The author discusses Aristotle's *Poetics* in paragraph 4 in order to

    Ⓐ describe a work of Renaissance era criticism
    Ⓑ exemplify ancient criticism
    Ⓒ illustrate the restoration efforts of Renaissance-era critics
    Ⓓ highlight an important work of criticism

11. According to the passage, what can be inferred about "The New Criticism"?

    Ⓐ It was founded by one individual.
    Ⓑ It was based on the works of Plato and Aristotle.
    Ⓒ It was similar to deconstruction.
    Ⓓ It did not form in only one place.

12. The word **it** in the passage refers to

    Ⓐ philosophy
    Ⓑ method
    Ⓒ criticism
    Ⓓ information

Literary Criticism

Students around the world study great literature in school. But sometimes they need the help of experts to better understand what they have read. It is the job of literary critics to study and discuss the works of authors. They think about and decide what the author meant. This kind of work is based on literary theory. However, it is important to note that not all critics are theorists.

These days, literary criticism often comes in an essay or book format. Academic critics teach classes on this subject. They also write their findings in academic journals. Ironically, their writings are sometimes longer than the books they are writing about. More popular critics have their work printed in magazines. Some popular magazines that print literary criticism are *The New York Times Book Review*, *The Nation*, and *The New Yorker*.

As long as literature has been around, there have been critics to discuss it. Aristotle and Plato wrote works that were highly critical of Greek poetry. **A** In the Middle Ages, classical critics focused on religious texts. **B** But around this time, it was dangerous to criticize the Holy Bible. **C** Critics' comments on holy books such as this were usually made with the official opinions of church leaders in mind. **D**

In the Renaissance, many new ideas about writing were formed. These ideas about form and content led to a new group of critics. These critics claimed that writing was at the center of all culture. They claimed that poets and authors were protectors of a long literary tradition. Some of these noble poets began restoring great works of the past. One classic work that was rescued was Aristotle's *Poetics*.

More new ideas about literature were brought to the field of literary criticism by the British Romantic movement. These critics of the early 19th century thought that the object of writing did not always have to be beautiful. They had no problem with it being common, gritty, or ugly. They thought that the act of creating literature itself could raise a common subject. The highest level a work could attain was that of the "sublime."

Then, in the early 20th century, a new group of critics began to publish their work. These critics, who came from Britain and America, called their work "The New Criticism." These critics thought the most important way to study writing was to read it very closely. They encouraged people to focus "on the words themselves." This method is still a very popular way of reading.

The New Criticism was the most common method of studying writing until the late 1960s. Around this time, university professors became highly influenced by Continental Philosophy. This new way of thinking led to a new style of criticism. Both this philosophy and method of criticism focus on the form of information. They look very closely at the way it is presented. The critic must go through a process of taking a work apart. This process is called "deconstruction."

Vocabulary Review

A Choose the word with the closest meaning to each highlighted word or phrase.

1. The engineer created a very primitive model for his experiment.
   - (A) excessive
   - (B) basic
   - (C) advanced
   - (D) complicated

2. The founder of the organization finally retired after thirty-five years as president.
   - (A) president
   - (B) manager
   - (C) creator
   - (D) discoverer

3. Bill Gates is a pioneer in the field of software.
   - (A) engineer
   - (B) discoverer
   - (C) opportunist
   - (D) leader

4. Everyone looked tense while they were waiting for the results to come in.
   - (A) upset
   - (B) disinterested
   - (C) nervous
   - (D) pleased

5. The question poses many potential problems for the people.
   - (A) presents
   - (B) answers
   - (C) asks
   - (D) manages

6. Jerusalem is a sacred city to people of several different religions.
   - (A) holy
   - (B) fascinating
   - (C) capital
   - (D) popular

7. We did not dispute what the man accused us of doing.
   - (A) agree with
   - (B) do
   - (C) argue
   - (D) state

8. Donald made it to the summit of the mountain after climbing for several hours.
   - (A) base
   - (B) bottom
   - (C) cliff
   - (D) top

B Match each word with the correct definition.

1. alignment •
2. improvisation •
3. seeing factor •
4. hypocrite •
5. dilemma •
6. allegory •
7. archaeology •
8. legend •
9. acclimate •
10. synthesize •

- • **a.** the ability to see something in a certain place
- • **b.** a very big problem
- • **c.** a story from the past that may or may not be true
- • **d.** the placement of something
- • **e.** to create; to make
- • **f.** creativeness; the act of creating new things
- • **g.** the science of studying ancient cultures
- • **h.** to become used to something
- • **i.** a person who says one thing but does the opposite
- • **j.** a story that uses symbols to convey meaning

PART 3

Reading to Learn

In this part, the reading comprehension questions include: prose summary and fill in a table. The learning objectives of these comprehension questions are to recognize the major ideas and the relative importance of information in a passage and to organize the main ideas and other important information in the appropriate categories.

Unit 9

Prose Summary

9 Prose Summary

Overview

■ Introduction

Prose Summary questions are a new type of question on the TOEFL iBT. In this type of question, you will be asked to complete a summary chart by choosing the three most important ideas from six choices. In order to solve Prose Summary questions, you should understand the overall theme of the passage and distinguish important ideas from minor ones in the passage.

■ Question Type

Directions: An introductory sentence for a brief summary of the passage is provided below. Complete the summary by selecting the THREE answer choices that express important ideas in the passage. Some sentences do not belong in the summary because they express ideas that are not presented in the passage or are minor ideas in the passage. *This question is worth 2 points.*

[An introductory sentence]

-
-
-

Answer Choices

1. XXXXXXXXXXXXXXXXXXXXXXXXXX
2. XXXXXXXXXXXXXXXXXXXXXXXXXX
3. XXXXXXXXXXXXXXXXXXXXXXXXXX

4. XXXXXXXXXXXXXXXXXXXXXXXXXX
5. XXXXXXXXXXXXXXXXXXXXXXXXXX
6. XXXXXXXXXXXXXXXXXXXXXXXXXX

■ Useful Tips

• Try to understand the overall structure of the passage.

• Write down the main idea of each paragraph on your scratch paper.

• Distinguish major points from minor details in the passage.

• Incorrect answer choices usually deal with the minor points of the passage or are not mentioned in the passage.

Sample iBT Question

Pennsylvania's Coal

Coal is a huge source of energy. Countries have spent lots of money getting at the coal they have. The eastern United States has a tradition of mining coal. Pennsylvania is one such place. It is the source of so much coal, but it is the home of a great mining disaster.

There are two ways to get at coal in the ground. The first way is to dig a hole below the surface of the earth. Miners make tunnels that can be miles long. The second way is called open mining. Miners will remove the surface of the earth over a huge area until they reach what they want.

Centralia, Pennsylvania has very high-quality coal. It burns hotter than most other kinds of coal. Many open mines are in that town. Sadly, the town garbage dump was near an old, open mine pit. In 1962, the garbage caught fire. It set the open mine on fire, too. The fire started burning underground, where it was impossible to put out. The fine quality of the coal made the disaster even worse. The fire has been burning underground for over forty years. No one knows how to stop it. They say it will burn for 250 years.

Directions: An introductory sentence for a brief summary of the passage is provided below. Complete the summary by selecting the THREE answer choices that express the most important ideas in the passage. Some answer choices do not belong in the summary because they express ideas that are not in the passage or are minor ideas in the passage. ***This question is worth 2 points.***

Pennsylvania has a great mining tradition and a sad history.
-
-
-

Answer Choices

1. The town garbage dump was near an old, open mine.

2. The coal near a town caught fire and has been burning for decades.

3. The town of Centralia has many open mines.

4. Pennsylvania uses open mining to get coal from the ground.

5. The fire will burn for 250 years.

6. There is good, quality coal in Pennsylvania.

 Correct Answer Choices 2, 4, and 6 are correct because they represent major ideas in the passage: Pennsylvania's open mining and the long-lasting burning fire. Choices 1, 3, and 5 are just minor ideas.

Prose Summary questions ask you to complete a summary chart with the most important ideas from the passage. The topic sentence will be given for the summary. You need to understand the overall theme of the passage first and then distinguish major points from minor ideas in the passage.

Portrait Painting

The painting of portraits is a kind of art. Its intent is to show a visual image of the subject, which is usually a person. The portrait is expected to show the true form of the subject. Portraitists create their portraits for someone who hires and pays them. They are sometimes inspired by strong feelings they have for the subject. A self-portrait is one in which the artists portray themselves. Portraits can show the subject's entire body, half of the person's body, or a bust, which covers from the shoulders to the top of the head. Animals, pets, and even houses are sometimes chosen to be subjects for portraits.

1. **Directions:** Complete the summary by selecting the TWO answer choices that express the most important ideas in the passage.

   This passage discusses the characteristics of portrait painting.
   -
   -

   (A) A portraitist is someone who paints portraits for money.
   (B) Portraits are created to show the true form of the subject.
   (C) Some people prefer self-portraits for the strong feelings they experience.
   (D) The subjects of portraits include humans, animals, and buildings.
   (E) Portraits of the bust show the subject from the shoulders to the top of the head.

Flatworms

Flatworms are a group of simple life forms with very soft bodies. These animals have no spine. They are found in saltwater, freshwater, and moist places. Most of them are free-living forms, but some species are parasitic and live on other animals. There are four classes of flatworm: Tematoda, Cestoda, Monogenea, and Turbellaria. The flatworm's soft body is ribbon-shaped. Flatworms are the simplest animals, with organs formed out of three germ layers. There are outer and inner layers and a middle layer between them. These worms have no true body cavity except for their gut. The inside of their bodies are filled with loosely spaced tissue.

2. **Directions:** Complete the summary by selecting the TWO answer choices that express the most important ideas in the passage.

   Flatworms' bodies are very basic.
   -
   -

   (A) Flatworms live in watery places.
   (B) Flatworms have ribbon-shaped, soft bodies without spines.
   (C) Flatworms have three germ layers to develop their body cavity.
   (D) Flatworms are classified into four different kinds according to their size.
   (E) Flatworms cannot survive without a nutrient supply from other animals.

Deltas

A delta is a landform that occurs where a river flows into an ocean, sea, desert, or lake. This flow builds a deltaic deposit in the outward direction of the flow. A delta is formed by sediment carried by the river. This sediment is deposited as the water current dissipates. Deltaic deposits of larger rivers that are heavy with sediment divide river channels into multiple streams. These streams divide and come together again to form a system of active and inactive channels. A deposit at the mouth of a river forms a shape that is roughly triangular. The blocking of the river mouth by silt causes the shape and increased width at the base of the delta.

3. **Directions:** Complete the summary by selecting the TWO answer choices that express the most important ideas in the passage.

   This passage describes how deltas are formed.
   -
   -

   Ⓐ Sediment carried by a river creates deltas.
   Ⓑ Rivers are often divided into multiple streams.
   Ⓒ Deltas are triangular in shape.
   Ⓓ The mouth of a river is blocked by silt deposits.
   Ⓔ Deltaic deposits build in the inward direction of a river flow.

Social Psychology

The field of social psychology is an ongoing study of how people behave in groups. It focuses on how they perceive, influence, and relate to others. Gordon Allport is credited with the classic definition of this study. He said it is an attempt to understand and explain how people are influenced by others. This can include their ways of dealing with the imagined or implied presence of other people. Much of the research done in this field is completed through the observation of small groups. These groups are assembled and given tasks to complete. Researchers observe the group interactions as they attempt to complete the assigned tasks.

4. **Directions:** Complete the summary by selecting the TWO answer choices that express the most important ideas in the passage.

   Social psychology examines the group dynamics of people.
   -
   -

   Ⓐ Social psychologists publish their research in different journals.
   Ⓑ Social psychology explains how people are influenced by others.
   Ⓒ Researchers often observe small groups of people doing tasks.
   Ⓓ Social psychology was first defined by Gordon Allport.
   Ⓔ Social psychology is a subfield of psychology and sociology.

Practice with Long Passages

A Read the following passage, and answer the questions.

Estuaries

Time Limit: 2 min. 40 sec.

An estuary forms at the tidal mouth of a river. It is a coastal body of water that is semi-enclosed. It also has a free flowing connection to the open sea. The main feature of an estuary occurs within this connection when seawater mixes with freshwater. The combining of seawater and freshwater from a stream or river creates a supply of brackish water. A tide must be present to create motion at the point where the two waters meet. In seas without a tide, the rivers naturally form deltas.

The tidal mouth of a river is the usual location of an estuary. Here there is often a lot of sediment deposits that consist of silt carried from runoff from the land. Estuaries occur more frequently on sunken coasts, where the land is situated lower, as the sea level has risen. Valleys are flooded by this process, which creates forms such as rias and fjords. If there is a stream or river flowing into them, they can become estuaries.

Brackish water created in estuaries is not as salty as seawater. But it is saltier than freshwater. This kind of water allows estuaries to harbor thriving ecosystems. One of the most well-known estuaries is the River Thames, which flows through London. It reaches to the town of Teddington, a few miles west of London. This area marks the limit of the tidal part of the Thames. But as far west as Battersea, it is still a freshwater river.

The fauna in this part of the Thames consists mostly of freshwater species. There are many fish found here, such as roach, dace, carp, perch, and pike. Between Battersea and Gravesend, the Thames becomes brackish. A limited number of freshwater and marine species populate this area. The salinity increases a little further east, and marine species completely replace the freshwater fish.

General Comprehension

1. **The word harbor in the passage is closest in meaning to**
   - (A) contain
   - (B) hide
   - (C) destroy
   - (D) create

2. **According to the passage, a tide must be present at an estuary in order to**
   - (A) build sediment deposits
   - (B) mix fresh and salty water into brackish water
   - (C) form a delta naturally
   - (D) maintain a thriving ecosystem

- **sediment (n)**
  dirt and silt from the bottom of a river
- **runoff (n)**
  rainwater that forms a stream rather than going into the ground
- **sunken (a)**
  beneath the water level
- **brackish (a)**
  somewhat salty
- **thrive (v)**
  to become successful or strong; to flourish
- **fauna (n)**
  animals in a particular area
- **populate (v)**
  to live in a certain place

3. **Directions:** An introductory sentence for a brief summary of the passage is provided below. Complete the summary by selecting the THREE answer choices that express the most important ideas in the passage. Some answer choices do not belong in the summary because they express ideas that are not in the passage or are minor ideas in the passage.

An estuary has many different features.

-
-
-

Answer Choices

(A) Freshwater species mostly live in estuaries.

(B) The River Thames is one of the most studied estuaries.

(C) Estuaries have lots of sediment deposits.

(D) Many different fish live in the Thames.

(E) Valleys can flood near sunken coasts.

(F) Estuaries are a combination of freshwater and seawater.

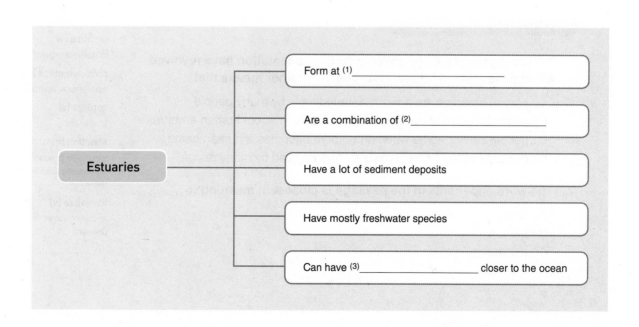

Estuaries

Form at (1)_____

Are a combination of (2)_____

Have a lot of sediment deposits

Have mostly freshwater species

Can have (3)_____ closer to the ocean

Read the following passage, and answer the questions.

The Embryo

Time Limit: 3 min.

The embryo is the earliest stage of development for multi-celled life forms. The development of the embryo begins with sexual reproduction. Once this is completed, a sperm fertilizes an egg. The zygote is the cell that results from this process. All the DNA of the two parents is contained within it. In this early stage, the human embryo does not possess consciousness. This point is hotly contested by groups that are for or against abortion rights.

For human embryos there are three major stages of development. From weeks 1 to 4, the embryo will begin to search for a place to attach to the wall of the uterus. It finds the right place and implants itself there. The mother and the embryo will begin to form their connections. The umbilical cord forms during this time.

During weeks 5 to 6, the embryo puts out chemicals. The woman's menstrual cycle is stopped by these. The brain begins to develop. Around the sixth week, brainwave activity begins. The heart begins to beat around this time. Stubs where arms and legs will grow later become visible. All of the main organs begin to grow.

Between weeks 7 and 8, the embryo's blood type is established. The embryo can move, and its eyes form. Most organs are fully developed or are in the process of developing. At the end of the eighth week, the embryonic stage ends. This marks the beginning of the fetal stage.

Much controversy and argumentation have revolved around the topic of human embryos. The question is at which point an embryo becomes a human with a consciousness and a soul. This question is central to the abortion issue in the United States. Many believe that the embryo is a human life and should be protected. They want abortion and scientific testing on embryos to be illegalized as a form of murder. But opponents believe that the embryo is merely undeveloped tissue. They believe women should be able to make their own decisions on whether or not to abort a human embryo before it enters the fetal stage.

General Comprehension

1. **In stating that much controversy and argumentation have revolved around the topic of human embryos, the author means that**

   Ⓐ human embryos are a much debated topic by many people
   Ⓑ there is a general consensus among people about human embryos
   Ⓒ people cannot agree when an embryo becomes a human being
   Ⓓ discussions about embryos are often enjoyed by many people

2. **The word opponents in the passage is closest in meaning to**

   Ⓐ allies
   Ⓑ helpers
   Ⓒ murderers
   Ⓓ enemies

fertilize (v)
to make pregnant

consciousness (n)
awareness; realization

contest (v)
to dispute

abortion (n)
a surgical process that terminates the life of a fetus

illegalize (v)
to make something unlawful

3. **Directions:** An introductory sentence for a brief summary of the passage is provided below. Complete the summary by selecting the THREE answer choices that express the most important ideas in the passage. Some answer choices do not belong in the summary because they express ideas that are not in the passage or are minor ideas in the passage.

The human embryo develops over the course of three stages.

-
-
-

Answer Choices

(A) Main organs, such as limbs and eyes, start developing relatively early.

(B) In the early stage, the embryo attaches itself to the mother's womb.

(C) The question of when a fetus becomes a baby is important to the abortion issue.

(D) The fetal stage begins as soon as the embryonic stage ends.

(E) Before the baby is born, the eyes are fully developed.

(F) The brain and the heart begin to activate in the middle stage.

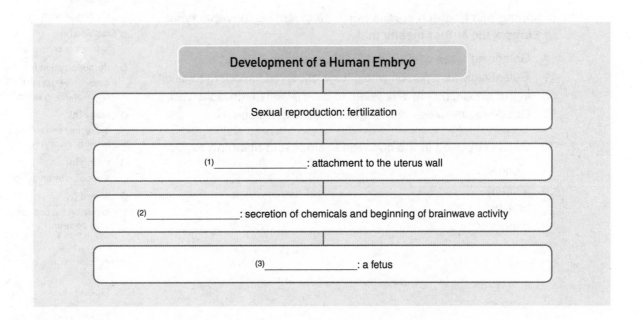

Development of a Human Embryo

Sexual reproduction: fertilization

(1)_____: attachment to the uterus wall

(2)_____: secretion of chemicals and beginning of brainwave activity

(3)_____: a fetus

Read the following passage, and answer the questions.

Johannes Gutenberg and Metal Type

Time Limit: 2 min. 40 sec.

Johannes Gutenberg was an inventor. He achieved fame for his invention of a printing press with movable type. His press had a type metal alloy, oil-based inks, and a mold for casting type. This invention led to the book becoming an item of use by the common man.

The exact origin of Gutenberg's first press is unknown. Tradition credits him with inventing movable type in Europe. It was an improvement on the block printing already in use there. By combining these components into a production system, he enabled the rapid printing of written materials. This led to an information explosion in across Renaissance Europe.

Gutenberg moved from his native town of Mainz to Strasbourg around 1430. He began experimenting with metal type after he moved. He knew that wood-block type involved a great deal of time and expense to produce because it had to be hand-carved. Gutenberg concluded that metal type could be reproduced much more quickly since it could be done once a single mold had been fashioned.

In 1455, Gutenberg made a demonstration of his printing press. He did this by selling copies of a two-volume Bible for just 300 German florins each. This was the same amount of money as three year's wages for an average clerk. But it was much cheaper than a handwritten Bible. One of those books normally took a single monk 20 years to write by hand.

Gutenberg had a partner named Johann Fust. The money Gutenberg earned from his press was not enough to repay Fust for his investments. Fust sued Gutenberg in court and won. The court's ruling bankrupted Gutenberg. It also awarded control of the movable type and his printing equipment to Fust. Gutenberg ran a small print shop until shortly before his death. But Fust became the first printer to publish a book with his name on it.

General Comprehension

1. **In stating that tradition credits him with inventing movable type in Europe, the author means that**

   (A) Gutenberg received payment for his invention
   (B) Gutenberg was a person who always observed important traditions
   (C) in Europe Gutenberg is believed to have invented movable type
   (D) Gutenberg invented many of the traditions of Europe

2. **The word fashioned in the passage is closest in meaning to**

   (A) planned
   (B) shaped
   (C) broken
   (D) decorated

○ **mold (n)**
a shape or form

○ **fashion (v)**
to make or create

○ **demonstration (n)**
a practical illustration of how something works

○ **wage (n)**
the money one receives for work; salary

○ **ruling (n)**
a decision by an authority

○ **award (v)**
to give on the basis of a legal decision

3. **Directions:** An introductory sentence for a brief summary of the passage is provided below. Complete the summary by selecting the THREE answer choices that express the most important ideas in the passage. Some answer choices do not belong in the summary because they express ideas that are not in the passage or are minor ideas in the passage.

Gutenberg's press influenced printing practices and society in important ways.

-
-
-

Answer Choices

(A) Movable type was invented in 1455.

(B) Books became available to common people because of the printing press.

(C) It took a monk twenty years to copy the entire Bible.

(D) Johann Fust was Gutenberg's partner.

(E) Metal type cut down on the amount of time and money spent on printing.

(F) Circulation of information increased rapidly over a short period of time.

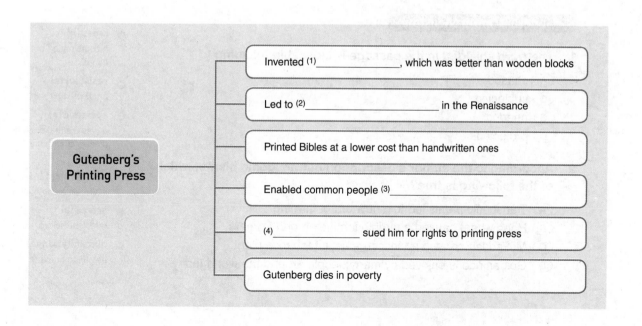

Gutenberg's Printing Press

- Invented (1)_____, which was better than wooden blocks
- Led to (2)_____ in the Renaissance
- Printed Bibles at a lower cost than handwritten ones
- Enabled common people (3)_____
- (4)_____ sued him for rights to printing press
- Gutenberg dies in poverty

Transgenic Plants

Time Limit: 2 min. 50 sec.

Transgenic plants share genes from different species. In the late 1800s, the first transgenic plant species was recorded. It was a cross between wheat and rye. This crossbreeding of two plant species marked a new era of farming. By moving genes from one plant to another, farmers can raise crops that are more resistant to diseases. These plants are protected from epidemics that can destroy many fields worth of food and income.

In the 1930s, E.S. McFadden bred a variety of wheat that had a transgene from wild grass. This variety was called Hope. It was resistant to a stem rust disease that was threatening to destroy the entire American wheat crop. This new kind of wheat saved farmers from ruin. Many people were also shielded from famine.

The growth of transgenic plants began through normal crossbreeding methods. But by the 1970s, scientists were performing DNA transplants between plant and even animal species. In 1985, a laboratory in Belgium created a genetically engineered tobacco plant that had an insect tolerance. This was done by adding genes encoded with proteins that could kill insects.

This development opened up the field of transgenic recombinant plants. This field has been the subject of controversy between several international bodies. These warring groups promote and oppose genetically modified crops and foods. This battle over the use of plant DNA has resulted in the creation of a new biological class. Members of this class are known as genetically modified organisms (GMOs).

One example of a useful transgenic plant is golden rice. This version of rice was created in a laboratory. It contains 23 times more vitamin A than regular white rice. Vitamin A is an important form of nourishment that is scarce in many parts of the world. This version of rice was created as a humanitarian tool to help people in these areas. But due to the opposition from various groups that are against transgenic foods, this rice is not available.

General Comprehension

1. **The word shielded in the passage is closest in meaning to**

    Ⓐ chased
    Ⓑ subjected
    Ⓒ needed
    Ⓓ protected

2. **According to the author's description of transgenic plants, which of the following is true?**

    Ⓐ Transgenic plants led to a new era of farming.
    Ⓑ Hope wheat caused a terrible famine among farmers.
    Ⓒ McFadden created an insect-resistant tobacco plant.
    Ⓓ Golden rice is enjoyed by many people around the world today.

cross (n)
a combination of two things

resistant (a)
unaffected by

epidemic (n)
a disease that spreads quickly among many people

nourishment (n)
sustenance; nutrition

scarce (a)
rare; insufficient

humanitarian (a)
helpful to humans

3. **Directions:** An introductory sentence for a brief summary of the passage is provided below. Complete the summary by selecting the THREE answer choices that express the most important ideas in the passage. Some answer choices do not belong in the summary because they express ideas that are not in the passage or are minor ideas in the passage.

Scientists have developed many different transgenic plants.

-
-
-

Answer Choices

Ⓐ A Belgian laboratory has made tobacco plants that can resist insects.

Ⓑ Some transgenic plants are causing controversy with different groups.

Ⓒ Transgenic plants are those that share characteristics with other species.

Ⓓ A strain of wheat called Hope helped save many American farmers.

Ⓔ Golden rice created in the laboratory is more nutritious than regular rice.

Ⓕ Since the 1970s, scientists have been creating transgenic plants.

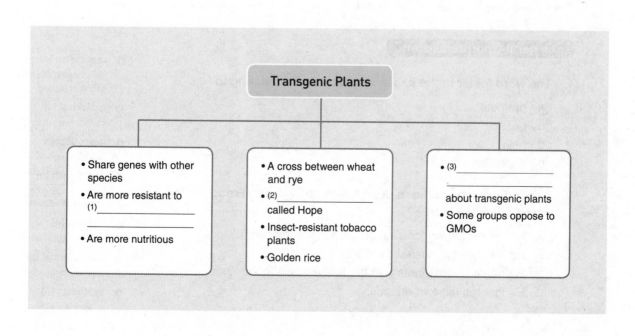

Transgenic Plants

- Share genes with other species
- Are more resistant to (1)_____
- Are more nutritious

- A cross between wheat and rye
- (2)_____ called Hope
- Insect-resistant tobacco plants
- Golden rice

- (3)_____ about transgenic plants
- Some groups oppose to GMOs

Sigmund Freud

Time Limit: 2 min. 50 sec.

Sigmund Freud was an Austrian neurologist. He was the founder of a new kind of psychology. He is best known for his theories about sexual desire and dreams. He is also famous for his studies of repression and the unconscious mind. He has been called by many "the father of psychoanalysis."

Freud was born in Freiberg in 1856. His family lived in a crowded apartment. But his parents made an effort to foster his intellect. He ranked first in his class in six of his eight years of schooling. He attended the University of Vienna at the age of 17.

Freud opened his own practice for patients with nervous and brain disorders. He tried using hypnotism with his most hysterical and neurotic patients. But he eventually gave up this practice. He found that he could get his patients to talk by an easier method. He put them on a couch and encouraged them to say whatever came into their minds. This process was termed "free association."

In his forties, Freud felt that he had many mental problems. He began to explore his own dreams. He also examined his own memories and the dynamics of his personality. During this self-analysis, he came to realize the hostility he felt towards his father. He also recalled his childhood feelings for his mother, who was attractive, warm, and protective. Scholars who have studied Freud consider this time of emotional difficulty to be the most creative time in his life.

Freud's theories and research methods were controversial during his life. A paper by Lydiard H. Horton called Freud's dream theory "dangerously inaccurate." Another of Freud's critics was Juliet Mitchell. She suggested that Freud's basic claim that our conscious thoughts are driven by unconscious fears and desires should be rejected. She said this because it challenges the possibility of making universal and objective claims about the world. Many critics think that Freud's ideas were a byproduct of his heavy cocaine use.

General Comprehension

1. **The word foster in the passage is closest in meaning to**

   Ⓐ promote
   Ⓑ destroy
   Ⓒ hide
   Ⓓ popularize

2. **According to the author's description of Sigmund Freud, which of the following is true?**

   Ⓐ He is best known for his theories about repression.
   Ⓑ He was born in Australia in 1856.
   Ⓒ He treated his patients with the free association method.
   Ⓓ He ignored his own dreams.

repression (n)
the stopping of some action or feeling

hysterical (a)
frantic; in a panic

neurotic (a)
unstable; nervous

association (n)
the connecting or combining of ideas

hostility (n)
hatred; unfriendliness

controversial (a)
divisive; contentious

byproduct (n)
a result; an effect

On the TOEFL Test

3. **Directions:** An introductory sentence for a brief summary of the passage is provided below. Complete the summary by selecting the THREE answer choices that express the most important ideas in the passage. Some answer choices do not belong in the summary because they express ideas that are not in the passage or are minor ideas in the passage.

Sigmund Freud made many advances in the field of psychology.

-
-
-

Answer Choices

Ⓐ He introduced the free association method.

Ⓑ He used drugs to get insight into dreams.

Ⓒ He almost always ranked at the top of his class.

Ⓓ He theorized about sexual desires and unconsciousness.

Ⓔ He opened and pioneered the field of psychoanalysis.

Ⓕ He treated his physical illness through self-analysis.

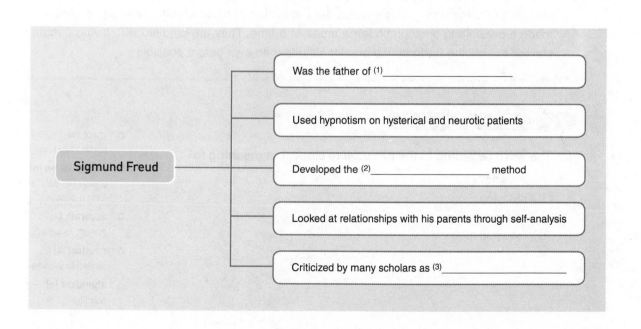

Sigmund Freud

- Was the father of (1)_____
- Used hypnotism on hysterical and neurotic patients
- Developed the (2)_____ method
- Looked at relationships with his parents through self-analysis
- Criticized by many scholars as (3)_____

Read the following passage, and answer the questions.

The History of Cartography

Time Limit: 2 min. 50 sec.

The study and practice of making maps or globes is called cartography. This has been an important part of human history as far back as can be traced. The first known maps were of the constellations of stars rather than the Earth. The night sky was found mapped out as dots dating to 16,500 B.C. These were found on the walls of the Lascaux Caves in France. Three bright stars, Vega, Deneb, and Altair, were included on these walls. The Pleiades star cluster was also mapped in these cave paintings.

In ancient Babylon, maps were made using very accurate surveying techniques. A clay tablet found in 1930 at Ga-Sur, near today's Kirkuk in northern Iraq, shows a map that is a good example. It is of a river valley between two hills. An inscription on this tablet shows that the plot of land belonged to someone named Azala. Scholars date this tablet to 2300 to 2500 B.C.

In ancient Egypt, maps were quite rare. But those that survived show a focus on geometric calculation and survey technique. The Turin Papyrus, which is dated to 1300 B.C., shows mountains east of the Nile. This was an important area where gold and silver were mined.

An early revolution in mapmaking occurred during the time of Claudius Ptolemy, who lived in the Hellenic Egyptian city of Alexandria from 90 to 168 AD. He began depicting the Earth as a sphere and outlined the concept of parallels of latitude and meridians of longitude that we use today.

Throughout the Middle Ages, mapmaking advanced. By the time of the Renaissance, cartographers from Portugal were making nautical charts for the navigation of ships. The oldest known nautical chart was made by Pedro Reinel in 1485. This chart had a scale of latitudes on it.

By 1569, a Flemish geographer named Gerardus Mercator published the first map based on his Mercator projection. This is an accurate map of the world in which the sphere of the globe is stretched out on a plane.

During the 1900s, maps became more abundant. This is due to improvements in printing and photography. These factors made the production of maps cheaper and easier. Airplanes made it possible to photograph large areas at a time. They are credited with giving people a chance to view the Earth from a greater altitude than ever before possible.

General Comprehension

1. **The word depicting in the passage is closest in meaning to**

   (A) erasing

   (B) studying

   (C) characterizing

   (D) referring to

trace (v)
to detect or find

constellation (n)
a group of stars which form a pattern

accurate (a)
correct; exact

nautical (a)
related to the sea

abundant (a)
plentiful

2. **According to the passage, which of the following is true about the history of mapmaking?**

   Ⓐ The practice of making maps and globes is called choreography.

   Ⓑ Accurate surveying techniques were used to make maps in ancient Babylon.

   Ⓒ The practice of mapmaking did not advance during the Middle Ages.

   Ⓓ Maps became more abundant in the 1900s due to space travel.

On the TOEFL Test

3. **Directions:** An introductory sentence for a brief summary of the passage is provided below. Complete the summary by selecting the THREE answer choices that express the most important ideas in the passage. Some answer choices do not belong in the summary because they express ideas that are not in the passage or are minor ideas in the passage.

   Maps have been made by people for a long time.

   -
   -
   -

Answer Choices

Ⓐ Maps became widely used by photographers in the 1900s.

Ⓑ Some maps on cave walls show various stars.

Ⓒ A map in Babylon from 2500 B.C. shows some land ownership.

Ⓓ Maps were common in ancient Egypt.

Ⓔ Mercator published a map using the projection he had invented.

Ⓕ Mapmaking was not allowed during the Middle Ages.

History of Cartography

Maps in the Lascaux Caves showing the stars and constellations

A Babylonian map showing (1)_____

Egyptian maps showing the location of a gold and silver mine

Ptolemy's concept of (2)_____ in 2nd century AD

(3)_____ in the Renaissance

Mercator's world map using the Mercator projection around 1569

Better and more maps thanks to better printing technology, photography, and airplanes in the 1900s

Building Summary Skills

The following summaries are based on the long passages you worked on earlier. Complete each of them by filling in the blanks with suitable words or phrases.

1. Estuaries

marine species	the tidal mouth of a river	the River Thames
somewhat salty	both saltwater and freshwater	

Estuaries are semi-enclosed bodies of water that form near (1)_____.
They combine (2)_____. The water formed is (3)_____.
Mostly freshwater species live in estuaries, but (4)_____ live in them closer to the ocean. (5)_____ is among the most famous estuaries in the world.

2. The Embryo

three major stages	eight weeks	abortion rights
the organ forming stage	multi-celled life forms	

The embryo is the earliest stage of development for (1)_____. There are (2)_____ of development in the human embryo. These stages include the connection forming stage, the brain forming stage, and (3)_____. This marks the point at which the embryo becomes a fetus. After (4)_____, the fetal stage begins. There is much controversy around the development of the embryo because of (5)_____
_____.

3. Johannes Gutenberg and Metal Type

metal type	an information explosion	handwritten ones
Johann Fust	moveable type	

Johannes Gutenberg invented (1)_____. This revolutionized Europe and led to
(2)_____. He used (3)_____ instead of wood-block type. In 1455, he sold copies of a two-volume Bible that were much cheaper than (4)_____.
However, Gutenberg's partner (5)_____ sued him and took the rights to his invention. Gutenberg died in poverty.

4. Transgenic Plants

modified	the genes of other species	transfer genes
more nutritious	genetically modified organisms	

Transgenic plants share [1]_____. Scientists [2]_____
from one plant to another to give the plants better resistance to disease or insects or to make
them [3]_____. Wheat, tobacco, rice, and even animals have had their genes
[4]_____. Some people are opposed to transgenic plants, which they call [5]_____
_____.

5. Sigmund Freud

his parents	the father of psychoanalysis	many critics
psychology	a neurologist	

Sigmund Freud was [1]_____ who founded a new kind of [2]_____.
He is often referred to as [3]_____. He had his own practice and soon
began to use free association methods with his patients. He also interpreted his dreams and his
relationships with [4]_____. He did, however, have [5]_____ during his
life and afterwards.

6. The History of Cartography

the stars and constellations	the Renaissance	cartography
Babylon and Egypt	accuracy and efficiency of mapmaking	

Making maps or globes is called [1]_____, and people have been making them for
thousands of years. Early maps just showed [2]_____ as in the wall
paintings of the Lascaux Caves. There were also early maps in [3]_____.
Mapmaking improved in the Middle Ages and [4]_____. Later mapmakers showed
lines of latitude and longitude and made maps for sailors. By the 1900s, advancements in
photography as well as the advent of airplanes and later, satellites, led to giant leaps forward in
the [5]_____.

1. **The word adorned in the passage is closest in meaning to**

    (A) etched   (B) decorated   (C) scribbled   (D) portrayed

2. **According to paragraph 3, which of the following is true about the black-figure period?**

    (A) The pottery looked black due to iron-rich clay.
    (B) The period concluded around 700 B.C.
    (C) It first started in Corinth.
    (D) The pottery had to be fired three times.

3. **The word process in the passage is closest in meaning to**

    (A) method   (B) delivery   (C) analysis   (D) instructions

4. **According to the passage, what can be inferred about ancient Greek pottery?**

    (A) Corinth and Athens made the best pottery.
    (B) The Greeks produced vases for special needs.
    (C) Black-figure period vases were of the highest quality.
    (D) Achilles Painter signed his name on the vases.

5. **The word it in the passage refers to**

    (A) the vase   (B) the paint   (C) the clay   (D) the design

6. **Directions:** An introductory sentence for a brief summary of the passage is provided below. Complete the summary by selecting the THREE answer choices that express the most important ideas in the passage. Some answer choices do not belong in the summary because they express ideas that are not in the passage or are minor ideas in the passage. *This question is worth 2 points.*

    Greek pottery often had many different paintings and pictures on it.

    -
    -
    -

    Answer Choices

    (A) In red-figure pottery, the painter created the design before the pot was fired.

    (B) Corinth and Athens produced high-quality pottery.

    (C) Many city-states made their own pottery.

    (D) Painters used refined clay to paint figures on the pottery.

    (E) Many different characters were often painted on the pottery.

    (F) Achilles Painter was one of the greatest painters.

Ancient Greek Pottery

Scholars have knowledge of ancient Greek art through the pottery that survives from that culture. While little else in the way of Greek painting or artwork still exists, there are over 100,000 Greek vases left. Many of these vases are adorned with paintings of Greek characters and scenes. These vases were common in every level of Greek society. This is because the Greeks produced many vases to be used for everyday needs such as drinking and cooking.

In the early periods of Greek civilization, small city-states produced their own pottery. But later, Corinth and Athens became the two great producers of these vases. The pottery from these cities became the standard all over the Greek world. It was so widely exported that it put an end to local varieties.

Two of the major periods of pottery in ancient Greece were the black-figure period and the red-figure period. The black-figure period began around 700 B.C. It originated in the city of Corinth. By this method, vases were made of pale, iron-rich clay. When fired, they became a reddish-orange color. The designs were outlined on the surface of the vase. Refined clay was then used to paint the figures that had been drawn. Finer details were added with an engraving tool, after which the vase was fired again. The second firing process left the painted designs a glossy black color.

Red-figure pottery was developed around 530 B.C. It became such a popular style that it was used over black-figure pottery. Even today, this style is thought to be the height of Greek pottery craftsmanship. The most highly valued surviving Greek vases are of this style. The process that resulted in a finished piece of this type of pottery required close cooperation between the potter and the painter. In this process, the painter would create a design on the vase before it was fired. Since the vase was unfired, the paint and the clay were the same color, and the painter had to create the design without being able to see it. After the potter fired the vase, the design would become visible. This process required the painter to work very quickly and precisely, relying only on his memory.

The painters of these vases rarely signed their names. So the only ways scholars of modern times can identify these artists are by the images they repeatedly painted. For example, one of the greatest vase painters is known as "Achilles Painter" since his most common subject choice was the Greek character of that name. Another way painters are identified is by the name of the potter they worked for. Potters often signed their names on the vases, so the painter who worked for Kleophrades is identified as "Kleophrades Painter."

7. **According to paragraph 1, which of the following is true of cliffs?**

   (A) They are always found along rivers.
   (B) They are not formed by igneous rocks.
   (C) They are formed through erosion.
   (D) They are not particularly vertical.

8. **The word vertical in the passage is closest in meaning to**

   (A) upright   (B) high   (C) unique   (D) elevated

9. **The author of the passage implies that**

   (A) humans are the only reason erosion occurs
   (B) it is impossible to repair land damaged by erosion
   (C) humans can cause erosion to occur faster
   (D) erosion happens quickly

10. **Why does the author mention waterfalls and rock shelters in paragraph 5?**

    (A) To state that they only appear on cliffs
    (B) To exemplify some features that cliffs sometimes have
    (C) To explain why they are eroding forces on cliffs
    (D) To emphasize how important they are to cliffs

11. **The phrase peters out in the passage is closest in meaning to**

    (A) increases in size   (B) becomes more dangerous
    (C) stops eroding   (D) comes to an end

12. **Directions:** An introductory sentence for a brief summary of the passage is provided below. Complete the summary by selecting the THREE answer choices that express the most important ideas in the passage. Some answer choices do not belong in the summary because they express ideas that are not in the passage or are minor ideas in the passage. *This question is worth 2 points.*

    Cliffs have many different features that are a product of forces of nature such as erosion.

    -
    -
    -

    Answer Choices

    (A) The highest cliff in the world is the east face of Great Trango.
    (B) The bases of cliffs are usually formed by erosion-resistant rocks.
    (C) Cliffs tend to peter out at the end of a ridge, leaving behind columns of rock.
    (D) Scarps are formed by the movement of geological faults or landslides.
    (E) There is sometimes ambiguity over whether or not a slope is a cliff.
    (F) Erosion can sometimes be slowed down by people using improved land use practices.

The Cliff and Erosion

A cliff is a geographic feature that consists of a sharply vertical rock exposure. Cliffs are created by the process of erosion and weathering. They are most common on coasts and in mountainous areas. The strong bases of cliffs are usually formed by rock that is resistant to erosion and weathering. Sedimentary rocks such as sandstone, limestone, chalk, and dolomite are most likely to form cliffs. Igneous rocks, such as granite and basalt, can also be found.

Erosion is described as the displacement of solids by the agents of wind, water, or ice. These solids can be soil, mud, rock, and other particles. The process of erosion occurs by down-slope movement in response to gravity. It can also be caused by living organisms. This is called bioerosion. Erosion is different from weathering, which is the breakdown of rock and particles through processes where no motion is involved. However, these two processes can occur at the same place and time.

Erosion is a process that occurs naturally. But it is increased by human land use in many places. Cutting down trees and allowing animals to overgraze are poor land use practices that lead to faster erosion. Unmanaged construction activity and road or railroad building also fall into this category. Erosion can be limited by improved land use practices. Activities like terrace building and tree planting can help rebuild damaged areas.

A type of cliff formed by the movement of a geologic fault or a landslide is called a scarp. Most cliffs have a talus slope at their bases. These are usually exposed jumbles of fallen rock in arid areas or under high cliffs. A soil slope may obscure the talus in areas with more water in the air.

Waterfalls and rock shelters also occur as features on cliffs. A cliff sometimes peters out at the end of a ridge. This might leave tea tables or other types of rock columns behind. A cliff does not have to be exactly vertical to be classified as such. So there can be some ambiguity about whether a slope is actually a cliff or not.

There are unique cliffs to be found all over the world. The highest cliff is said to be the east face of Great Trango. It exists in the Karakoram Mountains of northern Pakistan and is about 1,340 meters high. Kalaupapa, Hawaii, is home to the highest sea cliffs. These measure 1,010 meters high. Mount Thor on Baffin Island in Arctic Canada is the highest vertical drop at 1,370 meters in total. It has the longest purely vertical drop on Earth, which is 1,250 meters.

Vocabulary Review

A Choose the word with the closest meaning to each highlighted word or phrase.

1. There was a cluster of students gathered around the table.
   - (A) lot
   - (B) class
   - (C) group
   - (D) room

2. This was the central part of the project.
   - (A) secondary
   - (B) next
   - (C) confusing
   - (D) important

3. The businessman earned a lot of money last month.
   - (A) made
   - (B) spent
   - (C) borrowed
   - (D) used

4. Some trees are highly resistant to storm damage.
   - (A) destroyed
   - (B) exhausted
   - (C) resilient
   - (D) informal

5. Dr. Park's theory was very controversial.
   - (A) original
   - (B) divisive
   - (C) educational
   - (D) scholarly

6. The river carried the sediment down to the delta.
   - (A) water
   - (B) mud
   - (C) sand
   - (D) silt

7. All the students' answers on the test were accurate.
   - (A) exceptional
   - (B) correct
   - (C) mistaken
   - (D) wrong

8. The plane was traveling at a very rapid speed.
   - (A) fast
   - (B) moderate
   - (C) slow
   - (D) incredible

B Match each word with the correct definition.

1. brackish
2. fertilize
3. mold
4. hysterical
5. humanitarian
6. constellation
7. neurologist
8. trace
9. organ
10. nautical

   - a. important parts of the body like the heart, liver, and lungs
   - b. helpful to humans
   - c. a person who studies the nerves and nervous system
   - d. to detect or find
   - e. related to the sea
   - f. to make pregnant
   - g. a design that stars make in the sky
   - h. a shape or form
   - i. somewhat salty
   - j. frantic; in a panic

Unit 10

Fill in a Table

10 Fill in a Table

Overview

■ Introduction

Fill in a Table questions ask you to identify and organize major ideas and important supporting information from across the passage. Then, you should classify them into the appropriate categories. Passages used for this type of question usually have particular types of organization such as compare/contrast, cause/effect, or problem/solution. A five-answer table is worth 3 points, and a seven-answer table is worth 4 points.

■ Question Type

Directions: Complete the table below to summarize information about X discussed in the passage. Match the appropriate statements to the categories with which they are associated. TWO of the answer choices will NOT be used. *This question is worth 3 points.*

Answer Choices

1.
2.
3.
4.
5.
6.
7.

Category 1
-
-
-

Category 2
-
-

■ Useful Tips

- Look at the categories of information in the table first.

- Using your scratch paper, make an outline of the passage according to these categories.

- Distinguish between major and minor information in the passage.

- Wrong answers usually include information that is not mentioned in the passage or that is not directly relevant to the categories in the table.

Sample iBT Question

The Opossum

Marsupials are mammals that have a pouch. The female keeps its babies in the pouch until they are old enough to live outside it. The only marsupial in North America is the opossum.

The opossum is about the size of a large cat. Its fur is gray, and it has a pink nose, feet, and tail. They have large, black eyes for seeing at night when they move around the most. Even though they have fifty very sharp teeth, they are very gentle animals. They try to avoid any kind of fight.

Opossums are very adaptable. They can live in many places, including trees and underground. They eat all kinds of food, both plants and animals. They eat insects, mice, small snakes, grass, leaves, and berries.

The opossum has a variety of defenses. They are mostly immune to snake poison. They usually do not get rabies, a nasty disease, because of the temperature of their blood. Their most famous defense is to play dead. Because most animals do not eat dead things, it is a good defense. The opossum will turn on its back and show its teeth. It will produce a bad smell near its tail. Usually the other animal will go away.

Directions: Complete the table below to summarize information about the adaptability and defenses of opossums. Match the appropriate statements to the categories with which they are associated. TWO of the answer choices will NOT be used. ***This question is worth 3 points.***

Adaptability	Defenses
• •	• • •

Answer Choices

1. They have a variety of homes.

2. They are not affected by snake poison.

3. Their blood temperature prevents rabies.

4. They are as large as cats.

5. They avoid fights.

6. They can eat many different things.

7. They play dead.

 Choices 1 and 6 are concerned with the adaptability of opossums, and choices 2, 3, and 7 are about their defenses. Choices 4 and 5 are not relevant to the given categories.

Fill in a Table questions ask you to recognize and organize the important ideas of the passage into table categories. You need to understand what type of organization the passage uses: for example, compare/contrast, cause/effect, or problem/solution.

Classism

The term "classism" refers to a form of prejudice. It takes place against people who are in a lower social class. It is a form of social elitism. Individual classism is practiced by people. It happens when wealthy people disregard those who make less money than they do. It also happens when the rich receive advantages over the middle class or poor. Structural classism occurs in institutions. It happens when things are done in such a way as to exclude people from lower classes. Many people see this type of classism in American politics. This is because people who make the largest campaign contributions seem to have more influence in the government. This practice excludes the working class from having an equal level of influence.

1. **Directions:** Complete the table below by matching FOUR of the six answer choices with appropriate types of individual and structural classism.

Individual Classism	Structural Classism
•	•
•	•

(A) Rich people ignore those people with lower incomes.
(B) People from lower classes cannot find decent jobs.
(C) Bigger political campaign donors have more influence in the government.
(D) The rich receive advantages that the middle class or poor do not get.
(E) The children of the rich receive better gifts than the children of the poor.
(F) People from lower classes cannot participate in making decisions.

Mesopotamia

Mesopotamia is called the "cradle of civilization" because the first human societies began in this area. The area is located in a fertile zone between two rivers. This made it possible for humans to grow crops. Their prosperity led to the rise of cities. Once these cities existed, many discoveries were made. The first writing system was developed. The people of these cities also invented metal working. They were one of the first bronze-age peoples. They used copper, bronze and gold to decorate their palaces and temples. They also used astronomy. By studying the stars, they were able to calculate the length of an Earth year. This led to the accurate 60-minute hour and the 24-hour day that we still use today.

2. **Directions:** Complete the table below by matching FOUR of the six answer choices with the appropriate causes and effects of Mesopotamian discovery and innovation.

Causes	Effects
•	•
•	•

(A) Mesopotamians engaged in farming.
(B) Cities thrived in Mesopotamia.
(C) Mesopotamia was surrounded by a big river.
(D) A unique calculating system was invented.
(E) Mesopotamians were good astronomers.
(F) A day was divided into 24 hours.

Green Revolution

The term Green Revolution is used to describe a large change in farming. This took place in many developing nations between the 1940s and 1960s. It led to a large increase in cereal production. This change was the result of programs of agricultural research. The Green Revolution has had positive and negative impacts on society and the Earth. A positive impact is that famine was avoided. But this led to the negative effect of overpopulation in some areas. The Green Revolution is also credited with the success of large-scale farming. But this success has made it very difficult for small-scale farmers to profit. This shift in economics greatly hurt the socialist movement.

3. **Directions:** Complete the table below by matching FOUR of the six answer choices with the positive and negative effects of the Green Revolution.

Positive Effects	Negative Effects
•	•
•	•

- Ⓐ Agricultural research was widely encouraged.
- Ⓑ Fewer people suffered hunger.
- Ⓒ Some areas experienced a rapid increase in population.
- Ⓓ Large-scale farming took root in some countries.
- Ⓔ It became difficult for small-scale farmers to survive.
- Ⓕ Cereal production increased substantially in a few countries.

Natural Phenomena

A natural phenomenon is an event that is not caused by humans. It occurs in nature. But it can affect humans. Some natural phenomena can be described by physics. They are called physical phenomena. Lightning is an example of this type of event. The orbit of planets due to gravity is another example. Natural disasters that come from within the Earth are considered to be geological phenomena. A common example is a volcanic eruption. A tidal wave is also this type of event. These events cannot be controlled. Humans do not create them and cannot stop them. But these events can be understood through science.

4. **Directions:** Complete the table below by matching FOUR of the six answer choices with appropriate types of physical and geological phenomena.

Physical Phenomena	Geological Phenomena
•	•
•	•

- Ⓐ A wild fire is caused by humans.
- Ⓑ A flash of lightning strikes across the sky.
- Ⓒ A tsunami occurs in the ocean.
- Ⓓ A volcano explodes and spews hot lava.
- Ⓔ Gravity makes planets move in their orbits.
- Ⓕ An earthquake is simulated in the laboratory.

Practice with Long Passages

A Read the following passage, and answer the questions.

Emergence

Time Limit: 3 min. 20 sec.

The concept of emergence describes the way in which a complex pattern forms. This pattern arises from its basic parts. An emergent property comes from the relationships between these parts. This is a constantly changing process. It may occur over a long period of time. The evolution of the human body is a good example. Its form emerged over thousands of generations. The human body is very complex. But it is formed by millions of tiny cells, which are not.

Emergence occurs on disparate-size scales. An example is between neurons and the human brain. Interactions between many neurons produce a human brain. This brain is capable of thought. But none of the neurons that made it are capable of thought. The single brain that results from many neurons is much bigger than any of the single neuron parts that created it.

A common way of looking at emergence in nature is through structures. They can come from organic or inorganic sources. A good example of a living structure is a flock of birds. The flock takes a shape and has behavioral characteristics. But these properties are not exhibited by individual birds. Another example of an organic emergent structure is an ant colony. The ant colony is emergent because no single ant, including the queen, could organize such an effective colony of workers. Yet collectively, the colony structure arises. An example of an inorganic emergent structure is a hurricane. This storm system forms as a result of various factors. Some of these factors are pressure, temperature, and humidity. They combine to form a violent storm. But any single factor would not form the same storm.

Emergence also occurs in human culture. One place this kind of emergence has occurred on a large scale is in the stock market. As a system, it regulates the prices of companies around the world. But there is no single leader that controls the entire market. Agents only know of a limited number of companies and must follow strict rules of the market. Through these interactions, the complexity of the market as a whole emerges. Another type of this emergence is with the World Wide Web. In this case there is no central website, yet links between major and minor websites create the complex whole that is known as the World Wide Web.

General Comprehension

1. **The word regulates in the passage is closest in meaning to**

   (A) controls
   (B) limits
   (C) raises
   (D) maintains

property (n)
a characteristic

evolution (n)
the process by which organisms develop

disparate (a)
essentially different and distinct

colony (n)
a group of organisms

2. **Based on the information in the passage, which of the following best explains the term "emergence"?**

   Ⓐ the way in which a number of small units interact to form a very large structure

   Ⓑ the way in which simple components combine to form a complex system

   Ⓒ the way in which a complex organic system emerges from its basic parts

   Ⓓ the way in which various single units interlock to form a large system

On the TOEFL Test

3. **Directions:** Complete the table below by matching FIVE of the seven answer choices with structural and cultural emergence.

Structural Emergence	Cultural Emergence
• • •	• •

Answer Choices

Ⓐ The queen bee is fed by workers many times a day.

Ⓑ A flock of birds exhibits a shape and certain behavior.

Ⓒ Small and large websites are linked to create the World Wide Web.

Ⓓ The human brain is composed of numerous thinking neurons.

Ⓔ A hurricane is the result of various climatic factors.

Ⓕ The stock market forms a complex pattern.

Ⓖ Ants build an effective colony collectively.

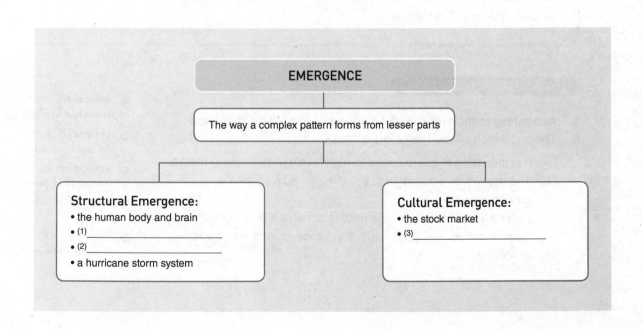

EMERGENCE

The way a complex pattern forms from lesser parts

Structural Emergence:
• the human body and brain
• (1)_____
• (2)_____
• a hurricane storm system

Cultural Emergence:
• the stock market
• (3)_____

The Media Influence Theory

Time Limit: 2 min. 50 sec.

The American entertainment industry has been heavily criticized. Critics are unhappy with the amount of pretend violent acts it shows. The Media Influence Theory explains this problem. It suggests that the rise in the rates of real violent acts is linked to entertainment.

This theory considers many acts of violence. High school shootings are the most common. It claims they are due to the high levels of violent acts in the media. This takes on various forms in popular entertainment.

The basis of the theory lies in the assumption that many people are exposed to a high level of violent content in media outlets. A small percentage of these people have trouble separating fantasy and reality about the violence they see. These people think that it is okay to commit violent acts.

The most frequent targets of the theory's advocates are video game companies. These companies produce many first-person shooter games. Most of these feature a high level of violence and gore. Advocates say these games make life seem cheap. These games reward the player for committing acts of violence.

Advocates also target musicians who sing hateful lyrics. They claim these artists incite violence. Violent movies too cannot avoid their accusation. They claim these kinds of movies make violence look glamorous. All of these are forms of entertainment, and people want the companies to take more responsibility for their products. They want them to label products that are extremely violent. They also want minors to have limited or no access to these products.

However, critics of this theory say that government should not regulate media. They say that it would harm American citizens' right to free speech. They compare statistics of violence between the United States and other countries. Some of these other countries have the same kind of violent media. But there are much fewer violent acts being committed. So these critics claim that the problem of violence in America is not due to the media. They say it is caused by the availability of weapons.

General Comprehension

1. **According to the author's description of the Media Influence Theory, which of the following is true?**

    (A) It is inevitable to get exposed to high levels of violence in media.
    (B) The most frequent targets of the theory's advocates are gun companies.
    (C) Hateful lyrics can encourage people to behave in a violent way.
    (D) Easy access to weapons causes violence among teenagers in America.

criticize (v)
to find fault with; to judge

pretend (a)
not real; imagined

assumption (n)
a supposition; belief

advocate (n)
a supporter

incite (v)
to provoke; to encourage

2. The word them in the passage refers to

Ⓐ advocates

Ⓑ musicians

Ⓒ people

Ⓓ companies

On the TOEFL Test

3. Directions: Complete the table below by matching FIVE of the seven answer choices with the appropriate claims made by advocates or critics of the Media Influence Theory.

Advocates	Critics
• • •	• •

Answer Choices

Ⓐ Artists who sing hateful lyrics incite violence.

Ⓑ High school punishment can lead teenagers to be violent.

Ⓒ Alcohol abuse causes people to shoot guns.

Ⓓ Media should not be controlled by the government.

Ⓔ Violent movies make violence look glamorous.

Ⓕ Violent video games cheapen human life.

Ⓖ Violence is caused by weapons being available.

Media Influence Theory

Advocates:
• Some people cannot tell imaginary violence from reality.
• Video games, music with hateful lyrics, and violent movies are responsible for violence in society.
• (1)_____ should be more responsible.
• Government should (2)_____ .

Critics:
• Reason for rising levels of violence
  – (3)_____
• Government should not control the entertainment industry.
• Other countries have similar violence in media but fewer real violent acts.

Read the following passage, and answer the questions.

The Great Chicago Fire

Time Limit: 2 min. 40 sec.

The Great Chicago Fire burned from October 8th to 10th in 1871. It had terrible effects. Hundreds of people were killed by it. Much of the city turned into ashes. It was one of the largest disasters in the U.S. during the 19th century. But the people of Chicago began to rebuild their city immediately. This led to Chicago's status as one of the most economically important American cities.

The fire began around 9 p.m. on Sunday, October 8th. It started in a small shed in an alley off DeKoven Street. The most commonly believed reason for the fire starting is that a cow kicked over a lantern in a barn. This barn was owned by Patrick and Catherine O'Leary.

It is now known that Mrs. O'Leary was used as a scapegoat. Historians think she was blamed for the fire because she was a woman, an immigrant, and a Catholic. All of these groups suffered persecution at this time in American history. The *Chicago Tribune*'s first post-fire issue claimed that Mrs. O'Leary's negligence was the cause. But later, the reporter who wrote the story admitted that he made it up. He said he did it because he thought it was a colorful story.

Richard Bales is an amateur historian. He believes the fire was started by Daniel Sullivan. He was the man who first reported the fire. Bales offered the theory that this man ignited some hay in the barn. He says Sullivan did it while trying to steal some milk.

But Anthony DeBartolo has recently reported some new evidence to the *Chicago Tribune*. He put forth the suggestion that a gambler named Louis M. Cohn may have started the fire. DeBartolo says he did this during a craps game. According to a book by Alan Wykes, a lost will by Cohn includes a confession that he started the fire.

General Comprehension

1. **The word ignited in the passage is closest in meaning to**

   (A) lit up
   (B) set fire to
   (C) blew up
   (D) put out

2. **According to the passage, which of the following is true about the Great Chicago Fire?**

   (A) It turned most of Atlanta into ashes.
   (B) It was one of the largest 18th-century disasters in the United States.
   (C) There are several theories about how it started.
   (D) People believe it was caused by Patrick O'Leary.

---

destroy (v)
to ruin; to demolish; to wreck

shed (n)
a small structure used for storage

scapegoat (n)
a whipping boy; the fall guy

persecution (n)
cruel and unfair treatment

a game of craps (phr)
a dice game that is usually played for money

3. **Directions:** Complete the table below by matching FIVE of the seven answer choices with the reported causes and effects of the Great Chicago Fire.

Reported Causes	Effects
• • •	• •

Answer Choices

Ⓐ It killed hundreds of people.

Ⓑ A lantern in a barn was kicked over by a cow.

Ⓒ Daniel Sullivan burned the barn while stealing some milk.

Ⓓ A milk thief kicked a torch and started the fire.

Ⓔ Many parts of Chicago were destroyed.

Ⓕ Anthony Debartolo found new evidence of how the fire started.

Ⓖ A gambler started the fire during a craps game.

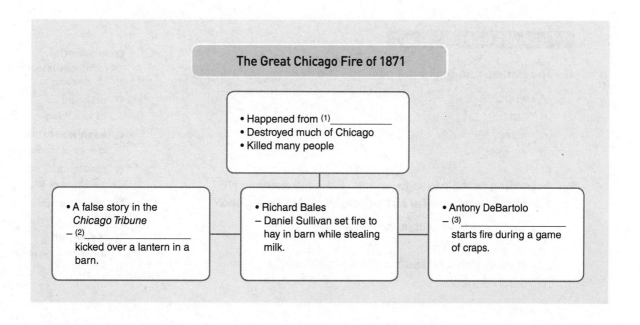

The Great Chicago Fire of 1871

- Happened from (1)_____
- Destroyed much of Chicago
- Killed many people

- A false story in the *Chicago Tribune*
  – (2)_____ kicked over a lantern in a barn.

- Richard Bales
  – Daniel Sullivan set fire to hay in barn while stealing milk.

- Antony DeBartolo
  – (3)_____ starts fire during a game of craps.

Differences in the Concept of Family

Time Limit: 2 min. 50 sec.

A family consists of a group of people who live together. They are linked by birth or marriage. They can also be linked by other legal ties. Some of these are domestic partnerships and adoption.

Many people think families are only related by "blood." But many social scientists say that the notion of "blood" should be taken metaphorically. Many societies define family through other concepts. Article 16 of the Universal Declaration of Human Rights calls family the natural group unit of society. It says that the family is entitled to protection by society and the State.

The structure of families is based on ties between parents and children. It is also based on links between spouses. Or it can be based on both. There are three major types of families.

A matrifocal family consists of a mother and her children. The children are usually the mother's biological offspring. But this does not rule out adoption. This type usually occurs in places where the woman has enough resources to raise their family alone.

A consanguineal family can be found in various forms. The most common form consists of a mother and her children and the family of the mother. Fathers are often not present. This is especially true when property is passed down through inheritance. When men own property, this type of family may include members of the husband's family.

A conjugal family is made up of one or more mothers and their children. It also includes one or more fathers. This kind of family is linked to the existence of a division of labor. Both men and women must do different types of labor in this form. Families in this situation have high mobility.

The nuclear family is a sub-group of the conjugal family type. This type has one woman and one husband. Together they raise their children. This type of family is the most common in modern industrialized society.

General Comprehension

1. **The phrase rule out in the passage is closest in meaning to**

   (A) illegalize
   (B) omit
   (C) allow
   (D) exclude

2. **According to the passage, which of the following is NOT a criterion by which the structure of families is defined?**

   (A) links between husband and wife
   (B) blood or legal ties
   (C) spousal links and ties between parents and children
   (D) parents-children ties

adoption (n)
taking legal responsibility for parenting

notion (n)
an idea; thought; concept

be entitled to (phr)
to deserve something

spouse (n)
a husband or wife

inheritance (n)
legacy

mobility (n)
the ability to move easily

3. **Directions:** Complete the table below by matching SEVEN of the nine answer choices with the types of families.

Matrifocal Family	Consanguineal Family	Conjugal Family
• •	• •	• • •

Answer Choices

Ⓐ Fathers are often absent from this type of family.

Ⓑ There is usually a division of labor in this type of family.

Ⓒ This kind of family has only children and no parents.

Ⓓ This type usually happens when the mother can support her family by herself.

Ⓔ The nuclear family belongs to this type.

Ⓕ A mother and her children and the family of the mother are the most common form of this type.

Ⓖ This type is composed of a mother and her children.

Ⓗ This type includes the husband's parents when he is poor.

Ⓘ There are one or more mothers or fathers in this type of family.

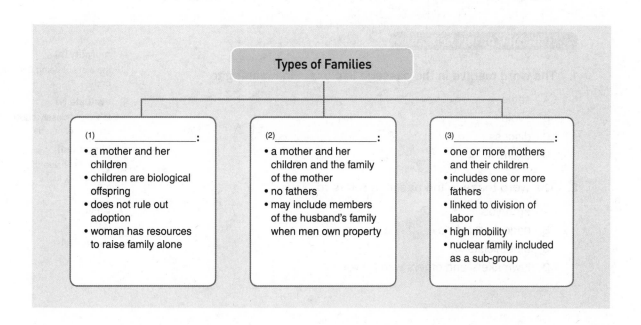

Types of Families

(1)_____:
• a mother and her children
• children are biological offspring
• does not rule out adoption
• woman has resources to raise family alone

(2)_____:
• a mother and her children and the family of the mother
• no fathers
• may include members of the husband's family when men own property

(3)_____:
• one or more mothers and their children
• includes one or more fathers
• linked to division of labor
• high mobility
• nuclear family included as a sub-group

Bioethics

Time Limit: 2 min. 50 sec.

Bioethics is a branch of applied philosophy. It looks closely at science and medicine. Its function is to ask questions about the morality of research and treatments. It also evaluates the ethics of the laws that regulate science. This field is very important because it protects the human race. Without it, advances by science and medicine could put humans in great danger.

The study of bioethics affects many laws. Many scientists react blindly against those who practice bioethics for this reason. These scientists believe that their work is ethical by nature.

Bioethics is an academic area that shows rapid growth. Its history as a formal study is only thirty years old. Many academic centers now offer degrees in bioethics. In the 1990s, a group of social scientists created a mode of discourse. This established the method of research about ethical issues. This method attempts to resolve these issues with society. This data compiled by bioethicists is subject to the same peer review as other social sciences.

There are some major questions about bioethics. Its validity as an area of academic inquiry is doubted. Why must it exist apart from philosophy? Is everyone not an ethicist? These questions are answered by the needs of institutions. Bioethicists put to work the enormous body of research and history. They apply it to questions of bioethics. They do it in a fair, honest, and intelligent way. They share a commitment to this goal.

Bioethicists research many topics. They often focus on issues that cause controversy in society. They compile data and publish reports. These reports are used to form public opinion. They also form policy. Some of the topics that bioethicists deal with are about abortion and cloning. They also cover the use of embryos in stem cell research. These are difficult ethical problems. They arise from questions about human life. Bioethicists try to educate lawmakers and others with power. These are the ones who draw boundaries. They decide what is acceptable in medicine and science.

General Comprehension

1. **The word resolve in the passage is closest in meaning to**

   (A) settle

   (B) avoid

   (C) discuss

   (D) examine

2. **The word these in the passage refers to**

   (A) embryos

   (B) ethical problems

   (C) bioethicists

   (D) lawmakers and others with power

○ **morality (n)**
the state of being good or bad

○ **evaluate (v)**
to look at closely based on a set of criteria

○ **blindly (ad)**
without considering, examining, looking, or thinking

○ **rapid (a)**
fast

○ **resolve (v)**
to solve

3. **Directions:** Complete the table below by matching FIVE of the seven answer choices with the topics examined by bioethicists and functions of bioethicists

Topics	Functions
• • •	• •

Answer Choices

(A) They examine the use of embryos in stem cell research.

(B) They compile data about social sciences.

(C) They examine the morality of research and treatments.

(D) They evaluate ethics of laws that regulate science.

(E) They express their opinions about abortion.

(F) They look at the ethics of cloning.

(G) They protect people from the development of science and medicine.

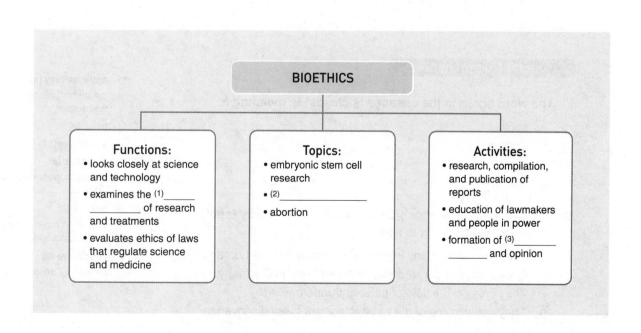

BIOETHICS

Functions:
• looks closely at science and technology
• examines the (1)_____ _____ of research and treatments
• evaluates ethics of laws that regulate science and medicine

Topics:
• embryonic stem cell research
• (2)_____
• abortion

Activities:
• research, compilation, and publication of reports
• education of lawmakers and people in power
• formation of (3)_____ _____ and opinion

Read the following passage, and answer the questions.

Paleoanthropology

Time Limit: 2 min. 50 sec.

The study of human and pre-human fossils is called paleoanthropology. It is a branch of physical anthropology. It focuses on tracing the evolution of humans through the ages. Scientists in this field trace anatomic, behavioral, and genetic linkages. These links show how humans developed from pre-humans. Scientists use these links to reconstruct a timeline for the rise of man. This timeline spans from prehistoric to modern times.

Paleoanthropologists are able to study early hominids by digging up fossil remains. They scour the earth digging up small traces. These bits they find give them impressions of ancient life. Preserved bones, tools, and footprints provide this type of fossil evidence.

Paleoanthropology began in the late 1800s when a few important discoveries were made that led to the study of human evolution. The first was made in 1856. A Neanderthal man was discovered in Germany. This was an important event. It led to the emergence of this science. Other notable events were the publication of two important books on this subject. The first was Thomas Huxley's *Evidence as to Man's Place in Nature*. The second important book was Charles Darwin's *The Descent of Man*.

Some of the most important discoveries in this field were made by the Leakey family. Their long list of important fossil discoveries began with Louis Leakey. He began digging in the Olduvai Gorge in Tanzania, Africa. In 1959 he and his wife found the remains of an early hominid skull.

After Louis's death in 1972, his wife Mary Leakey continued his research. One of her most notable discoveries was the Laetoli footprints. She found these in Tanzania in 1976. These footprints were preserved in volcanic ash. They were dated back to 3.7 million years ago. They represent the most conclusive proof that early pre-humans walked on two legs.

The Leakey's son Richard is also credited with some important fossil discoveries. In 1972, his group found the skull of a Homo habilis in Tanzania. Then in 1975, his group also found the skull of a Homo erectus in Kenya.

General Comprehension

1. **The word scour in the passage is closest in meaning to**

   Ⓐ spoil
   Ⓑ explore
   Ⓒ search
   Ⓓ study

2. **According to the author's description of the Leakey family, which of the following is true?**

   Ⓐ They published many important books about pre-humans.
   Ⓑ They discovered a Neanderthal man fossil in Germany.
   Ⓒ They created the field of paleoanthropology.
   Ⓓ They made some of the most important fossil discoveries.

anthropology (n)
the study of people and their culture

trace (v)
to track down; to find

anatomic (a)
relating to the body of an organism

linkage (n)
something that connects two separate things

conclusive (a)
convincing; without doubt

3. **Directions:** Complete the table below by matching FIVE of the seven answer choices with the places where major discoveries were made.

Kenya	Tanzania	Germany
•	• • •	•

Answer Choices

Ⓐ The remains of an early hominid skull were found in 1959.

Ⓑ Preserved prehistoric tools were discovered in the 1800s.

Ⓒ The remains of a Neanderthal man were discovered in 1856.

Ⓓ The skull of a Homo habilis was found in 1972.

Ⓔ Fossil bones of a hominid were found in 1852.

Ⓕ The skull of a Homo erectus was discovered in 1975.

Ⓖ The Laetoli footprints were found in 1976.

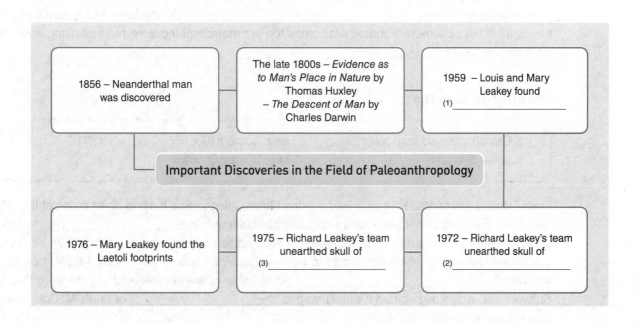

1856 – Neanderthal man was discovered

The late 1800s – *Evidence as to Man's Place in Nature* by Thomas Huxley – *The Descent of Man* by Charles Darwin

1959 – Louis and Mary Leakey found (1)_____

Important Discoveries in the Field of Paleoanthropology

1976 – Mary Leakey found the Laetoli footprints

1975 – Richard Leakey's team unearthed skull of (3)_____

1972 – Richard Leakey's team unearthed skull of (2)_____

Building Summary Skills

The following summaries are based on the long passages you worked on earlier. Complete each of them by filling in the blanks with suitable words or phrases.

1. **Emergence**

> cultural   organic and inorganic structures   the World Wide Web
> a complex pattern   ant colonies or flocks of birds

Emergence is the concept that describes how (1)_____ forms from lesser parts. A good example is the human body, which has developed over thousands of successive generations. Emergence is evident in all forms of (2)_____.
Scientists who study emergence look at the characteristics of organic emergent structures such as (3)_____ and at inorganic structures such as hurricanes. Another form of emergence is (4)_____, in which some form of human organization results in a highly complex structure that is more than the sum of its parts. (5)_____ and the stock market are prime examples of the sort of phenomenon in which simple components combine to form a complex whole.

2. **The Media Influence Theory**

> reality   the availability of weapons   regulated by the government
> many acts of violence   rising levels of violence

The Media Influence Theory states that (1)_____ in society are attributable to individuals who see violence depicted in entertainment and are unable to distinguish it apart from (2)_____. Advocates of this theory target video games, music with hateful lyrics, and movies as being responsible for (3)_____. They want to see these forms of entertainment heavily (4)_____. On the other hand, critics of this theory think the government should not control the entertainment industry and that rising levels of violence are due to (5)_____.

3. **The Great Chicago Fire**

> a Catholic, female immigrant   steal some milk   1871
> a game of craps   Mrs. O'Leary's cow

From October 8th to 10th in (1)_____, the Great Chicago Fire burned down much of the city and killed hundreds of people. The fire was originally blamed on (2)_____ kicking down a lantern in the barn. But the reporter who wrote this story later said he made it up because it sounded interesting, which led people to believe that Mrs. O'Leary was made a target because she was (3)_____. Some other possible causes of the fire were Daniel Sullivan, who may have started it while trying to (4)_____, or Louis M. Cohn, who is said to have started it during (5)_____.

4. Differences in the Concept of Family

the conjugal family   genetic or other types of bonds   blood relation
the nuclear family   matrifocal, consanguineal, and conjugal

A family consists of people who live together and are linked by (1)_____.
Although (2)_____ defines many families, it is not the only thing that can link
people together. There are three major types of families: (3)_____.
The most common type of family in modern society is a sub-group of (4)_____
called (5)_____.

5. Bioethics

the human race   public opinion   the ethics of scientific
politicians   bioethics programs

Bioethics is a branch of applied philosophy that looks closely at (1)_____
_____ and medical practices. This field is very important because it asks questions about
and examines policies and treatments that greatly affect (2)_____. It is also an
area of academic growth, as many universities have created (3)_____.
Although bioethicists' roles are often questioned, they do many activities such as researching
and compiling reports that greatly affect (4)_____ and the policies made by
(5)_____.

6. Paleoanthropology

the late 1800s   the skull of a hominid   the Leakeys
the Laetoli footprints   a Homo habilis and a Homo erectus

The study of human and pre-human fossils is paleoanthropology. This field began with several
important discoveries and publications in (1)_____, including the discovery of
Neanderthal man fossils. Some of the most important discoveries in this field have been made
by a family named (2)_____. Their long list of discoveries began in the 1950s when
Louis and Mary Leakey found (3)_____ in Tanzania. But Mary Leakey's
most important discovery came after her husband's death, when she found (4)_____
in 1976. These footprints offered conclusive evidence that early man walked upright on two legs.
Their son, Richard, also found the skulls of (5)_____.

1. The word **levied** in the passage is closest in meaning to

   Ⓐ saved   Ⓑ pointed at   Ⓒ imposed   Ⓓ exempted

2. According to paragraph 1, which of the following is true of a partnership?

   Ⓐ It is not a very good form of business because it is outdated.
   Ⓑ People who want to work with their friends find this form of business useful.
   Ⓒ A partnership can only be established between people with the same college degrees.
   Ⓓ It is used for businesses such as bakeries and pubs.

3. According to paragraph 2, which of the following is NOT true of partnership?

   Ⓐ A partnership agreement may exist between partners.
   Ⓑ A declaration of partnership may be made between partners.
   Ⓒ A partnership cannot be available for public inspection.
   Ⓓ A partnership is a legal entity in many countries.

4. The word **others** in the passage refers to

   Ⓐ charities   Ⓑ partnerships   Ⓒ businesspeople   Ⓓ partners

5. Which of the following best expresses the information in the highlighted sentence?

   Ⓐ People about to start a partnership must decide which form they like best.
   Ⓑ Partners must always think about the possible forms of business.
   Ⓒ Partners must make many choices about their new business.
   Ⓓ Business partners should always make choices together.

6. **Directions:** Complete the table below by matching SEVEN of the nine answer choices with the appropriate forms of partnership and the criteria for a partnership to exist. TWO of the answer choices will NOT be used. *This question is worth 4 points.*

Answer Choices	Criteria
Ⓐ The partners must have known each other for at least ten years.	•
Ⓑ A general partnership is the most basic kind.	•
Ⓒ There must be a valid agreement between parties.	•
Ⓓ A view to profit is necessary.	•
Ⓔ The ability to manage the business is given up by limited partners.	
Ⓕ Unknown partners are not aware of each other's existence.	**Forms**
Ⓖ A limited liability partnership is the third kind.	•
Ⓗ A business must be carried on.	•
Ⓘ Rights such as interest and obligation must have some mutuality.	•

Partnership in Business

A partnership is a type of business. In it, partners share profits and losses with two or more members. Partners are people who have united to take part in the same business. This form of business is good for people who want to work with their friends or people they trust. It is also useful for two or more people who have different specialties. By forming a partnership, they can combine their skills. A partnership can also be made between existing companies.

Partners may have a partnership agreement. Or they may make a declaration of partnership. In some jurisdictions, such agreements must be registered. After doing this, they are made available for public inspection. In many countries, a partnership is a legal entity.

Partnerships are often favored over corporations for taxation purposes. This makes a partnership more useful for businesses that face heavy taxation. A partnership structure may eliminate the dividend tax. This tax is levied on profits made by the owners of a corporation.

A general partnership is the most basic form. In this style, all partners manage the business. They are all personally liable for the company's debts. There are two other forms of partnership as a business. One of them is the limited partnership. With this style, certain "limited partners" give up their ability to manage the business. They trade this ability in order to receive limited liability for the partnership's debts. The other kind is a limited liability partnership. In this style, all partners accept some degree of liability.

According to the Partnership Act 1958, there are four criteria for a partnership to exist. The first is a valid agreement between the parties. The second is for them to carry on a business. This is defined in the agreement as any trade, occupation, or profession. The third is that they must be in common. This means there must be some mutuality of rights. This includes interests and obligations. Finally, there must be a view to profit. This is the reason charities cannot be partnerships.

The businesspeople who are going to form a partnership must choose which form best suits them. Some partners may want more control. They may be willing to risk greater liability. Others may want to lessen their liability. They may be willing to forego some ability to control the business. The balance between control, profit and liability must be found by the new partners. But the most important ingredient for a successful relationship between partners is trust.

7. **The word partitioned in the passage is closest in meaning to**

    Ⓐ separated   Ⓑ distinguished   Ⓒ formalized   Ⓓ constructed

8. **The author's description of Cliff Palace mentions which of the following?**

    Ⓐ It is a possible site of a war against the Aztec Empire.
    Ⓑ It is the most beautiful palace in the United States.
    Ⓒ It is located in the southwest corner of Colorado.
    Ⓓ It is a dangerous place to visit because of snakes.

9. **According to paragraph 2, which of the following is NOT true about Cliff Palace?**

    Ⓐ It occupies a space in an empty sandstone cliff.
    Ⓑ There were probably about 120 storage rooms.
    Ⓒ Not every room in it had a hearth.
    Ⓓ Some Anasazi people still live there.

10. **Which of the following can be inferred about Cliff Palace?**

    Ⓐ Rooms without hearths were used by animals.
    Ⓑ It is the only structure of its kind in this area.
    Ⓒ Tourists are not allowed to take pieces of the stone structure.
    Ⓓ The Anasazi people fled because of tourists.

11. **Look at the four squares [■] that indicate where the following sentence can be added to the passage.**

Another possibility suggested by some archaeologists familiar with the mysterious structure is that it was used to hold prisoners.

Where would the sentence best fit?

12. **Directions:** Complete the table below by matching FIVE of the seven choices with the appropriate characteristics of the storage rooms, towers, and kivas of Cliff Palace. TWO answer choices will NOT be used. ***This question is worth 3 points.***

Answer Choices	Storage Room
Ⓐ These were built high to be safe from moisture and pests.	•
Ⓑ The structure is partitioned by walls.	•
Ⓒ This room has a self-heating bathtub.	**Kiva**
Ⓓ There is no way to access it through doorways or portals.	•
Ⓔ There are some abstract designs.	•
Ⓕ People accessed these rooms with removable ladders.	**Tower**
Ⓖ This room has a beautiful view of the backyard of Cliff Palace.	•

The Anasazi Architecture of Cliff Palace

The largest cliff dwelling in North America is named Cliff Palace. This is an ancient Pueblo structure. It is located in Mesa Verde National Park. This park is in the southwest corner of Colorado. It was an ancient home to the Anasazi peoples.

Cliff Palace is a large ruin that many people find amazing. It was built into an empty space in a sandstone cliff. This alcove is approximately 40 meters deep and 25 meters high. This stone structure is about 130 meters long. Cliff Palace has 150 rooms. But not all of these rooms had hearths. A hearth used for building fires shows that a room was a living space for people. Only about 25 to 30 of Cliff Palace's rooms have these. The remaining rooms were probably used for storage.

Cliff Palace has many open areas and rooms whose functions are still not understood. Nine storage rooms are built on the upper level. These were built high. They are safe from moisture and pests. The surplus harvest was probably stored here. Removable ladders allowed people access these rooms.

Scientists have made a guess as to how many people lived there. They based their guess on the number of rooms with hearths. It is estimated that Cliff Palace was home to between 100 to 150 Anasazi.

At Cliff Palace there are a few towers. These are square and round structures that go up a few stories. Some of the finest stonework in the ruin is contained in these towers. The interior of a four-story tower at the south end of the complex contains some abstract designs. These are painted on original plaster within the tower.

Cliff Palace also contains round sunken rooms of ceremonial importance. These are called kivas. One kiva is located in the center of the ruin. The entire structure at this point is partitioned by a series of walls. It has no doorways or other access portals. The walls of this kiva were plastered with one color on one side, and a different color on the opposing side. **A** Archaeologists have studied this strange structure. **B** They think that two communities lived here. **C** This kiva may have been used to integrate the two communities. **D**

Archaeologists can tell the age of Cliff Palace through tree ring dating. This indicates that construction and refurbishing of Cliff Palace was continuous. It took place from 1190 AD to 1260 AD. They also figure that a major portion of the building was done during a time span of twenty years. Cliff Palace was abandoned by 1300 AD for reasons that are still unknown.

Vocabulary Review

A Choose the word with the closest meaning to each highlighted word or phrase.

1. Scientists examined several properties of the strange phenomenon.
   - (A) characteristics
   - (B) vehicles
   - (C) owners
   - (D) colors

2. His dream was to move to New Mexico and join an art colony.
   - (A) house
   - (B) school
   - (C) group
   - (D) list

3. He had a poor reaction after viewing pretend violence.
   - (A) real
   - (B) necessary
   - (C) negative
   - (D) imaginary

4. She was a strong advocate of the Media Influence Theory.
   - (A) critic
   - (B) supporter
   - (C) not sure
   - (D) enemy

5. The police found many linkages between the crime scene and the suspect.
   - (A) fingerprints
   - (B) witnesses
   - (C) similarities
   - (D) connections

6. She suddenly got the notion that he wanted to ask her on a date.
   - (A) hope
   - (B) expectation
   - (C) idea
   - (D) worry

7. The morality club engaged in much discourse about current issues.
   - (A) questioning
   - (B) argument
   - (C) fighting
   - (D) ethics

8. The doctors were able to reconstruct his nose after the accident.
   - (A) rebuild
   - (B) help
   - (C) replace
   - (D) remove

B Match each word with the correct definition.

1. anthropology •   • **a.** someone who is blamed for a problem, usually unjustly
2. surname •   • **b.** cells that process and transmit information in the brain
3. scapegoat •   • **c.** the visual aspect of blood or murder
4. assumption •   • **d.** a certificate of accreditation from a university or college
5. evolution •   • **e.** the practice of parents raising a child that is not genetically theirs
6. adoption •   • **f.** objects or money that is passed from someone who dies to someone else
7. inheritance •   • **g.** the study of people and their culture
8. neurons •   • **h.** the process by which organisms develop
9. gore •   • **i.** the name shared by family members or people who are related
10. degree •   • **j.** a belief that is created by looking at various information

This part provides lists of important vocabulary words in each unit. They are essential words for understanding any academic texts. Many of the words are listed with their derivative forms so that students can expand their vocabulary in an effective way. These lists can be used as homework assignments.

Vocabulary Wrap-up

→

Unit 1 • Vocabulary

⊙Step A

- [ ] affection
- [ ] analysis
- [ ] anthropologist
- [ ] archaeologist
- [ ] banish
- [ ] consensus
- [ ] conservation
- [ ] constant
- [ ] constitution
- [ ] despot
- [ ] distinct
- [ ] drought
- [ ] ennoble
- [ ] era
- [ ] expel
- [ ] expose
- [ ] flourish
- [ ] hereditary
- [ ] impoverish
- [ ] initiative
- [ ] intestine
- [ ] launch
- [ ] microbe
- [ ] monarchy
- [ ] nonrenewable
- [ ] opulence
- [ ] overthrow
- [ ] perspective
- [ ] populate
- [ ] precede
- [ ] predictability
- [ ] prestigious
- [ ] prominence
- [ ] proponent
- [ ] rampant
- [ ] ratify
- [ ] reign
- [ ] sovereign
- [ ] thrive
- [ ] treason

⊙Step B

Noun	Verb	Adjective	Adverb
☐ abundance	☐ abound	☐ abundant	☐ abundantly
☐ adherence	☐ adhere	☐ adhesive	☐ adhesively
☐ anatomy	☐ anatomize	☐ anatomical	☐ anatomically
☐ circulation	☐ circulate	☐ circulative / -atory	
☐ colony	☐ colonize	☐ colonial	☐ colonially
☐ competition	☐ compete	☐ competitive	☐ competitively
☐ contrast	☐ contrast	☐ contrastive	☐ contrastively
☐ experiment / -ation	☐ experiment	☐ experimental	☐ experimentally
☐ extortion	☐ extort	☐ extortive	
☐ identification	☐ identify	☐ identifiable	☐ identifiably
☐ inspiration	☐ inspire	☐ inspiring	☐ inspiringly
☐ oppression	☐ oppress	☐ oppressive	☐ oppressively
☐ patron	☐ patronize	☐ patronizing	☐ patronizingly
☐ prediction	☐ predict	☐ predictable	☐ predictably
☐ stability	☐ stabilize	☐ stable	☐ stably

Unit 2 • Reference

⊙ Step A

- [ ] abnormal
- [ ] affect
- [ ] approximately
- [ ] biodiversity
- [ ] carnivorous
- [ ] catastrophic
- [ ] condense
- [ ] corpse
- [ ] deadly
- [ ] decline
- [ ] ecology
- [ ] ecosystem
- [ ] equatorial
- [ ] estuary
- [ ] exotic
- [ ] fend for
- [ ] fungus
- [ ] hibernate
- [ ] impose
- [ ] indigenous
- [ ] inertia
- [ ] inhale
- [ ] meteorology
- [ ] momentum
- [ ] nutrient
- [ ] offspring
- [ ] opaque
- [ ] parasite
- [ ] parched
- [ ] phenomenon
- [ ] unprecedented
- [ ] unrestrained

⊙ Step B

Noun	Verb	Adjective	Adverb
☐ accumulation	☐ accumulate	☐ accumulative	☐ accumulatively
☐ aggression	☐ aggress	☐ aggressive	☐ aggressively
☐ conduction	☐ conduct	☐ conductive	☐ conductively
☐ deduction	☐ deduce	☐ deductive	☐ deductively
☐ deprivation	☐ deprive	☐ deprivable	☐ deprivably
☐ dissipation	☐ dissipate	☐ dissipative / -ted	☐ dissipatively / -tedly
☐ diversity	☐ diversify	☐ diverse	☐ diversely
☐ domination	☐ dominate	☐ dominant	☐ dominantly
☐ epidemic		☐ epidemic(al)	☐ epidemically
☐ estimation	☐ estimate	☐ estimative / -mable	☐ estimably
☐ evaporation	☐ evaporate	☐ evaporative	☐ evaporatively
☐ falsification	☐ falsify	☐ falsifiable	☐ falsifiably
☐ fertilization	☐ fertilize	☐ fertile	☐ fertily
☐ need	☐ necessitate	☐ necessary	☐ necessarily
☐ precipitation	☐ precipitate	☐ precipitate	☐ precipitately
☐ regulation	☐ regulate	☐ regulative / -tory	☐ regulatively / -torily
☐ sustenance	☐ sustain	☐ sustainable	☐ sustainably

Unit 3 • Factual Information

⊙Step A

☐ acrobatics	☐ assassinate	☐ awareness	☐ botany
☐ bounce	☐ cede	☐ civic	☐ centennial
☐ disfavor	☐ drastic	☐ glacial	☐ hygiene
☐ integrity	☐ internal	☐ majestic	☐ massacre
☐ monument	☐ nitrogen	☐ optical	☐ propaganda
☐ refined	☐ sleet	☐ splice	☐ sulfur / sulphur
☐ summon	☐ supreme	☐ thereof	☐ tuberculosis
☐ transparent	☐ treaty	☐ unrest	☐ wade

⊙Step B

Noun	Verb	Adjective	Adverb
☐ absorption	☐ absorb	☐ absorptive	☐ absortively
☐ commemoration	☐ commemorate	☐ commemorative	☐ commemoratively
☐ conclusion	☐ conclude	☐ conclusive	☐ conclusively
☐ controversy	☐ controvert	☐ controversial	☐ controversially
☐ corruption	☐ corrupt	☐ corruptive	☐ corruptively
☐ deduction	☐ deduct	☐ deductive	☐ deductively
☐ delight	☐ delight	☐ delightful	☐ delightfully
☐ eruption	☐ erupt	☐ eruptive	☐ eruptively
☐ exaggeration	☐ exaggerate	☐ exaggerative	☐ exaggeratively
☐ immigration / -rant	☐ immigrate	☐ immigrant	☐ immigrantly
☐ incorporation	☐ incorporate	☐ incorporative	☐ incorporatively
☐ induction	☐ induct	☐ inductive	☐ inductively
☐ inscription	☐ inscribe	☐ inscriptive	☐ inscriptively
☐ proclamation	☐ proclaim	☐ proclamatory	☐ proclamatorily
☐ repeal	☐ repeal	☐ repealable	
☐ symbol	☐ symbolize	☐ symbolic	☐ symbolically
☐ transmission	☐ transmit	☐ transmissive	☐ transmissively

Unit 4 • Negative Factual Information

⊙ Step A

☐ annual	☐ arid	☐ array	☐ camouflage
☐ carbon	☐ caterpillar	☐ commodity	☐ comprise
☐ circadian	☐ crude	☐ current	☐ deposit
☐ epilepsy	☐ evaporation	☐ fertile	☐ fragment
☐ habitat	☐ manufacture	☐ metabolism	☐ nectar
☐ neurology	☐ photic	☐ physiologist	☐ precipitation
☐ reputation	☐ specimen	☐ spherical	☐ vegetation

⊙ Step B

Noun	Verb	Adjective	Adverb
☐ assembly	☐ assemble	☐ assembled	
☐ assumption	☐ assume	☐ assumptive	☐ assumptively
☐ competition	☐ compete	☐ competitive	☐ competitively
☐ conversion	☐ convert	☐ convertible	☐ convertibly
☐ domination	☐ dominate	☐ dominant	☐ dominantly
☐ elimination	☐ eliminate	☐ eliminative	☐ eliminatively
☐ externalization	☐ externalize	☐ external	☐ externally
☐ generation	☐ generate	☐ generative	☐ generatively
☐ illustration	☐ illustrate	☐ illustrative	☐ illustratively
☐ inherence	☐ inhere	☐ inherent	☐ inherently
☐ inheritance	☐ inherit	☐ inheritable	☐ inheritably
☐ invention	☐ invent	☐ inventive	☐ inventively
☐ migration /-rant	☐ migrate	☐ migrant	☐ migrantly
☐ modification	☐ modify	☐ modifiable	
☐ obtainment	☐ obtain	☐ obtainable	☐ obtainably
☐ replacement	☐ replace	☐ replaceable	☐ replaceably
☐ reproduction	☐ reproduce	☐ reproductive	☐ reproductively
☐ visibility	☐ view	☐ visible	☐ visibly

Unit **5** • Sentence Simplification

⊙Step A

☐ adept	☐ auditory	☐ binary	☐ concentric
☐ conflict	☐ deciduous	☐ defecation	☐ deficit
☐ edible	☐ entrepreneur	☐ foster	☐ immoral
☐ in disrepair	☐ inflation	☐ latitude	☐ maize
☐ mammal	☐ molecular	☐ mollusk	☐ monetary
☐ olfactory	☐ overt	☐ permanent	☐ protein
☐ rank	☐ staple	☐ substantial	☐ temperate
☐ territory	☐ tissue	☐ tropical	☐ unethical
☐ urination	☐ variant	☐ wayfarer	☐ whereas

⊙Step B

Noun	Verb	Adjective	Adverb
☐ adjustment	☐ adjust	☐ adjustable	☐ adjustably
☐ alternation	☐ alternate	☐ alternate	☐ alternately
☐ contradiction	☐ contradict	☐ contradictory	☐ contradictorily
☐ cultivation	☐ cultivate	☐ cultivatable	
☐ domestication	☐ domesticate	☐ domestic	☐ domestically
☐ elaboration	☐ elaborate	☐ elaborate	☐ elaborately
☐ enactment	☐ enact	☐ enactive	
☐ extinction	☐ extinguish	☐ extinct / -tive	☐ extinctively
☐ mutation	☐ mutate	☐ mutational	☐ mutationally
☐ preservation	☐ preserve	☐ preservative	
☐ prevalence	☐ prevail	☐ prevalent	☐ prevalently
☐ radiation	☐ radiate	☐ radiational	
☐ reference	☐ refer	☐ referent / -tial	☐ referentially
☐ regeneration	☐ regenerate	☐ regenerative	☐ regeneratively
☐ residence / -dent	☐ reside	☐ resident	
☐ restriction	☐ restrict	☐ restrictive	☐ restrictively

Unit **6** • **Rhetorical Purpose**

⦿ Step **A**

☐ accuracy	☐ amplify	☐ aspect	☐ astronomy
☐ causal	☐ celestial	☐ cope with	☐ component
☐ confederate	☐ decade	☐ disabled	☐ epoch
☐ feat	☐ fulcrum	☐ embrace	☐ magnetic
☐ infantry	☐ metaphysics	☐ outermost	☐ predatory
☐ probe	☐ prominent	☐ region	☐ retrograde
☐ shift	☐ solitary	☐ transcontinental	☐ vivid

⦿ Step **B**

Noun	Verb	Adjective	Adverb
☐ ceremony		☐ ceremonial	☐ ceremonially
☐ civilization	☐ civilize	☐ civilizational	☐ civilizationally
☐ contribution	☐ contribute	☐ contributive	☐ contributively
☐ convection	☐ convect	☐ convective	☐ convectively
☐ convergence	☐ converge	☐ convergent	☐ convergently
☐ deformity	☐ deform	☐ deformative	
☐ divergence	☐ diverge	☐ divergent	☐ divergently
☐ exertion	☐ exert	☐ exertive	
☐ foundation	☐ found	☐ foundational	☐ foundationally
☐ influence	☐ influence	☐ influential	☐ influentially
☐ inhibition	☐ inhibit	☐ inhibitive	
☐ intensity / -sification	☐ intensify	☐ intense	☐ intensely
☐ notability	☐ note	☐ notable	☐ notably
☐ representation	☐ represent	☐ representative	☐ representatively
☐ revelation	☐ reveal	☐ revealing	☐ revealingly
☐ suspicion / -pect	☐ suspect	☐ suspicious	☐ suspiciously
☐ theory	☐ theorize	☐ theoretical	☐ theoretically
☐ transportation	☐ transport	☐ transportable	

Unit **7** • Inference

⊙Step A

☐ agriculture	☐ appendage	☐ aquatic	☐ cartilage
☐ cerebellum	☐ complement	☐ complex	☐ dart
☐ disclaim	☐ echolocation	☐ fissure	☐ forage
☐ geological	☐ horizontal	☐ lyric	☐ mechanical
☐ misconception	☐ niche	☐ parallel	☐ parasite
☐ playwright	☐ pollen	☐ render	☐ rupture
☐ sensory	☐ skeptically	☐ spontaneity	☐ suffrage
☐ symmetrical	☐ temporal	☐ thrust	☐ verbal

⊙Step B

Noun	Verb	Adjective	Adverb
☐ accompaniment	☐ accompany	☐ accompanying	
☐ attachment	☐ attach	☐ attachable / -ched	
☐ confirmation	☐ confirm	☐ confirmative	☐ confirmatively
☐ diminishment	☐ diminish	☐ diminishing	☐ diminishingly
☐ distinction	☐ distinguish	☐ distinct	☐ distinctly
☐ diversification	☐ diversify	☐ diverse / -sifiable	☐ diversely
☐ emergence	☐ emerge	☐ emergent	☐ emergently
☐ emphasis	☐ emphasize	☐ emphatic	☐ emphatically
☐ emission	☐ emit	☐ emissive	
☐ impulse	☐ impel	☐ impulsive	☐ impulsively
☐ initiation	☐ initiate	☐ initiatory	☐ initiatorily
☐ perception	☐ perceive	☐ perceptive	☐ perceptively
☐ prohibition	☐ prohibit	☐ prohibitive	☐ prohibitively
☐ resolution	☐ resolve	☐ resolute	☐ resolutely
☐ separation	☐ separate	☐ separate	☐ separately
☐ significance	☐ signify	☐ significant	☐ significantly
☐ volunteer	☐ volunteer	☐ voluntary	☐ voluntarily

Unit 8 • Insert Text

⊙ Step A

- ☐ acclimate
- ☐ carbohydrate
- ☐ doctrine
- ☐ entity
- ☐ groundbreaking
- ☐ maritime
- ☐ primitive
- ☐ revive
- ☐ tense

- ☐ alignment
- ☐ commission
- ☐ dormant
- ☐ explicit
- ☐ hypocrite
- ☐ notion
- ☐ proceed
- ☐ sacred
- ☐ unmanned

- ☐ allegory
- ☐ diameter
- ☐ embodiment
- ☐ faculty
- ☐ influx
- ☐ observatory
- ☐ radioactive
- ☐ submission
- ☐ vanish

- ☐ burlesque
- ☐ dispute
- ☐ ensure
- ☐ fictional
- ☐ legend
- ☐ pioneer
- ☐ repeal
- ☐ summit
- ☐ wane

⊙ Step B

Noun	Verb	Adjective	Adverb
☐ attainment	☐ attain	☐ attainable	☐ attainably
☐ consistence	☐ consist	☐ consistent	☐ consistently
☐ conveyance	☐ convey	☐ conveyable	
☐ cremation	☐ cremate	☐ crematory	
☐ criticism	☐ criticize	☐ critical	☐ critically
☐ derivation	☐ derive	☐ derivative	☐ derivatively
☐ hierarchy		☐ hierarchical	☐ hierarchically
☐ immortality	☐ immortalize	☐ immortal	☐ immortally
☐ improvisation	☐ improvise	☐ improvisational	☐ improvisationally
☐ isolation	☐ isolate	☐ isolated	☐ isolatedly
☐ moderation	☐ moderate	☐ moderate	☐ moderately
☐ organization	☐ organize	☐ organizational	☐ organizationally
☐ persistence	☐ persist	☐ persistent	☐ persistently
☐ pursuit	☐ pursue	☐ pursuable	
☐ recollection	☐ recollect	☐ recollective	☐ recollectively
☐ synthesis	☐ synthesize	☐ synthetic	☐ synthetically

Unit **9** • **Prose Summary**

⊙Step A

☐ adorn	☐ ambiguity	☐ brackish	☐ byproduct
☐ calculation	☐ cartography	☐ consciousness	☐ constellation
☐ craftsmanship	☐ delta	☐ epidemic	☐ embryo
☐ engraving`	☐ era	☐ estuary	☐ famine
☐ fauna	☐ fetus	☐ geometric	☐ germ
☐ granite	☐ hostility	☐ humanitarian	☐ hysterical
☐ inscription	☐ mold	☐ nautical	☐ navigation
☐ neurotic	☐ objective	☐ obscure	☐ organ
☐ pottery	☐ ruling	☐ runoff	☐ scarce
☐ sediment	☐ spine	☐ trace	☐ transplant
☐ triangular	☐ umbilical	☐ vertical	☐ zygote

⊙Step B

Noun	Verb	Adjective	Adverb
☐ abortion	☐ abort	☐ abortive	☐ abortively
☐ association	☐ associate	☐ associative	☐ associatively
☐ assignment	☐ assign	☐ assignable	☐ assignably
☐ erosion	☐ erode	☐ erosive	☐ erosively
☐ demonstration	☐ demonstrate	☐ demonstrative	☐ demonstratively
☐ displacement	☐ displace	☐ displaceable	
☐ illegalization	☐ illegalize	☐ illegal	☐ illegally
☐ nourishment	☐ nourish	☐ nourishing	☐ nourishingly
☐ opposition	☐ oppose	☐ opposing	☐ opposingly
☐ portrayal	☐ portray	☐ portrayable	
☐ promotion	☐ promote	☐ promotive	☐ promotively
☐ recombination	☐ recombine	☐ recombinant	☐ recombinantly
☐ repression	☐ repress	☐ repressive	☐ repressively
☐ resistance	☐ resist	☐ resistant	☐ resistantly

Unit **10** • **Fill in a Table**

⊙ Step A

☐ anatomic	☐ collectively	☐ commitment	☐ conjugal
☐ corporation	☐ disparate	☐ dividend	☐ entitle
☐ evolution	☐ flock	☐ glamorous	☐ gore
☐ hominid	☐ humidity	☐ impact	☐ incitement
☐ jurisdiction	☐ levy	☐ liability	☐ linkage
☐ metaphorically	☐ mobility	☐ morality	☐ outlet
☐ paleoanthropology	☐ prejudice	☐ property	☐ refurbish
☐ scapegoat	☐ scour	☐ skull	☐ span
☐ spouse	☐ statistics	☐ surplus	☐ validity

⊙ Step B

Noun	Verb	Adjective	Adverb
☐ adaptation	☐ adapt	☐ adaptable	
☐ adoption	☐ adopt	☐ adoptive	☐ adoptively
☐ advocacy	☐ advocate	☐ advocative	☐ advocatively
☐ compilation	☐ compile	☐ compilatory	
☐ definition	☐ define	☐ definitive	☐ definitively
☐ descent	☐ descend	☐ descendent	☐ descendently
☐ exhibition	☐ exhibit	☐ exhibitive	☐ exhibitively
☐ evaluation	☐ evaluate	☐ evaluative	☐ evaluatively
☐ ignition	☐ ignite	☐ ignitable	
☐ immunization	☐ immunize	☐ immune	☐ immunely
☐ impression	☐ impress	☐ impressive	☐ impressively
☐ integration	☐ integrate	☐ integrative	☐ integratively
☐ persecution	☐ persecute	☐ persecutive / -tory	
☐ pretense	☐ pretend	☐ pretended / -ing	☐ pretendedly / -ingly
☐ prosperity	☐ prosper	☐ prosperous	☐ prosperously
☐ reconstruction	☐ reconstruct	☐ reconstructive	☐ reconstructively

Reading Section **Directions**

This section measures your ability to understand academic passages in English. It consists of three passages and a set of questions about each of them.

Most questions are worth 1 point, but the last question in each passage is worth more than 1 point. The directions indicate how many points you may receive.

Some passages include <u>underlined</u> words or phrases in shade. You can see a definition or an explanation at the end of the passage.

While working on the questions, you can go to the next question by clicking on **Next**. You may skip questions and go back to them later. If you want to return to previous questions, click on **Back**. You can click on **Review** at any time, and the review screen will show you which questions you have answered and which you have not answered. From this review screen, you may go directly to any question you have already seen in the Reading section.

You may now begin the Reading section. You will read 3 passages. You will have 60 minutes to read the passages and answer the questions.

Actual Test

1. **The word precursor in the passage is closest in meaning to**

   (A) summary
   (B) sequel
   (C) forerunner
   (D) framework

2. **Look at the four squares [■] on the above passage that indicate where the following sentence could be added to the passage.**

   But no one had succeeded in organizing the elements in a format that showed those patterns.

   Where would the sentence best fit?

   Click on a square [■] to add the sentence to the passage.

3. **Which of the following best expresses the essential information in the highlighted sentence in paragraph 3?** *Incorrect* **choices change the meaning in important ways or leave out essential information.**

   (A) Elements with the same number of protons do not react with each other.
   (B) Periodicity refers to an element's tendency to periodically gain an extra proton.
   (C) An element has protons and neutrons in the nucleus of its atoms.
   (D) The properties of elements tend to reoccur at fixed intervals of their atomic weights.

Periodic Table

Humans have always known about certain elemental substances, such as gold and silver, that occur in nature and cannot be broken down into other substances. **A** Other chemical elements were discovered gradually beginning in 1669, when a German merchant, Hennig Brand, accidentally found phosphorus while attempting to find a way to create gold out of more common metals. **B** By 1809, the number of known elements had increased to 47. **C** Chemists studying the elements began to notice patterns in the way chemicals reacted. **D**

The first modern chemistry textbook was written in 1789 by Antoine-Laurent de Lavoisier. He listed the known elements, which he classified into metals and nonmetals. But his listing omitted the gases and included some things that were not substances, such as light and calories. Thus, his list was not accepted as an accurate organizing system.

An important trait of elements is their periodicity: similarly acting elements tend to occur at regular intervals when arranged by their atomic weight (the number of protons plus neutrons in the nucleus). A French geologist, Alexandre-Emile Beguyer de Chancourtois, was the first to notice this periodicity. He designed a precursor to the periodic table, the telluric helix. That system arranged the elements on a spiral-shaped cylinder in order of their atomic weight. The elements with similar physical properties appeared vertically on the cylinder. But because Chancourtois's 1862 paper used geological terms and did not include drawings, his periodic system was not accepted by those in the field of chemistry.

4. According to the passage, the first chemist to notice periodicity was

- (A) Mendeleev
- (B) Chancourtois
- (C) Lavoisier
- (D) Newlands

5. The word breakthrough in the passage is closest in meaning to

- (A) discovery
- (B) quest
- (C) experiment
- (D) goal

6. Why does the author mention the card game of solitaire?

- (A) To name the favorite game of Mendeleev
- (B) To identify the source of the organizing plan of the periodic table
- (C) To describe the solitary nature of chemistry studies
- (D) To give an example of a precursor to the periodic table

7. According to the passage, Mendeleev's main discovery was that

- (A) some elements have similar physical properties that reoccur at regular intervals of their atomic weights
- (B) an element's atomic weight and number could be shown in a single table
- (C) similarly acting elements appear in groups of eight
- (D) the rarest elements have the lowest atomic weights

As new elements were discovered through the first half of the 1800's, chemists confirmed the regular repetition of the physical properties of the elements. Chemists studied ways to classify the elements in order to reflect this periodicity. In 1863, an English chemist, John Newlands, divided the 56 known elements into groups, each sharing the same characteristics. As each group seemed to contain eight elements, he referred to his system as the Law of Octaves, after the eight keys in an octave on the piano. But Newlands's idea was ridiculed and his theory dismissed. Not until 1919 did it become accepted that the elements should be grouped by eights.

But the underlying concept of the periodicity of the elements was adapted to better effect in 1869 by the Russian chemist Dmitri Mendeleev. His great breakthrough was to see that the two key characteristics of an element—atomic weight and atomic number (the number of protons in the nucleus)—could be combined in a single table. His table came to be called the *periodic table*.

Mendeleev's table was inspired by the card game of solitaire, in which cards are arranged horizontally by suit and vertically by number. Borrowing the same organizing patterns, Mendeleev arranged the elements in groups of seven. He grouped them horizontally by their atomic number in ascending order and vertically by their similar qualities in groups of seven. Thus similar metals such as gold, silver, and copper appear in the same vertical column. Similarly reacting gases such as helium, argon, and neon appear in another column. The most common elements (hydrogen, helium, lithium) have lower atomic

Actual Test

8. **The word their in the passage refers to**

    (A) the most common elements

    (B) lower atomic numbers

    (C) the rarest elements

    (D) protons

9. **Which of the following can be inferred about hydrogen?**

    (A) Its atomic number is less than uranium's.

    (B) It appears in a vertical row.

    (C) It reacts with helium.

    (D) Its atomic weight is greater than lithium's.

10. **The word valid in the passage is closest in meaning to**

    (A) studied

    (B) misleading

    (C) legal

    (D) accurate

11. **All of the following are true about the periodic table EXCEPT:**

    (A) It is constantly changing as new elements are found.

    (B) It originally predicted that more elements would be discovered.

    (C) It will never contain more than 120 elements.

    (D) It arranges elements according to their physical properties.

numbers and thus appear near the beginning of the table in the first horizontal row. The rarest elements (uranium and plutonium) have the greatest number of protons in their nuclei. They are ordered near the end of the table.

In Mendeleev's time, only 63 elements had been discovered. The brilliance of his periodic table, however, was that it predicted that new elements would be found to fit into the missing slots in his original table. Today the table shows 120 elements, 92 naturally occurring and 28 created in the laboratory. Scientists believe that many more will be found. The periodic table has been called "the most elegant organizational chart ever devised."

Mendeleev's chart remains valid today. But it has been modified by the continual discovery and manufacture of new elements. And in 1914, Henry Mosely discovered a relationship between an element's X-ray wavelength and its atomic number. Thus, he rearranged the elements by electric charge. Another important improvement was suggested by Glenn T. Seaborg in 1945: the addition of a vertical group of certain heavy elements called the actinide series.

12. Directions: An introductory sentence for a brief summary of the passage is provided below. Complete the summary by selecting the THREE answer choices that express the most important ideas in the passage. Some answer choices do not belong in the summary because they express ideas that are not in the passage or are minor ideas in the passage.
This question is worth 2 points.

This passage explores the history of the periodic table.
-
-
-

Answer Choices

(A) Chancourtois was the first to notice the periodicity of elements.

(B) The periodic table is constantly changing as new elements and new ways of classifying them are discovered.

(C) Lavoisier's list of elements included light and calories.

(D) By 1809, there were 47 known elements.

(E) The most common elements appear near the end of the table while the least common are near the beginning.

(F) Mendeleev organized the elements into a table based on their atomic weight.

Drag your answer choices to the spaces where they belong.
To remove an answer choice, click on it. To review the passage, click **View Text**.

Actual Test

13. The phrase **keep track of** in the passage is closest in meaning to

- (A) preserve
- (B) account for
- (C) describe
- (D) line up

14. According to paragraph 1, the first signs of counting were found in

- (A) tallies
- (B) sheep
- (C) rocks
- (D) animal bones

15. According to paragraph 2, Egypt's counting system used which of the following to show numbers?

- (A) tallies
- (B) pictographs
- (C) place values
- (D) an inverted U

16. The author mentions **the number 236** in order to

- (A) illustrate the importance of the zero in the place-value system
- (B) explain how the Arabs invented Arabic numerals
- (C) identify the first numeral that was written with place values
- (D) show a number that does not contain a zero

History of Counting

The earliest signs of counting have been found in ancient hunting artifacts. Notches in animal bones from 30,000 B.C. may have been a tallying system. Tallies were used to keep track of things. A sheepherder would put a pebble in a pile each time a sheep was let out to graze. When the sheep returned at night, the owner would remove the pebble. Any pebbles that remained represented missing sheep. But such tallying was not true counting. It merely compared two sets of objects.

Egypt was one of the first civilizations to adopt a real number system. Beginning in about 3000 B.C., Egyptians expressed numbers with pictographs, or symbols to represent numbers. Thus, the numbers from one to nine were combinations of vertical strokes. Ten was an inverted U, 100 was a coiled rope, and 1000 was a lotus flower.

Different cultures used different base numbers for their counting systems. Many, such as the Egyptians, used a base 10, a reflection of the numbers of fingers on both hands. Others, like the Babylonians, used a base 60. But that system was awkward because it required either separate symbols for each number up to 60 or clusters of 10 numbers. But the base of 60 survives today in geometry (60 seconds and minutes of angular measurement, 360 degrees in a circle, and 180 degrees in a rectangle) and in time-keeping (60 seconds in a minute and 60 minutes in an hour).

The first great advance in numbering was the place-value concept. Invented by the Babylonians, place values were needed to show the value of each digit in a numeric notation. For example, without place values, the number 236 was complicated to write in

17. The word complicated in the passage is closest in meaning to

- (A) precise
- (B) difficult
- (C) simple
- (D) definite

18. The author's description of zero mentions which of the following?

- (A) It was invented by the Babylonians.
- (B) It was first expressed with Roman numerals.
- (C) It was needed to make place values accurate.
- (D) It was used widely by 3000 B.C.

19. According to the passage, all of the following are true about place values EXCEPT:

- (A) They were invented by the Babylonians.
- (B) They show the value of each digit in a multiple-digit number.
- (C) They allowed calculations with written numerals.
- (D) They were included in the system of Roman numerals.

20. In paragraph 7, why does the author mention the abacus?

- (A) To contrast it with written numbers regarding speed of calculating
- (B) To give an example of the means of counting used after the year 1600
- (C) To describe how sheepherders kept track of their sheep
- (D) To mention a device invented by Al-Khwarizmi

most systems, as it required multiple symbols and strokes. But with a value assigned to each place (in a system based on 10), we know that the digit 6 represents 6 ones, the digit 3 represents 3 tens, and the digit 2 represents 2 hundreds.

For place value to accurately reflect a number, a "zero" was needed to eliminate any confusion over, for example, whether the digits 236 were intended to represent 236 or 2360 or 2036 or 2306. The zero or "empty" place value was originally indicated by leaving a gap between numbers, as in 23_6 to mean 2306. Eventually, a special symbol was designed to show zero, the "0" digit that we use today. That symbol was invented for the Arabic counting system and was in common use by about 650 A.D.

For zero and place values to be useful in mathematics, it was necessary to invent a symbol for each number up to the base figure. Thus, different symbols for one through nine were adopted, with the zero added after each symbol to reflect another 10 (10, 20, 30, 40, and so on). And multiple zeros were added to represent even larger numbers (100, 1000, and 10,000).

Arabic numerals ultimately replaced the Roman numerals that had dominated Western European history until the seventeenth century. Those are the numerals used in most of the world today. Early forms of Arabic numbers appeared in India by 200 B.C. Indian mathematicians found that a place-value system that included a symbol for zero allowed them to perform mathematical operations by writing down and manipulating numerals. That was faster than the abacus, a mechanical device that had been the principal means of counting. Using written

269

Actual Test

21. According to the passage, Al-Khwarizmi's treatise was unknown in Europe until the twelfth century because

(A) it was not yet translated into Latin

(B) printing was not invented until then

(C) Arab mathematicians wanted to keep it secret

(D) European mathematicians were not interested in other counting systems

22. The word supplanted in the passage is closest in meaning to

(A) revised

(B) replaced

(C) reinforced

(D) resurrected

23. According to the passage, which of the following is true of algorism?

(A) It was a mechanical device for counting.

(B) It was the Roman system of counting.

(C) It was the Arabic number system.

(D) It was not used after printing was invented.

numerals to calculate did not become known outside India until the ninth century, when an Arab mathematician, Al-Khwarizmi, wrote a treatise about numbers. But his work was not translated into Latin until the twelfth century and thus did not become known in Europe until then. An Italian, Leonardo Fibonacci, popularized the Arabic numbering system (called "algorism") by writing books about it that were read by bookkeepers and merchants. They started to use the system in their commercial transactions.

For a few hundred years after Fibonacci, scholars and merchants debated the merits of algorism versus the abacus. With the invention of printing, books about algorism became widely known, leading to its becoming the accepted method from about 1500 and after. By about 1600, Roman numerals had been supplanted by Arabic numerals for performing most computations.

24. Directions: Complete the table below to summarize information about the two ideas that permitted counting with written numerals. Match the appropriate statement to the idea with which they are associated. *This question is worth 3 points.*

> Drag your answer choices to the spaces where they belong.
> To remove an answer choice, click on it. To review the passage, click **View Text**.

Place value　　　　　　　　**Select 3**
-
-
-

Zero　　　　　　　　**Select 2**
-
-

Answer Choices

Ⓐ Computation required that a number show the value of each digit.

Ⓑ Tallying was used to keep records.

Ⓒ Numbers were complicated to write.

Ⓓ A special symbol was needed to show an empty place value.

Ⓔ The idea was first invented by the Babylonians.

Ⓕ Roman numerals were replaced by Arabic numerals.

Ⓖ The symbol was first used by the Arabs.

Actual Test

25. According to paragraph 1, which of the following is a characteristic of minerals?

(A) crystal structure   (B) organic matter
(C) hardness   (D) smooth surface

26. The word the latter in the passage refers to

(A) mineral   (B) diamond
(C) graphite   (D) carbon

27. Which of the following best expresses the essential information in the highlighted sentence? *Incorrect* answer choices change the meaning in important ways or leave out essential information.

(A) The sheets of graphite's carbon atoms slide past the sheets of diamond's carbon atoms.

(B) Graphite contains a network of carbon atoms that create a strong crystal structure.

(C) Diamond is harder than graphite because of its carbon atoms' interlocking structure.

(D) The networks of carbon atoms in diamond and graphite make each mineral very hard.

28. The word identical in the passage is closest in meaning to

(A) similar
(B) complex
(C) same
(D) contrasting

Minerals

Minerals are naturally occurring solid substances formed by geologic movements in the Earth. Their main defining characteristics are that 1) they are inorganic (composed of non-living matter); 2) they have a crystal structure; and 3) they have a unique chemical composition. The type of mineral is determined both by its crystal structure and its chemical composition. A crystal structure occurs when the atoms inside the mineral are ordered in a geometric pattern that repeats itself throughout the mineral. All crystal structures fit into one of 14 possible "lattice"—regular pattern—arrangements of atoms, which lattices can be detected by X-rays.

A mineral's physical traits are influenced by its crystal form. For example, both diamond and graphite are composed of the same element (carbon), but the former is the hardest mineral while the latter is soft. This is because graphite's crystal structure arranges the carbon atoms in sheets that can slide past each other, while diamond's carbon atoms are arrayed in a strong, interlocking network.

Two minerals with identical crystal structures can have different chemical compositions. Thus, halite and galena share the same crystal structure but are composed of different chemicals. Conversely, two minerals with the same chemical ingredients can differ in their crystal structure. For example, pyrite and marcasite both are made of iron sulfide, but the arrangement of their atoms differs.

According to the International Mineralogical Association, 4,000 minerals have been identified to date. Only about 150 of them

29. According to the passage, two minerals with the same crystal structure can be different because

(A) they have different specific gravities
(B) they are found in different locations
(C) they were formed by different geologic processes
(D) they have different chemical compositions

30. According to paragraph 3, halite and galena are different elements because

(A) they have the same crystal structure
(B) they have different chemical compositions
(C) they were formed by different geologic processes
(D) they have different rankings on the Mohs scale

31. The word hospitable in the passage is closest in meaning to

(A) welcoming
(B) hostile
(C) comparable
(D) reactive

32. Why does the author discuss the role of volcanic movements in creating rocks?

(A) To give an example of one of the Earth's geologic forces
(B) To identify a factor that determines what kinds of minerals are found in rocks
(C) To explain why some rocks contain silicon
(D) To criticize the theory that minerals are created only by chemical reactions

are plentiful, and about 50 are classified as "occasional." The remainder are rarely found, some consisting of only small grains of rock.

Minerals are often found as components of rocks, which may contain organic matter as well. Some rocks consist wholly of one mineral, such as calcite in limestone rock. Other rocks may host many minerals. Almost all of the rocks visible today contain one or more of a group of about 15 minerals, including quartz, mica, and felspar.

The kinds of minerals found in any given rock are determined by three factors. First, the rock's chemical composition must be hospitable to a particular mineral. For example, rocks containing silicon will likely contain quartz. Second, the conditions under which the rock was formed will influence the kinds of minerals found in the rock. Thus, rock born from volcanic movements at high temperatures and pressures may contain granite. Third, mineral distribution is affected by the geological stages through which the rock passed before reaching its present state. For example, exposure to moisture and acids may decay some minerals and cause others to take their place. During the changes from one ecological stage to another, the rock may disintegrate into sand or soil.

Mineralogists classify minerals according to either physical properties or chemical composition. Minerals have numerous measurable physical properties. *Hardness* is measured on the "Mohs scale," which ranks hardness from one to 10. Any mineral can be cut or marked by a mineral with a higher ranking on the Mohs scale. Thus a diamond,

Actual Test

33. The word disintegrate in the passage is closest in meaning to

- (A) decompose
- (B) imbed
- (C) pressurize
- (D) decline

34. Which of the following can be inferred about minerals on the Mohs scale?

- (A) Graphite is softer than gypsum.
- (B) Quartz can cut a mineral with a rank of 8.
- (C) Diamond can cut a mineral with a rank of 9.
- (D) The hardest minerals are metals.

35. According to the passage, all of the following are properties of minerals EXCEPT:

- (A) cleavage
- (B) luster
- (C) streak
- (D) weight

36. The word residue in the passage is closest in meaning to

- (A) engraving
- (B) picture
- (C) outline
- (D) remains

with a rank of 10, can cut into quartz, with a rank of 7. *Luster* measures the reflection of light by the surface of the mineral. Metals have a higher luster than gypsum, which has a porous surface. *Cleavage* refers to the way a mineral splits apart along its natural grain, and *fracture* refers to its breakage against its natural cleavage planes. *Streak* is the color of the residue left by a mineral as it is rubbed across a special plate. *Specific gravity* measures the density of the mineral; it is computed by comparing the mass of the mineral to the mass of an equal volume of water.

Minerals can also be classified by their chemical characteristics. The most frequently occurring minerals are called *silicates* because of their large shares of silicon and oxygen. Almost all rocks fit this category. The second most common minerals are *carbonates*, which contain carbon and oxygen. Carbonates are found on the ocean floor as the deposits of decayed plankton. Another grouping, *halides*, are found where water has evaporated, as in dried lake beds and landlocked seas such as the Great Salt Lake in Utah. Other common classes include *sulfates*, *oxides*, *sulfides*, and *phosphates*.

37. Directions: An introductory sentence for a brief summary of the passage is provided below. Complete the summary by selecting the THREE answer choices that express the most important ideas in the passage. Some answer choices do not belong in the summary because they express ideas that are not in the passage or are minor ideas in the passage. *This question is worth 2 points.*

This passage discusses the characteristics of minerals.

-
-
-

Answer Choices

(A) When a mineral is exposed to moisture and acid, it may decay and allow a new mineral to form.

(B) Minerals are classified by their physical properties or chemical composition.

(C) The kind of mineral is defined by its crystal structure and its chemical composition.

(D) Carbonates are deposits of dead plankton that are found on the ocean floor.

(E) Minerals are often found in rocks, and each rock may host one or many minerals.

(F) Cleavage is the property of minerals that concerns the way it breaks along its natural cleavage planes.

Drag your answer choices to the spaces where they belong.
To remove an answer choice, click on it. To review the passage, click **View Text**.

How to
Master Skills ^{for the}

TOEFL iBT
Reading

Intermediate

Answer Book

Unit 1 Vocabulary

Skill & Drill

1. Ⓑ

巴卡族

巴卡是游牧民族，他们居住在喀麦隆、刚果、加蓬以及中非共和国的热带雨林中。他们平均身高 1.5 米左右，因此人们将其界定为矮人。但是，相对于这个并不悦耳的称呼，他们更乐于被叫做巴卡人——以其部落名命名。

巴卡人以捕猎、采集为生。他们住在临时以树枝为框架，以树叶为顶棚搭起的小屋里，并形成群落。男人们用毒箭和毒矛捕猎林中的动物；女人们采集水果和坚果，并且还要照顾孩子和养蜂。巴卡人实行公社自治，他们在作出任何决定之前都会听取全族人的意见。

2. Ⓑ

细菌

细菌是最常见的生物。它们生活在土壤和水中，或者寄生在其他生物体内。总的来说，大部分细菌微小得人眼很难直接观察到。但是有些大的细菌可以长到 0.5 毫米以上。细菌有类似植物和真菌细胞的细胞壁。多数细菌通过挥动鞭毛移动。

对于人类和动物而言，细菌有益亦有害。一些细菌会引起诸如霍乱、麻风等可怕的疾病。但是，寄生在人体肠道内的细菌却对人有益，因为它们可以分解大肠内的有害微生物，阻止其在人体内生长。

3. Ⓓ

干旱

干旱是指持续时间极长的一段非正常的干燥天气。在这段时间内，没有足够的水源来满足农业、城市和环境的需求。干旱通常与较长一段时期内降水量低于正常水平有关，但任何造成水循环水减少的因素都可能引发干旱。

人类无法控制天气，所以就无法消除引起干旱的因素。最常见的起因是缺水和高温。许多科学家认为，近几年的干旱都是由全球变暖造成的。他们宣称，如果我们能减少对臭氧层的破坏，就能减少干旱的发生。

4. Ⓒ

隐喻

隐喻是一种将两个无关的事物直接进行比较的语言修辞方法。两种事物通过隐喻在一定程度上被等同起来。隐喻有很多不同的类型，比如混杂隐喻、活隐喻、死隐喻。

混杂隐喻通过结合两个普通的隐喻来制造一种荒诞的比喻。例如，"他走近盘子抓住了牛角。"活隐喻在日常生活中并不常用。例如："你是我的太阳。"死隐喻指的是比较俗套的隐喻方式。例如："破冰"（打破尴尬局面）。

5. Ⓒ

伊丽莎白一世

从 1558 年到 1603 年，伊丽莎白一世作为女王统治着英格兰和爱尔兰。同时她也被认为是法国的女王，尽管她的管辖范围并不包括那里。她是都铎王朝第五位，也是最后一位统治者。她终身未婚，因此也被称为"童贞女王"。

伊丽莎白一世统治时期被称为伊丽莎白时代。在其统治下，许多伟大成就应运而生：莎士比亚的戏剧创作，弗朗西斯·德雷克爵士的环球旅行，以及英国人对北美的殖民统治。伊丽莎白一世逝世后不久，英国在美洲建立了以弗吉尼亚为名的殖民地。使用这一名称便是为了纪念这位童贞女王。

6. Ⓐ

草履虫

草履虫是一种有机生物，因其身体形状像草鞋底而得名。草履虫是单细胞纤毛科生物的代表，该科生物因全身被类似尾巴的纤毛覆盖而得名。这些纤毛便是它们细小的翼，它们通过不断摆动纤毛来运动。草履虫有一个深深凹入细胞内的"口沟"，它也被纤毛覆盖着，相当于"嘴巴"，帮助草履虫排水。草履虫通常生活在淡水水域，尤其是有浮垢的地方。它们喜酸性环境。

Practice with Long Passages

Ⓐ　　**1. Ⓒ**　　**2. Ⓒ**　　**3. Ⓑ**　　**4. Ⓑ**

¹ Absolute / ² Symbolic / ³ Constitutional

欧洲的君主制

君主制是指由一人担当国家最高统治者的政体形式。它是世界上最古老的政体形式之一。最高统治者通常是国王或者女王，但也可以是首领、皇帝，或者另有其他称谓。在日本等一些国家，君主只不过是一个象征、一个没有实权的傀儡罢了；而在另外一些国家，君主却掌握着相当大的权力。目前，世界上共有 29 个国家实行君主制。

世袭君主制是最常见的一种继位方式，世界上大部分君主制国家均采用这种形式。如此一来，所有的国王及女王均来自同一家族。由同一个家族统治的时代叫做一个王朝。王冠在家族成员间传递下去。世袭制具有稳定性高、延续时间长、可预测的优点。同时，对家族的热爱和忠诚也是维持其稳定的因素之一。

多个世纪以来，大多数欧洲国家都实行君主制。英国、丹麦以及挪威至今仍沿用君主立宪制。在君主立宪制中，国王或者女王的统治必须建立在其本人遵守国家宪法的基础之上。这种政体形式极大地限制了君主的权力。

英格兰在 17 世纪成为君主立宪制国家。当时的国王查理一世签订了一份协议，协议规定：只有在议会通过的前提下，国王才有权征收新税、颁布新的法规或者发动战争。但是，协议签完之后，查理一世对其置若罔闻，并试图掌控所有实权。后来，他因叛国罪被送上断头台。至此，君主立宪制的时代拉开了序幕。

沙俄帝国是欧洲的一个完全君主制国家。第一任统治者是出身于罗曼诺夫家族的彼得一世。他在 1682 年成为沙皇。"沙皇"是俄语，意为皇帝。罗曼诺夫家族对沙俄的统治直至 1917 年的俄国二月革命才被人民推翻。当时在位的沙皇——尼古拉斯二世，被迫放弃王位。1918 年，尼古拉斯二世及其家族被行刑队枪决。

B   1. Ⓐ   2. Ⓓ   3. Ⓑ   4. Ⓑ

[1] Hard energy path / [2] Soft energy path

可替代能源

矿物燃料是引发诸多环境问题的元凶。其造成的严重污染直接导致了全球变暖。并且，由其引发的争夺油田的战争接连不断。作为一种不可再生能源，它终有枯竭的一天。而能源危机的到来必将引发社会问题。

那么，太阳能能否完全替代矿物燃料呢？尽管太阳能清洁、安全并且价格低廉，但是用它替代矿物燃料的想法却完全不切实际。就目前的情况来看，太阳能电池技术仍不够发达，太阳能电池也不够可靠。它们在阴雨天及夜晚会完全失效。同时，它们占据了大量的空间，却难以制造出足够的能量。

软能源是一种替代矿物燃料的不错选择，使用它就相当于保护能源。相对于有害且不可再生的硬能源（其中包括矿物燃料和核能），软能源指的是可再生并且环保的能源，包括太阳能、风能、生物能及地热能。

软能源有众多支持者。他们认为，解决能源问题的根本在于运用新方法开发能源。第一步便是实施对硬能源技术的保护；其次，随着软能源技术的发展，会有更多新型软能源投入使用。

但是，有评论家指出，这一举措将影响所有的能源生产。他们指出了矿物燃料的重要性及其使用对工业的益处，并希望尽可能多地控制石油生产。

加拿大、瑞典等国家目前正在实施软能源计划。加拿大正在逐步减少对汽油的依赖。若干年之后，加拿大国内所有汽油将含有生物能源的成分。瑞典也已表态，要在 2020 年以前将石油使用率减少 40%。

C   1. Ⓐ   2. Ⓒ   3. Ⓓ   4. Ⓐ

[1] Nickname / [2] Tom Wills / [3] August 7, 1858 / [4] How to Play the Game

澳式橄榄球史

澳式橄榄球有许多不同的昵称。其球迷仅仅称其为"橄榄球"或者"footy"。与其他形式的橄榄球相区别，它被称为"澳式橄榄球"或者"AFL"。AFL 即澳式橄榄球联赛，是澳大利亚最著名的联赛。

汤姆·威尔斯在 1858 年发明了澳式橄榄球。他发明这项运动的初衷是希望板球球员能够在冬季保持身体健康。他向一份体育杂志致信说明了自己的意向并呼吁开办一个橄榄球俱乐部。1858 年，威尔斯与其他球员进行了一场实验性的比赛——那是历史上第一场澳式橄榄球比赛。然而，人们对这场比赛的细节却知之甚少。

1858 年 8 月 7 日，发生了两件对这项运动至关重要的大事。首先，世界上最早的橄榄球俱乐部之一——墨尔本橄榄球俱乐部成立了。另外，墨尔本文法学校和苏格兰学院之间进行了一场举世闻名的橄榄球比赛，由汤姆·威尔斯担任裁判。同年 8 月 21 号，双方又进行了第二次较量，然后是第三次；一直到 9 月 4 日进行决赛。从此以后，这两个学校每年都会组织橄榄球比赛。

澳式橄榄球参赛双方各 18 名队员，比赛场地为同样适用于板球比赛的椭圆形赛场，长约 185 米。这几乎是其他形式橄榄球比赛场地的 4 倍。

当球越过得分线并且落在高柱与侧柱之间时，得 1 分。当球在落入两个高柱之间时碰到了任何一个队员的某一部位，也可得 1 分。落入两个高柱之间得 6 分，落入高柱和侧柱之间得 1 分。

D   1. Ⓐ   2. Ⓒ   3. Ⓑ   4. Ⓑ

[1] the human genome / [2] 1990 / [3] liver and Alzheimer's disease

人类基因组计划

人类基因组计划（HGP）是一个重大科研项目。它旨在绘制出人类所有的基因图谱和基因序列。人类基因一共有 30 亿个遗传密码。尽管它们已经全部被识别出，但仍需进一步排序。而基因组计划同时也会识别出所有现存基因。

1986 年，查尔斯·德里斯首次提出了国际基因组计划。1987 年的一份报告中指出："该计划的最终目的是了解人类的染色体组。对人类染色体组的认知在医药学及其他保健科学中的作用，同人类解剖学对现阶段医药发展的作用一样重要。"

这项耗资 30 亿美元，预期历时 15 年的项目在 1990 年正式启动。全世界的遗传学家都参与了这次国际合作。

最近有媒体报道，人体基因组图谱已全部绘制完成。但是，就 2006 年来讲，还不能说全部完成。如此一来，这个项目耗费的时间已远超出预期。每一条染色体的中间部分都是高度繁琐的 DNA 序列。正因如此，仅凭目前的技术水平，对其进行排序具有很大难度。

目前，92% 的基因组图已绘制完成。随着绘图技术的发展，这项任务会变得越来越容易，并很有希望在不久的将来圆满完成。

一张清晰的基因组图能给医生提供很多有用信息，进而推动医学的发展。它对乳腺癌的早期诊断有着不可估量的推动作用。同时，它也会提高我们对肝病及老年痴呆症的医治能力。

分析基因组为人类进化研究开辟新道路奠定了基础。人类 DNA 顺序图目前存储在一个叫做"基因库"的网上数据库中，供所有人自由浏览。

E　1. Ⓑ　2. Ⓐ, Ⓓ　3. Ⓒ　4. Ⓐ

[1] disadvantaged youths / [2] crimes / [3] die or desert (run away)

黑帮与暴力

许多来自底层社会的年轻人会加入黑帮。帮指的是有着共同身份的一群人。一些人类学家认为，帮是人类历史上最早的组织形式之一，他们通常与犯罪活动有关。

来自低收入贫困家庭的年轻人倾向于加入街头黑帮。然而，一些来自中上层社会的人则会选择加入组织严格的犯罪团伙，例如黑手党。

黑帮通常在一个城市或者郊区有自己的势力范围。在行话中被称为"地盘"。在其势力范围内最常见的犯罪活动便是"收取保护费"。这是最常见的一种敲诈方法，即一个黑帮收取当地居民的保护费，以保证其免受该黑帮内部成员的威胁。

从 20 世纪 70 年代开始，许多黑帮开始贩卖毒品。其中以纯可卡因最为危险。与此同时，他们也会实施入室盗窃、盗车以及持枪抢劫。

匪徒，通常指的是黑帮中的个体成员。一些人在青少年时便加入黑帮成为匪徒。一般来说，这是由过早接触毒品和暴力所致。低收入家庭及贫困社区是黑帮存在并迅速发展的摇篮。

新加入的成员有时需要接受"欢迎礼"。此时，其他黑帮成员会殴打新成员以检验其献身精神和忠诚度。有时，新成员还需要先进行抢劫、强奸或谋杀等犯罪活动才得以加入黑帮。

一旦加入黑帮，想要退出，只有两种方法。一种是死，一种是逃离组织。但是这种逃离组织的行为通常会招致来自黑帮其他成员的杀身之祸。

黑帮成员的寿命通常很短。正因如此，道德早已被置之脑后。暴力犯罪行为并不是一种禁忌，而是一种在帮内赢得尊重和威望的方式。

F　1. Ⓒ　2. Ⓒ　3. Ⓓ　4. Ⓐ

[1] mass produced items / [2] middle class / [3] locally produced materials

美国工匠式建筑

美国工匠式建筑是盛行于 20 世纪前 30 年的一种建筑设计类型。它改变了美国的建筑风格。

工匠式风格最早产生于欧洲。19 世纪 60 年代时，英国艺术式和工匠式崭露头角。其独特的设计旨在提高普通百姓的地位。相较于批量生产的物品来说，人们更喜欢手工制品。但是这种英式风格依然是维多利亚女王时代的产物，并且仅是富豪们的专有物。

1897 年，一群波士顿的建筑学家将这种手工制造风格引入了美国。他们举办了一场手工制品展览，取得了巨大成功。他们由此看到了手工制品的发展潜力，并于 1897 年 6 月 28 号成立了工艺协会。该协会的口号是"鼓励发展更高水平的手工艺"。

在维多利亚时代末期，美国风格开始崛起。它强调手工技术，非常重视原创性和简约性。本地材料和手工制品的质量也不容忽视。这些特点都旨在使中产阶级平庸的住所更显尊贵。

这些简约的工艺品都是用当地生产的玻璃和木材制成的，显得极为典雅。金属制品是维多利亚时期阔绰生活的体现。越来越多批量生产的房屋建筑材料遭到人们的摒弃。美国工匠式建筑往往线条简洁，结构坚固，并尽可能多地使用天然材料。

这种工艺风格改变了许多美国中产阶级家庭。工艺家们为没有佣人的家庭设计了新的室内格局，这也成为新型中产阶级的一个特征。厨房由"幕后"走向"台前"。另一个进步是早餐厅的设计。这个新创造出的地方使得一家人可以在任何时候都有地方碰头。

另外，莎克和米申家具是受到工匠式的启发而产生的，美国工匠式建筑也引领了 20 世纪 30 年代的装饰艺术运动。

Building Summary Skills

1. Monarchy in Europe

Monarchy is a form of [1] government in which there is [2] a single ruler. Some forms of monarchy are symbolic, absolute, and constitutional. In a symbolic monarchy, the ruler has [3] no power. In an absolute monarchy, the ruler has [4] total power. In a constitutional monarchy, the ruler must follow [5] the laws of the constitution.

2. Alternative Energy Sources

[1] Fossil fuels cause many problems, such as [2] pollution and wars. But [3] solar cell technology is not currently advanced enough to replace fossil fuels. Many proponents say societies should adopt the [4] soft energy path. This is a plan for reducing [5] fossil fuel consumption while adopting new clean energy technologies as they emerge. Some countries are already adopting the soft energy path.

3. The History of Australian Rules Football

[1] Australian Rules Football is a popular game in Australia. It was created by [2] Tom Wills in [3] 1858. The game went through many steps before it became popular. It is played between two teams of 18 on [4] a cricket field. A goal is worth [5] six points, and a "behind" is worth one point.

4. The Human Genome Project

The Human Genome Project is an important effort to [1] identify and sequence the human genome. After working on it for over [2] fifteen years, the project is still [3] incomplete. But this project is so important that it must be completed. Once completed, [4] knowledge of the genome will lead to many advances in [5] medicine.

5. Gangs and Violence

Many young people from [1] poor homes join street gangs. The gangs offer them [2] a violent and short life. The life of a gang member is filled with [3] crime and drugs. The only way to escape the gang lifestyle is to [4] die or desert the gang forever. The gang lifestyle ignores [5] morality.

6. The American Craftsman Style

The American Craftsman style was the American version of [1] the British Arts and Crafts Movement. It was brought to North America by [2] prominent architects. This movement sought to create a [3] unique, simple, and elegant American style of home. It introduced many design changes to [4] middle-class homes of the time. This style [5] influenced a later style as well.

Mini TOEFL iBT

1. Ⓑ   2. Ⓑ   3. Ⓐ   4. Ⓓ   5. Ⓒ
6. The Great Man Argument Ⓐ, Ⓓ, Ⓕ /
   The Black Plague Theory Ⓑ, Ⓔ
7. Ⓑ   8. Ⓓ   9. Ⓒ   10. Ⓒ   11. Ⓐ   12. Ⓑ

意大利文艺复兴时期的艺术

文艺复兴时期是欧洲中世纪之后，宗教改革运动之前的一段历史时期，大约从 14 世纪一直持续到 16 世纪。

文艺复兴的主要特点是艺术技法方面的革新。意大利是这些革新的聚焦点，而弥漫着古典文化气息的佛罗伦萨就成为这场启蒙运动的中心。艺术家们一直渴望振兴雅典和罗马的共和理想。

鲁切拉曾写道：他属于一个伟大的时代。列奥纳多·布鲁尼在《佛罗伦萨颂歌》中也表达过类似的情感。

雕塑艺术在这一时期有了很大进步。雕塑家运用了一些经典主题的罗马模型，并创作出大量展示人类尊严的裸体雕塑。

绘画艺术同样繁荣发展，乔托和弗拉·安吉利科等艺术家对此作出了突出贡献。由于当时的教会是这些艺术家的主要客户，所以他们的作品几乎都与宗教有关，但也有一些简单的象征性主题的作品。

艺术家一般都会用神话和宗教来表达主题。例如，他们有时会借助《圣经》中亚当和夏娃的形象来表现裸体的男性和女性，这也使其能在道义上被接受。一片无花果叶常被用来遮住人物的性器官。

透视画法的应用也逐渐风靡起来。绘画作品第一次成为透视空间的窗口，这也加强了建筑物作品的真实感。透视画法带动了画家使用更为统一的创作元素。

印刷机也是在这一时期发明的，这促进了柏拉图和亚里士多德的许多人文哲学类书籍的印刷和普及，也造就了文艺复兴的理性氛围。

关于文艺复兴运动兴起的原因有几种不同的说法。一种理论称，强大的梅迪奇家族引发了这场运动。他们资助了许多佛罗伦萨的艺术家。但是批评家指出，文艺复兴始于 15 世纪早期，而那时，梅迪奇家族还没有掌控权势。

另一种理论被称为"伟人"理论。这种理论说，是艺术家个人的才华点燃了这个伟大的时代。多纳泰罗、伯鲁乃列斯基等伟大的艺术家带动了其他的艺术家。佛罗伦萨的艺术家们是站在列奥纳多·达·芬奇和米开朗基罗的肩膀上的。但是这个说法却无法直接解释为什么这些天才的艺术家与其他任何时期的艺术家不同。

另一个是"黑死病"理论。14世纪，三分之一的欧洲人死于黑死病，上至国王、牧师，下至穷苦百姓，都不能幸免。在这场灾难面前，基督信仰没有使任何人得到保护。这动摇了基督教徒的世界观，人们开始更多地思考现世，而不是来生。

法国大革命

法国大革命是西方文明史上的一个重要时期。在此期间，法国的君主专制被共和政府所取代。同时，罗马天主教会也被迫放弃了许多权力。

革命结束后的75年里，法国仍然在共和国、君主制帝国间摇摆不定。但是，这一时期也成为法国最终进入民主制的重要转折时期。

革命的爆发有许多政治、社会、经济原因。旧的统治者毁于自己统治的僵化。与此同时，受启蒙运动的影响，崛起的中产阶级与工人和穷人结为同盟。

在革命爆发前的几个月，法国国内食物短缺。面包的价格已经高到普通工人难以承受的程度；失业率直线上升；很多人冒着被斩首的危险去偷盗。而路易十六却没能有效地解决这些问题。

随着革命的发展，国王对部下展开了大规模的血腥杀戮。整个国家陷入了债务危机。而这也直接导致了赋税的激增。

此时，路易十六企图关闭国民大会。因此，国民大会在一个网球场上召开了会议并宣誓在法国宪法出台之前决不休息。

1789年7月11日，路易国王要驱逐改良大臣内克尔，此举引起了众多巴黎市民的公开暴动。7月14日，他们攻占巴士底狱并杀死了狱长。随后，他们放出所有囚犯并杀死了巴黎市长。他们威胁国王，使他同意签署一份协议，为人民颁布一部宪法，以此为条件暂时保证他的安全。

巴黎革命中"自由、平等、博爱，或死亡！"的口号一直沿用至今。它已成为所有试图推翻暴政的人民的团结口号。

与此同时，法国的贵族们也自身难保。一些人穿着仆人的衣服掩饰自己的真实身份；另一些人干脆逃出法国。各地发生着翻天覆地的变化——市镇已经丧失了征税的权力，而教会也失去了大部分势力和土地。

1793年，路易十六因"密谋危害公众自由与安全"的罪名被判死刑。1月21日，他被送上了断头台。同年10月16日，皇后玛丽·安托瓦内特也步其后尘。

1795年，新的宪法最终被颁布。它确立了一个名为督政府的、由500名代表构成的新的立法机关。与此同时，一位名叫拿破仑·波拿巴的将军赢得了越来越多的威望。1799年，他发动政变。五年之后，他自命为皇帝。至此，法国大革命的共和国阶段宣告结束。

Vocabulary Review

A 1. Ⓑ 2. Ⓓ 3. Ⓒ 4. Ⓓ
5. Ⓑ 6. Ⓐ 7. Ⓒ 8. Ⓑ

B 1. h 2. c 3. a 4. i 5. g
6. j 7. d 8. b 9. f 10. e

Unit 2 Reference

Skill & Drill

1. Ⓑ

雾的形成

雾是指与地面接触的云状物。雾与其他云状物的唯一区别在于，它与地球表面相接触。大多数雾在地面相对湿度达到100%时形成。雾可以骤然形成，而且根据露点温度不同，它的消散也可快可慢。蒸发雾和降水雾是雾的两种类型。前者由汽化引起；后者则源于降水。

位于加拿大纽芬兰省的大浅滩是世界上最多雾的地方。来自北部的拉布拉多寒流和来自南部的墨西哥湾暖流在该地交汇，从而形成此处多雾的特性。

2. Ⓐ

蜻蜓

蜻蜓是昆虫的一种。硕大的复眼使它具有360度的视野。同时，它有着舒展的身体和两对透明且有力的翅膀。

蜻蜓一般以蚊子、苍蝇和其他小昆虫为食。以害虫为食的习性也使其受到人类的喜爱。它们生活在湖泊、池塘、小溪或者湿地附近。它们的幼虫，也称为若虫，是水生的。

从卵到成虫死亡，蜻蜓的一个生命周期一般会持续6个月到6、7年不等。但其中大部分时间是处于若虫形态。在这一阶段，若虫通过腮呼吸并且以蝌蚪或鱼类为食。

3. Ⓑ

生态学

生态学主要研究生物及其栖息地，即研究物种生存在特定地域的原因及某一地域能够存活的物种个数。同时，生态学还研究物种之间的相互作用。

生物的生存环境包括各种自然因素，例如日照、天气以及地质等。同一栖息地的其他生物也是影响因素之一。

生态学的范围很广。行为生态学就是其中的分支之一，主要研究单个生物对其栖息地的适应性。另一个分支是研究单一生物物种的种群生态学。生态学还有许多其他分支。

4. Ⓒ

假设

假设是指针对一个科学尚未解决的事件所提出的联想性的解释。它通过推理的方式联想两个或两个以上现象之间可能存在的联系。科学家一般将假设建立在观察或理论的基础上。

科学的方法要求验证假设。但是科学界许多专家认为，假设也可能被证明为错。

一个经典的假设是：某人到了一个新的国家，只看到了白色的羊，因此他假设这个国家所有的羊都是白色的。但是，如果出现一只黑羊，这个假设就会被证明是错的。

5. Ⓑ

牛顿运动定律

牛顿运动定律是三个物理学定律。为了理解第一定律，假设桌上放着一个苹果，如果不推它，它就一直保持静止。

对于第二定律，假设用手轻轻推动同一个苹果，令其移动一小段距离；如果此时加大力量用手猛击它，这一击产生的冲力将会使苹果沿施力方向撞到墙上。

苹果撞到墙上时的反作用可作为牛顿第三定律的例子。每一个作用力都存在与之等量反向的反作用力。在这个例子中，反作用力可能造成的结果是——墙被撞出一个坑或者苹果被撞烂。

6. Ⓑ

生物界

1735 年，卡罗勒斯·林尼厄斯出版了一本关于生物界的书。书中，他把生物划分为两大生物界——动物界和植物界。世间万物，必能归入其一。不久之后，他又创造了第三界"无机物界"的概念。

许多年之后，人们发现了细菌。生物学家意识到，细菌不属于上述三类的任何一个。于是，生物学家为其专门创立了一个分类，命名为"原核生物界"。

随着科技的进步与发展及对生物认识的深入，人们不断需要创立新的分类。1969 年，罗伯特·惠特克为真菌创立了第五个生物界分类。1980 年，为了分离更加微小的有机体，人们又创立了一个分类。

Practice with Long Passages

A　**1.** Ⓐ　**2.** Ⓑ　**3.** Ⓒ　**4.** Ⓓ
¹ El Nino / ² La Nina

厄尔尼诺与拉尼娜现象

厄尔尼诺现象与拉尼娜现象是指在全球范围内，发生在大洋与大气间的现象。在太平洋的热带区域，海水表面的水温会有明显变化。在温度变化能维持 5 个月以上的前提下，水温上涨幅度大于等于 0.5 摄氏度的现象称为厄尔尼诺；水温下降幅度大于等于 0.5 摄氏度的现象称为拉尼娜。

受该气候变化影响的主要是南美和非洲的第三世界国家。这些国家的经济主要依赖于农业和渔业，它们是国家食品供应、国内就业、对外贸易的主要来源。因此，如果能采取新的方法来预测这两种气候变化，必将对这些国家的社会经济产生巨大影响。

厄尔尼诺现象与拉尼娜现象的发生没有规律可循。近些年来，它们的发生周期为 2 至 7 年不等并持续 1 到 2 年。厄尔尼诺现象的影响很广。许多地区会因此出现反常天气。一些地方甚至因为强降雨而遭遇可怕的洪灾；长时间干旱也造成了一些地区的森林大火。而另一方面，拉尼娜现象的影响也在全世界范围内逐渐扩大。拉尼娜现象发生时，信风风力会大增，并且，太平洋中部和东部会产生比通常温度低的寒流。

在通常的太平洋海洋大气循环系统中，赤道风首先聚集，然后暖流会汇合并向西流去，寒流会沿着南美洲海岸上涨，由于鱼类会跟随富含营养的寒流，这就会将一部分鱼带向海岸，从而促进当地的渔业。

当厄尔尼诺现象开始发挥作用时，暖流会流向南美洲海岸。由于冷水的缺失，海水会变暖。如此一来，鱼类非但没有被带向海岸，反而被重新带回了海洋中，这就会严重破坏当地的渔业。

虽然厄尔尼诺现象与拉尼娜现象的起因仍不明确，但是众多科学家正致力于更加深入地去了解这种全球气候现象。

B　**1.** Ⓑ　**2.** Ⓒ　**3.** Ⓑ　**4.** Ⓒ
¹ Threats / ² Effects / ³ Decline

生物种类的衰减

生物多样性是指一个地区生物种类的范围。在过去的

100 年间，科学家见证了生物多样性的大幅衰减。这对于地球的管家——人类来说，是巨大的损失。

研究表明，目前有 1/8 的植物物种濒临灭绝。据估计，每年约有 14 万种植物物种灭绝。其中许多植物本可以被用来制造药物，抗击疾病。而它们的灭绝，是由不可持续发展的生态实践造成的。

在过去的几千年间，大部分物种的灭绝都是人类造成的。其中最主要的原因就是对热带雨林的乱砍滥伐。这些生物的栖息地被开辟成牧场放养食用牛，开垦成农田种植用来做面包的小麦，或建成果园种植水果来满足人们的消费需求。

外来物种的引进是另一个威胁。当一个外来物种侵入某个生物栖息地时，它们会试图不断壮大自己的物种数量，因此威胁到该地原有物种的生存。这些外来物种可能是捕食者，也可能是寄生者，或者干脆就是侵略者。它们夺走了当地生物的营养。因为当地生物没有机会进化，它们总是缺少防御，所以根本无法与外来物种抗衡。

地球上的物种非常丰富，这仅仅是源于海洋这一难以逾越的障碍。然而，由于人类发明了船和飞机，物种便有了接触的可能。人们不顾其适应性，不断将不同地域的物种进行结合。如此一来，地球的生态系统将会迅速被一少部分侵略型的超级物种所占据。

为了解决这些问题，人类需要最大限度地减少消耗。要减少对牛肉及其他会破坏自然环境的产品的消费。另外，针对破坏自然资源以及引进外来物种的行为，政府应制定严格的法律。

C 1. ⓒ 2. Ⓐ 3. Ⓑ 4. Ⓑ

¹ electricity / ² nuclear power / ³ the Rance Tidal Power Plant

潮汐发电站

潮汐能可以用来发电。海潮推动海水运动时所产生的大量能量都被潮汐发电系统利用起来。这种方法的生态效应仍有待商榷，目前全球只有少量潮汐发电站正被人们使用。然而，许多国家政府已经将建设更多的潮汐发电站提上日程。其中，美国、墨西哥、加拿大三国计划建造 8 座。

世界上第一个潮汐发电站是位于法国布列塔尼大区拉朗斯河上的拉朗斯潮汐发电站。建造该发电站就必须将周围地区的水抽干。两个水坝在两年间建成。

1963 年 7 月 20 日，发电站的建造正式开始。此时，拉朗斯河已经完全被两座水坝阻隔住。发电站于 1966 年竣工。1967 年 12 月 4 日，拉朗斯潮汐发电站成功与法国国家电力网络连接。该发电站的建造耗资 5 亿 2 千 4 百万欧元，它向布列塔尼大区供给 3% 的用电量。这项工程耗资巨大，但这笔花费不是没有回报的。潮汐发电站发电的成本要小于核能发电。

发电站的水坝导致泥沙不断淤积，对拉朗斯河流域的生态系统产生了影响。玉筋鱼和欧鲽已经绝迹，海鲈和墨鱼返回河中。潮水依然涌入河口。发电站的操作人员也一直试图将其对生态的影响降至最低。

北美第一座也是唯一一座潮汐发电站是位于加拿大安纳波利斯罗亚尔的安纳波利斯潮汐发电站。这座发电站建于 1984 年，其目的是寻求新的发电方式。但它也改变了当地的环境——当地的水质及气温均有所变化。此外，泥沙的沉积形式发生了改变，河坝两旁的河岸有所延长。

D 1. ⓒ 2. Ⓑ 3. Ⓐ 4. Ⓐ

¹ Largest lizard / ² Indonesian islands / ³ 6,000

科莫多巨蜥

科莫多巨蜥是世界上尚存的最大的蜥蜴。其体长通常为 2 至 3 米。野生的成年科莫多巨蜥重 70 公斤左右，它是巨蜥家族中的一员。

科莫多巨蜥生活在印度尼西亚的众多群岛上。1910 年，欧洲首次报道发现了科莫多巨蜥。1912 年，爪哇岛茂物的动物学博物馆馆长彼得·欧文斯发表了一篇关于这种动物的论文，使人们对其有了更广泛的认识。1980 年，科莫多国家公园成立，以协助保护科莫多巨蜥种群。

科莫多巨蜥是食肉动物。尽管它们喜食动物尸体，但也捕食活物。捕食时，它们先悄悄接近目标，然后突然发起进攻。此时，其速度能达到每小时 20 千米以上。

科莫多巨蜥不分泌毒液，但其牙齿上寄生着 50 多种细菌。如果第一次咬杀猎物没能成功，猎物也会因致命的细菌感染而在一周之内丧命。然后科莫多巨蜥会沿着味道找到猎物并将其吃掉。

科莫多巨蜥在幼年时经常会借助其巨大的爪子爬到树上，避免被成年蜥蜴吃掉。但当它们长大后，利爪则主要被用做武器。

科莫多巨蜥的捕猎范围很广，包括野猪、山羊、鹿和水牛。在野外，人们也观察到它们捕食小蜥蜴。有时，它们也吃人和人类的尸体。在过去的 100 年间，已有超过 12 人被其咬伤致死。

科莫多巨蜥是濒危物种，目前世界上仅存大约 6000 只。5 月到 8 月是它们的交配季节，9 月为产卵期。为了使得受到保护，雌性蜥蜴将卵产至地下或树洞中，通常它们一次产卵 20 个左右。科莫多巨蜥从出生到成年一般需要 5 年，其寿命能够达到 30 年。

E 1. ⓒ 2. Ⓓ 3. Ⓐ 4. ⓒ

¹ Uses / ² Risks

纳米技术

纳米技术是应用科学的一个新领域。人们利用它成功研制出了以纳米为单位的微型机器。纳米是测量单位，代表10^{-9}米。人们用它来描述非常小的东西。

纳米技术在现代科技中实际应用的一个例子便是以分子结构为基础的聚合物的形成。另一个实例是以表面科学为基础的电脑芯片板的设计。

在纳米状态下，许多物质的属性会发生变化。例如，铜会由不透明体变为透明体；固态金在常温下会变为液态；硅等绝缘体会变成导体。所有这些变化都有潜在的风险。

因为其状态的改变，纳米粒子会变得更加活跃，并更容易与其他物质发生反应。纳米粒子可通过被吸入、吞食、由皮肤吸收和注射四种途径进入人体。一旦它们进入人体，就会变得异常活跃。

事实上，人们尚未完全了解这些粒子在生物体内如何发生反应。但是科学家猜测，这些微粒能轻易使生物的免疫细胞超负荷工作，从而降低生物体对疾病的抵御能力。人类非常容易失去对这种小颗粒的控制，而这很有可能引发大规模的流行病，导致疾病和死亡的蔓延。

纳米技术的另一个隐患是其给环境带来的风险。一项报告详述了它可能带来的灾难——地球将被一种灰色黏稠物质所笼罩。而这是由一种能控制自己的纳米机器人引起的。它们会通过无限制的自我复制而最终引发灾难。

因此，科学家在获准制造纳米机器人之前，需要收集尽可能多的资料。而纳米机器人的生产，也应受法律的严格控制——只有获得批准的科学家才有权进行安全的试验。

F 1. Ⓐ 2. Ⓒ 3. Ⓓ 4. Ⓐ
[1] November 11, 1933 / [2] May 11, 1934 /
[3] April 14, 1935

尘暴

尘暴，指的是 20 世纪 30 年代中后期，发生在美国与加拿大中部的一系列沙尘暴。大面积干旱和几十年来错误的耕种方法是导致尘暴的元凶。耕地时的除草造成大平原上肥沃土壤的裸露。

干旱时节，土地沙化，变成尘土被吹走。尘土在风的作用下形成大片黑云向东移动，致使一路直至芝加哥的天空都呈现黑色。最终，尘土被吹入太平洋中，造成土壤流失。

尘暴始于 1934 年，一直持续到 1939 年。1933 年 11 月 11 日，一场猛烈的沙尘暴刮走了久经干旱的南达科他州农田的表层土壤。而这只是当年多场灾难性沙尘暴中的一场。

1934 年 5 月 11 日，一场持续了两天的强沙尘暴席卷了大平原，带走了大量表层土壤，这是尘暴中破坏性最强的一场。这些尘雾再一次一路移至芝加哥。污垢落在这座城市中，像下雪一样。

1935 年 4 月 14 日被称为黑色星期天。尘暴中最可怕

的"黑色暴风雪"在这一天降临。它将白昼变为黑夜，造成了巨大的损失。目击者称，他们当时甚至看不见距离自己5 英尺的东西。

由于大量草皮因种植小麦而遭到破坏，数百万公顷的表层土壤被风吹走。野牛群也无法给原有的草地施肥。这场生态灾难迫使很多居民从得克萨斯州、阿肯色州、俄克拉何马州以及大平原周边迁出，从而导致超过 50 万的美国人无家可归。他们其中多数移居西部寻找工作。尽管他们并不都是俄克拉何马州人，但依然被称为"俄克拉何马州民（Okies）"。

Building Summary Skills

1. El Nino and La Nina

El Nino and La Nina are major [1] temperature changes that affect a large portion of the world's climate. The economies of many nations in [2] South America and Africa are strongly affected by these climate changes. El Nino and La Nina occur [3] irregularly and can cause some damaging effects such as [4] drought, flooding, and forest fires. These changes also affect the [5] migratory patterns of fish, which affects the fishing industry. Scientists do not fully understand El Nino and La Nina yet, but they are studying them very closely.

2. The Decline of Biodiversity

[1] Biodiversity, which describes the range of [2] living things, has been declining rapidly over the past century. Many species of plants are becoming extinct because of [3] unsustainable environmental practices. Humans are the biggest cause of these environmental problems, mainly because they chop down so much of the [4] rain forests. Another threat to biodiversity is the introduction of [5] foreign species, which overtake local species. Humans need to take strong steps to stop the decline of biodiversity.

3. Tidal Power Plants

Tidal power plants are a method of [1] generating electricity through the power of [2] moving water and are gaining popularity around the world. The Rance Tidal Power Plant in France is the world's first power plant that uses this method. The construction of the Rance Tidal Power Plant took a lot of [3] time and money, but it has generated enough power to cover its costs. Tidal power plants do affect the [4] local ecosystem, and scientists are still studying how. The first and only tidal power plant in North America is in [5] Annapolis Royal in Canada.

4. The Komodo Dragon

Komodo dragons are the [1] largest living lizards in the world today. They live on [2] the islands of Indonesia. They eat meat, which they kill by a bite that [3] infects the prey and kills it over a period of days. Komodo dragons eat a wide range of other animals, including [4] their own species. Today, the [5] population of Komodo dragons is not very large.

5. Nanotechnology

[1] Nanotechnology is the risky science of building [2] microscopic machines. This technology could be very useful, but it is [3] unpredictable since the properties of many materials change at the microscopic level. Some scientists worry that machines this small could easily enter [4] human bodies and cause effects that nobody can predict. Another concern is that [5] self-replicating nanobots could damage the environment on a very large and unexpected scale. Experiments with nanotechnology should be done in a very cautious fashion as regulated by the government.

6. The Dust Bowl

The Dust Bowl was [1] a series of terrible storms in the 1930s that damaged the farming industries in [2] America and Canada. Farming was damaged because the fertile layer of topsoil was [3] blown away by powerful winds, leaving only [4] dusty, infertile ground. Some of these storms were so bad that the sky was turned black and no one could see the sun. Many farmers were made homeless by this [5] natural disaster and were forced to travel west looking for work.

Mini TOEFL iBT

1. Ⓑ 2. Ⓓ 3. Ⓒ 4. Ⓒ 5. Ⓐ
6. Ⓑ 7. Ⓐ 8. Ⓑ 9. Ⓐ 10. Ⓑ
11. Ⓓ 12. Ⓒ

气象学

气象学主要研究地球的大气现象，包括观测天气变化并对其进行预测和解释。这些气象变化主要受包括气温、气压、水蒸气在内的大气因素的影响。这些因素相互作用，构成各种气象模式。

公元前350年，亚里士多德创造了"气象学"这个词。他是观察并记录水分蒸发过程的第一人。他观察到，炽热的阳光将水变为雾；第二天，它又在冷空气的作用下回到地面。

1607年，伽利略制造了第一个测量温度的工具。数年之后，其助手发明了第一个气压计。1648年，帕斯卡尔发现了气压随海拔下降而下降的现象。同时他还猜测，大气层之上是真空层。

1667年，罗伯特·胡克发明了测量风速的仪器。不久之后，埃德蒙·黑利为水手绘制了信风地图。他同时推断，大气变化受日照影响。

20世纪，科学家开始理解越来越多重要的大气现象。其中最为重要的或许是，科学家掌握了地球自转对大气循环的影响。这个巨大的力叫做"科里奥利效应"。

1904年，一位挪威科学家表示，若以自然法则为前提，通过计算，我们是有可能预测天气的。这就为日后的天气预报奠定了基础。

20世纪50年代，电脑开始被应用于天气预测中。早期的电脑帮助天气预测员完成了很多实验。最早的天气预测应用了高温低温模型。

大约十年之后，人类发射了第一颗天气卫星。此举标志着全球性天气信息时代的到来。卫星已成为研究从森林大火到厄尔尼诺现象等各类问题的重要工具。它们令科学家对地球有了更深层的认识。

最近，科学家通过建立气象模型，比较往年的气象数据，将历史数据与现今的气象状况互相关联。这就为科学家研究长期的气象变化提供了依据。例如，全球变暖效应日前就得到了更好的解释。目前，功能强大的新型超级计算机的应用使建立大气流通模型成为可能。

许多人工天气预测方法也仍在使用。这些方法的应用主要依靠天气预测员的技术和判断。其中很多方法的准确率可达50%以上。

当今社会，许多人都依赖气象信息。这些信息不仅提高了农产品产量，还可以对自然灾害进行预测以减轻伤亡。人类对天气的准确预测能力，已达到了史无前例的程度。

花鼠

地球上数以百万计的物种中，每一种都在脆弱的地球生态系统中占有重要的位置。花鼠是一种生活在北美及亚洲森林中的小型啮齿类动物。它个头虽小，但对一个栖息地的生态健康有着至关重要的意义。花鼠一共有25种。其中绝大多数都有一个共同的特征——它们长着红棕色的毛，浑身布满黑白相间的花纹。

与众多啮齿类动物不同的是，花鼠一年中有两个繁殖期。第一个由二月至四月；第二个由六月至八月。花鼠平均一次生四个幼仔，但也有一窝至少一个，多至九个的情况。雌性花鼠将幼仔藏在地下的巢穴中直至六周之后它们能自立为止。它们的天敌包括猫、狗、隼、鹰、狐狸、郊狼和狼。野生花鼠的寿命通常只有一年，但也有活到五年的花鼠。

除了交配季节以外，花鼠多数时间独自修巢、觅食并躲避天敌。它们经常爬上树去觅食。

花鼠是传统的贮藏食物的动物。为了熬过漫长的冬季，它们会在春、夏季将各种坚果、种子、昆虫、浆果以及其他一些食物储藏进巢穴。其食物来源还包括菌类、鸟蛋、谷物和蠕虫。

花鼠的面颊是它们最显著的特征之一。花鼠头部两侧有特殊的颊囊，可以被拉伸，盛装食物。当颊囊被装满时，面颊每一边都会和花鼠的头一样大。这种能力使它们能轻松往返于洞穴运送大量食物。

像其他小型啮齿类动物一样，花鼠也被称为"播撒者"。它们能够播撒种子、真菌和其他植物。通常情况下，花鼠运往洞穴的食物总是会有一部分剩下或掉在路上。这些种子就开始生长，从而为该生物系统中的其他动物提供了更多的食物和掩护。

无论作为种子的播撒者还是其他动物的猎物，花鼠都是其栖息地生态系统的重要组成部分。它们是自然界不断进化的生物循环中的重要一环。

Vocabulary Review

A 1. ⒷＢ   2. ⒸＣ   3. ⒶＡ   4. ⒸＣ
      5. ⒹＤ   6. ⒷＢ   7. ⒶＡ   8. ⒹＤ
B 1. d   2. i   3. e   4. b   5. a
      6. c   7. j   8. f   9. h   10. g

Unit 3 · Factual Information

Skill & Drill

1. ⒸＣ

观点

观点是指持有者对某件重要的事所坚持的思想或理念。它并不是一个事实，故无对错之分。但是在美国联邦最高法院中，"观点"这个词却有另一层含义。在法律上，一个观点就是一项决议，它确立了一项法律在未来的执行手段。在 1971 年罗对韦德的案子中，法庭作出了堕胎合法的裁决。这项决议使美国的孕妇堕胎成为可能。而这也是一例引起争议的决议。法庭作出裁决之后，争议一直持续了很多年。

2. ⒶＡ

缝被

传统上，被褥是用来铺床的保暖效果最好的毯状物。但如今，许多被褥却成为艺术品，被挂在墙上进行展示。在殖民时期，大多数女性整日编织、制衣。但富有的女性则有时间缝制质量上乘的被褥，于是她们组织了"大家缝"活动。在婚礼或迎接新生儿的重大活动中，她们通常会利用刺绣技术将重要的日期或人名缝入被褥中以作纪念。她们还会将某人衣服的一角或者一面重要的旗帜缝入被褥中，作为历史记载。

3. ⒹＤ

药物史

1960 年，在一个史前人的陪葬品中发现了最早的药物存在的证据。在他的陪葬物中有八种不同的植物，它们的药用价值一直延续至今。在全世界不同的文化背景中，医药的发展也各不相同。在中国传统医术中，医生通过改变病人体内能量的流动治病。印度的医生则试图通过恢复病人身心和灵魂的协调来达到治疗的目的。西医最早产生于欧洲。欧洲的医生主要强调饮食结构和卫生对恢复健康的重要性。如今，随着科技的发展，世界也变小了，医生博采世界各地医药的精华来治病。

4. ⒷＢ

报刊业新闻工作

报刊业新闻工作可被划分为若干种，包括报纸、新闻杂志、大众杂志以及商业和业余爱好杂志。同时，它还包括业务通讯、私人出版物、新闻网页和博客。

报纸记者使用倒金字塔的写作结构。这种结构主要用于正统、严格的新闻报道而非专题报道。在写严肃的报道时，首先需要列出所有重要信息，而不需要过于重视文字修饰。当空间不够时，新闻中的故事成分可以全部被删去。专题报道的写作结构则比较自由。

Practice with Long Passages

A   1. ⒶＡ   2. ⒷＢ   3. ⒸＣ   4. ⒹＤ

¹ long distances / ² lighter than copper / ³ cheaper

光纤

　　光纤是由玻璃或塑料制成的细而透明的纤维。它们用于传送带有光和信息的光学信号。光纤广泛应用于通信系统。

　　研究光纤及其应用的学科叫做纤维光学。光纤利用全内反射的科学原理实现光信号的传播。根据该原理，由于光纤的外层厚于内层，所以光信号可以在光纤内部不断反射前进。

　　光纤的历史始于英国的维多利亚时期。那时的科学家应用全内反射原理为公共喷泉安装了光纤灯。20世纪中叶，光纤技术被应用于医学。医生发明了一种叫胃镜的工具以观察病人的胃部和肠道。1977年，电信公司开始利用光纤电缆传送远程电话信号。

　　过去，用于传送电子信号的主要是铜制电缆。但是，光纤凭借其优势变得更受欢迎。光纤在传送远程信号时损耗较小，并且比铜制电缆轻。7公斤的光纤与20吨铜制电缆的传输能力相当。这在航空领域具有很大用途。

　　光纤的唯一不足是在短程传输时，少量光缆的费用大于铜制电缆；并且它更难接合且无法在传送信号的同时传输能量。

　　在当今的计算机时代，人们对带宽的需求越来越大。因光纤能够远程传送大量的数据，光纤科学也变得更加有用了。

B　1. Ⓒ　2. Ⓑ　3. Ⓑ　4. Ⓐ

[1] Boston Massacre / [2] Boston Tea Party /
[3] Declaration of Independence

美国独立战争

　　美国独立战争结束了英国对美国的殖民统治。1776年，美利坚合众国建立。

　　美国独立战争源于思维观念的转变——美国人对英国的君主制政体不满。托马斯·杰斐逊和塞缪尔·亚当斯等先驱引导了新的思维方式。各个阶层的人们都希望在政府决策中拥有发言权。人们视不诚实为最大恶行，视公民道德为最高善行。一个人的家庭出身不再决定其社会地位。

　　三个事件所引发的暴动最终导致了独立战争的爆发。第一个事件是，1765年英国议会通过了《印花税法案》。该项税法要求对所有纸质商品征收税款以支持英国驻美军队。此举引起了殖民地人民的强烈不满，因为在此之前英国政府为了镇压当地人民已经征税充当军费开支。由此引发的越来越多的反抗最终使得该项税法被废除。

　　第二件大事发生在1767年。英国议会通过了《唐森德税法》，该项税法规定向玻璃、油画和纸张等物品征税。殖民地居民组织了针对这些商品的抵制运动，这引来了更多英军进入波士顿，一场暴力运动最终爆发。英军对暴动群众开枪致使五名居民丧生。这就是历史上的波士顿惨案。

　　第三个导致独立战争的事件发生在1773年。尽管当时的英国政府废除了《唐森德税法》，但是茶税依然被保留下来。一群愤怒的波士顿市民冲上一艘英国货船，将船上的所有茶叶倒入海中。这就是波士顿倾茶事件。

　　英国政府与美国殖民地人民的矛盾已达到不可调和的地步。1775年，战争在莱克星顿爆发。1776年，美国通过了《独立宣言》。1781年，战争结束，英国军队从美国撤出。

C　1. Ⓒ　2. Ⓓ　3. Ⓑ　4. Ⓐ

[1] the telegraph / [2] New York Times /
[3] Yellow journalism

19世纪的美国报纸业

　　1844年，电报被广泛应用。因此，报纸可以得到很远地方的新闻报道。一个名为美联社（AP）的新闻通讯社成立并开始收集各地新闻。因为每天都有新的报道，地方报纸业在全美发展起来。其中，纽约为报纸业的中心。

　　全美的报纸业进入了一个蓬勃发展的时期。这一状况一直持续到1861年美国内战爆发。在这段时间内，报纸业水平显著提高——印刷和运输方法得到完善；新闻撰写和报道也变得更加清楚、生动。在塞缪尔·鲍尔斯和霍勒斯·格里利等编辑的带领下，社论再一次盛行起来。当时，社论曾一度遭市民厌恶。大多数人认为它们只是政党的宣传工具。格里利通过社论成为了反对奴隶制的先锋人物。

　　1851年，亨利·J·雷蒙德基于对其他报纸的改进，创立了《纽约时报》。人们认为由格里利主编的《纽约论坛》过于政治化；而由詹姆斯·G·贝内特主编的《纽约先驱论坛报》又太过浮华，只注重卖出更多份报纸。而《纽约时报》既有新闻报刊所秉承的正直诚实，又不失视觉上的吸引力。它凭借自身脱俗的高品质成为全美最受欢迎的报纸。这一状况一直延续至今。

　　直到1895年，约瑟夫·普利策和威廉·伦道夫·赫斯特统治着媒介帝国。两人都在全美很多城市拥有报业。在纽约，普利策的《纽约世界》与赫斯特的《纽约日报》为争夺更多市场份额激烈竞争。然而，它们都因过于注重犯罪和死亡事件而受到谴责，人们认为它们在夸大头条以吸引读者的好奇心。这一行为后被称为"黄色新闻"。之所以称其为"黄色"，主要有两个原因。其一，二者都刊登了一个名为"黄孩儿"的流行卡通形象；其二，"黄色"这个词表示怯懦和虚伪。许多人认为，这个问题在当代新闻业中依然存在。

D　1. Ⓐ　2. Ⓒ　3. Ⓓ　4. Ⓑ

[1] Statue of Liberty / [2] Liberty Bell

自由女神像与自由钟

　　在美国，有两座不朽的建筑代表了这个国家对自由理想的尊崇。自由女神像与自由钟从两个不同的方面象征着自由——自由女神像为美国移民带来了自由的希望；而自由钟纪念了历史上美国人民为争取自由所作的斗争。

过去，当人们乘船靠近美国时，自由女神像是他们最先看到的建筑。它的高度超过45米，是1885年法国专门选在美国独立100周年纪念日时送给美国的礼物。

自由女神像用铜建造。其内部骨架由曾经设计了著名的以其名字命名的巴黎埃菲尔铁塔的古斯塔夫·埃菲尔完成。自由女神像坐落在纽约港的自由岛上。自由女神右手举着火炬，代表用其照亮美国大陆上的自由之路；左手紧握刻有1776字样的铭板，以此纪念1776年美国摆脱英国统治，宣布独立。人们可以进入雕塑内部。很多人喜欢爬上楼梯，进入女神的头部和火炬中。

自由钟坐落于宾夕法尼亚州的费城。它在1776年7月8号被敲响以召集市民聆听《独立宣言》的首次公开宣读，并因此闻名于世。1774年它也曾被敲响以宣布美国第一次大陆议会的召开。在自由钟的内部刻着《圣经·利未记》25章10节中的一段话——"在遍地给一切的居民宣告自由"。自由钟最初于1752年铸造完成。众所周知，1753年自由钟在第一次敲响时就破裂了。

1965年，美国联邦调查局侦破了一起企图破坏自由女神像和自由钟的恐怖主义活动，及时制止了这场破坏美国和平象征的恐怖袭击。

E　1.　Ⓓ　2.　Ⓐ　3.　Ⓑ　4.　Ⓒ

[1] Sulfur and nitrogen gases / [2] rivers, lakes, and streams / [3] acidity levels

酸雨

当硫和氮气被释放到空气中时，会形成酸雨。这些化学物质一旦进入空气，就会被雨云吸收，然后这些受到污染的小水滴再以雨、雪或雨夹雪的形式落到地面。这样不仅增强了土壤的酸度，也影响了湖和河的化学平衡。

美国环保总局表示，酸雨目前已经成为影响美国和加拿大大部分地区的严重问题。它会损害河流、小溪、湖泊和森林。

冰川是酸雨增多的最好证据。科学家们发现，自工业革命之后，冰川的酸度一直在急剧增加。

工业酸雨问题也一直是中国、东欧国家以及俄罗斯存在的严重问题。处于这些地区下风向的国家，如韩国和日本，受到了这一问题所带来的消极影响。

英国的曼彻斯特，作为英国工业革命时期的重要城市之一，最早报道了酸雨现象。但是直到20世纪60年代末，人们才开始仔细地研究酸雨问题。一位名叫哈罗德·哈维的加拿大科学家首次调查了一个"死"湖。20世纪90年代，《纽约时报》刊登了关于酸雨效应的报道，这才引起了公众的注意。

自然灾害，例如火山爆发，是引起酸雨的原因之一。但是主要原因还是工业发展和矿物燃料的燃烧。其中，工厂、机动车以及发电是造成酸雨问题的最大元凶。

酸雨会夺取鸟类、鱼类以及昆虫等许多生物的生命。它还会损坏建筑物，人们甚至怀疑它会对人类的健康产生不利影响。此外，酸雨还会破坏土壤，影响农民耕种。

科学家正在尝试找到解决酸雨问题的方法。人们试图通过签订国际条约来解决这一全球性问题。其中，《长程越界空气污染公约》的签订就旨在保护人类环境，减少空气污染。

F　1.　Ⓑ　2.　Ⓒ　3.　Ⓐ　4.　Ⓓ

[1] opener, headliner, and chaser / [2] movie theaters / [3] The Great Depression

歌舞杂耍表演

在收音机、电影、电视出现之前，人们喜欢到杂耍剧场去。在美国，这种娱乐表演被称为歌舞杂耍表演。"歌舞杂耍表演"这个词来源于法语的"voix de ville"，意为"城市之声"。只需要5美分，人们就可以欣赏到包括音乐、喜剧、魔术、动物表演、杂技甚至演讲在内的各种流行的娱乐表演。

常规的歌舞杂耍表演通常以滑稽表演开场，例如杂技或者自行车技，以便让那些来晚的观众找到座位。演出在中间部分明星出场时达到高潮，这同时也是演出最精彩的部分。演出以追逐表演收尾。这一表演从特色的角度讲，算是成功，但是它又的确无聊，很多观众这时会退场。

1880年至1920年间，歌舞杂耍表演风行一时。工业的蓬勃发展使得美国人民可以花更多的钱娱乐。许多剧院都试图以文雅和家庭为中心作为吸引中产阶级观众的噱头。演员不能吐脏字，甚至连"地狱"这个词都不能说。但是，许多演员常常不遵守这个规定，而此举却取悦了观众。

成功的剧院老板都极力确保他们的剧院既体面又辉煌。他们给剧院配备了上好的红色天鹅绒帷幕和座位套以及镀金边的精致木制品。这一切都让剧院看起来像宫殿一般。但这里依然会上演杂耍狗等滑稽表演。到19世纪90年代，歌舞杂耍表演达到鼎盛时期。它变得与教堂和公立学校一样受大众拥戴，成为人们聚会的最佳场所。

歌舞杂耍表演并没有一个明确的衰亡时间。但是1910年，随着电影院的出现，观看歌舞杂耍表演的观众数量持续缩减，人们更愿意以较低的价格享受电影。具有讽刺意味的是，电影最早恰恰就是在歌舞杂耍表演剧院中放映的。到20世纪30年代，随着美国大萧条的到来，歌舞杂耍表演最终消亡了。

美国许多著名电影、电视明星都是在歌舞杂耍表演的舞台上崭露头角的。像活宝三人组、马克思兄弟、巴斯特·基顿以及朱迪·嘉兰这些演员都是在歌舞杂耍表演剧院开始自己的表演生涯的。

Building Summary Skills

1. Optical Fiber

Optical fibers are made of [1] glass or plastic and are very useful for sending [2] light and information. The study of fiber optics has shown that light can be bounced continuously down an optical fiber. The concept behind optical fibers was discovered [3] in England and later adapted into [4] medical equipment. An optical fiber has many advantages over [5] copper cable. In this age of information, an optical fiber is very useful.

2. The American Revolution

The American Revolution was the war that ended [1] British rule over the colonies of North America and established [2] the United States as a country. The revolution began with a shift in ideology that was led by great men such as [3] Thomas Jefferson and Samuel Adams. Three main events led up to [4] the Revolutionary War. These events were the Stamp Act of 1765, the Townshend Acts of 1767, and [5] the Boston Tea Party in 1773. By 1781 the fighting ended, and the British withdrew from North America.

3. American Newspapers in the 19th Century

In the middle of the 1800s, the wide use of [1] the telegraph enabled newspapers to get reports from far away. This led to a new age of growth in [2] the newspaper industry. During this time, everything from [3] the writing and visual presentation to the delivery of newspapers improved. New York was the most competitive place, and the [4] *New York Times* emerged as the most respected newspaper in the country. Meanwhile, two newspaper owners, [5] William Randolph Hearst and Joseph Pulitzer, battled to win readers, giving rise to the unethical practice of yellow journalism.

4. The Statue of Liberty and the Liberty Bell

Two monuments are the best symbols of [1] America's ideal of freedom: the Statue of Liberty and the Liberty Bell. The Statue of Liberty was given to the United States by France as a gift in 1885 to mark [2] the 100-year birthday of the United States. It was designed by [3] Gustave Eiffel and stands about 45 meters tall in New York Harbor. The Liberty Bell is located in [4] Philadelphia, Pennsylvania, and was most famously rung on July 8, 1776, to announce the first public reading of [5] the Declaration of Independence. It has a crack which was made when it was rung for the first time.

5. Acid Rain

[1] Acid rain is a pollution problem caused by the release of [2] sulfur and nitrogen gases into the air. This problem has been observed in many [3] industrialized countries. Acid rain causes many problems such as [4] the poisoning of bodies of water, killing animals, damaging soil, and harming [5] the health of humans. Scientists are searching for ways to reduce this problem.

6. Vaudeville

Vaudeville was a form of [1] inexpensive live entertainment that was very popular in the United States in [2] the late 1800s and early 1900s. Vaudeville entertained the audience with [3] a variety of acts, including trained animals, acrobats, magic, comedy, musical performances, and lecturers. A typical vaudeville show began with an opener, peaked with [4] a headliner, and closed with a chaser. At the height of its popularity, vaudeville theaters were among the most popular places for people to gather. By the early 1900s, movie theaters and [5] the Great Depression caused vaudeville to disappear.

Mini TOEFL iBT

1. Ⓑ 2. Ⓓ 3. Ⓑ 4. Ⓐ 5. Ⓒ
6. Ⓐ 7. Ⓐ 8. Ⓒ 9. Ⓓ 10. Ⓐ
11. Ⓓ 12. Ⓒ

安德鲁·杰克逊总统

安德鲁·杰克逊是美国的第七位总统。他也是佛罗里达州的第一位州长。杰克逊是一个强悍的军人。他强硬的作风使他得到了"老山胡桃"的绰号。

杰克逊13岁时参军，在美国独立战争中参加抗英斗争。他和兄弟都在战争中被俘虏。因拒绝为英国士兵擦靴子，杰克逊的脸和手都被划伤。此后，杰克逊一直非常憎恨英国人。被释放后，他的兄弟不幸去世。当他回到家中时，发现母亲和其他亲人也都去世了。

在 1815 年的新奥尔良之战中，杰克逊带领 6000 名美军打败了 12000 名英军。2000 名英军阵亡，而美军只牺牲了 8 个人。

1817 年，杰克逊带领军队在佛罗里达州大败西班牙和塞米诺尔印第安人。他击溃了塞米诺尔印第安人的军队，然后，命令西班牙交出佛罗里达州的管辖权。他也成为了该州的第一位州长。

1824 年，安德鲁·杰克逊参加了美国总统大选。包括托马斯·杰斐逊在内的许多人认为杰克逊过于桀骜不羁的性格不适合总统的职位，因此他在竞选中输给了约翰·昆西·亚当斯。在 1828 年的大选中，安德鲁·杰克逊卷土重来，并最终打败亚当斯成为美国总统。

杰克逊在任期间，最受争议的事情是他对美国印第安人的态度。1830 年，他起草的《印第安人迁移法》生效。在此期间，45000 名彻罗基印第安人被迫离家西迁。数以千计的人在这次后来被称为"血泪之路"的迁徙中丧命。一位历史学家称那段时间为"美国历史上最不幸的篇章"。

1835 年 1 月 30 日，一个名为理查德·劳伦斯的精神病患者试图暗杀杰克逊总统。他持手枪悄悄靠近总统并向其开了两枪。子弹并没有打中杰克逊。随后，杰克逊用手杖制服了劳伦斯。

安德鲁·杰克逊与和前夫离异的雷切尔结婚之后，许多人非议雷切尔的贞洁。为了保护妻子的名誉，杰克逊与别人决斗了 103 次。在决斗中他只杀死过一个名叫查尔斯·迪肯森的人。由于他侮辱杰克逊的妻子，两人进行了决斗。迪肯森首先开枪击中了杰克逊的肋骨，然后杰克逊开枪击毙了迪肯森。杰克逊在无数的决斗中受了许多次伤，这些伤一直困扰着他的余生。他时常咳血。最终，他在 78 岁时死于肺结核和心力衰竭。

亚里士多德与古希腊科学发展

西方科学起源于古希腊。亚里士多德是那一时代伟大的思想家。尽管他不是最早的科学家或哲学家，但确实是最有影响力的。他是柏拉图的学生同时也是亚历山大大帝的老师。

在他 18 至 37 岁的学生时代，亚里士多德在柏拉图开办的柏拉图学园求学。之后，他四处游历并在各类岛屿上研究生物学。不久之后，马其顿的菲利普国王请求亚里士多德教授自己 13 岁的儿子，亚历山大。数年后，亚历山大离开亚里士多德前去征服亚洲。亚里士多德重返雅典并办了吕克昂学园来培养科学家。

亚里士多德通晓从科学到艺术的各个领域，他的著作也涵盖了各个学科。尽管其著作没有一本能够完整地保留下来，但他的研究还是奠定了西方哲学和科学的基础。

亚里士多德推崇通过五种感官认识事物。他利用自己的判别力和辩证法追寻真理。这种辩证法由柏拉图首创，而亚里士多德将其深化。他将这种辩证法建立在逻辑思考之上，即用一个问题回答另一个问题，而最终的答案将指向真理。这种方法被称为归纳逻辑与演绎逻辑。

科学方法即建立在亚里士多德的逻辑法之上。这种方法通常为科学家所用。他们首先提出假设，然后用实验验证。科学方法是现代西方科学中最重要的方法。亚里士多德自己没有做过很多实验，但是他的逻辑体系却引导其他科学家有了众多发现。艾萨克·牛顿爵士和伽利略正是受到了亚里士多德的影响，利用科学方法，有了许多发现。

亚里士多德也创造了分类这个概念。他研究了所有可以研究的科学分支，并将其分门别类。从动物学到地质学，他无不精通。他的作品是希腊文明的重要组成部分。

亚里士多德同时也受到了很多批评。许多学者认为他不尊重女性；另一些人认为他的作品太令人费解。他自己甚至都经常不遵守自己的逻辑方法。中世纪时期，他那些被奉为权威的作品被用于镇压百姓。然而，几千年来，人们一直参考亚里士多德的作品，其研究成果是现代社会的支柱。

Vocabulary Review

A 1. Ⓑ   2. Ⓒ   3. Ⓓ   4. Ⓐ
   5. Ⓑ   6. Ⓐ   7. Ⓒ   8. Ⓐ

B 1. e   2. i   3. h   4. j   5. a
   6. d   7. b   8. g   9. c   10. f

Unit 4 Negative Factual Information

Skill & Drill

1. Ⓒ

毛毛虫

毛毛虫是蝶类或蛾类的幼虫。它们的身体又长又软，而且是分节的。这种生理特性能使其消耗大量食物并像气球一样迅速生长。当毛毛虫准备进入化蛹阶段时，它们就成了吃食机器。

与所有昆虫一样，毛毛虫不用嘴呼吸，而是通过身体两侧的管状器官吸入空气。它们的视力非常差，所以它们通过触角定位食物。

毛毛虫有许多防御鸟类和其他动物的方法。它们的身体非常适合伪装。有些毛毛虫看起来像蛇或者树叶。还有些毛毛虫通过吃有毒的树叶使自己也变得有毒。

2. B

冰箱

冰箱是一项改变人类日常生活的发明。在该发明出现之前，人们每天需要耗费大量时间来搜集新鲜的食物。冷藏食品的唯一途径就是把一个大冰块搬回家中。这样即昂贵又麻烦。

1911年，第一台家用电冰箱上市。那时，一台电冰箱的价格几乎是一辆新车价格的两倍。早期的电冰箱在家中占的空间很大，有时甚至需要占用两个房间。

直到1927年，通用电气公司推出了"监视器顶端"冰箱。这是第一款被广泛使用并一直沿用至今的电冰箱。

3. A

风的种类

风是地球表面的空气运动。它是由于大气的受热不均而产生的。对风的两个主要影响因素是：赤道和两极的温差以及地球自转。

根据引起风的原因可以将风分为不同种类。盛行风，例如信风、西风、喷气流等，都是由全球环流引起的；天气学中的风是由冷暖气团锋面相撞形成的；中型风是由雷暴引起的；微风是突然形成的一小股气流。

风是最常见却影响力巨大的自然力。它每天都在影响着我们的生活和我们的地球。

4. D

蜂鸟

蜂鸟以其能够通过快速摆动翅膀在空中停留的特性而闻名。蜂鸟的振翅速度为每秒15至80次。这样它们就能在吮吸花朵时保持身体位置不变。之所以被称之为蜂鸟，是因为它们的翅膀会发出"嗡嗡"的声音。

吸蜜蜂鸟是世界上最小的鸟类，它们体重仅为1.8克。褐蜂鸟的重量更具代表性，重3克。而巨型蜂鸟的体重可以达到24克。

除昆虫之外，蜂鸟的新陈代谢速度是所有动物中最快的。它们的心跳速度能达到每分钟1260次。为了维持如此快速的新陈代谢，它们每天必须消耗大于自己体重的食物。

Practice with Long Passages

A　1. B　2. D　3. B　4. A

¹ photic zones / ² mild wave action / ³ Threats

珊瑚礁

珊瑚礁生长在热带海洋中有足够阳光照射的区域。为了生存下来，珊瑚礁一般都生长在海浪运动比较温和的区域。温和的海浪运动既不会太强以至于破坏了珊瑚礁，又有足够的强度促进海水运动为珊瑚礁运送食物和氧气。

珊瑚礁是由数以百万计的名叫珊瑚虫的小动物的骸骨组成的。珊瑚虫死后，海浪和鱼类会分解掉它们的遗骸，然后这些碎片会沉淀在珊瑚礁上使其长大。海藻以这些骸骨为食，并将其转化成石灰岩。石灰岩在珊瑚礁上沉淀进而形成一层保护壳。这些海藻在干净的浅水中生长得最好。

世界上绝大多数珊瑚礁都位于太平洋和印度洋的热带海域。南北美洲和非洲的西海岸几乎没有珊瑚礁。这主要是由当地强劲的沿岸寒流造成的。

珊瑚礁保障了很多种生物的生长。它为许多鱼类和植物的繁衍创造了栖息地。若没有珊瑚礁，许多这样的物种将面临灭绝。

目前，全球的珊瑚礁受到了一些威胁。其一是许多从工厂和农场排出的污染物导致珊瑚礁死亡。通常该区域的水质会变得有毒，致使珊瑚礁和寄生在珊瑚礁上及其周围的生物死亡。

另一个威胁是人类的过度捕捞和破坏性捕鱼业。许多捕鱼者为了捕到奇特的鱼卖往宠物店而不惜使用氰化物麻醉猎物。这一做法会减短被捕的鱼的寿命，而且也会毒害珊瑚礁。炸鱼也是一种破坏珊瑚礁生态系统的捕鱼方法。它破坏了良好的珊瑚礁群。许多保护组织正积极致力于对全球珊瑚礁的保护。

B　1. C　2. D　3. A　4. B

¹ assembly lines / ² 93 minutes / ³ 15 million

批量生产和 T 型福特车

批量生产是指在流水线上生产大批量产品。这种生产线的出现改变了20世纪人们工作和生活的方式。然而，直到1908年亨利·福特的福特汽车公司开始生产 T 型汽车时，这种生产方法才开始流行起来。

亨利·福特是汽车的发明者，同时也是福特汽车公司的董事长。他总是不断寻求更为高效的生产方法。1913年，他将运动流水线引进到自己生产车间。到1914年，福特流水线的高效程度已达到每93分钟生产一辆 T 型汽车，每3分钟就有一辆汽车下线。因此，福特公司生产出的汽车总数比其所有对手生产的汽车数量总和还要多。

另外，福特的流水线还提高了对工人安全的保障。工人可以停留在一个指定的位置，这样就减少了意外事故。同时，震惊全国的是，福特公司还史无前例地开出了每位工人每天5美元的工资。为了吸引到更多有才能的工人，福特公司将工人的最低工资提高了一倍以上。

1908年，一辆T型汽车的价格为825美元，此后逐年下降。到1916年，该车的单价已经降至360美元。此时街上跑的T型汽车比其他车都多。黑色是该款汽车唯一的颜色，因为黑漆便宜并且干得快，这样就可以节约成本。亨利·福特曾经开玩笑说道："消费者可以买到他想要的任何颜色的汽车，只要这颜色是黑的就行。"

截至20世纪20年代，福特公司已生产了1500万辆T型汽车。这一记录一直保持了30年。许多人学驾驶都是从T型车开始的。他们都有与这一车型有关的美好记忆。

T型车革命改变了世界各地人们的工作与出行方式。如今，流水线早已深入每一个工业国家。同时，人们的日常生活也时刻需要用到汽车。

C 1. Ⓑ 2. Ⓒ 3. Ⓑ 4. Ⓐ
¹ Ancient Greece / ² Anatomy of the Brain /
³ a brain tumor

神经学的先驱

神经学的历史要追溯到古埃及时代——最早的古书中记载了大脑紊乱的病症。当时的人对神经系统已经有了初步的认识。古埃及人甚至进行了简单的脑部手术。

在古希腊，著名内科医生希波克拉底始终坚信癫痫是由生理原因引起的。而在他之前，人们认为这是上帝对人的惩罚。另一位古希腊内科医生盖伦观察了标本的神经系统，他切割下人猿脑部的一块神经组织，发现该人猿无法再出声。

1664年，托马斯·威利斯出版了《脑部解剖学》。在该书中，他描述了能使血液在脑部循环的脑底动脉环。他也是率先使用"神经学"一词的人。18世纪，贝利和克拉维尔赫出版了第一个脑部图解。这一图解帮助医生和科学家开始理解如中风带来的脑损伤等病症。

1837年，J·E·浦肯野第一次通过显微镜观察到神经细胞。这标志着通过手工绘图研究神经学的时代的结束。著名哲学家勒内·笛卡尔通过研究脑部得出一个关于生物行为的理论。他认为，动物的每一种活动都是对外界刺激所作出的必要反应。一些医生通过在病人身上进行实验，更好地了解了神经系统。

此后，巴甫洛夫，一位俄国生理学家对神经行为有了新的理解。他训练自己的狗在听到响铃时分泌唾液。这一试验证明，高级脑功能可以改变简单的反射。

到1878年，威廉·麦克尤恩成功摘除了一位患者的脑部肿瘤。这位患者此后活了很多年。手术期间，麦克尤恩使用了腱锤等工具。此后不久，X射线和CT机也相继出现。这些发展都推动了今天有助于人类的神经学的出现。

D 1. Ⓒ 2. Ⓓ 3. Ⓐ 4. Ⓑ
¹ Antarctica / ² Regs / ³ Ergs

沙漠性气候的影响

沙漠是一类降水量极小的地区。沙漠地区的年降水量一般小于250毫米。但是例如图森、亚利桑那等地，其年降水量虽然大于250毫米，但由于蒸发率较高，这些地区仍被称为沙漠地区。

许多环境学家表示，沙漠面积在不断扩大。这一过程被称为沙漠化。在这种情况下，有用的土壤被风刮走，然后气温上升，最终导致曾经肥沃的土地变成沙漠。环境学家将之归咎于全球变暖以及人类的过度发展，二者也是目前威胁人类的最主要问题。

严格意义上的沙漠中很少有植被。这些沙漠位于地球上鲜有降雨的最干旱的地区。

人们通常认为在沙漠中生物难以存活。但是这种认识并不属实——沙漠中有许多白天潜伏的动物。地球上大约五分之一的地区被沙漠覆盖。

沙漠地貌的表面主要由沙子和岩石组成。沙漠中通常会有沙丘和多石的表面。冷沙漠也有以上特征，但是那里并不降雨，而是降雪。南极洲是世界上最大的冷沙漠，而最大的热带沙漠是撒哈拉大沙漠。

多数沙漠昼夜温差非常大。夜晚的气温极低，这是因为干燥的空气几乎不能储存热量，所以太阳一落沙漠温度就会骤降。同时，无云的天空也加速了夜晚热量的散失。

地球上的沙漠只有大约20%被沙粒覆盖。沙漠可分为6种：一种是山地或盆地沙漠；一种是由高原地貌构成的石岩沙漠；一种是由石戈壁形成的砾质沙漠；一种是由沙海形成的沙质沙漠；还有形成于高海拔地区的山间盆地；最后一种是干旱的重蚀地，其土壤成分主要是黏土。

E 1. Ⓐ 2. Ⓓ 3. Ⓑ 4. Ⓒ
¹ Migrate / ² Two populations / ³ Hawaii

黑脉金斑蝶的迁徙

黑脉金斑蝶最早发现于北美洲。19世纪以来，在新西兰、澳大利亚和加那利群岛也发现了这种蝴蝶。同时，它们也迁徙到了亚速尔群岛、葡萄牙和西班牙。在某些地方，黑脉金斑蝶也被称为迁徙蝶。

黑脉金斑蝶主要以长距离迁徙著称。它们在每年的8月到10月成群向南部迁徙，然后春天再飞回北方。

雌性蝶会在迁徙期间完成产卵。北美的黑脉金斑蝶分为两个种群。一种主要活动在落基山脉东部，这一种群通常飞往墨西哥的米却肯过冬；而另一个种群生活在西部，它们通常在加州中部，主要是太平洋丛林和圣克鲁斯过冬。

黑脉金斑蝶迁徙的时间甚至长于单只蝴蝶的寿命。初夏出生的蝴蝶寿命一般不超过两个月，而夏天的最后一代蝴蝶可以存活 7 个月。这段时间它们会飞往过冬的地区，直到春天离开过冬地区时才繁殖后代。

令科学家百思不得其解的是，这一物种如何在跨代后依然能回到同一栖息地过冬。科学家一直致力于研究这项课题。目前的推测是，它们的飞行模式是遗传的。有研究显示，该模式是生理节律和太阳方位变化共同作用的结果。一项新的研究表明，黑脉金斑蝶有一种特殊的紫外线感光器官，它能使蝴蝶有方向感。

一些黑脉金斑蝶在环境适宜的时期也在英国出现。也有一些生活在夏威夷群岛。这些蝴蝶并不迁徙。如果植物园中有足够多产蜜的花来维持其生存，它们能存活 6 到 8 周。

F   1. Ⓐ   2. Ⓑ   3. Ⓓ   4. Ⓒ

[1] Writing Ball / [2] IBM Selectric typewriter / [3] daisy wheel

打字机的发展

打字机不是由一个人发明的，而是许多人共同努力的结果。1714 年，亨利·米尔获得了一项类似于打字机的机器的专利。但除此之外，人们对其一无所知。另一位名叫图里的早期发明家发明了能让盲人打字的机器，他同时还发明了复写纸。

1829 年，威廉·奥斯汀·伯特获得了排字机的专利。有些人认为这就是第一台打字机。但是其速度慢于手写。

1865 年，雷韦恩特·汉森发明了书写球（the Writing Ball）。它成为第一台投入生产的打字机，但是其打字速度依然很慢。1867 年，肖尔斯和格利登共同研制出第一台速度快于手写的打字机。他们将该专利卖给了雷明顿，后者在 1873 年开始生产该款打字机。

可见性是早期打字机存在的一个问题。由于铅字连动杆挡住了版面，打字员无法看到他们已经打出的字。1895 年，随着"可视"打字机的生产，该问题也迎刃而解。早期的打字机直到 1915 年才最终退出市场。

20 世纪时，IBM 公司开始生产带有球形字锤的字球式电动打字机。这种打字机随后迅速占领了市场。铅字球是一项重要的技术改进。它消除了同时按两个键时出现的堵塞现象。许多这样的机器一直沿用至今。

20 世纪 80 年代，最后一个最重要的技术改进出现

了。铅字球被菊花轮取代。它比铅字球更简单、更便宜，但是使用寿命更短。

如今，人们有时仍然会使用打字机。当无法或不方便使用电脑时，打字机仍然有用。Smith Corona、Olivetti 和 Brother 等公司依然生产打字机。但是总体来讲，打字机已经被电脑所替代。

Building Summary Skills

1. Coral Reefs

Coral reefs grow best in photic tropical zones with [1] mild wave action. Reefs are made of the skeletons of millions of [2] tiny polyps that have been turned into limestone by algae. These reefs are most common in [3] the tropical Indian and Pacific Ocean regions. Reefs are important because they support a wide range of species that would otherwise [4] become extinct. There are many threats to reefs, such as [5] pollution, over-fishing, and destructive fishing that conservation groups are fighting against.

2. Mass Production and the Ford Model–T

[1] Henry Ford changed the way people worked and lived in the 20th century with his Ford Model-T and the mass assembly line it was produced on. After beginning Ford Motor Company and inventing [2] the Model-T car, Ford introduced [3] moving assembly lines in his production plants. These were so effective that the Model-T car became common around the world and the price [4] became lower every year. [5] By the 1920s, there were more Model-Ts on the road than any other car, and people around the world worked on assembly lines and drove cars.

3. Pioneers in Neurology

The ancient [1] Egyptians and Greeks were the first to experiment on and begin to understand the brain. Scientists such as [2] Thomas Willis created the study of neurology and furthered knowledge of the brain by [3] describing its anatomy. By the 1800s, scientists and doctors, such as J.E. Purkinje began using [4] microscopes to expand their knowledge of the human nervous system. By 1878, [5] successful brain surgery was performed, leading the way to a modern age of neurological understanding and treatment.

4. The Effects of Desert Weather

Deserts are regions that [1] receive little precipitation. [2] Desertification is the process by which fertile land becomes desert. Many environmentalists argue that temperature increases due to [3] global warming are accelerating the rate of desertification around the world. Deserts are capable of [4] supporting life forms that have adapted to their harsh environments. There are six kinds of deserts, including mountain or basin deserts, hamada deserts, regs, ergs, [5] intermontane basins, and badlands.

5. The Migration of the Monarch Butterfly

The Monarch butterfly is found in some parts of the world, including [1] North America. Scientists wonder how the Monarch is able to [2] migrate so far every year. New generations of the Monarch return to [3] the same winter location every year even though they were not [4] alive at the time of the last migration. Scientists are curious about the fact that Monarchs have [5] very different life spans based on their place in the seasonal migration cycle.

6. The Development of the Typewriter

[1] No single person invented the typewriter, but many people have contributed to its creation [2] over the years. The history of the typewriter is [3] full of small improvements made over the years. When problems such as the type bar blocking the typist's view arose, new improvements corrected them. These days the typewriter has been replaced by [4] the computer. But some people still use [5] typewriters, and some companies still make them.

Mini TOEFL iBT

1. Ⓑ 2. Ⓐ 3. Ⓓ 4. Ⓑ 5. Ⓒ
6. Ⓒ 7. Ⓒ 8. Ⓐ 9. Ⓓ 10. Ⓑ
11. Ⓑ 12. Ⓐ

黑猩猩

黑猩猩有两种。普通的黑猩猩居住在非洲西部和中部；其远亲是生活在刚果共和国森林中的倭黑猩猩或侏儒黑猩猩。刚果河是这两个种群的分界线。

成年的雄性黑猩猩重达 35 至 70 公斤，直立时身高通常为 0.9 到 1.2 米。雌性黑猩猩一般重约 26 到 50 公斤，直立身高为 0.66 到 1 米。野生黑猩猩的寿命一般不超过 40 岁。但人工饲养的黑猩猩可活到 60 岁。

非洲人与黑猩猩的接触已有千年的历史。有记录的欧洲人与黑猩猩最早的接触发生在 17 世纪。葡萄牙航海家杜阿尔特·帕切科·佩雷拉的日记中记载了黑猩猩使用简单工具的行为。

17 世纪时，黑猩猩由安哥拉被带往欧洲。最早一只在 1640 年到达欧洲，被作为礼物送给了奥兰治世家的王子。当时的科学家着迷于黑猩猩与人类之间的相似点。在后来的 20 年间，又有大批黑猩猩被运往欧洲。

1859 年，达尔文的《进化论》出版。该书的出版进一步激发了人们对人类与黑猩猩之间的关系的强烈兴趣。当时的研究者对黑猩猩的行为很感兴趣，他们希望找到其与人类行为的共通之处。这些研究者的主要目标就是探索黑猩猩是否生来就是"好的"。然而这一设想并未能付诸于实践。当时的科学家倾向于极大地夸大黑猩猩的智慧，甚至曾经制定出使黑猩猩成为劳动力的计划。他们希望黑猩猩能承担工厂内最低等的工作。

20 世纪，人们开始对黑猩猩展开更加严谨的科学研究。1960 年之前，人们对自然环境下黑猩猩的生活习性几乎一无所知。随后，简·古多尔前往坦桑尼亚的贡贝森林，与黑猩猩共同生活并观察其生活习性。她发现黑猩猩可以自己制造工具。这一发现具有开创性，之前人们一直认为只有人类能制造工具。

普通黑猩猩有时会攻击人类。在乌干达，许多小孩都曾遭到黑猩猩的攻击。而这些攻击对于小孩子来说通常都是致命的。它们攻击人类的原因之一，是错把这些小孩当成一种叫红髯猴的动物。而红髯猴恰恰是其最喜欢的食物之一。

人类在黑猩猩旁边时必须非常小心，因为它们视人类为敌人，并且黑猩猩上身的平均力量是一个成年男性的 5 倍。这一点在美国前全国运动汽车竞赛协会车手圣詹姆斯·戴维斯身上得到了证实。他曾遭遇黑猩猩攻击并险些丧命。

玻璃制造术

玻璃是一种均匀的非晶体固态物质。它主要由二氧化硅构成。二氧化硅是沙粒的主要成分。如果原料中含铁量达到 1%，玻璃就会显现颜色。所以精密玻璃制厂会增大玻璃中硅的含量使其更加纯净。

自然形成的玻璃通常呈绿色。这是由于其中含有铁元素。但是吹玻璃的工人可以通过向玻璃中添加粉末状金属来改变玻璃的颜色。通过添加硫元素和碳元素，玻璃能呈现淡黄色或黑色；锡的氧化物能使玻璃呈现白色；钴元素则能使玻璃呈深蓝色；而如果加入一点硒元素，玻璃则会呈现明亮的硒红色。

黑曜石是一种自然产生自炽热的岩浆流的玻璃。自石器时代开始，这种玻璃就被用于制造尖刀、箭头和其他一些工具。据历史记载，最早开始制造玻璃的是腓尼基人。他们早在公元前 3000 年前就开始用玻璃做陶器的保护壳。

大约公元前 1500 年，古埃及人就开始制造玻璃罐和玻璃珠。这些玻璃珠由金属棒外层包裹着一层熔制玻璃制成。当时的玻璃珠是珍贵的财产，人们认为它有神力。

罗马人发明了很多新的制造玻璃的技术。同时，他们还把玻璃的用途传至遥远的中国和不列颠群岛。

在公元约 1000 年的北欧，人们发明了一种新的玻璃制造法。含碳酸钾的玻璃取代了之前的钠玻璃。这一点非常重要，因为碳酸钾的存量更加丰富，它可以从木灰中获取。从此，北欧和地中海的玻璃制品之间有了明显的区别。

11 世纪时，德国人发明了薄玻璃制法。我们目前用来制造房屋和建筑物窗户的现代玻璃制造法即以它为基础。14 世纪，威尼斯成为精致玻璃制品的中心。这座城市里所有的奢侈品，例如镜子、餐具和花瓶等均由玻璃制成。

人工吹制玻璃至今仍被视为商品。一些最著名的精致玻璃艺术大师包括戴尔·奇休利，勒内·拉里克，路易斯·康福特·蒂法尼。他们的作品被收藏在如史密斯索尼安这样的博物馆中，一些以高价出售。

人们应用冷却技术将玻璃转化为精致的水晶。爱丁堡水晶和沃特福德水晶等水晶制造商都用金刚石割刀切割玻璃并刨光，将其制成漂亮的成品。

Vocabulary Review

A	1. B	2. C	3. D	4. A
	5. A	6. B	7. C	8. A
B	1. e	2. f	3. g	4. a	5. j
	6. i	7. b	8. c	9. d	10. h

Unit 5 Sentence Simplification

Skill & Drill

1. B

民间医学

民间医学指用于医治疾病和外伤的传统医疗方法。它还被用于辅助分娩和保健。尽管它是一套区别于现代医学的知识体系，但二者在同一文化背景下可共存。在有人收集之前，民间医学通常不被书写下来，而是口口相传。在一种文化中，许多成年人都熟知当地的民间医学知识。医生和患者负责提供和收集这些知识，而接生婆、巫医和药贩子也会使用它们。这些药方没有系统的归类，许多治疗方法甚至相互矛盾。

2. A

陪审团的选择

在美国，对一些刑事或民事案件的审判需要陪审团。陪审团的成员是从该法庭管辖区域内的成年人中随意挑选出来的。陪审团的成员被称为陪审员。一个陪审团通常由 6 到 12 个陪审员组成。对陪审员的选择取决于他们公正审理的能力。由于一些陪审员会因健康或其他原因中途退出审判，所以经常会任命一些候补陪审员。他们通常全程跟随审判但不参与最终的裁决。

3. C

栎树

"栎树"是几百种乔木和灌木的统称。它原生于北半球，包括生长在寒带、亚洲热带地区和美洲的落叶乔木和常青树。

栎树的叶子呈螺旋状，叶缘较钝；也有一些栎树树叶呈锯齿状或者整片树叶叶缘都较为光滑。栎树开的花是柔荑花，盛开于春季；所结的果实是一种叫做橡果的坚果，呈杯状。每一个橡果中都含有一粒种子，种子长成成熟的栎树需要 6 到 18 个月，具体时长取决于栎树的种类。常青类栎树叫做槲树，但是这种树并不是一个明确的独立群体，当中有些种类也分布在其他种属中。

4. A

木料工业

被砍伐成木头的树称为木材，被制成木板的木材叫做木料。木料分为毛木料和成品木料。毛木料是制作家具的原材料，它来源于各种木材，但以硬木为主。成品木料有标准的大小规格，一般用于建筑工业。木料工业是美国最早兴起的工业之一，其中以缅因和纽约为首。后来，该工业逐渐扩展至密歇根、俄勒冈、华盛顿和加利福尼亚。那些伐木并将其制成木料的工人被称为伐木工人，他们是美国早期民间故事中常出现的角色。

Practice with Long Passages

A 1. Ⓒ 2. Ⓓ 3. Ⓑ 4. Ⓐ

¹ Six / ² human food / ³ cash crop

小麦的生产

小麦的种植遍及全球。作为在全世界为人类提供粮食的最重要的谷物，它的产量居全球谷物产量的第二位，仅次于玉米，排在第三的是水稻。小麦是面粉的原料，面粉可制成蓬松的面包、饼和馒头，或者饼干、蛋糕、通心粉、面条和蒸粗麦粉。另外，小麦还是啤酒或伏特加等酒类的原料。如今，人们还将小麦应用于生物燃料中。在磨面粉时分离出来的稻壳叫做麦麸。人们还留出一部分小麦当做家畜的饲料；麦秆可以当做喂养家畜的草料或者用于修建天窗。

收割的小麦要根据其特性按商品市场的需求进行分类，然后买主根据这些分类来决定最终购买哪一种小麦。每一类都有特定的用途。在这种分类体制下，小麦生产者会决定生产哪一种小麦能使利润最大化。

小麦之所以作为一种经济作物被广泛种植，是因为其单位面积的产量颇高。即便在较短的生长周期中，它也能在温和的气候条件下有很好的产量。人们将其制成优等的面粉用于烘烤（面包等）。多数面包是以小麦面粉为原料烤制的，包括很多以含有的小麦种类命名的面包，如黑麦面包和燕麦面包。还有其他很多深受人们欢迎的食物都是以小麦面粉为原料制成的。因此，人们对小麦的需求量非常大，甚至在一些有大量粮食剩余的地方也不例外。

美国目前种植的小麦主要有六种：一种是浅色质硬的硬质小麦；一种是呈红褐色且蕴含大量蛋白质的硬粒红春麦；另一种是与之相似的，生长在堪萨斯州的硬粒红冬麦；还有质软且蛋白质含量低的软粒红冬麦；颜色较浅呈白垩色的白色硬粒小麦；以及几乎不含蛋白质且生长在温和潮湿地区的白色软粒小麦。

B 1. Ⓑ 2. Ⓐ 3. Ⓓ 4. Ⓒ

¹ Proponents / ² Critics

人体冷冻法

人体冷冻法是将尸体器官组织冷冻的做法。它被应用于近期死去的人或动物，希望在不久的将来他们能复活。法律规定，人体冷冻必须以法医鉴定该人正式死亡为前提。许多科学家和医生认为人体冷冻法完全违反道德准则，但它也有许多支持者。

人体冷冻法的支持者希望随着未来科技的发展，尤其是原子技术的发展，人们可以预防早期的临床死亡。人们希望通过原子技术修复非常微小的组织并使受损伤的组织和器官再生。他们还设想在未来的某一天能够消除疾病和衰老。

支持者希望储存近期死亡的人大脑中的记忆和特征。人体冷冻法尝试通过使用一种保护大脑的液体来实现这一设想。在尸体冷冻之前用这液体能阻止大脑损伤。这种冷却液体能保存大脑内储存记忆和特征的部位的完整细胞结构。

而人体冷冻法的批评者却认为，以当代科技的发展水平，这种尝试只会浪费时间和金钱。尽管细胞、组织、血管以及一些小型动物器官的确能够被保存，甚至在零上几度的温度下，一些青蛙仍然能够在身体部分被冻住的状况下生存数月。但这并不能证明低温冷冻的可行性。没有任何证据表明，人死后，其个性特征和记忆仍可被恢复。

批评者还指出，如果真能使死人复活，这必将引发诸如人口过剩等许多社会问题。并且在许多人看来，起死回生是一种有悖于上帝旨意的不道德行为。

C 1. Ⓒ 2. Ⓓ 3. Ⓓ 4. Ⓑ

¹ the right to use the roads / ² according to law

罗马的道路法

道路是罗马帝国壮大过程中不可或缺的一部分。这些道路使罗马军队能够快速高效地行进。甚至有一条谚语叫"条条大路通罗马"。在其鼎盛时期，罗马整个道路系统共长 53000 英里，包含大约 372 条交通线路。罗马人非常擅长建造道路（罗马人称为"viae"）。

历史上最早的成型道路是罗马的街道。在公元前约450 年颁布的《十二铜表法》中详细规定道，一条道路在直道处应有 8 英尺宽，在拐弯处有 16 英尺宽。法典指挥罗马人修路，并规定行人有权由未修路的私人土地上经过。因此，修建无需不断返修的道路成为当时人们的共识。

罗马法律规定使用道路的权利为道路所有权（罗马人称为"servitus"）；使用私人土地上小路的权利为行走权；驾驶马车经过的权利为驾驶权。一旦仲裁者确认一条道路具有合适的宽度，这条道路就同时具有行走权和驾驶权。道路的法定最小宽度为 8 英尺。在这些非常严格的法律中，公共利益远高于个人利益，这就成为共和体制的特征。

罗马人无论何时都讲求事物的标准化。在公元前 20 年被任命为常任道路委员之后，奥古斯都在农神庙附近修建了一座黄金里程碑。其上列出了罗马帝国所有的城市以及它们到罗马的距离。这座碑后被称为"罗马之脐"。

罗马的道路不仅对罗马帝国的稳定性的维持和扩张有着至关重要的作用，它们也为当时的罗马军团提供了非常多的好处。这些道路在千年之后依然被使用。但是在罗马帝国衰落之际，也正是这些道路指引了野蛮人的入侵，最终导致罗马帝国大败。

D 1. Ⓓ 2. Ⓑ 3. Ⓒ 4. Ⓐ

¹ Visual / ² Olfactory / ³ Auditory

动物的领地权

"领地"一词指的是某个动物所保卫的一片区域。这些保卫领地的动物是领土的保卫者。"动物领地"这一概念最早由埃利奥特·霍华德在其1920年的著作中提出。20世纪30年代，玛格丽特·莫尔斯·尼斯通过对北美歌雀的研究进一步扩展了这一概念。不久之后，罗伯特·阿德里的著作《领地法则》使之更加流行。但同时，这本书的畅销也导致了人们对领地重要性的过分夸大。这一概念曾被认为属于社会生态学。然而实际上，只有一小部分物种拥有存在明显边界的领地并在其中生活和寻找需要的资源。

领地的概念在鸟类和鱼类中体现得最为明显。这些动物通过艳丽的外表警告其他动物不要接近自己的领地。欧亚鸲和暹罗斗鱼就是通过这种身体颜色来保护领地的。其领地里通常有它们的巢穴并有充足的食物提供给它们及其后代。

领地的保卫很少通过打斗进行。一般来讲，动物的领地设有明显的标志。这种标志可能是视觉标志——如知更鸟红色的前胸；也可能是听觉标志——如许多鸟的歌声和长臂猿的啼叫；或者是嗅觉标志——如一些动物排尿、排便留下的臭迹。狗就是这样标记它们的领地的。另外，一些动物还通过用带有特殊臭腺的身体部位摩擦领地中的物体来标记领地。猫通过将它们的面部和胁腹部与其他物体摩擦来标记领地。

E 1. Ⓐ 2. Ⓑ 3. Ⓓ 4. Ⓐ

¹ Old Style / ² Current Style

美国经济活动的流动

美国的经济在全球实力最强大。然而，自20世纪80年代早期起，美国发生了变化。它曾是全球最大的债权国，而如今它负担高额经常项目赤字及巨额国债。现在，国债已占当前美国GDP的约64%，这是自20世纪50年代以来的最高值。

目前，联邦政府正在引导经济的稳步发展。与此同时，政府还致力于提高就业率和稳定物价。减缓或加速经济增长可通过调整财政支出和政府税收实现，也可通过管理财政供给和控制信贷实现。而这一过程也会影响价格水平和就业。

20世纪30年代的大萧条曾严重影响美国经济。经济缓慢增长期和高失业率被视为当时美国经济的最大威胁。经济衰退现象严重。政府试图通过增加政府开支、减少税收来鼓励消费者消费，刺激经济发展，从而促成财政供给的快速增长。

另外，在20世纪70年代，美国遭遇物价飞涨，尤其是能源价格。这引起了人们对通货膨胀的恐惧并导致物价全面上涨。于是，国家领导者将重心逐渐转变为抑制通货膨胀。

20世纪60年代至90年代间，美国经济经历了许多变化。60年代时期，美国政府极力推崇财政政策。总统和国会在指导经济发展中起到了重要作用。但是高通货膨胀与高失业率使公众逐渐对他们失去了信心，经济整体放缓也损坏了他们的形象。如今，美国中央银行，即美国联邦储备委员会利用货币政策来控制经济活动的流动，这在很大程度上独立于总统和国会。

F 1. Ⓓ 2. Ⓒ 3. Ⓐ 4. Ⓓ

¹ two African types / ² 120kg at birth / ³ 6 hours and 50km

象的进化

象是其所在生物目中仅剩的一种动物。目前共有3种类型的象，它们分别是普通非洲象、森林非洲象和亚洲象。自最后一个冰川期开始，其他种类的象就已经灭绝了。

象是目前存活在陆地上的最大的哺乳动物。其孕期是22个月，是所有陆生动物中最长的。幼象出生时体重一般为120公斤。象的寿命可达70岁，甚至更长。有记载的最大的象是1956年在安哥拉被射杀的一头重达12,000公斤的公象。最小的象是一种史前物种，约有小牛或体型较大的猪那么大，它们生活在公元前5000年至公元前3000年的克里特岛。

象的生存正受到人类越来越严重的威胁。象与人类之间的冲突往往是致命的。在亚洲，每年有150头象和多达100人死于这些冲突。从1970年至1989年，非洲象的数目由最初的300万头降至后来的60万头，并在此后不断减少。到2000年，世界上仅存非洲象27.2万头。近些年来，人类致力于拯救象，才使其数目开始增加。象现在属于全球保护动物。人们制定了各种有利于象的法规，严格限制对其捕杀和驯养并控制象牙等商品的交易。

一些科学家认为，象和海牛有远亲关系。同时，他们还认为象和蹄兔之间有一定联系。尽管没有化石证据证明这一假设，但一些基因证据却表明了这种联系。其中一种理论表明，这些动物曾经大部分时间生活在水中并能用象鼻作为水下呼吸管进行呼吸。现在的象依然具有这种能力，而且人们知道象也是那样在水中游动并可以持续游动6个小时，约50千米。

Building Summary Skills

1. Wheat Production

Wheat is one of the most [1] widely grown and important crops in the world. It has many important uses by humans. Wheat grain is harvested according to a [2] classification system that determines [3] the quality and price. Wheat is a very [4] profitable crop because it is used so widely in products that are consumed daily. There are [5] six classes of wheat grown in the United States.

2. Cryonics

[1] Cryonics is the controversial process of [2] freezing animals or humans immediately after death in hopes of reviving them at a later date. Although reversing death is [3] not possible through current scientific methods, practitioners of cryonics hope future advances will make it possible. Their current goal is to [4] preserve the memory and identity of those who die. Critics of cryonics think it is [5] unethical as well as a waste of time.

3. Road Law in Rome

Roads were a very important part of the Roman Empire, and the Romans were very advanced at [1] building and administering laws to control them. [2] Roman roads were built to very strict measurements, and laws protected travelers when roads were not available or [3] in disrepair. There was even a point from which all roads to Rome led, called [4] the golden milestone. Roman roads eventually enabled barbarians to [5] invade and conquer Rome, but its roads still exist today.

4. Animal Territoriality

Animals defend areas called [1] territories, which are important to them. This concept was introduced [2] in the early 20th century although it was greatly exaggerated. Many animals develop [3] bright colors or strong smells to protect their territories. [4] Few animals fight over territory. Many common animals [5] mark their territory with their own smell.

5. The Flow of Activity in the U.S. Economy

[1] The U.S. economy was once the most powerful in the world, but it is now the most indebted. The federal government controls many factors that change [2] the direction of the economy. During [3] the Great Depression, the federal government shifted its economic philosophy from creating growth to holding back prices. Because of these changes, the public has lost faith in [4] the president and Congress's role in influencing the economy. [5] The nation's central bank now independently attempts to guide the economy.

6. The Evolution of the Elephant

There are only [1] three species of elephants still living today. They are the largest of all land mammals and have [2] the longest pregnancy period. These days, elephants have been endangered [3] by humans, but efforts are being made to [4] increase their numbers. Scientists think elephants are genetically related to [5] sea cows and possibly hyraxes although there is not enough evidence to prove this.

Mini TOEFL iBT

1. (B)	2. (B)	3. (D)	4. (C)	5. (A)
6. (B)	7. (A)	8. (C)	9. (C)	10. (B)
11. (C)	12. (D)			

美国工业发展

美国独立战争之后，尽管美国工业依然落后于欧洲，但差距并不算太大。在之后的 150 年间，随着新发明的不断涌现，美国工业得以迅速发展，并因此促使美国成为世界上最大、最现代化的经济强国。

在独立战争期间，美国尚未进入工业时代。当时，大多数制造业是以家庭为单位完成的。英国已完成工业革命，美国却落后了。1811 年，弗朗西斯·卡伯特·洛厄尔前往英国并记下了制造动力织布机的方法。他与同伴回到美国后，在波士顿建立了一些纺织厂。其中最有名的纺织厂建于 1822 年，坐落于马萨诸塞州的卢威尔市。卢威尔生产系统雇佣了许多"纺织女工"。她们住在集体宿舍中，便于返回工厂工作。

新英格兰是纺织工业发展的发源地，也是美国第一个经历如此高速发展的地区。另外，宾夕法尼亚州也经历了同样的迅速发展，钢铁工业推动了这一进程，其速度甚至超越了新英格兰。

从 1810 年开始一直到 19 世纪 60 年代，美国的工业发展开始转向新的方向。工厂仍然在不断扩大，但是发明创造领域的发展却更加显著。得益于这些有实用价值的发明，美国的制造业和农业水平大幅提升。理查德·切内沃斯发明了铸铁犁具，其有用性主要体现为它的零件具有可拆卸、可更换性。约翰·迪尔发明了钢制犁具，这一发明由于不粘土而大大提高了耕作效率。伊莱·惠特尼发明的轧棉机和夹具带动了美国南部棉花产业的发展。塞缪尔·莫尔斯发明的电报机开创了远程通讯的新纪元。伊莱沙·奥蒂斯发明的客用电梯促成了现代摩天大楼的建造。最后，乔治·普尔曼发明的火车中的卧铺车厢使远途旅行成为可能。

从19世纪50年代开始，美国掀起工业热潮。随着美国内战以北方的胜利告终，北方的企业家们开始跃跃欲试，政府也迫切希望看到工业扩张。上述革新带动了工业的迅猛发展。由于要向全国各地运送货物，人们对铁路的需求也迅速增大——很多南方人要将他们生产的棉花运送到北方和英国。

20世纪初期，人们对汽车的需求不断扩大，这大大促进了汽车工业的长足发展。20世纪20年代，亨利·福特制造出T型汽车，开创了流水生产线这一现代生产模式。

微生物

在人类发现微生物之前，食物为什么在长时间存放后会变质一直是个谜。人们不知道为什么葡萄能酿成酒，牛奶可以制成奶酪。人们甚至从未想过我们的食物上还会有小到人们肉眼看不到的生物在工作着。1676年，一位荷兰科学家发现了这些微生物。

现在我们对微生物的认识不断加深。专门从事其研究的科学家观察到了这些微型生物的各种形式，有细菌、真菌、古细菌以及真核生物。由于病毒不能单独存活，所以它不能被归为微生物。微生物有单细胞和多细胞两种。有几种被称为原生生物的单细胞微生物是肉眼可见的。

微生物一般生存在沸点以下的水或其他液体中。科学家从温泉、海底甚至地壳深层都提取到了微生物的样本。这些微生物是地球许多生态系统的重要组成部分；并且，它们在营养物质循环方面起到了重要作用，也是氮循环中的重要组成部分。

科学家认为，世界上最早的单细胞微生物出现在40亿年前，它们是地球上最早的生命形态，也是此后30亿年间地球上的唯一一种生命形态。微生物不仅能迅速、大量繁殖，不同物种的微生物之间还可以进行毫无障碍的基因交换。它们加速突变，这也使得它们可以快速进化以适应新的生存环境。微生物的这种快速进化能力也带来了麻烦——可抵御现代抗生素药物的"超级病菌"因此产生。

细菌是最简单的微生物。它们同时也是地球上最常见的生物群体。细菌在温度低于140摄氏度的所有环境中均能生存，它们存在于海水、土壤、甚至人体的胃和肠道中。细菌的基因结构是DNA单链结构。细菌有细胞壁，并通过二分裂进行繁殖，它们靠不断分裂完成繁殖。有些细菌在最适宜的条件下可以每十分钟分裂一次。

古细菌是另一种微生物。它们是一种无细胞核的单细胞生物。这种微生物普遍存在于各种生存环境中，包括一些极端的环境。不同于细菌和古细菌，真核生物是一种有细胞器的多细胞有机体，它的DNA储存在细胞核中。

嗜极生物是一种最有趣的微生物。它们能适应极端艰苦的环境。这些生命力极强的生物生活在南极、北极、沙漠和深海中。它们甚至能在距地球表面7公里处生存。有些嗜极生物能在真空下存活，还能抵御辐射。据此，科学家认为，它们能在太空中生存。

Vocabulary Review

A	1. Ⓓ	2. Ⓒ	3. Ⓑ	4. Ⓓ
	5. Ⓑ	6. Ⓐ	7. Ⓒ	8. Ⓓ

B	1. i	2. f	3. h	4. j	5. a
	6. d	7. c	8. g	9. e	10. b

Unit 6 Rhetorical Purpose

Skill & Drill

1. Ⓒ

栉水母

栉水母是一种海洋生物，但因其并无毒螫针，所以算不上真正的水母。目前全世界共有超过100种的栉水母生活在海洋中，占浮游生物中的很大一部分。其中一种是生活在北海的海醋栗，它们的数量非常多，经常会塞满渔民的渔网。很少有其他物种会出现这种情况。但是，由于栉水母的构造极其脆弱，科学家很难对其进行研究，也就无法收集它们寿命方面的数据。但目前知道的是，栉水母在成年之前就开始进行繁殖了，科学家因此推断它们的生命周期较短。

2. Ⓑ

白矮星和棕矮星

质量较小或中等质量的恒星衰亡时会变为白矮星。在此之前，这些恒星会经历红巨星阶段，之后它们将外层物质脱落。白矮星大小和地球相当，但密度却近似于太阳。它是太空中除了黑洞、中子星和夸克星之外密度最大的物质。但是，与白矮星不同的是，棕矮星的密度却非常小，它主要由气体构成，有时很难与大行星区别开来。

3. Ⓓ

蜘蛛的群居性

　　蜘蛛是捕食类动物。通常情况下，在交配之后，雌性蜘蛛会吃掉雄性蜘蛛，有些种类的雌性蜘蛛甚至会吃掉它们的后代。大多数蜘蛛属于非群居生物，但是仍有少数种类共同织网并生活在大群落中。尽管它们会表现出群居性，但是它们并没有进化为像蜜蜂和蚂蚁这样的群居昆虫。Anelosimus Eximius 可以算作蜘蛛中群居性最强的物种。它们最大的群落可由近 5 万只蜘蛛构成。很多蜘蛛仅能活一到两年，但是鸟蛛却通常能活 20 年左右。

4. Ⓒ

手工艺品

　　手工艺品是实用又好看的物品。它们通常以手工制造，有时会用到简单的工具。这个词通常指传统的产品制造方法。手工艺品独特的风格很重要。这些物品经常蕴含文化及宗教意义。大规模或机械化生产的产品不是手工艺品。不同于一般的装饰艺术和工艺品，手工艺品是用来使用和穿着的物品。它们的价值不仅仅是简单的装饰，通常还被认为是更加传统的作品，是人们日常生活的一部分。

Practice with Long Passages

A 　1. Ⓓ　2. Ⓑ　3. Ⓐ　4. Ⓒ

[1] 7,000°C / [2] hydrogen, helium, and methane / [3] 13 moons

海王星

　　海王星是太阳系的第 8 颗，也是离太阳最远的一颗行星。它的直径长度在 8 颗行星中居第 4 位，质量居第 3 位，是地球的 17 倍。尽管它与天王星近似于双子星，但是海王星质量更大一些。海王星是根据罗马海神命名的。

　　海王星上的大气主要由氢和氦组成。其中也有微量的甲烷。这些化学元素使得海王星呈现比天王星更加明显的蓝色，尽管后者的大气中也有近似含量的甲烷。因此，科学家认为，海王星的这种颜色是由一种未知成分引起的。

　　海王星的许多奇异的特征令科学家对它很感兴趣。其中一个就是：海王星上的风力是太阳系所有行星中最大的，风速能达到 2500 千米 / 小时。另外，已证实有 13 颗卫星围绕海王星的轨道运行，其中特里顿卫星以其逆行轨道

著名。该卫星上的大气由氮和甲烷构成且气温很低。

　　海王星云层最高点的气温一直维持在零下 210 摄氏度左右，它也因此成为太阳系最冷的行星之一。低温的主要原因是海王星与太阳的距离相当遥远。该行星中心极度炽热的气体和岩石使得其中心温度达到 7000 摄氏度左右，这比太阳表面的温度还要高。但是海王星最外层却极度寒冷。

　　1989 年，"旅行者 2 号"探测器飞过海王星，并在该行星的南半球上发现了类似于木星上大红斑的大暗斑。另外，科学家还在该行星周围检测到了微弱的环，比土星环小得多。这些海王星环是由爱德华·吉南带领的研究小组发现的。他们起初认为这些环是不完整的，它们在环绕海王星一圈之前就慢慢褪去了。但是"旅行者 2 号"传送来的完整海王星环的照片却否定了他们最初的想法。

B 　1. Ⓐ　2. Ⓓ　3. Ⓑ　4. Ⓓ

[1] Material Cause / [2] Formal Cause / [3] Efficient Cause / [4] Final Cause

亚里士多德的形而上学

　　亚里士多德是历史上最有影响力的思想家之一。在科技尚未出现的时代，他创立了众多学科，形而上学就是其中之一。他主张，万物的起因都能通过追溯其源头找到，在了解一个事物的起因时，我们就能了解到一些科学的知识。了解一个事物的存在要了解其存在的理由。他是指引了所有后来偶然建立起的理论的第一人。根据亚里士多德的理论，所有起因都能归在几个不同的类别中。

　　他将事物的起因分为四个主要类别：质料因是指一个事物靠其各部分的组合而产生。以干酪三明治为例，它是由肉、面包和干酪组合而成的。任何一个单独的成分都无法构成干酪三明治，但它们合起来就成为干酪三明治存在的起因。形式因阐明了物质的定义。洪水的形式因是过剩的水。动力因描述了物质变化的原因。例如一团熊熊燃烧的火焰被雨水浇灭，雨水使大火终止。目的因是指做某事的原因。例如，一个国家为了保卫边界开战，这就是战争的起因。

　　亚里士多德的形而上学还研究了物质的概念。他总结道，一种特定物质是物质本身和物质形式的结合体。他还定义了五种主要元素：火——热而干；土——冷而干；气——热而湿；水——冷而湿；最终，他将"以太"定义为组成天球和天体的圣物。

　　亚里士多德的这些分类法为现代物理学开辟了道路。他的著作可以被看做是现代物理学的坚实基石。

C 1. Ⓒ 2. Ⓑ 3. Ⓓ 4. Ⓐ

¹1809 / ²1821 / ³1823

塞阔雅

塞阔雅是美洲印第安彻罗基族人，也被称为乔治·吉斯特。他是一个银匠，但是却以发明了彻罗基族书写文字而闻名。他也因此在文字书写体系发明者的名人堂中占有令人尊敬的一席之地。

塞阔雅的出生地和准确出生日期不详，因为当时没有文字记录。历史学家们猜测他生于1760至1776年之间，出生地可能为田纳西州、佐治亚州、北卡罗来纳州、亚拉巴马州或南卡罗来纳州。詹姆斯·穆尼是一位著名的研究彻罗基族的历史学家，他引述塞阔雅一位远亲所言，说塞阔雅和他的母亲早年生活在田纳西州的塔斯克吉村。

塞阔雅的名字来源于彻罗基语，意思是"猪"。这可能是指其儿时畸形，或者后来的因伤致残。

塞阔雅的父亲有可能是白人，或者白人和美洲印第安人的混血，但是塞阔雅不会说英语。这也许能证明他和母亲被他的白人父亲遗弃这一猜测。塞阔雅大概在1809年的某个时间搬到了亚拉巴拉罕州的威尔斯村开始从事银匠工作。

白人殖民者的书写令塞阔雅印象深刻，他把写有英文的纸叫做"会说话的叶子"。约1809年，塞阔雅开始为彻罗基族语创造书写系统。历时12年，他创出85个字母来表示不同的音节。

然后，塞阔雅开始教自己的女儿如何用自己创造的这套新系统阅读和书写。当地人为之惊奇，但部落的巫医却称塞阔雅被恶魔附了身。于是，塞阔雅只能先把这套系统介绍给一些武士，然后部落的其他人才开始慢慢接受。到1823年，所有彻罗基族人都完全接受了这套新的文字系统，并利用它记录史实供后人参考。

D 1. Ⓓ 2. Ⓒ 3. Ⓐ 4. Ⓓ

¹ Union Pacific Line / ² Central Pacific Line

第一条横跨大陆的铁路

世界上第一条横跨大陆的铁路建于19世纪60年代的美国，它横跨北美大陆，将美国东部和加利福尼亚州的铁路网络连接起来。1869年5月9日，该铁路举行了通车仪式，即著名的"黄金道钉"仪式。这条铁路的开通标志着美国全国范围内的旅行的开始。它改变了美国西部的人口和经济状况，并使美国彻底告别了马车运输的时代。

该铁路的建设经由1862年的《太平洋铁路法》的认可，并得到了美国联邦政府的大力支持。它是人们几十年努力的成果，也是亚伯拉罕·林肯总统伟大的功绩之一。该铁路在林肯去世四年后竣工，耗费了大量的物力和人力。它穿越高山平原，由联合太平洋铁路和中太平洋铁路构成。这两条铁路都是由地方承建，但都得到了联邦政府的支持，它们分别通向美国西部和东部。

这条铁路的建设，旨在将处于内战冲突中的美国联合起来。它使人们大批迁往西部，也造成这些地区印第安人的大量减少。

联合太平洋铁路大部分由爱尔兰劳工修建，同时还有美国的退伍军人、南部联邦军队以及摩门教徒参与修建工作。大部分的中太平洋铁路是由中国劳工修建的。最初，人们认为中国人体力太弱，无法胜任这项工作。但是不久，大量中国劳工被从中国带入美国。当时多数工人的日工资为1到3美元，而中国工人的工资却低得多。最终，他们举行了大罢工，此举为之赢得了工资的小幅上涨。

E 1. Ⓑ 2. Ⓓ 3. Ⓑ 4. Ⓒ

¹ a lever / ² the Colt revolver / ³ assembly lines

机械化

机械化是指从人类劳动生产向机器生产的转变。它彻底改变了人类的历史。机器使得人类能用更少的力气做更多工作。在有文献记载之前，人类就已经开始制造结构简单或复杂的机器了。

最简单的一种机器就是杠杆。它是位于物体底下的一根棍子，棍子底下面放一块石头或者其他东西。下面的物体起到支点的作用，使棍子产生杠杆效应。当人用力压下棍子的一端时，它下压支点并举起棍子上方的物体。在这一过程中，人的力量被杠杆增大了。人可以用较少的力量举起质量较大的重物。这是所有机器发展中的指导原则之一。如此一来，人只施加一点力，机器就能为人工作了。

一种重要的机器是蒸汽车床。相较于金属和木质机器，这种设备在速度和精确度上都有了明显提高。另一个重要机器是蒸汽机，这使得蒸汽船和蒸汽火车的出现成为可能，并促成了后来的交通运输革命。作为第一支可连发的机械手枪，柯尔特左轮手枪的出现增强了战争的致命性。20世纪初，福特公司启用了流水线汽车制造法，实现了机械化。它改变了人们工作和出行的方式。

"机械化"这个名词也使用在军事方面。在军事上，它指履带装甲车的使用。装甲运兵车就是其中的一种，它通常被用来快速转移战场上的大量军队，尽可能降低去往战场的途中士兵的伤亡。在此之前，许多士兵在未抵达战场时就阵亡了。机械化大大提高了军队的流动性和战斗力。在现代化国家，所有的军事力量都以全机械装备的步兵团为基础。

猛犸象

猛犸象化石是最常见的史前化石。猛犸象是大象的一种，现已灭绝。其象牙长且弯曲，又被称为长牙。北方的猛犸象全身被浓密的皮毛覆盖。它们主要活动在约 160 万至 1 万年前的更新世。

猛犸象与现代亚洲象的血缘最近，另外两种非洲象的基因和猛犸象的基因匹配度并不高。约 600 万到 730 万年前，亚洲象和猛犸象共同的祖先从非洲象的种群中分离出来。50 万年之后，亚洲象和猛犸象也相互分离开来。

科学家认为，猛犸象的进化最早发生在 480 万年前的北非。在乍得、利比亚、摩洛哥以及突尼斯已经发现了那时的猛犸象的骸骨。在南非和肯尼亚的遗迹中也同样发现了远古的遗骸。这些遗骸被认为属于最古老的物种。

此后，非洲猛犸象开始迁移。化石记载显示，它们最终北迁至欧洲。于是一个新的物种——南方猛犸象便在不久之后产生了，在亚洲和欧洲各处均有分布。研究显示，南方猛犸象后来穿越了现已沉没的白令海峡大陆桥到达北美大陆。这一寒冷的大陆区域通过连接现在的西伯利亚和阿拉斯加连通了那时的亚洲和美洲大陆，并将猛犸象带到了北美大陆。

大约 70 万年前，温暖的气候开始改变——欧洲、亚洲和北美的热带稀树草原逐渐变为贫瘠阴冷的干草原。南方猛犸象成为最早灭绝的物种。30 万年前，一个新的物种——长毛象产生，其全身覆盖着的浓密皮毛使它能应付冰川期极度寒冷的天气。

Building Summary Skills

1. Neptune

Neptune is ¹ the outermost planet of the solar system and is ² the fourth largest in diameter and the third largest in mass. Its atmosphere is composed mostly of gas, and it has ³ a vivid blue appearance. There are many strange facts about the planet, such as its high winds, 13 moons, and ⁴ hot core temperature that make it interesting to scientists. The only human probe ever to visit and collect information of Neptune was ⁵ Voyager 2.

2. The Metaphysics of Aristotle

Aristotle was one of the most important thinkers of all time because he created many fields of study, one of which is ¹ metaphysics. He created the guidelines for understanding ² the causes of things, of which there are ³ four major categories. He made many conclusions about ⁴ the substance of matter and form as well as defining five major elements. His classifications laid important foundations for ⁵ modern science that are used today.

3. Sequoyah

Sequoyah was a ¹ Cherokee Native American who is famous for creating the first system of writing for the Cherokee people. His exact place and date of birth are unknown because his people lacked ² a system of writing for recording historical data. After 12 years of work, Sequoyah created a writing system for the Cherokee language that used ³ 85 characters to represent the sounds of the language. This system was at first rejected by the Cherokee people, but they later accepted it after Sequoyah taught it to ⁴ a group of respected warriors. This system gave the Cherokee people a way to ⁵ record their history for future generations.

4. The First Transcontinental Railroad

The first transcontinental railroad to ¹ run across North America was completed in 1869 and commemorated with the famous Golden Spike event. The railroad was heavily backed by ² the federal government and stands as one of the great achievements of ³ President Abraham Lincoln. The building had many effects, such as bringing the Union states together during the Civil War as well as leading to the decline of ⁴ Native Americans in the West by populating it with white settlers. Much of the railroad was built by immigrant laborers from ⁵ Ireland and China as well as by veterans of the Union and Confederate armies and Mormons.

5. Mechanization

¹ Human history has been changed by the shift from human labor to ² mechanization. A good example of a simple machine that relieves a human of labor is ³ the lever. Some very important machines were ⁴ the steam-powered lathe, steam-powered trains, the Colt revolver, and the mechanization of car assembly lines. Military forces have also mechanized their forces, which results in many advantages in ⁵ warfare.

6. The Mammoth

The mammoth was [1] a prehistoric variety that is now extinct and whose fossil remains are the most commonly found. Mammoths are most closely related to [2] the Asian variety of elephant, having genetically split off from the African varieties of elephant [3] over 7 million years ago. Due to fossil evidence, scientists believe the mammoth originally evolved in [4] North Africa and then migrated around the world, ending up in North America. Mammoths began to die off due to [5] climate changes that began 700,000 years ago.

Mini TOEFL iBT

1. Ⓑ   2. Ⓓ   3. Ⓑ   4. Ⓓ   5. Ⓐ
6. Ⓒ   7. Ⓑ   8. Ⓓ   9. Ⓓ   10. Ⓐ
11. Ⓒ   12. Ⓑ

太阳黑子

太阳黑子是太阳表面的黑色区域。几千年来，它一直是天文界的难解之谜。公元前 28 年，中国天文学家曾记载了黑子的相关信息。当中亚沙漠的沙粒被风吹起挡住了太阳的光芒时，他们看到了最大的黑子群。西方人在中世纪时曾看到一个大的太阳黑子，但它的奥秘直到 1612 年才被伽利略解释清楚。

自公元 1700 年起，天文学家就开始记录所观察到的太阳黑子。如今，科学家已经能够估测出公元前 11000 年太阳黑子出现的整个过程。最近一次的太阳黑子高峰期从 1900 年开始一直持续到 20 世纪 60 年代。太阳上一次相似的活跃期在 8000 多年前。

太阳黑子区域的温度低于其周围区域的温度。它们同时出现强磁活动，进而抑制太阳的正常对流。如此一来，太阳上就出现了表面低温区。但是这些区域的亮度依然很高，无法直视。太阳上其他区域的温度为 5700 开氏度，而黑子区域的温度只有 4000 开氏度。这种温差主要由这些清晰可见的黑色区域引起。除太阳之外的其他星球上所出现的类似区域被称为恒星黑子。

人们还没有完全弄清太阳黑子的形成原因。但毋庸置疑，它们是太阳对流区中可见的类似磁通管的物质。这些磁通管是由差动自转"卷绕"而成的。当磁通管所承受的压力达到一定限度时，它们像橡皮圈一样卷起来然后穿透太阳的表面。在这些穿刺点上的对流就会受到抑制，于是太阳内部流出的能量减少，进而降低了太阳表面的温度。

黑子的数量与太阳辐射的强度有关。自 1979 年科学家能用卫星检测辐射以来，这种联系就被记录了下来。因为太阳黑子颜色较暗，所以科学家自然而然地推测黑子数量与辐射强度成反比。然而，太阳黑子周围区域却更明亮。因此，总体效果是更多的太阳黑子使得太阳更加明亮。但是这种明亮度的微小变化是肉眼无法观察到的。"蒙德极小期"表示太阳上几乎没有黑子的一段时间。这段时间，地球上的温度下降了大约 1 摄氏度。

雷暴的频率

雷暴发生时通常伴有雷和闪电，因此被称为雷电。这种猛烈的风暴是由一种会带来强降水和冰雹的积雨云引起的。在冬季较罕见的情况下，积雨云还有可能带来降雪，即雷雪。

当空气在不稳定的环境下急剧冷凝时，就会形成雷暴。在一股强劲的上升气流的作用下，雷暴会带来大范围的降雨和冰晶。雷暴产生时伴有三个特征：首先是低空的湿度大幅上升，这反映为露点的升高。其次，它还会带来空气温度的大幅下降和高度的上升，这叫做干绝热递减率。第三，它会产生例如力学辐合的自然力。这种自然力沿冷锋产生并使上升力集中。

世界各地都有雷暴现象，甚至包括极地在内。暴风雨出现最频繁的地区是热带雨林地区，其频率可达到一天一次。据说乌干达的坎帕拉和托罗罗是地球上出现雷暴最多的地区，另外，印度尼西亚爪哇岛上的茂物也是地球上的多雷暴区。在温带地区，雷暴一般发生在春季，但是它也可能在一年中任何时候随着冷锋的形成而产生。佛罗里达州是除热带地区外雷暴发生最频繁的地区。在夏季，强烈的暴风雨每天都会袭击佛罗里达州的中南部。

美国的暴风雨最强烈且最危险，尤其是在中西部以及南部的各个州。这些暴风雨会带来大范围冰雹和强龙卷风。虽然雷暴在美国西海岸并不常见，但它却是内陆地区的常客，加州的萨克拉门托和圣华金山就经常遭遇雷暴。西北地区雷暴的情况与中西部的相类似，但频率和强度要小很多。

早期人类文明很大程度上受到雷暴频率的影响。罗马人认为雷暴是宙斯神发动的战争，他向人类投掷火神制造的闪电。频繁的雷暴使罗马人忧心忡忡，他们宰杀了许多动物作为祭品，来安抚这位暴怒的天神。美洲印第安人认为雷暴与伟大神灵的仆人有关，而其频率与神灵的怒气有关。如今，风暴追逐者每年春天都会前往美国大平原和加拿大大草原，并在夏天通过观察暴风雨和龙卷风进行科学研究。对于这些追求刺激的人来说，暴风雨越多越能满足他们对冒险的渴望。

Vocabulary Review

A 1. Ⓐ 2. Ⓒ 3. Ⓑ 4. Ⓐ
　　5. Ⓐ 6. Ⓒ 7. Ⓑ 8. Ⓑ

B 1. d 2. h 3. j 4. c 5. b
　　6. g 7. f 8. i 9. e 10. a

Unit 7　Inference

Skill & Drill

1. Ⓓ

海绵

海绵是一种动物，是海绵动物门的一种。它们是生存在海底的最原始的滤食动物。它们能够通过身体将水吸入，过滤出食物粒子。海绵是最简单的动物之一，它们没有真正的组织，也没有肌肉、神经和内部器官。地球上现已发现 5000 多种海绵，多数存于岩石表面和潮间带。在地下 8500 米及更深的区域都能发现海绵。化石记录显示，在前寒武纪时期海绵就已经存在了，但是现在仍不断有新的种类被发现。

2. Ⓐ

特诺奇蒂特兰

特诺奇蒂特兰是阿兹特克帝国的古都，位于现今墨西哥城所在地。该古城建在特斯科科湖的群岛上。它的建设基于一个对称型的构建图——城市被分为四个部分，每个部分都被称作 campans。运河贯穿在城市间，用于交通运输。整座城市的建设依据的是一套以宗教领域为中心的既定方案。高达 60 米的特诺奇蒂特兰大金字塔屹立在这座城市中。城中的房屋由木材和黏土建成，屋顶由芦苇搭建。但是金字塔、寺庙和宫殿通常是用石头建造的。

3. Ⓑ

电子乐

电子乐由各种低耗能的电子设备创造出来。在电子音乐出现之前，许多作曲家希望通过使用高科技来创造音乐。人们也发明了一些利用新型电子机械设计的乐器，穆格键盘就是其中之一。在 20 世纪 70 年代的一部名为《发条橙》的电影作品中，这种键盘被用来录制电影中贝多芬的音乐。它也造就了最早的电子乐唱片。20 世纪 90 年代末期，又有许多音乐类型从电子乐中分离出来。这些音乐的

风格多种多样，也没有严格的标准和界限。

4. Ⓓ

洋流

洋流的产生源于流入大洋中的水流的不断运动。洋流可持续流动数千千米。这种现象通常出现在邻近大洋的区域。湾流就是其中最典型的例子。这种洋流使得欧洲西北部的气候相较于同纬度的其他地区而言更加温和。另一个例子是夏威夷群岛。得益于加利福尼亚洋流，夏威夷群岛的气温相较于同纬度的其他热带岛屿来说更加凉爽。掌握表面洋流的相关知识也很重要。了解这些信息可以大大缩减海运费用。这是因为洋流的运动可以推动船只航行，这样便可以大幅降低燃料费。

Practice with Long Passages

A　1. Ⓒ　2. Ⓑ　3. Ⓓ　4. Ⓐ
[1] Megabats / [2] Microbats

蝙蝠与回声定位

蝙蝠是哺乳动物。其前肢演化为翼，这使得它们成为世界上唯一一种会飞的哺乳动物。现今全球约有 1100 种蝙蝠。

蝙蝠又可被分为两个亚目——大蝙蝠和小蝙蝠。但并不是所有大蝙蝠的体型都大于小蝙蝠。二者最主要的区别有两点：小蝙蝠通过回声定位确定方向和寻找食物。大蝙蝠则不具备这样的能力。但它们却有着小蝙蝠没有的长在第二只脚趾和前翼上的尖爪。

大蝙蝠通常以水果、花蜜和花粉为食。小蝙蝠主要以昆虫、大型动物的血液、小型哺乳动物和鱼类为生。小蝙蝠所使用的回声定位是生物声呐的一种。海豚和鲸也使用这样的声呐。

回声定位是指动物向其周围区域发出信号，借助周围不同物体反射回来的声波判断这些物体的位置、范围进而识别的过程。它们通过测量动物的声音和返回的声波之间的时间差来进行测距。小蝙蝠用耳朵完成这一工作。

1794 年，一位科学家在蝙蝠身上进行了一系列试验。他得出的结论是：蝙蝠通过它们的听觉飞行。但是当时的科学界否定了他的发现。1938 年，另一位科学家描述了蝙蝠所使用的超声波回声定位。

小蝙蝠通过回声定位在黑暗中飞行和觅食。太阳下山后，它们就从洞穴或栖息地中出来，然后在晚上捕捉昆虫，以之为食。这种能力使它们在捕食时处于独特的地位，因为这时经常有很多昆虫出现。由于夜晚捕食者较少，许多昆虫选择在夜晚出来活动。而且此时对食物的竞

争并不大，并且以蝙蝠为食的动物也很少。

B 1. Ⓑ 2. Ⓓ 3. Ⓒ 4. Ⓑ
[1] Emphasized the new over the traditional /
[2] Eduard Manet, Claude Monet, and Gustave Eiffel

现代主义

现代主义是一项寻求进步发展的运动。20世纪时，它席卷了各个文化领域。它强调人的力量并鼓励人们摒弃传统的方式。现代主义者相信他们可以通过应用科学技术，形成、推进，甚至重新塑造自己的生活以及整个世界。

现代主义的重要性体现在它所代表的观念的转变。它体现了工业革命对人类思想的影响。并且，它也是艺术、哲学与科技的交汇点。

现代主义的历史是由一系列运动所构成的，现代主义者们试图谋求进步。现代主义于19世纪中叶由法国画家发起，其中最早的是一些印象派画家，诸如埃多瓦·马奈和克劳德·莫奈。他们表明，人们在欣赏油画时，并不是欣赏画作中的物体本身，而是接受光影效果所传递的图像。另一位早期的现代主义者是古斯塔夫·埃菲尔，他设计的埃菲尔铁塔改变了人们对建筑以及建筑学发展前景的看法。

然而，现代主义者们最主要的问题是，他们之间总是相互否定，在各种相关问题上发生争执。他们会争论谁是某一种风格的开创者或者谁的风格与另一位著名现代主义者的风格更为接近。然而他们的争论绝大多数情况下难分孰是孰非，不过是在浪费时间与精力罢了。

一些历史学家将20世纪分为现代时期和后现代时期。他们认为，后现代主义者将现代主义风格和原则用于消费产品中。现代派风格不仅被用于商品中，还被用于唱片封面的艺术设计、明信片设计，甚至伦敦地铁站中各种标志的图案设计中。

但是也有人将现代派与后现代派归为一类。他们都用怀疑的目光审视一切，并且致力于找到一切"阻碍"进步的事物，然后将其剔除。取而代之的是一种可达同样目的的新方法。而"新"，即意味着"更好"。

C 1. Ⓑ 2. Ⓐ 3. Ⓒ 4. Ⓑ
[1] ancient India and Greece / [2] the church in the Middle Ages / [3] Germany and Britain

音乐剧

音乐剧是一种娱乐形式，通过歌曲、言语和舞蹈的形式讲述故事。这种娱乐形式的起源要追溯到几千年以前，一些早期的音乐剧发源于古印度和古希腊。希腊人在当时流行的舞台剧的基础上又加入了音乐和舞蹈。一些伟大的希腊剧作家甚至亲自为自己的剧作谱曲。

几百年后的公元前3年，这种音乐剧形式再度出现。罗马喜剧作家普劳图斯将歌曲、舞蹈以及管弦乐曲加入到自己的剧作中。为了使舞步声足够响亮以便在开阔的剧院也能让全场观众听到，演员在各自的鞋上装上了铁片。这便是最早的踢踏舞鞋。

中世纪，戏剧成为教堂传播教义的工具。他们通过以赞美诗为主体的宗教意味的戏剧教授礼拜仪式。这些戏剧变得越来越流行，最终脱离教堂成为一种娱乐方式。其形式在散文对话与礼拜赞美诗之间不断转换以吸引观众。

这种形式一直发展到文艺复兴时期并成为意大利的传统。滑稽的小丑表演贯穿整场戏剧，表演普通人皆知的故事，这种娱乐形式被称为喜歌剧。这种新的传统在17世纪时传入法国。法国伟大作家莫里哀成功将他的部分喜剧改编为音乐剧，其中的音乐创作由琼·巴普蒂斯特·吕里完成。

这种娱乐形式在欧洲大陆盛传并不断被改进。18世纪的英国和法国出现了两种不同的音乐剧——一种是民谣歌剧，这种歌剧的剧作家通过借用当时的流行歌曲，根据自己的需要改写歌词；另一种是喜剧歌剧，这种歌剧的不同之处在于，它们的配乐和情节主线均为原创并且充满浪漫主义色彩。

D 1. Ⓓ 2. Ⓓ 3. Ⓒ 4. Ⓐ
[1] speed and control / [2] small movements /
[3] momentum / [4] turning

鱼鳍

所有鱼的身体都呈流线型，这使它们可以在水中自由游动。鳍的出现就是鱼类进化过程中的一部分。鱼鳍是鱼类的附肢，呈扁平状，由软骨构成并被鱼鳞覆盖。鱼类不同的身体部位有不同类型的鱼鳍，以控制它们在水中的游动。这些鱼鳍能使鱼类在水中转弯、减速、加速、停住或者在某处保持静止。

背鳍长在鱼背的中间，有的尖有的钝。尖的背鳍用于加速；而钝的背鳍可以使小鱼在激流中控制住身体。鱼类最多有三个背鳍，它们由刺状或者柔软型两种不同的软骨鳍条支撑着，背鳍可包含任何一种或同时包含两种鳍条。刺状鳍条，因为有锐利甚至有毒的尖，有时也可被当做防御武器。

另外，尾鳍、胸鳍以及腹鳍都是由鳍条支撑着。这些鳍虽小，却能使鱼类很好地控制身体，反应迅速，快速游动。正因为这些鱼鳍，鱼类可以寻找合适的位置进行觅食或者与其他鱼组成鱼群。尾鳍位于鱼类身体的尾部，在肛门的后方。

胸鳍位于鱼身两侧，就像鸟类的翅膀一样。其鳍条的结构，与陆生动物的前肢构造有异曲同工之妙。一对腹鳍位于胸鳍的下方和后方，与陆生动物的后肢相仿。通过这些鱼鳍的摆动, 鱼类即可在水中游动。

尾鳍(tail fins)(也被称做 caudal fins)能使鱼类在水中转弯以及加速。一些鱼类之所以游得很快, 是因为它们的尾鳍前部有一个横向龙骨尾鳍, 使尾部形成一个突起, 这样就提高了游动的速度以及稳定性。

E 1. Ⓐ 2. Ⓒ 3. Ⓐ 4. Ⓒ

¹ parietal lobe / ² occipital lobe / ³ cerebellum

人脑的功能

人类的大脑被一道裂沟分为左右两边。大脑一边的结构与另一边完全对称, 但是其主要功能却各有不同。这曾经导致了"人们只用左脑或右脑"这一没有依据的理论的形成。但是这种理论是一种误解, 因为一个正常人只有在左右脑的协调工作下才能完成各种技能和工作。

人脑由五部分组成, 它们是顶叶、额叶、枕叶、颞叶和小脑。顶叶的主要作用是收集由身体各个部分传来的感官信息, 以及通过视觉判断空间。这是人对大脑了解最少的一个区域。

大脑的额叶由脑回和运动皮质层组织构成。大脑通过该组织控制身体的随意运动。另外, 人们还发现额叶可以管理冲动控制、判断力、记忆、语言、运动功能、问题解决能力、性行为、社交行为以及自发行为。许多身体活动都受到额叶的控制。

枕叶的作用是处理视觉信息。它是四个脑叶中最小的一个, 位于大脑后方。它主要用于处理颜色、空间以及运动知觉。如果枕叶受到损伤, 人会视力下降甚至失明。

颞叶位于大脑两边的较低的位置, 由听觉皮质层组成。它不仅控制着人类听和处理声音的能力, 还控制着诸如语言等高级信息的处理。它主要管理理解、非文字记忆、列举及语言功能。

小脑位于大脑基部, 与脊髓交于一点。这一区域的主要作用是感官知觉与肌肉控制通过神经系统的交汇点。

F 1. Ⓓ 2. Ⓒ 3. Ⓐ 4. Ⓑ

¹ Cotton and cattle / ² Northern areas / ³ Hogs and corn

美国的农业

农业是美国发展的基础。这项产业养活了全美国人民, 并向世界其他国家出口粮食。然而, 这项产业的发展绝非一日之功, 几个世纪以来的不断改进, 才最终创造出足以养活全美人民的农业基础。

西进的殖民地运动促进了农场在美国的盛行。殖民者到达一个新的地方, 就在该地建立自己的农场。他们的努力也使新的城镇发展起来。通往这些地区的供应链最终发展成为全美四通八达的公路。

由于适于在寒冷地区生长, 小麦成为北方地区粮食种植的首选。人们通常会在新的殖民地上种植小麦, 这些地区也因此被称为"小麦边境"。多年来, 这些新开垦的小麦田不断向西移动, 更加多样的农田取代了之前的小麦田。

在中西部地区, 玉米种植业和养猪业是常见的农业组合形式。二者之所以互为补充, 是因为在运河和铁路出现之前, 向市场运送谷物非常困难, 而猪的运送却容易得多。因此, 谷物就被用来当做喂猪的饲料。

在温暖的南方地区, 棉花的种植以及肉牛的饲养最为盛行。原因是二者都是耐热性生物。烟草种植在南方也很常见。美国内战之前, 农活一直由奴隶完成。在美国东北部的农业生产中也会用到奴隶。这种情况一直持续到 19 世纪早期。但是, 1787 年《自由法案》的颁布废除了中西部的奴隶制。

大萧条期间, 土地大面积荒芜。这是由于尘暴的侵袭使中西部地区大片土壤无法再被耕作。后来, 这些地区被改建为国家森林。但 20 世纪 40 年代, 为了支持第二次世界大战的粮食供应, 这些土地又重新被用来耕作。

Building Summary Skills

1. Bats and Echolocation

Bats are ¹ the only mammals that can fly. There are two suborders of bats: ² megabats and microbats. These bats are different from each other. Megabats have a claw on their legs and are typically ³ herbivorous. Microbats use ⁴ ultrasound echolocation to get around and hunt insects, small animals, and fish. They usually ⁵ hunt at night when there are a lot of insects, much less competition for food, and fewer enemies.

2. Modernism

¹ Modernism was an important movement in ² the twentieth century. It encouraged people to forget about traditional ways and to try to ³ improve their lives. Its members, like ⁴ Eduard Manet and Gustave Eiffel, wanted to create progress. But sometimes they got into ⁵ useless arguments. Still, the effects of modernism can be seen everywhere today.

3. Musical Theater

The musical theater is a kind of ¹ entertainment that is very old. It goes back to ² ancient India and Greece. Over the years, it has undergone a number of different changes. The church in the Middle Ages used it to tell [3] religious stories. Other cultures created [4] musical theater productions that were [5] comedies or dramas.

4. The Fins of Fish

An important evolutionary development in fish is their fins. [1] Dorsal fins are located on the back and help the fish [2] control its speed. The anal, pectoral, and pelvic fins let the fish [3] dart quickly through the water. The pectoral fins [4] on the side of fish help give them momentum. And the tail fins let the fish [5] turn in the water.

5. The Functions of the Human Brain

The human brain is divided into two separate halves, [1] the left and right. There are five different sections: the parietal, frontal, occipital, and temporal lobes and the cerebellum. [2] The parietal lobe controls sensory information, while the frontal lobe controls [3] the body's movements. [4] The occipital lobe controls vision, and the temporal lobe controls hearing. The cerebellum controls [5] the senses and muscles.

6. Agriculture in America

[1] Agriculture has long been important in America for a number of reasons. As people [2] moved west across the country, they lived by [3] farming the land. Various regions in the country raised different [4] crops and animals, including cotton, wheat, corn, hogs, and cattle. Some parts of the country have gone back and forth between being [5] farmed and unfarmed.

Mini TOEFL iBT

1. (A)　　2. (B)　　3. (C)　　4. (D)　　5. (B)
6. Endoparasites (B), (D), (F) / Ectoparasites (A), (E)
7. (A)　　8. (D)　　9. (C)　　10. (C)　　11. (D)
12. (B), (C), (E)

寄生

寄生描述了两个不同形式物种之间的关系，其中一种对另一种有害。存在寄生关系的两个物种必须是长时间生活在一起的，但不包括动物捕食猎物以及蚊子以寄主为生的情况。

寄生虫大致分为两种——内寄生虫和外寄生虫。内寄生虫寄生在寄主体内。钩虫就是其中一种，它寄生在人或动物的胃中。大部分内寄生虫是被动地找到寄主的。它们寄生在寄主的肠道中并产卵。这些卵随着寄主的排泄物排至体外，在一些卫生条件不好的地方再寄生到其他人或动物体内。

外寄生虫寻找新寄主的方式多种多样。一些水蛭通过其运动传感器来定位寄主，并通过体温和化学信号来判断寄主的身份。一旦确定了目标，水蛭就会利用其钩状的牙齿依附至寄主身上，然后深入皮层以下开始吸血。

寄生虫的寄生方式也可分为两种——死体营养型和活体营养型。死体营养型寄生虫不断消耗其寄主组织直至寄主因缺乏组织和营养而最终死亡。而对于活体营养型寄生虫来说，一旦寄主死亡，其自身也无法存活。因此，它们必须确保寄主活着以保全自己。许多病毒属于活体营养型寄生虫，它们利用寄主的基因和细胞变化过程来繁殖。

活体寄生是一种生物存活的普遍方式。至少有一半的动物都经历过寄生的阶段，包括人类的胎儿寄生在母体的子宫中。寄生在植物与菌类中也很常见。所有非寄生生物都是一种或多种寄生虫的寄主。

一些寄生虫属群居类。它们懂得如何利用群居类寄主的行为。一些寄生性昆虫，如线虫，会寄生于蚂蚁群或白蚁群中。它们寄生于整个蚁群，直到这个蚁群衰弱并最终灭亡。许多种类的杜鹃鸟以偷寄主的食物为生。它们甚至将蛋产在其他鸟类的巢穴中让其为之抚养后代。因此，成年的杜鹃鸟只会为自己捕食，而幼年的杜鹃鸟则由别的成年鸟类抚养。

泛古陆

20 世纪初科学家提出了大陆漂移学说。他们称，我们今天所熟知的七大洲在许多年前其实是一个庞大的整体。一位名叫阿尔弗雷德·韦格纳的科学家将其命名为泛古陆。"泛古陆"来源于希腊语，意思是"所有的土地"。

该学说引起了巨大争议。该理论的年表与当时盛行的地球只有几千年历史的观点相悖。相较于自然的力量，人们更倾向于相信是上帝缔造了地球。韦格纳在 1920 年以大陆漂移学说反驳了人们的观点。

泛古陆的地形呈"C"状，它沿赤道分布开来。月牙状部分由大片水域填充，被称为特提斯海。环绕在大陆周围的大洋被称为泛古洋。

泛古陆的陆地非常广阔。由于缺水，其内陆地区非常干旱。动物可以随意从北极迁徙至南极。

泛古陆的分裂主要经历了 3 个阶段。一个普遍认同的观点是它在 1 亿 8 千万年前，即侏罗纪时代开始分崩离析。经过几百万年，它最终分裂形成了我们如今熟知的七大洲。

最早的大陆断裂大约始于 1 亿 8 千万年前大陆上出现的一道巨大断层线。地震和火山喷发引发了大陆运动。自特提斯海一直向东的泛古陆形成了一条裂纹，就在现在的北美洲和非洲之间。第一次大陆分裂形成了两块较小的大陆。南部的被称为冈瓦纳大陆；北部的被称为劳亚大陆。

大陆断裂的第二阶段发生在大约 1 亿 5 千万至 1 亿 4 千万年之前。当时较小的冈瓦纳大陆又分裂成四块大陆，也就是后来的非洲、南美洲、印度和澳大利亚。

第三次也是最后一次分裂发生在约 6 千万至 5 千 5 百万年之前。北美大陆从欧亚大陆脱离出来，挪威海也就此形成。

但是该理论的支持者同时表示，泛古陆并非最早的大陆。通过追溯地球的地质历史，他们又增加了一些其他的大陆形成阶段。其中距离泛古陆最近的阶段是潘诺西亚大陆。科学家认为该大陆形成于 6 亿年前并在 5 千万年之后再次分裂。再之前的大陆被称为罗迪尼亚大陆，科学家认为该大陆形成于 11 亿年前并在 7 千 5 百万年后分裂。哥伦比亚大陆可能是最早的大陆，科学家认为它存在于 18 亿至 15 亿年前。

Vocabulary Review

A 1. (A) 2. (C) 3. (B) 4. (B)
5. (A) 6. (D) 7. (B) 8. (D)

B 1. d 2. f 3. i 4. c 5. j
6. h 7. e 8. b 9. a 10. g

Unit 8 Insert Text

Skill & Drill

1. **C**
分子

分子由两个或两个以上的原子构成，由键的作用结合在一起。这些物质通常不能再被分为单位更小的同等物质。分子被认为是物质组成中最小的颗粒。在这种状态下，分子依然有自己的结构和化学性质。很多物质最好被认为由原子和离子构成。科学家就是这样看待物质的，而不是只看到分子结构。分子是包含两个或两个以上原子的稳定体。分子这个概念最早由一位名叫阿伏伽德罗的科学家于 1811 年提出。

2. **C**
食

eclipse(食)这个词来源于希腊语的"消失"一词，它是一种天文景观。当一个天体进入另一个天体的阴影部分时，就会产生食。食一般指的是日食，它是月亮的阴影遮住阳光，落在地球表面时所产生的。而月食，则是当月亮进入地球的阴影部分时所产生的。食也指发生在地月系统之外的天文景观，例如当行星穿过其卫星的阴影部分时所产生的景观，或者也可能指卫星进入其围绕运行的恒星的阴影，或者就是一个卫星进入另一个卫星的阴影部分。

3. **A**
爵士乐

爵士乐是一种起源于美国的音乐形式。20 世纪初期，新奥尔良首先奏响了爵士乐。爵士乐起源于美国黑人音乐。后来它还与西方音乐技术和理论相结合。爵士乐包含蓝调、摇摆乐、"呼"与"应"以及即兴演奏。自其最早在美国黑人圈内兴起之后，爵士乐在 20 世纪 20 年代开始传播开来。它影响了很多其他音乐类型。爵士乐中最基本的乐器由世纪之交时游行乐队和舞蹈乐队所使用的乐器构成，包括贝斯、簧片、鼓和西方十二音音阶。但是"爵士"这个词从何而来却尚无定论。

4. **B**
索福克勒斯

索福克勒斯是古希腊三大悲剧戏剧家之一。有文献记载，他共创作了 123 部剧作。他在戏剧比赛中赢得的冠军数无人能及。他提交给戏剧节的四部剧作中有三部是悲剧。最后一部叫做羊人剧。另外，他在未取得第一的比赛中都位居亚席。公元前 468 年，他赢得了生平第一个冠军，尽管当代的学者认为这并不是他第一次参加比赛。目前完整保存下来的索福克勒斯的悲剧仅剩七部，这其中最著名的是三部关于俄狄浦斯和安提戈涅的剧作，统称为《俄狄浦斯环》。

Practice with Long Passages

A 1. (D) 2. (C) 3. **1A** 4. **2C**
[1] Astronomy Precinct / [2] Clean, dry air / [3] 12 telescopes

冒纳凯阿火山天文台

冒纳凯阿火山上坐落着 11 座研究站，这里是全世界观测星象的最佳地点。在夏威夷语中，"冒纳凯阿"的意思是"白色的山"。这座山是夏威夷岛上的一座休眠火山，它不仅是太平洋盆地的最高点，也是世界上最高的岛山。冒纳凯阿火山距洋底 9750 米，海拔为 4205 米。其最高峰在地球大气厚度的 40% 之上。

冒纳凯阿火山上方的空气非常干燥、清新，这是因为顶峰下有浮动的云层。这些云层将顶部的空气与较低处潮湿的海洋性气团分隔开来，保证了顶峰空气的纯净和干燥。同时它们也保护了顶峰的空气免遭污染。

山顶的晴朗使其成为研究星象的最佳地点。这里晴朗的夜晚数量居全球之最，能见度很高。星辰清晰可见的另一个原因是冒纳凯阿火山远离城市的灯光。全岛强制实施的照明法保证了极其漆黑的夜空。

冒纳凯阿火山的天文区创立自 1967 年。它位于一片受保护的土地上。该区域之所以受保护，是因为它在夏威夷文化中的神圣地位。该天文区被建成了一个供天文学家前来观测星象的国际中心。

科学家驻地位于顶峰下大约海拔 3000 米的位置。游客信息站位于其下 100 米处。科学家及游客需要在海拔较低处停留 30 分钟左右，以便在到达顶峰之前稍作适应，避免高原反应。

山顶一共设有 12 台望远镜，由来自不同国家的企业和机构赞助。其中，夏威夷大学控制着两台；凯克天文台拥有其中的两台孪生望远镜；斯巴鲁公司拥有并管理一台；英国拥有一台红外线望远镜；加拿大和法国共享一台；加州理工大学拥有并操控一台。这些组织都在努力为人类更好地理解太空作出贡献。

B 1. ⓒ 2. ⓓ 3. **1A** 4. **2C**

[1] element 104 / [2] element 106 / [3] element 105

元素命名之争

20 世纪 60 年代，美国和苏联的关系一度非常紧张。甚至连两国的科学家都开始争执。那时，许多科学家都在相互竞争，希望成为元素合成的第一人以获得元素的命名权。一个争议也由此产生，直到 1997 年才得以解决。问题开始于一些科学家表示他们在同一时间合成了同一种元素。这其中主要的科研实验室是美国伯克利的一个实验室和苏联杜伯纳的一个实验室。

当苏联科学家合成了第 104 号元素时，他们以苏联"原子弹之父"伊戈尔·库尔恰托夫的名字为其命名。但是美国科学家强烈反对这一做法，他们不能忍受用发明攻击美国武器的人的名字来命名一种元素。但是他们也因此被冠以伪君子之名，因为之前他们曾以"爱因斯坦"命名一种元素，而爱因斯坦也曾致力于研究原子武器。

此后，国际元素命名委员会成员拒绝了美国将第 106 号元素以科学家格伦·T·西博格的名字命名的请求。因为他依然健在，并且他分发印有自己名字的元素周期表，这

违反了委员会规定。1994 年，委员会提出了一套新名字以解决这一纠纷。他们希望以苏联杜伯纳实验室的名字命名第 104 号元素以取代其之前的名称；并且提议拒绝用西博格命名第 106 号元素。

这一提议遭到了美国化学协会的反对，他们认为自己有按自己的意愿命名第 106 号元素的权利。国际委员会最终决定命名权应由伯克利和杜伯纳共享。但是杜伯纳还未提供一个名字，与此同时，许多美国的书中已经使用了之前的名字。

最终，在 1997 年，双方就命名问题达成一致。但是 1999 年，西博格仍然质疑第 105 号元素名称的修改。它已经由 hahnium 变为了 dubnium。他说他们并未真正发现与该名称对应的元素。但是杜伯纳小组拒绝让出他们的命名权。伯克利的一些科学家依然称 105 号元素为 hahnium。

C 1. ⓒ 2. ⓓ 3. **1B** 4. **2A**

[1] Aristocles / [2] the early dialogues / [3] the *Republic*

柏拉图

柏拉图出生于古希腊的黄金时代。他原名阿里斯托克勒，历史学家认为他之所以得到柏拉图的绰号是因为其思想宽阔，在希腊语中，"柏拉图"的意思是"宽阔"。还有一种说法是柏拉图有着宽大的前额。他的父母在雅典很有影响力。柏拉图起初跟随苏格拉底学习。苏格拉底去世后，柏拉图去了埃及和意大利学习，随后返回雅典并开办了自己的学堂。他努力传播苏格拉底式的思考模式，引导学生发现真理。

柏拉图试图通过记录老师的语录来传播苏格拉底式教学。这些对话是关于苏格拉底史实的首要来源。早期的对话着眼于单一的问题，但是却鲜有结论。其中一篇柏拉图的对话叫做《尤西弗罗篇》，它讲述了诉诸权威与坚持道德判断的两难问题。《申辩篇》描述了哲学生活。这一描述是苏格拉底在雅典陪审团面前所作的陈述。

在柏拉图的对话中，苏格拉底是一个虚构的人物。但柏拉图在对话中也表达了自己关于哲学问题的看法。在《美诺篇》中，柏拉图介绍了苏格拉底"没有人会故意犯错"的观点。他还引入了关于回忆的学说，并试图以此探索美德是否可以被教授。《斐多篇》发展了柏拉图式思想，展示了形式论。这些论证都用以体现人类灵魂的不朽。

《理想国》是柏拉图这些对话中最伟大的作品。它以一段关于"正义的性质"的对话为开头，由此延伸至对正义、智慧、勇气和稳健的讨论。他着眼于这些品质对个人以及整个社会的不同影响。其中关于洞穴的寓言充分展示了人类生活的各种可能性。对话以对各种体制政府的评论收尾。柏拉图还在其中详细阐述了只有哲学家适合掌权的理想国度。同时，他还试图说明正义是优于非正义的。

D 1. Ⓑ 2. Ⓐ 3. 1C 4. 2A

¹ modern dance / ² new dance movements /
³ French fans

洛伊·富勒

洛伊·富勒是现代舞领域的先驱。她同时还是照明技术领域的革新者。她生于芝加哥，以当儿童演员开始了自己的演艺事业。之后，她开始在滑稽歌舞杂剧、歌舞杂耍表演以及马戏团表演中表演舞蹈。她同时也是自由舞表演的先驱。她的舞蹈均为原创，动作自然。她还创造了即兴表演，将舞蹈动作与丝绸服装的飘动相结合。这些在其设计的彩色灯光下大放光彩。

富勒以其作品"蛇舞"在美国一炮走红。但是她却因自己不被大众认真对待而闷闷不乐。她感到人们仍然把她当演员看待。巴黎的人民热情地接纳了她，于是她留在法国继续自己的事业。她是法国女神游乐厅剧场的固定演员，通常会表演"火焰舞"。后来，成为新艺术运动的代表人物。

许多法国艺术家和科学家都被富勒这种开拓性尝试所吸引。她的舞迷包括诸如朱尔斯·谢雷特、亨利·德·图卢兹-洛特雷克以及玛丽·居里在内的大人物。她还获得了许多关于舞台灯光的专利权，包括利用化合物制造彩色凝胶。她甚至还是法国天文协会的成员。

富勒为早期的现代舞蹈演员安排了很多欧洲巡演。她是第一位在欧洲表演的美国现代舞演员。她将伊莎多拉·邓肯引荐给巴黎的观众。其闻名之处还在于，她使得现代舞蹈作为一种严肃的艺术形式被人们接受。

富勒偶尔会返回美国，她在学生的鼓励下重新回到舞台演出。这些学生被称为"Fulleret"或者缪斯。她在巴黎度过余生，于 1928 年死于乳腺癌。火化之后，她的骨灰被埋在了巴黎。

E 1. Ⓐ 2. Ⓒ 3. 1D 4. 2A

¹ Norman Lockyer / ² Gerald Hawkins /
³ Alexander Thom / ⁴ Euan Mackie

古天文学

许多古代社会研究星象。现在，又有很多科学家研究那时的天文学实践。他们也研究早期社会人们所制造的用来观察星象的工具。如今，这种考古学和天文学相结合的研究形式已经正式成为科学的一个分支，但最初却备受争议。很多人并不相信原始人类能够理解天文学。

19 世纪末，一位名叫诺曼·罗克耶的天文学家在该领域异常活跃。他的研究涵盖了巨石阵和埃及金字塔，他试图让这门研究作为科学的正式分支被广泛接受。但是在不列颠群岛，对这个领域的研究越来越少。20 世纪 60 年代，

天文学家杰拉德·霍金斯提出，巨石阵是石器时代的计算机。这一有趣的观点又重新燃起人们对这一领域的兴趣。

大约在同一时期，一位名叫亚历山大·汤姆的工程师公布了其研究结果。他在论文中指出，在古代文明中，人们在精密天文学方面有着广泛的实践。他还说，古时候的巨石阵被应用于不列颠群岛上。霍金斯的观点遭到普遍反对，但是汤姆的分析却引出了一个问题，它挑战了当时史学方面的学术界观点。克莱夫·格拉斯对汤姆的调研作了重新定位，希望证明其说法的错误性。但是，人们对于石器时期遗址的天文学研究的广泛兴趣已成为不争的事实。

只有一位科学家——尤安·麦凯认同汤姆的理论需要验证。他分别在 1970 和 1971 年前往阿盖尔郡 Kinstraw 石阵遗址，考察汤姆关于石阵上平台的观测准确性的预言是否正确。他分别在考察了这些平台同石阵排成的直线后，发现预言是正确的——汤姆的结论被接受了。这些都被记录在英国新的史前发现中。这些坚忍不拔的科学家们证实了古时候的人们确实能够研究星象并得出精确的结果。历史从此被改写。

F 1. Ⓑ 2. Ⓒ 3. 1A 4. 2D

¹ the Calvin cycle / ² photosynthesis / ³ carbon-14

梅尔文·卡尔文

梅尔文·卡尔文是一位伟大的化学家，他将永远被世人铭记。他一生致力于探索与发现。他和他的团队一同发现了卡尔文循环——即碳元素在植物内的循环路径。这一发现之所以闻名世界，是因为其解开了"植物光合作用之谜"。而他也因此获得了 1961 年的诺贝尔化学奖。

卡尔文于 1937 年进入伯克利加州大学工作。1963 年，他获得分子生物学教授头衔。他是生化力学实验室的创始人兼主管。他同时还是伯克利放射实验室的副主管。

据民间传言，二战时日本投降当天，实验室的主管找到卡尔文说："现在是让放射性碳发挥作用的时候了。"他指的是 1940 年发现的碳的同位素，该同位素曾被应用于袭击日本的原子弹的制造中。卡尔文随即组织了一个放射性元素科研小组，开始研究光合作用的过程。绿色植物通过这一过程将太阳能转化为化学能。

卡尔文及其研究小组利用碳 14 作为同位素指示剂，并据此绘制了碳在植物中运动的完整路径。这一过程从其吸收空气中的二氧化碳开始，以合成碳水化合物结束。卡尔文小组证明，阳光在这一过程中作用于植物的叶绿素，并为有机化合物的合成提供能量。在此之前，人们一直认为阳光仅作用于植物中的二氧化碳。

这些试验使卡尔文一生都对能量生产感兴趣。他还多年致力于研究生命的化学进化，他在 1969 年出版的书中就主要探讨了这一问题。直至晚年，卡尔文依然不懈地进

行科学研究。他研究了产油植物的应用并将其列为可再生能源。卡尔文还分析了月球岩石。他是个热爱科学的人，对他来说，科学本身比他得到的众多荣誉更加重要。

Building Summary Skills

1. The Observatories at Mauna Kea

There are many research stations located on [1] Mauna Kea in Hawaii. These observatories are located there because of [2] the air quality and the fact that the night skies are [3] very dark and clear. The Astronomy Precinct there was established in [4] 1967. There are [5] twelve telescopes located there that are run by different countries or corporations.

2. The Element Naming Controversy

[1] In the 1960s, tensions between [2] the USA and Soviet Union even caused problems between scientists. There were [3] naming controversies over various elements that different laboratories created. The Americans objected to [4] the Soviet name, and the Soviets objected to the American name. Finally, an agreement on the name was arrived at, but some [5] American scientists still use the old name.

3. Plato

Plato was a great [1] Greek philosopher who lived in Athens and studied with Socrates. After Socrates died, Plato opened his own school and tried to imitate [2] the Socratic method of philosophy. Many of [3] his early dialogues looked at single issues but never came up with answers. His middle dialogues stopped using Socrates as a character and expressed [4] Plato's own thoughts. [5] The *Republic* was one of Plato's greatest works.

4. Loie Fuller

Loie Fuller was a pioneer in the field of [1] modern dance. She created many new dance movements through [2] improvisation. She became famous in America, but she [3] felt unappreciated, so she moved to France, where she had many fans. She had many [4] important French fans, including Jules Cheret, Henri de Toulouse-Lautrec, and Marie Curie. She toured Europe and also [5] helped other artists to do so.

5. Ancient Astronomy

Nowadays, many scientists study [1] the stargazing practices of ancient societies. [2] Norman Lockyer was an early scholar who looked into these practices. Gerald Hawkins also looked at [3] Stonehenge and noticed how it was connected to astronomy. Most people discounted Hawkins's work, but [4] Alexander Thom produced new evidence to support it. Euan Mackie went to Stonehenge and proved that [5] Thom's conclusions were correct.

6. Melvin Calvin

Melvin Calvin was [1] a great chemist who won a Nobel Prize. He discovered [2] the Calvin cycle, which helped to unlock [3] the secrets of photosynthesis. He worked at [4] UC Berkeley, where he was a professor. He used [5] the carbon-14 isotope to trace the route of carbon through the plant. He studied many different things through the course of his life.

Mini TOEFL iBT

1. Ⓒ	2. Ⓑ	3. Ⓓ	4. **B**	5. Ⓐ
6. Ⓒ	7. Ⓐ	8. Ⓑ	9. **C**	10. Ⓒ
11. Ⓓ	12. Ⓓ			

炫财冬宴

炫财冬宴是美洲一些印第安部落举行的宗教仪式。该仪式对其社会结构有极其重要的作用。这些部落位于太平洋西北海岸地区，从美国一直延伸至加拿大的英属哥伦比亚。这些部落包括海达族、辽鹤族、赛利希族和特林基特族。

"炫财冬宴"这个词来源于奇努克语，但参与这一仪式的每个群体对其都有不同的称呼。这个奇努克词语的发音与英语的"罐（pot）"和"闩（latch）"相近，但和这两样东西没有任何联系。

最初，举办炫财冬宴是为了纪念一些重要事件，如一位德高望重的长者的离世或者一个新生儿的诞生。美洲印第安人的社会阶层是有限定的。所以当一个人的社会阶层得到提升时，大家必须目睹其过程才能接受这一事实。

炫财冬宴是一种仪式型的盛宴。传统的炫财冬宴上会有海豹肉或大马哈鱼。宴席间，各个团体之间的等级关系通过交换礼物、舞蹈表演以及其他仪式得以确立和加强。主办家族通过分发财物以显示其财富。而这也会刺激那些地位显赫的客人举办自家的炫财冬宴作为回馈。

在欧洲人到来之前，炫财冬宴上的礼物可能是储存的食物、船只或者奴隶。18世纪末至19世纪，诸如毛毯和铜等新的物品的涌入却对炫财冬宴产生了消极影响。一些团体开始把炫财冬宴当做战争的角斗场。人们展开了对地位的激烈争夺。有时，人们收下礼物后会随即毁掉它们。

1885年，加拿大宣布炫财冬宴为非法。而在19世纪末，在传教士和政府官员的强烈要求下，美国也将其定为非法活动。他们认为炫财冬宴是一个愚蠢的习俗。在他们看来，炫财冬宴既浪费财物又不能创造生产价值，并且对参与者毫无裨益。但是，尽管已被明令禁止，炫财冬宴依然秘密进行了很多年。

多年之后，许多部落请求政府解除禁令。他们将炫财冬宴比做圣诞节，称炫财冬宴就像圣诞节一样是一个可以相互交换礼品的宴会。20世纪以来，炫财冬宴已不再是严重的问题，所以，最后禁令被解除了。

如今，许多种族学家致力于研究炫财冬宴，他们被这项节日活动深深吸引着。炫财冬宴的赞助者会分发许多珍贵的物品以此换得声望。而这种声望会随着炫财冬宴的豪华程度而增加。

文学评论

世界各地的学生都在学校学习伟大的文学作品。但有时他们也需要专家的帮助以更好地理解阅读过的作品。研究并探讨各个作家的文学作品是文学评论家的工作。他们思考并判断作家的意思，这种工作以文学理论为基础。但需要特别注意的是，并非所有评论家都是理论家。

如今，文学评论常以论文或者书的形式出现。学术评论家不仅教授这方面的课程，还将其研究成果发表在学术期刊上。具有讽刺意味的是，他们的评论文章的长度有时甚至超出了被评论的作品本身。更多的知名评论家将其作品发表在杂志上。其中一些比较流行的刊登文学评论的杂志有《纽约时报书评》、《民族》和《纽约客》。

从文学产生之初就有评论家对其进行讨论。亚里士多德和柏拉图都曾写书对古希腊诗歌进行尖锐的批评。中世纪，古典评论家主要将注意力集中于宗教经文上。但当时，批评《圣经》是非常危险的。评论家关于一些诸如《圣经》的圣书的评论通常需要与教会领袖的官方观点保持一致。

文艺复兴时期，许多写作方面的新想法不断产生，这些关于行文结构和内容的观点促使一批新的评论家产生。这些评论家认为写作是一切文化的核心，他们还表示，诗人和作家是悠久的文学传统的保护者。一些德高望重的诗人开始重新搜集过去的伟大作品。这其中被拯救的一部经典作品便是亚里士多德的《诗学》。

英国浪漫主义文学运动为文学评论领域带去了许多新的观念。19世纪早期的文学评论家认为写作的主体不需要华美，普通、粗糙甚至丑陋都没有关系。他们认为创造文学本身就是一个普遍的主题。文学作品所能达到的最高境界是"崇高"。

到了20世纪早期，一群新生文学评论家开始发表他们的作品，这些来自美国和英国的评论家称自己的作品为"新批评"。这些评论家认为研究写作最重要的方法就是字斟句酌地去阅读它。他们鼓励人们关注"文字本身"。这一阅读方法至今仍然非常流行。

20世纪60年代之前，新批评一直是研究写作最普遍的方法。之后，大学教授受到"大陆哲学"的深刻影响。这种新的思维方式催生出一种新的文学评论。这种哲学和评论方式都着眼于信息的结构。他们细致地研究这种结构的呈现方式。文学评论家必然经历一个叫做"拆析"的解构文学作品的过程。

Vocabulary Review

A　1. Ⓑ　　2. Ⓒ　　3. Ⓓ　　4. Ⓒ
　　　5. Ⓐ　　6. Ⓐ　　7. Ⓒ　　8. Ⓓ

B　1. d　　2. f　　3. a　　4. i　　5. b
　　　6. j　　7. g　　8. c　　9. h　　10. e

Unit 9　Prose Summary

Skill & Drill

1. Ⓑ, Ⓓ

肖像画

肖像绘画是一种展示主体视觉形象的艺术形式，这一主体通常指人。它同时还要求展示主体的真实形态。肖像画家为花钱雇佣他们的人创作肖像画。他们有时会受到对主体的强烈感情的启发。自画像指的是艺术家为自己所创作的肖像画。肖像画可以包括主体的整个身体或者身体的一半，也可以是从肩膀到头顶的胸像。肖像画选择的主体有时也可以是动物、宠物甚至房屋。

2. Ⓑ, Ⓒ

扁虫

扁虫是一种简单的生命形态，其身体柔软，无脊椎。它们生活在咸水、淡水及潮湿的环境中。多数扁虫为非寄生虫，但也有部分扁虫属寄生类，依靠其他动物为生。扁虫可被划分为四个纲——吸虫纲、绦虫纲、单殖纲和涡虫纲。扁虫柔软的身体呈丝带状。它是结构最简单的生物，其器官由三个胚层发育而来，分别是内胚层、外胚层和中胚层。扁虫除了内胆外没有真正的体腔。其体内充满着排列疏松的组织。

3. (A), (D)

三角洲

三角洲是在河水流入洋、海、沙漠或者湖的入口处形成的一种地貌。这些水流在向外扩散时形成三角洲沉淀。河流带来的沉淀物最终形成了三角洲。随着水流减缓，这些沉淀物就会沉积下来。一些大河的三角洲沉淀中有很多沉积物，这些沉积物会将河道分为许多支流。这些支流先分开再最终汇合，形成了既有活跃河道又有不活跃河道的系统。河口沉积的形状大体呈三角状。淤泥将河口堵住使这一形状最终形成并增大了三角洲底基的宽度。

4. (B), (C)

社会心理学

社会心理学主要研究人在群体中的表现，这一领域目前仍在不断发展。它着眼于个体如何认知、影响及与他人产生关联。戈登·奥尔波特为这项研究的经典定义作出了重大贡献。他说，社会心理学尝试理解并解释人与人之间是如何相互影响的，其中包括他们处理想象的或暗示的他人存在的方式。这一领域的大部分试验都是通过对一些小群体的观察完成的。这些群体被集中起来并给予一些任务去完成。在他们试图完成这些规定任务的过程中，研究者便展开对群体成员之间相互作用的观察。

Practice with Long Passages

A   1. (A)   2. (B)   3. (A), (C), (F)
[1] the mouths of rivers / [2] freshwater and seawater /
[3] marine species

河口

河口一般在河流的潮汐口形成。它是一个半封闭的海岸水体，并且与海洋水流自由联通。当海水与淡水交汇时，河口在这种联通中最突出的特征也就体现出来了。这种海水与来自溪流或河流的淡水的结合会形成微咸水。但其前提是在二者交汇时，必须有潮汐运动为其提供动能。因此在没有潮汐运动的海洋中，河流入海处一般会形成三角洲。

河口一般位于河流的潮口处。河流从地表径流带来的土壤淤泥通常会在该处形成沉淀。在一些低洼的海岸，即那些因海面升高而下沉的海岸处，更易形成河口。而这一过程会淹没山谷，进而形成溺湾和峡湾。如果这时有溪流或者河流流入这些区域，就会形成河口。

河口处形成的微咸水没有海水那么咸，但比淡水要稍咸一点。这种水使得河口的生态系统繁荣发展。最有名的河口之一是流经伦敦最终到达伦敦西部特丁顿镇的泰晤士河。泰晤士河在上述地区会受到潮汐的影响，但当其向西到达巴特西时，又变成淡水河。

位于泰晤士河这一区域的动物群多为淡水物种，包括许多鱼类——如欧鲤、条鱼、鲤鱼、鲈鱼和狗鱼。在巴特西和格雷夫森德之间的泰晤士河水域是微咸水，这里只有为数不多的淡水和海洋物种。随着河流稍微向东，河水的咸度也在不断升高，最终海洋物种彻底取代了淡水鱼。

B   1. (A)   2. (D)   3. (B), (D), (F)
[1] Weeks 1~4 / [2] Weeks 5~6 / [3] Week 8

胚胎

胚胎时期是多细胞生物发育的最初阶段。胚胎的发育开始是有性生殖。一旦这一阶段结束，一个精子就与一个卵细胞结合使之受精，形成一个受精卵。这个受精卵中含有父母双方的全部DNA。在这个早期阶段，人类的胚胎并无知觉。而这也成为堕胎权的支持者和反对者争执的焦点。

人类的胚胎发育一般会经历三个主要阶段。从第一周到第四周，胚胎需要找到一个可以依附子宫壁的位置。一旦它找到合适的位置，它就会自动移植过去。母体和胚胎开始结合，脐带即在这一阶段形成。

第五周至第六周，胚胎开始释放化学物质使母体停止月经，胎儿的大脑开始发育。大约第六周左右，胚胎开始有脑波和心跳活动。那些以后会逐渐长出胳膊和腿的地方开始显现出来。所有主要器官开始发育。

第七周到第八周之间，胚胎的血型确定下来，胚胎可以开始活动，眼睛也已形成。大多数器官要么已发育完全，要么正处于发育期。在第八周结束时，胚胎期结束，这标志着胎儿阶段的开始。

人们围绕胚胎的话题展开了许多讨论和争论，主要围绕着"胚胎何时变为有知觉和灵魂的人"这一问题展开。这一问题是美国的堕胎问题的核心。许多人认为胚胎就是一条人命，理应得到保护。他们认为法律应视堕胎和对胚胎进行的科学试验活动为非法，并将其列为谋杀罪的一种。但反对者认为，胚胎只不过是未发育的组织结构。他们认为，在胚胎进入胎儿期之前是否堕胎应由母亲自己决定。

C   1. (C)   2. (B)   3. (B), (E), (F)
[1] movable metal type / [2] an information explosion /
[3] to own books / [4] Johann Fust

约翰尼斯·古登堡和金属活字

约翰尼斯·古登堡是一位发明家，他因发明了活字印刷机而闻名世界。他发明的印刷机有一个活字金属合金、油基印墨和一个铸造活字的模子。这一发明使书籍成为大众普遍使用的物品。

古登堡制造的第一台印刷机的准确情况无从考证。但是传统上人们认为他在欧洲发明了活字。这是对当时已被使用的模板印刷术的一大改进。他将这些原件都组装至一个生产系统，从而大大提高了文字材料的印刷速度。这引起了欧洲文艺复兴时期的信息大爆炸。

1430 年左右，古登堡从他的家乡美因茨搬到了斯特拉斯堡。随后他便开始尝试发明金属活字印刷术。他知道木制模板印刷术因要靠手工刻板，所以耗时长且费用高。于是古登堡得出结论：金属活字印刷术速度要快得多，因为只要制成一个模板就可以了。

1455 年，古登堡向世人展示了他发明的印刷机。他以每本仅 300 德国弗罗林的价钱出售两卷的《圣经》，这相当于一个普通公务员 3 年的工资。但这已经比之前的手抄本《圣经》便宜了很多。这些手抄本书籍通常需要一个僧人花费 20 年的时间来完成一本的抄写。

古登堡有一位名叫约翰·福斯特的搭档。但是古登堡通过印刷机赚来的钱却不足以偿付福斯特的投资费用。福斯特因此起诉了古登堡并胜诉。法院的裁决使得古登堡最终破产，法院还将其活字和印刷设备的管理控制权判给了福斯特。古登堡在去世以前一直经营着一家小型印刷店，而福斯特却成为第一个出版印有自己名字的书的印刷者。

D 1. Ⓓ 2. Ⓐ 3. Ⓐ, Ⓓ, Ⓔ

[1] diseases and insects / [2] A wheat variety /
[3] International controversy

转基因植物

转基因植物拥有不同种类植物的基因。19 世纪末，第一株转基因植物被载入史册，它是小麦和黑麦的杂交品种。这种两种植株的杂交培养方式标志着一个农业的新纪元。通过将一种植物的基因移植到另一种植物中，农民们可以培养出抗病性更强的庄稼，它们能抵御流行病的侵害，进而大大减少粮食和财产的损失。

20 世纪 30 年代，E·S·麦克法登培育出一种含有从野草中提取的基因的小麦。这一品种被命名为希望，它可以抵御小麦茎锈病。这种疾病一度威胁着全美的小麦作物。这种小麦将农民从绝境中解救出来，并解决了许多百姓的饥荒问题。

转基因植物的培养从一般的杂交培育开始，但是到了 20 世纪 70 年代，科学家不但在植物种类之间，还开始在动物种类之间试验 DNA 移植培育。1985 年，在比利时的一个实验室中，科学家通过基因工程技术，将能够合成具有杀虫性的蛋白质的基因添加到烟草植物的基因中，创造出一种有耐虫性的烟草植物。

这项发展开启了转基因植物重组的新领域。但是一些国际机构却对这一领域的发展产生了分歧。双方争执的焦点集中在转基因农作物和食物上。这场针对植物 DNA 的利用的交锋促成了一个新的生物门类的产生。这一门类中的生物被称为转基因生物。

黄金稻米就是一例成功的转基因植物。这种稻米是在实验室创造出来的。它所含的维生素 A 是普通白米的 23 倍。维生素 A 是一种非常重要但在世界上很多地区都较为缺乏的营养物质。这种稻米的创造是人道主义的体现，它帮助了这些地区的百姓。但是因为遭到许多反对转基因食物的组织的抗议，这种稻米目前仍无法供应。

E 1. Ⓐ 2. Ⓒ 3. Ⓐ, Ⓓ, Ⓔ

[1] psychoanalysis / [2] free association / [3] inaccurate and too subjective

西格蒙德·弗罗伊德

西格蒙德·弗罗伊德是奥地利的精神分析学家。他创立了一种新的心理学学派。他因其关于性欲和梦的理论而闻名于世。他关于压抑和潜意识的研究也同样有名。很多人称他为"精神分析学之父"。

弗罗伊德于 1856 年出生在弗赖贝格。他们一家人住在一所狭小的公寓中，但是他的父母却致力于对其智力的培养。他上学的 8 年间，6 年都在班上名列第一。他在 17 岁时考入维也纳大学。

弗罗伊德后来开始为有神经紊乱和大脑紊乱的病人治病。他将催眠术应用于多数歇斯底里和神经过敏的病人身上。但是他最终放弃了这些尝试。他发现他可以用更简单的方式使他的病人开口说话。他让他们安坐在沙发上，然后鼓励他们说出他们脑中的所有想法。这一过程被称为"自由联想"。

进入 40 岁后，弗罗伊德发现自己有许多精神问题，于是他开始探索自己的梦，并开始研究自己的回忆以及自己人格的动态性。在这种自我剖析中，他逐渐意识到他对自己的父亲怀有敌意。他还想起了儿时对母亲的感觉——有吸引力、温暖而有安全感。一些研究弗罗伊德的学者认为，弗罗伊德经历情感困惑的这一时期，是其生命中最富创造力的时期。

弗罗伊德的理论及研究方法在他的一生中都饱受争议。利迪亚德·H·霍顿发表的论文中指出弗罗伊德的梦的解析理论"具有危险的不准确性"。另一位弗罗伊德批评家叫朱丽叶·米切尔。她认为弗罗伊德提出的"人们有意识的思考受到潜意识中的恐惧和欲望的驱动"的基本理念应该被摒弃。她称这是因为这一理念减弱了对世界作出整体客观的评论的可能性。许多评论家认为弗罗伊德的这些思想是由于他大量吸食可卡因而产生的。

F 　1. Ⓒ　2. Ⓑ　3. Ⓑ, Ⓒ, Ⓔ
[1] land ownership / [2] latitude and longitude / [3] Nautical charts

制图学的历史

研究并进行地图绘制或地球仪制作的学科称为制图学。自人类可追溯的历史以来，制图学一直是人类历史中一个重要的组成部分。最早闻名于世的地图并非地球地图，而是关于星座的天体图。在可追溯至公元前 16500 年的一幅天体图上，整个夜空被各个点标出，这幅图被发现刻在法国拉斯科岩洞的岩壁上。织女星、天津四星和牛郎星这三颗亮星都包含在图中。昴宿星团也在这幅岩壁图中被标了出来。

在古巴比伦王朝，人们使用非常精确的测量技术来绘制地图。1930 年在珈瑟（即今天位于伊拉克北部的基尔库克）发现的一块泥板上所绘制的地图就是一个很好的例子。地图描绘的是两座山之间的一个河谷。泥板上的铭文表示这片土地归一个叫阿扎拉的人所有。专家认定这块泥板制作于公元前 2500 年至公元前 2300 年。

在古埃及，地图很稀少。但是那些保存下来的地图却展示了古埃及人对几何演算和测量技术的重视。可追溯至公元前 1300 年的图林纸草，描绘了尼罗河东部的山脉，那里是有着丰富的金矿和银矿的重要地区。

克罗狄斯·托勒密时期发生了制图学早期的革新。托勒密生活在公元 90 年至 168 年间埃及的亚历山大城。他将地球描绘成一个球体，并绘制出我们今天所使用的平行的纬线和经线。

制图技术在整个中世纪不断发展。文艺复兴时期，葡萄牙的制图学家为船舶导航绘制出航海图。目前知道的最古老的航海图是由佩德罗·赖内尔在 1485 年绘制的。这张航海图上标明了纬度。

1569 年，一位名叫杰拉德斯·麦卡托的佛兰德斯地理学家根据他的麦卡托投影制作了第一张地图。这是一张十分精确的世界地图。地球的球形被展开并投射在一个平面上。

20 世纪，地图变得更加丰富。这是由于印刷术和摄影技术的发展使地图的制作越来越便宜而且容易。飞机使得人们可以一次拍摄很大一片区域，这就为人们提供了前所未有的机会，使人们可以从更高的高度观察地球。

Building Summary Skills

1. Estuaries

Estuaries are semi-enclosed bodies of water that form near [1] the tidal mouth of a river. They combine [2] both saltwater and freshwater. The water formed is [3] somewhat salty. Mostly freshwater species live in estuaries, but [4] marine species live in them closer to the ocean. [5] The River Thames is among the most famous estuaries in the world.

2. The Embryo

The embryo is the earliest stage of development for [1] multi-celled life forms. There are [2] three major stages of development in the human embryo. These stages include the connection forming stage, the brain forming stage, and [3] the organ forming stage. This marks the point at which the embryo becomes a fetus. After [4] eight weeks, the fetal stage begins. There is much controversy around the development of the embryo because of [5] abortion rights.

3. Johannes Gutenberg and Metal Type

Johannes Gutenberg invented [1] movable type. This revolutionized Europe and led to [2] an information explosion. He used [3] metal type instead of wood-block type. In 1455, he sold copies of a two-volume Bible that were much cheaper than [4] handwritten ones. However, Gutenberg's partner [5] Johann Fust sued him and took the rights to his invention. Gutenberg died in poverty.

4. Transgenic Plants

Transgenic plants share [1] the genes of other species. Scientists [2] transfer genes from one plant to another to give the plants better resistance to disease or insects or to make them [3] more nutritious. Wheat, tobacco, rice, and even animals have had their genes [4] modified. Some people are opposed to transgenic plants, which they call [5] genetically modified organisms.

5. Sigmund Freud

Sigmund Freud was [1] a neurologist who founded a new kind of [2] psychology. He is often referred to as [3] the father of psychoanalysis. He had his own practice and soon began to use free association methods with his patients. He also interpreted his dreams and his relationships with [4] his parents. He did, however, have [5] many critics during his life and afterwards.

6. The History of Cartography

Making maps or globes is called [1] cartography, and people have been making them for thousands of years. Early maps just showed [2] the stars and constellations as in the wall paintings of the Lascaux Caves. There were also early maps in [3] Babylon and Egypt. Mapmaking improved in the Middle Ages and [4] the Renaissance. Later mapmakers showed lines of latitude and longitude and made maps for sailors. By the 1900s, advancements in photography as well as the advent of airplanes and later, satellites, led to giant leaps forward in the [5] accuracy and efficiency of mapmaking.

Mini TOEFL iBT

1. Ⓑ   2. Ⓒ   3. Ⓐ   4. Ⓐ   5. Ⓓ
6. Ⓐ, Ⓓ, Ⓔ   7. Ⓒ   8. Ⓐ   9. Ⓒ
10. Ⓑ   11. Ⓓ   12. Ⓑ, Ⓒ, Ⓓ

古希腊的陶器制造

学者们从古希腊文化存留下来的陶器中了解到古希腊的艺术发展。虽然当时的画作和艺术品几乎都没有保存下来，但却有超过10万只希腊花瓶流传至今。很多花瓶上都画有希腊人物和风景作为装饰。因为希腊人会制造各式各样的瓶子用于喝水、做饭等日常家务，所以这些瓶子在希腊社会的每一个阶层都很常见。

在希腊文明早期，小的城邦生产他们自己的陶器。但不久之后，科林斯和雅典就从中脱颖而出成为两个最大的花瓶产地。这里制造的陶器成为希腊社会的陶器制造标准。其大量出口也使各地制造的本土陶器退出舞台。

古希腊陶器制造的两个重要阶段分别是黑彩陶器阶段和红彩陶器阶段。黑彩陶器阶段始于约公元前700年的科林斯城。在这个阶段，花瓶用灰白色且含铁丰富的黏土制成。烤制时，它们会变成红橙色。设计的图案会在花瓶表面显现出轮廓。然后人们用精炼的黏土来涂绘已经画好的图案，并用雕刻工具来完成细节部分。这些工作完成之后，瓶子需要再被烤制一次。这一过程中陶器上的设计图案就变成了亮黑色。

红彩陶器在约公元前530年开始发展。它风靡一时并取代了黑彩陶器的地位。即便是如今，人们也认为红彩陶器制造技术是古希腊陶器工艺的最高峰。保存下来的古希腊花瓶中价值最高的就是红彩陶器。红彩陶器的制作过程需要陶艺家和画家的密切合作。首先画家需要在花瓶烤制之前在花瓶上创作一个设计图案。由于还未烤制，颜料和黏土的颜色难以区分，也就是说，画家需要在看不见其设计图案的情况下进行创作。当陶艺家将陶器烤制后，设计图案才能显现出来。这一过程要求画家凭借其记忆力快速、准确地创作。

参与陶器制作的画家很少署上自己的名字。因此当代学者只能通过重复出现的设计图案来辨别这些艺术家。例如，其中一位最伟大的希腊花瓶画家被称为"阿基利斯画家"，因为他在作画时最常选用的主体就是叫这个名字的希腊人物。另一个辨别这些画家的方法是通过他们为之工作的陶艺家的名字。陶艺家经常将自己的名字属在这些花瓶上，所以为克莱奥弗拉德斯工作的画家就被称为"克莱奥弗拉德斯画家"。

峭壁与侵蚀

峭壁是一种地貌形态，它由一个尖锐、垂直的岩石露头构成。悬崖的形成是侵蚀和风化的结果，它们一般位于海岸或者山区。峭壁坚固的根基是由抗腐蚀、抗风化的岩石构成的。沉积石（如砂石、石灰石、白垩和白云石）最容易形成峭壁。火成岩（如花岗岩和玄武岩）也能形成峭壁。

侵蚀，是指在风力、水力或者冰的作用下，固态物质的移动。这些固态物质包括土壤、泥土、岩石以及其他固态颗粒。在重力的作用下，这些固态物质发生下滑运动，于是发生侵蚀。侵蚀现象也可能由一些有机生物引起，这叫做生物侵蚀。侵蚀不同于风化。风化是指岩石或其他固态颗粒的分解，这一过程不涉及物体的运动。但是，侵蚀和风化两者可以同时在同一地点发生。

侵蚀是自然现象。但是由于人类用地的增加，侵蚀现象出现得越来越频繁。不断伐木以及过度放牧这些不当的土地利用导致侵蚀速度的加快。另外，无管理的建筑工程以及道路、铁路的修建也是元凶之一。人们可以通过改善土地利用来控制侵蚀。建造梯田和植树造林等做法都可以帮助重建受损土地。

地质断层或者山体滑坡所形成的峭壁叫做scarp。大多数峭壁的根基处都有岩屑坡。它们通常暴露在外，由干旱地区和高崖下部滚落的岩石构成。一座土坡可能会使空气潮湿地区的岩屑失去光泽。

峭壁处有时会形成瀑布和岩洞。有些峭壁随着山脉的走向在山脉的尽头消失。这就可能留下桌状或其他类型的岩柱。峭壁并不一定都像定义的那样呈垂直状，所以斜坡是否是峭壁这一问题是没有统一定论的。

世界各地有很多独特的峭壁。最高的峭壁据说位于大川哥岩峰群东麓，属于巴基斯坦北部的喀喇昆仑山脉的一部分，大约 1340 米高。最高的海蚀崖位于夏威夷的卡劳帕帕，约 1010 米高。位于加拿大北极区巴芬岛上的索尔山是世界上最高的陡直悬崖，约 1370 米高。它同时还是世界上长度最大的纯陡壁，约 1250 米长。

Vocabulary Review

A 1. Ⓒ 2. Ⓓ 3. Ⓐ 4. Ⓒ
    5. Ⓑ 6. Ⓓ 7. Ⓑ 8. Ⓐ

B 1. i 2. f 3. h 4. j 5. b
    6. g 7. c 8. d 9. a 10. e

Unit 10   Fill in a Table

Skill & Drill

1. Individual Classism Ⓐ, Ⓓ
Structural Classism Ⓒ, Ⓕ

阶级歧视

    "阶级歧视"一词指的是一种对社会阶层较低的人的偏见。它是一种社会精英主义。人们通常有个人阶级歧视。比如，一些富人瞧不起收入不如自己高的人。再比如，比起穷人和中等收入的人，富人可以受到优待。社会制度中也存在结构性阶级歧视，即人们有意做一些事情来排斥阶级较低的人。这种阶级歧视通常出现在美国政坛，这是因为在竞选中出资最多的人似乎在政府中更有影响力。而这一举措就使得工薪阶级无法获得同等的影响力。

2. Causes Ⓐ, Ⓔ / **Effects** Ⓑ, Ⓕ

美索不达米亚

    美索不达米亚被称为"人类文明的摇篮"。这是因为最早的人类社会始于这里。美索不达米亚位于两河之间的一片土地肥沃的区域，这使得人们可以种植农作物。他们的繁荣发展促使了城市的出现，进而促进了许多发明、发现的产生，如第一个书写系统。那里的人们还发明了金属加工。而他们也是最早进入青铜时代的人——他们用铜、青铜和黄金来装饰自己的宫殿和神庙。他们还运用天文学——通过观察星象来计算地球上一年的时长。如今仍在使用的"1 小时 60 分钟，1 天 24 小时"的精确计时法即起源于那里。

3. Positive Effects Ⓑ, Ⓓ
Negative Effects Ⓒ, Ⓔ

绿色革命

    绿色革命是指在 20 世纪 40 年代至 60 年代间，发生在许多发展中国家的一次大型农业革新运动。这次革新通过农业研究项目的开发利用，大大提高了谷物的产量。但绿色革命对社会和地球来说是一把双刃剑。其有利的一面是饥荒得到缓解；但是其消极影响在于这会造成一些地区的人口过剩。绿色革命的一大功劳在于大规模农业生产的成功，但这也使得小规模生产的农民很难获利。这种经济转变很大程度上妨害了社会主义运动。

4. Physical Phenomena Ⓑ, Ⓔ
Geological Phenomena Ⓒ, Ⓓ

自然现象

    自然现象是不受人类影响而发生的事情。它发生在自然界，却会对人类产生影响。有些自然现象是物理作用的结果，因此被称为物理现象。闪电就是其中一例；在重力作用下形成的天体运行轨道是另一个例子。因地球内部活动引起的自然灾害被称为地质现象。一个常见的例子是火山爆发，还有海啸。这些事件都无法控制。人类既不能创造它们也无法阻止它们，但却可以通过科学对它们进行理解。

Practice with Long Passages

A 1. Ⓐ 2. Ⓑ

    3. Structural Emergence Ⓑ, Ⓔ, Ⓖ /
    Cultural Emergence Ⓒ, Ⓕ
    ¹ a flock of birds / ² an ant colony / ³ the World Wide Web

突生

    "突生"这一概念描述的是一种复杂模式的形成。这种模式源其基本组成部分。各部分之间的关系会催生出物质的自然属性，这是一个长期的、不断变化的过程。人体的进化便是一例，人体形态经过了几千代的演变。人体虽然复杂，但构成人体的数百万个微小的细胞并不复杂。

    突生发生的规模也有大小之分。以神经细胞和人脑为例。神经之间的相互作用形成大脑，大脑有思考的能力，但是组成大脑的任何一个单独的神经细胞并不能思考。这些神经细胞组成的大脑要比任何一部分单独的神经结构作用都大。

    在自然界中，我们一般可以通过结构来观察突生。这些结构可能来源于有机物质也可能来源于无机物质。生物结构的一个典型例子就是鸟群——一群鸟会形成群体并表现出一些行为特征，然而这些特征并不在个体鸟身上表现出来。另一个关于生物突生结构的例子是蚁群——蚁群就是一种突生，因为没有任何一只蚂蚁（包括蚁王）能够组织起如此高效的蚁群。但是如果这些蚂蚁聚集起来，就能建立一个蚁群结构。一个关于非生物突生结构的例子是飓风。飓风系统的形成是各种因素共同作用的结果，包括气压、气温和湿度。它们结合在一起形成了强烈的风，但是任何一个单独的因素都无法形成飓风。

突生也存在于人类文明中。其中一个大范围产生突生的例子是股票市场：作为一个系统，它能调控全世界公司的股价，但是该系统中却没有一个领导可以控制整个市场。经纪人只了解数量有限的企业并且必须严格遵守市场规定。通过这些相互作用，市场作为一个整体的复杂性就产生了。另外一个例子是万维网：万维网中没有一个中心网站，而是通过各种大大小小的网站之间的联系构成一个复杂的整体。

B 1. Ⓒ 2. Ⓓ

3. Advocates Ⓐ, Ⓔ, Ⓕ / Critics Ⓓ, Ⓖ

[1] Entertainment companies / [2] control the entertainment industry / [3] availability of weapons

媒体效应理论

美国的娱乐业遭到了严厉的谴责。批评家对各种节目中过多的暴力行为十分不满。媒体效应理论就解释了这一问题，即现实生活中不断增多的暴力行为与娱乐界有很大关系。

这一理论涉及许多暴力行为，其中最普遍的便是高中校园枪击事件。该理论将其归咎于媒体大量出现的各种形式的暴力场面。

这一理论的假设基础是，许多人现在通过媒体接触到大量的暴力内容，其中有一小部分人缺乏对这些暴力行为的虚构性与真实性的辨别能力。于是这些人就认为可以实施暴力。

这一理论的拥护者通常将矛头指向电脑游戏公司。这些公司会发行很多第一视角射击游戏，其中包含了大量的血腥、暴力场景。媒体效应理论的拥护者认为，这些游戏让生命看起来很廉价，而且它还对实施暴力的行为进行奖励。

拥护者还将矛头直指一些歌词内容充满仇恨的歌手，他们认为这些人在宣扬暴力。暴力电影也难辞其咎，拥护者认为这类电影使暴力看起来很有魅力。而这些都是娱乐的不同形式，人们希望娱乐公司能对自己的产品负责，标注极端暴力的产品并禁止未成年人群购买此类产品。

然而，这一理论的批评者却指出，政府不应该管制媒体，因为这会损害美国国民的言论自由权。他们通过对比美国与其他国家的暴力数据发现，其他一些国家也有同样的暴力传播，但其暴力行为却远没有美国这么多。所以这些批评者指出，美国的暴力问题并不能归咎于媒体，而是由普通公民也可拥有武器造成的。

C 1. Ⓑ 2. Ⓒ

3. Reported Causes Ⓑ, Ⓒ, Ⓖ /
   Effects Ⓐ, Ⓔ

[1] Oct. 8th to 10th / [2] Catherine O'Leary's cow / [3] Louis M. Cohn

芝加哥大火

1871 年的芝加哥大火从 10 月 8 号一直持续到 10 号。它造成了灾难性的后果——数以百计的百姓丧生，芝加哥城大部分地区在大火中化为灰烬。这是 19 世纪美国最大的灾难之一。但人们却立刻开始重建芝加哥城，使芝加哥最终发展成为美国最重要的经济城市之一。

大火发生在 10 月 8 号（星期天）早上大约 9 点，在德科文大街旁一个小巷子的棚屋里。目前普遍认可的原因是一头奶牛踢翻了牲口棚的一只灯笼。这个粮仓归帕特里克和凯瑟琳·奥利里所有。

现在人们都知道奥利里夫人不过是替罪羊而已。历史学家认为，她之所以被指责要为那次起大火负责，只是因为她是一个女人、一个移民、一个天主教徒。在美国历史上的这一时期，这些群体都是受迫害的。《芝加哥论坛报》在大火过后的第一篇报道就声称奥利里夫人的疏忽就是这场大火的起因。其实不久之后，这篇报道的记者承认这都是他编造出来的。而他之所以这么做，是因为他觉得这是一个吸引人的故事。

理查德·贝尔斯是一个业余历史学家，他认为造成这场大火的罪魁祸首是最先报告这场大火的人——丹尼尔·沙利文。他表示，就是这个人在试图偷牛奶的时候点燃了粮仓中的干草。

但是近日，安东尼·德巴尔托洛向《芝加哥论坛报》提供了一些新的证据。他认为，是一个叫路易斯·M·科恩的赌徒在一场掷骰子游戏中引起了这场大火。根据艾伦·威克斯写的一本书中显示，科恩在遗嘱中承认了自己是纵火者。

D 1. Ⓓ 2. Ⓑ

3. Matrifocal Family Ⓓ, Ⓖ /
   Consanguineal Family Ⓐ, Ⓕ /
   Conjugal Family Ⓑ, Ⓔ, Ⓘ

[1] Matrifocal / [2] Consanguineal / [3] Conjugal

"家庭"的观念差异

家庭由住在一起的一群人组成，并由婚姻、血统或其他法定关系(例如同居关系和领养关系等)联系在一起。

许多人认为家庭只与"血缘"有关。但许多社会学家认为，"血缘"这个概念应该有更深的隐含意义。许多社会用其他概念来定义"家庭"。《世界人权宣言》第16条将家庭定义为天然的社会单元，并指出家庭应受到社会和国家的保护。

家庭结构以配偶之间、父母与子女之间的关系为基础。家庭主要分为三类。

母主家庭一般由一位母亲与和她有血缘关系的子女组成，但并不排除领养的可能性。当一位女性有足够能力独自支撑家庭时，才会形成母主家庭。

血亲家庭有多种形式，其中最常见的组合是：一个家庭由母亲、她的子女以及母亲的家族成员组成，通常没有父亲。这种组合通常发生在遗产继承的家庭背景下。当男性掌控财产时，这一类型就可能还包括丈夫的家族成员。

夫妇家庭包括一个或多个母亲、她们的子女以及一个或多个父亲。这一类型强调的是家庭分工。男性和女性都需要完成不同类型的劳动。这种类型的家庭具有高迁移率。

核心家庭是夫妇家庭的一个分支。这类家庭只包括一个妻子和一个丈夫，他们共同抚养子女。这种类型是现代工业化社会最普遍的家庭类型。

E　1. Ⓐ　　2. Ⓓ
　　　3. Topics Ⓐ, Ⓔ, Ⓕ /
　　　　 Functions Ⓒ, Ⓓ
　　　 [1] morality / [2] cloning / [3] public policy

生命伦理学

生命伦理学是应用哲学的一个分支。它主要着眼于科学和医学，质疑一些研究和治疗方法的道德性。它还会评估用以规范科学的法律的伦理性。这一领域保护着人类，因而至关重要。生命伦理学的缺失将会使科学和医学的进步发展对人类构成巨大的威胁。

生命伦理学的研究对许多法律的制定产生了影响。也正因如此，许多科学家盲目反对这些生命伦理学的实践者。这些科学家认为他们的工作本身就是符合伦理道德的。

生命伦理学是一个迅速发展的学术领域。它成为正式科学研究的历史不过30年。现在许多学术中心都设有生命伦理学学位。20世纪90年代，一个由社会学家组成的团体制定了一套论文写作范式，确立了伦理问题研究的方法。该方法试图解决这些社会问题。同其他社会科学一样，生命伦理学家的研究所依据的数据也会受到其他生命伦理学家的检视。

对于这门学科，现在仍存在一些重要的疑问。其作为一个学术研究领域的有效性遭到质疑。为什么它要脱离哲学独立存在？难道不是每个人都是伦理学家吗？制度建立的需要正好回答了这些问题。生命伦理学家调动了大量的研究和历史，并将其应用于生命伦理学的问题中。他们在研究中秉持公正、诚实、理性的原则，并为此共同努力着。

生命伦理学家研究各种主题，他们主要着眼于那些在社会上引起争议的问题。他们搜集数据并发表报告。这些报告会指导公众观点甚至政府政策的形成与制定。他们研究的话题包括堕胎、克隆以及胚胎在干细胞试验中的使用问题。这些都是从人们生活中产生的非常棘手的道德伦理问题。生命伦理学家还试图教育引导立法者和其他掌权者，因为他们才是划分界限的人，决定着什么在医学和科学中才是合法的。

F　1. Ⓒ　　2. Ⓓ
　　　3. Kenya Ⓕ / Tanzania Ⓐ, Ⓓ, Ⓖ /
　　　　 Germany Ⓒ
　　　 [1] early hominid skull / [2] Homo habilis / [3] Homo erectus

古生人类学

研究人类和史前人类化石的学科叫做古生人类学，它是体质人类学的一个分支，主要追溯随时代变迁的人类进化过程。该领域的科学家追踪人体结构、行为以及基因上的联系，而这些联系即能表明人类是如何从史前人类进化而来的。科学家通过这些联系构建了一个时间表，反映了从史前到现代的人类崛起。

古生人类学家搜遍整个地球挖掘出一些残遗化石，他们通过这些小的线索来研究早期的远古人类。他们找到的这些残遗化石，如保存下来的骸骨、工具和足迹，让他们了解那些古老的生命。

19世纪末，一些重大发现促使人们开始研究人类的进化，古生人类学也应运而生。第一个重大发现发生在1856年，人们在德国发现了一具尼安德特人遗骸，这一重大发现导致了古生人类学的出现。其他重大事件包括两本相关方面著作的发表：一本是托马斯·赫胥黎的《人类在自然界中的地位》，另一本是查尔斯·达尔文的《人类的起源》。

利基家族在这一领域有许多重大发现。其中路易斯·利基发现了第一个重要化石，为之后无数重大化石发现奠定了基础。1959年，他和他的妻子在非洲坦桑尼亚的奥杜瓦伊峡谷的挖掘中发现了早期原始人头骨的遗骸。

1972年路易斯去世后，他的妻子继续他的研究。其中最为重大的发现之一是雷托立足迹。她于1976年在坦桑尼亚的一处火山灰中发现了它们。这些足迹可追溯到370

万年前，它们为"史前人类用双腿行走"这一说法提供了最有力的证据。

他们的儿子理查德·利基也成绩斐然，他发现了许多重要的化石。1972 年，他带领的小组在坦桑尼亚发现了能人的头盖骨。1975 年，该小组又在肯尼亚发现了直立人的头盖骨。

Building Summary Skills

1. Emergence

Emergence is the concept that describes how [1] a complex pattern forms from lesser parts. A good example is the human body, which has developed over thousands of successive generations. Emergence is evident in all forms of [2] organic and inorganic structures. Scientists who study emergence look at the characteristics of organic emergent structures such as [3] ant colonies or flocks of birds and at inorganic structures such as hurricanes. Another form of emergence is [4] cultural, in which some form of human organization results in a highly complex structure that is more than the sum of its parts. [5] The World Wide Web and the stock market are prime examples of the sort of phenomenon in which simple components combine to form a complex whole.

2. The Media Influence Theory

The Media Influence Theory states that [1] rising levels of violence in society are attributable to individuals who see violence depicted in entertainment and are unable to distinguish it apart from [2] reality. Advocates of this theory target video games, music with hateful lyrics, and movies as being responsible for [3] many acts of violence. They want to see these forms of entertainment heavily [4] regulated by the government. On the other hand, critics of this theory think the government should not control the entertainment industry and that rising levels of violence are due to [5] the availability of weapons.

3. The Great Chicago Fire

From October 8th to 10th in [1] 1871, the Great Chicago Fire burned down much of the city and killed hundreds of people. The fire was originally blamed on [2] Mrs. O'Leary's cow kicking down a lantern in the barn. But the reporter who wrote this story later said he made it up because it sounded interesting, which led people to believe that Mrs. O'Leary was made a target because she was [3] a Catholic, female immigrant. Some other possible causes of the fire were Daniel Sullivan, who may have started it while trying to [4] steal some milk, or Louis M. Cohn, who is said to have started it during [5] a game of craps.

4. Differences in the Concept of Family

A family consists of people who live together and are linked by [1] genetic or other types of bonds. Although [2] blood relation defines many families, it is not the only thing that can link people together. There are three major types of families: [3] matrifocal, consanguineal, and conjugal. The most common type of family in modern society is a sub-group of [4] the conjugal family called [5] the nuclear family.

5. Bioethics

Bioethics is a branch of applied philosophy that looks closely at [1] the ethics of scientific and medical practices. This field is very important because it asks questions about and examines policies and treatments that greatly affect [2] the human race. It is also an area of academic growth, as many universities have created [3] bioethics programs. Although bioethicists' roles are often questioned, they do many activities such as researching and compiling reports that greatly affect [4] public opinion and the policies made by [5] politicians.

6. Paleoanthropology

The study of human and pre-human fossils is paleoanthropology. This field began with several important discoveries and publications in [1] the late 1800s, including the discovery of Neanderthal man fossils. Some of the most important discoveries in this field have been made by a family named [2] the Leakeys. Their long list of discoveries began in the 1950s when Louis and Mary Leakey found [3] the skull of a hominid in Tanzania. But Mary Leakey's most important discovery came after her husband's death, when she found [4] the Laetoli footprints in 1976. These footprints offered conclusive evidence that early man walked upright on two legs. Their son, Richard, also found the skulls of [5] a Homo habilis and a Homo erectus.

1. Ⓒ   2. Ⓑ   3. Ⓒ   4. Ⓓ   5. Ⓐ

6. Criteria Ⓒ, Ⓓ, Ⓗ, Ⓘ / Forms Ⓑ, Ⓔ, Ⓖ

7. Ⓐ   8. Ⓒ   9. Ⓓ   10. Ⓑ   11. ▣Ⓓ

12. Storage Room Ⓐ, Ⓕ / Kiva Ⓑ, Ⓓ / Tower Ⓔ

商务合伙关系

合伙关系是商业活动的一种。在该关系中，两个或两个以上的合作人共享收益，共担损失。合作人是指那些共同参与同一商业活动的人。这种形式的商业活动适用于希望同自己的朋友和致信一起工作的人。它同时还适用于各有所长的两个或两个以上的个体，他们通过建立合伙关系各取所长。已成立的企业之间也可建立合伙关系。

合伙人需要签订一份合伙契约，或者对其合伙关系发出声明。一些司法权中规定，合伙双方必须登记合伙契约，以供公众审查。在许多国家，合作关系就是一个法律实体。

企业对建立合伙关系的热衷往往源于一些税收目的。对于面临巨额税务的公司来说，合伙关系就显得更为有用。建立合伙关系能消除股息税。股息税是对一个企业股东的收益所征收的税款。

一般合伙关系是最基本的形式。在这种合伙关系中，所有成员都要管理企业。每个人都对公司债务负有责任。除此之外还有其他两种合伙关系：一种是有限合伙关系，这种关系中，一些"有限合伙人"放弃其对企业的管理权，这样做是为了只对合伙债务承担有限的责任。另一种是有限责任合伙关系，这种关系中，所有合伙人都要承担一定的责任。

1958年颁布的《合伙法》中规定，合伙关系的建立需要达到四个标准：一、合伙人之间需要签订一份有效协议；二、他们需要共同经营一项生意——如协议中指定的任何贸易、职业或者专业项目；三、他们必须有共同之处，也就是说要存在权利的共有性，包括利益、义务；最后，他们必须以盈利为目的，这也是为什么慈善机构不是合伙关系的原因。

需要建立合伙关系的商人必须选择适合自身的合伙关系形式。一些合伙人想掌握更多的控制权，那么他们就需要承担更多的义务；而另一些人想少承担义务，那么他们就要放弃一部分对企业的控制权。刚刚成为合伙人的各方需要找到控制权、利益与义务之间的平衡点。但是对于成功的合伙关系来说，最重要的因素是相互信任。

峭壁宫殿中的阿纳萨奇建筑

北美最大的位于悬崖上的住所叫做峭壁宫殿。它是一座古普韦布洛建筑，位于梅萨维德国家公园。这座公园坐落于科罗拉多州的西南角，是古时阿纳萨奇部落人的居住地。

峭壁宫殿是一处令人惊叹的历史遗迹。它建在一处砂岩峭壁中镂空的区域中。该壁龛用石头搭建，约40米深，25米高，120米长。峭壁宫殿中共有150个房间，但并不是所有房间都配有壁炉。壁炉用来生火，它表明该房间供人居住。宫殿中仅有约25到30个房间配有壁炉。剩下的房间可能被用做储藏室。

峭壁宫殿中有许多开放的区域和房间，它们的作用还不得而知。在宫殿上层建有9个储藏室。因其建在高处，所以有防潮、防虫的作用。当时的人可能会把丰收时的盈余部分储藏在那里。他们使用可移动的梯子进入储藏室。

根据配有壁炉的房间数量，科学家大概估算出了居住在峭壁宫殿里的人数。他们估计，约有100到150个阿纳萨奇人曾居住在这里。

峭壁宫殿中还有一些用做会堂的圆形地下室，人们称之为大地穴。其中一个大地穴位于遗迹中央。整个大地穴被一些墙壁分隔开来，没有门或其他入口。这些墙一面涂成一个颜色，背面涂成另一个颜色。考古学家研究了这种奇特的建筑结构后认为，可能有两个不同的部落居住在这里，而这个大地穴是其汇合的地方。

考古学家根据树的年轮判断出了峭壁宫殿的年龄。结果显示，从公元1190年到1260年，峭壁宫殿一直在进行建造和翻新。他们还推算出该宫殿一个主要部分的建造历时20年。峭壁宫殿在公元1300年被废弃，原因不详。

Vocabulary Review

Ⓐ	1. Ⓐ	2. Ⓒ	3. Ⓓ	4. Ⓑ	
	5. Ⓓ	6. Ⓒ	7. Ⓓ	8. Ⓐ	
Ⓑ	1. g	2. i	3. a	4. j	5. h
	6. e	7. f	8. b	9. c	10. d

Actual Test

1. Ⓒ   2. ▣Ⓓ   3. Ⓓ   4. Ⓑ   5. Ⓐ

6. Ⓑ   7. Ⓑ   8. Ⓒ   9. Ⓐ   10. Ⓓ

11. Ⓒ   12. Ⓐ, Ⓑ, Ⓕ   13. Ⓓ   14. Ⓓ

15. Ⓑ   16. Ⓐ   17. Ⓑ   18. Ⓒ   19. Ⓓ

20. Ⓐ   21. Ⓐ   22. Ⓑ   23. Ⓑ

24. Place value Ⓐ, Ⓒ, Ⓔ / Zero Ⓓ, Ⓖ

元素周期表

人们一直都知道一些自然界天然存在的无法继续分解的物质，例如金和银。1669年，一位名叫亨宁·布兰德的德国商人在试图用一些普通金属冶炼出金子的时候，偶然发现了磷。从此，一些其他化学元素逐渐被发现。到1809年，已被发现的化学元素增加到了47种。研究元素的化学家们开始关注化学反应的模式。

1789年，安东尼·劳伦特·拉瓦锡编写了当代第一本化学课本。他列举出所有已发现的元素，并将其分为金属类和非金属类。但是这个列表中漏掉了气体，却加入了诸如光和卡路里的非化学物质。因此，这份列表并未成为一个准确的规范系统。

化学元素一个很重要的特性是其周期性：如果将元素按原子质量（质子和中子数之和）排列，反应特征类似的元素会有规律地间隔出现。元素的这种周期性最早由一位名叫亚历山大-埃米尔·贝吉耶·德·尚古尔多阿的法国地质学家发现。他设计了《螺旋图》，这是元素周期表的前身。这一体系根据元素的原子质量，将它们排列在一个螺旋形的圆柱上。有相似物理性质的元素在该柱体上竖直排成一列。然而，由于尚古尔多阿于1862年发表的论文中使用的是地质学的术语并且没有图表展示，他设计的周期体系并没有被化学界接受。

19世纪上半叶，随着新的元素不断被发现，化学家们证实了元素物理性质的规律性重复出现，并致力于研究能反映元素周期性的分类方法。1863年，一位名叫约翰·纽兰兹的英国化学家将56个已知元素分组，每一组有相同的特性。因为每一组都含有8个元素，这与钢琴上的8个音度非常相像，因此他将该体系称为"八音律法则"。但是当时的人们认为纽兰兹的理论纯属无稽之谈，不予接受。直到1919年，这种8个一组的元素分组法才开始被普遍接受。

1869年，俄国化学家德米特里·门捷列夫将这种元素周期性的基本概念发展得更为成熟。其中最重大的突破是：一个元素的两种最重要的特性——原子质量和原子序数（原子核中的质子数），可以用一个表格表示出来。这一表格后来即被称为元素周期表。

门捷列夫的周期表是受到一种单人纸牌游戏的启发。这种纸牌按同花色排成横行，按数字排成纵列。就是借用这种排列方法，门捷列夫将每7个元素分为一组。横排，他按照元素序数递增排列；纵行，按照元素相似的性质将其分为7组。因此，性质相似的金属，如金、银、铜被归在同一列。而性质相似的反应气体，如氮、氩、氪被归在另一列。一些最常见的元素（氧、氢、锂）因为原子质量较低，因此出现在周期表每一横行的首位。而稀有元素（铀、钍）因为原子核中的质子数最大，因此被安排在周期表的最末尾处。

在门捷列夫的年代，已发现的元素只有63个。而其元素周期表的卓越之处在于，它预示着，还会有新的元素被发现，来填补这张表剩下的空缺。如今，元素周期表一共有120个元素，其中92个是天然存在的，另28个是在实验室中产生的。而科学家坚信，还会有更多的元素被发现。化学元素周期表被称为"人类创造的最优雅的组织结构图"。

门捷列夫的元素周期表在今天依然适用。但是随着新元素的不断发现和产生，周期表也在不断被改动。1914年，亨利·莫斯利发现了元素序数与元素的X射线波长之间的关系，因此，他根据元素的电荷重新排列了这些元素。1945年，格伦·T·西博格也对周期表作出重大改进——他加入了一纵列锕系重金属。

计数的历史

最早反映人类开始计数的证据发现于古代的捕猎工具中。那些可追溯至公元前3万年的刻在动物骨骸中的刻痕就可以被视为一个记录系统。人们用符木记录事物。每把一只绵羊放出羊圈食草，牧羊人就会将一块鹅卵石放进一堆鹅卵石中；当羊在晚上回来时，牧羊人会把那块石头拿出来。剩下的那些石头就代表丢失的羊。但是这样的记录方式并不是真正的计数，它只是把两种物体做了一个比较而已。

埃及是最早使用真正的计数系统的古文明之一。大约从公元前3000年开始，埃及人用象形文字或者符号来表示数字。因此，那时的数字1到数字9都是由竖线组合成的。10是一个倒着的U，100是卷曲的绳索，1000是一朵莲花。

不同的社会，其计数系统的基数也各不相同。以埃及为代表的许多国家都以10为基数，这正好是左右手指个数之和。以巴比伦为代表的其他国家则以60为基数。但是这种计数系统却难以操作，因为它需要60个不同的符号来表示60个数，或者由10个数字组成的一连串数字。但是这种60进制的计数方法在如今的几何学（例如角度测量中的60秒和分；圆周的360度和矩形的180度）和计时（1分60秒，1小时60分钟）中仍被使用。

计数发展过程中，第一个重大进步是"位值"这个概念的产生。这个概念是由巴比伦人首先提出的，它被用来说明每一个数字在数字记号法中的数值。比如，如果没有位值，236这个数字在很多系统中会很难写出来，因为它需要复合的符号和笔画。但是如果每一位都有一个数值对应（在十进制的计数系统中），那么就是 6 代表 6 个 1，3 代表 30，2 代表 200。

为了使位值可以精准地表示一个数字，人们需要一个"零"来消除所有的困惑。例如，236 到底表示的是 236，还是 2360，还是 2036，或者 2306？"零"，或者说"空"位值，最早是用两个数字之间的空隙表示的。如 23_6 表示 2306。最后，人们设计了一个特殊的符号来表示零，那就是我们现在用的"0"。这个符号是为阿拉伯计数系统创造出来的，它在公元 650 年左右开始被普遍使用。

因为零和位值在数学中的重要用途，人们需要为基数中每一个数字发明一个对应的符号。因此，从 1 到 9 每一个数字都有了不同的符号，并以在每个数字后增加 0 的方式表示十位（10、20、30…）；用多个 0 表示更大的数（100、1000、10,000）。

到 17 世纪，阿拉伯数字彻底取代了长期统治西欧国家的罗马数字。目前全世界普遍使用阿拉伯数字。早期的阿拉伯数字出现在公元前 200 年的印度。当时的印度数学家发现，位值系统中如果含有表示"零"的符号，就可以使他们通过记录和运用数字来完成一些数学运算。其运算速度比算盘（一种最基本的计数工具）还要快。直到 9 世纪，这种数字运算方法才被一位名叫阿尔-花剌子模的阿拉伯数学家传出印度。他写了一篇关于数字的论文，但是这篇论文直到 12 世纪才被翻译成拉丁文，进而才在欧洲流行开来。一个名叫莱昂纳多·斐波那契的意大利人写了一些关于阿拉伯计数系统（也被称为"十进制计数法"）的书使其得到推广。簿记员和商人在阅读了这些书之后，开始将这种计数法应用在其商业买卖活动中。

在斐波那契去世后的几百年间，学者和商人针对阿拉伯计数法和算盘各自的优点一直不断辩论。随着印刷术的发明，关于阿拉伯计数法的书籍越来越普及，这也就使其成为自 1500 年至今的公认的计数法。到 1600 年左右，阿拉伯数字以其便于计算的优点，彻底取代了罗马数字。

矿物

矿物是在地球地质运动过程中自然形成的固态物质。它们主要的特征是：1) 它们是无机物（由非生物物质组成）；2) 它们都有晶体结构；3) 它们有着独特的化学成分。当矿物中的原子按照一定的几何图形重复排列时，就会出现晶体结构。所有的晶体结构都可以被归在 14 个"晶格"（即有规律的原子排列法）中，这些"晶格"能被 X 射线检测出来。

矿物的晶体结构会影响其物理性质。例如，金刚石和石墨都由同一种元素（碳）组成，但是前者是矿物中质地最硬的而后者却质软。这是因为石墨的晶体结构是由碳原子形成的层状结构，各个层之间会产生滑动；而金刚石中的碳原子却形成了环环相扣的牢固的网状结构。

有相同晶体结构的两种矿物却会有不同的化学成分。因此，岩盐和方铅矿虽然有相同的晶体结构，却是由不同的化学物质构成的。反过来，两种由相同化学元素构成的物质，其晶体结构也可能不同。例如，黄铁矿和白铁矿都是由硫化亚铁组成，但其原子排列方式却不同。

国际矿物学会表示，迄今为止，已有 4000 种矿石被发现。其中只有 150 种存量丰富；50 种被界定为"不常见"；剩下的都很稀少，有些只是一些沙粒。

矿物通常为岩石的组成部分，这些岩石中还可能有有机物。有些岩石中只含有一种矿物，例如石灰岩中的方解石；有些岩石中则可能含有多种矿物。迄今发现的几乎所有岩石中都含有一组或多组矿物（每组有 15 种矿物），包括石英、云母石和长石。

岩石中发现的矿物的种类由三个因素决定。首先，该岩石的化学成分一定是接受某种特定矿物的。例如，含有硅元素的岩石中很可能会有石英。其次，形成岩石的环境也会对其含有的矿物种类产生影响。因此，在高温、高压的火山运动中形成的岩石就可能含有花岗岩。最后，在岩石最终定型前所经历的那些地理阶段也会对矿物的分布产生影响。例如，长期暴露在潮湿或酸性的环境中，会使一些矿物被腐蚀，继而被其他矿物所取代。随着生态阶段的变迁，岩石也会分解成砂石和泥土。

矿物学家根据矿物的物理性质或化学组成将其分类。矿物有很多用以界定物理性质的衡量尺度。用"莫式硬度"将硬度划分为 1 到 10 十个等级来衡量矿物的硬度。任何一种矿物都可以被比其莫式硬度高的矿石切开或者划刻。因此，莫式硬度为 10 的金刚石就可以切开莫式硬度为 7 的石墨。光泽用于衡量矿物表面的反光性。金属的光泽比石膏强是因为后者表面呈多孔状。解理是指一种矿物沿着其天然纹理裂开的方式，断口是指矿物沿其解理层的断裂。条痕是指一种矿物划过一种特质薄板后留下的残渣的颜色。比重用以测量矿物的密度，通过比较矿物的质量和同体积的水的质量来对其进行计算。

也可以通过矿物的化学性质来将其分类。最常见的矿物是硅酸盐，因为其中含有大量的硅和氧，几乎所有岩石都可被归入此类。第二种最常见的矿物是碳酸盐，它由碳和氧组成。碳酸盐主要存在于海底浮游生物腐烂后的沉淀物中。另一种是卤化物，其主要存在于湖、海水蒸发后的干涸河床和内陆海中，例如犹他州的大盐湖。其他常见的分类包括硫酸盐、氧化物、硫化物和磷酸盐。

《ETS 新托福考试官方指南》

（第 3 版）（含光盘 1 张）

ETS（美国教育考试服务中心）编著

◎ ETS 中国唯一授权版本
◎ 新托福考试的必备权威辅导书
◎ 数百道托福考试题目及写作题库

定价：88 元　开本：16 开　页码：464 页

《新托福考试综合教程》

（含互动模考光盘 1 张 + 9 张 CD）

Deborah Phillips 著　张洪伟 等译

◎ 8 套专项训练题目，全方位强化应试技能
◎ 2 套完整的全真模拟试题，帮助考生熟悉真实考试形式

定价：148 元　开本：16 开　页码：672 页

《新托福考试备考策略与模拟试题》

（含光盘 1 张）　**Nancy Gallagher 著**

◎ 36 个包含阅读、听力、口语及写作的语言技能训练单元
◎ 4 套完整的全真强化试题
◎ 为考生设置了 15 周的学习计划，提供大量练习资料

定价：98 元　开本：16 开　页码：716 页

《新托福考试全真模考题与精解》

（含 MP3 和模考盘各 1 张）

Pamela J. Sharpe 著

◎ 详细说明听说读写四部分的特点及有效的应试策略
◎ 含 650 分钟录音光盘 1 张，包含书中所有音频内容
◎ 含模考光盘 1 张，模拟真实考试情景

定价：118 元　开本：16 开　页码：832 页

《新托福考试冲刺试题》

（含光盘 1 张）　**Nancy Gallagher 著**

◎ 6 套完整全真冲刺试题，600 道经典测试题目，体现托福考试的最新特色
◎ 文章题材、出题角度、考题类型以及话题内容等与实际考试一致
◎ 随书配有 360 分钟录音光盘 1 张，语境逼真，契合真实考场情景

定价：58 元　开本：16 开　页码：396 页

《新托福考试阅读技能与考点精练 1》

（含光盘 1 张）

Bruce Rogers 著　张洪伟 郝春梅 译

定价：38 元　开本：16 开　页码：232 页

《新托福考试阅读技能与考点精练 2》

（含光盘 1 张）

Bruce Rogers 著　张洪伟 王惠玲 译

定价：38 元　开本：16 开　页码：240 页

《新托福考试阅读技能与考点精练 3》

（含光盘 1 张）

Bruce Rogers 著　张洪伟 王惠玲 译

定价：38 元　开本：16 开　页码：264 页

◎ 所收文章题材广泛，涵盖新托福阅读的选材范围
◎ 每单元针对一种阅读技能，强化训练，解析技巧
◎ 精心设计测试题目，题材与题型分类结合
◎ 书后附习题参考答案、听力原文和单元测试
◎ 配 MP3 光盘，包含所有文章录音和听力练习

《新托福考试口语胜经》

翟少成 编著

◎ 深入剖析各个口语题型，点拨回答技巧
◎ 3 份真题详解 + 4 套模拟试题 + 5 个核心章节 + 6 大实用模板 = 实现托福口语高分

定价：49 元　开本：16 开　页码：320 页

《新托福考试听力胜经》

许杨 编著

◎ 各个听力题型深入剖析，点拨做题技巧，帮助考生重点突破，轻松应对
◎ 归纳托福听力常见概念、听力必备词汇、句型及习语、俚语，托福考点一网打尽，有的放矢

定价：45 元　开本：16 开　页码：260 页

《新托福考试写作剖析及高分范文》

包凡一 王文山 著

◎ 紧扣新托福作文考试最新趋势编写，契合中国考生备考托福作文特点

◎ 深入剖析新托福综合与独立写作考试

◎ 提供切实有效的应试技巧和备考策略

定价：48 元　开本：16 开　页码：360 页

《新托福考试写作高分速成》

陈向东 著

◎ 详细阐述托福综合写作解答的 7 大步骤及 5 大写作原则，给出独立写作 3 大写作策略和 5 大解题原则

◎ 深刻剖析写作思路，并提供解题策略及思维训练，解读真题

◎ 精心打造托福写作题型、解答原则与黄金模板

定价：35 元　开本：16 开　页码：280 页

《新托福考试核心语法》

（含光盘 1 张）

Nancy Gallagher 编著

◎ 全书涵盖 20 个重要的英语语法点，紧扣新托福考试语法要点

◎ 结合经典的例子，对各个语法点进行精辟深入的讲解

◎ 提供大量模考练习，设有计时测验

定价：50 元　开本：16 开　页码：308 页

《新托福考试阅读特训》（第二版）

Ji-Yeon Lee 著

◎ 62 篇精选文章，题材广泛，全面满足备考需求

◎ 特设仿真阅读试题，体验真实考试情境

◎ 全书结构编排科学合理，实用性强

定价：55 元　开本：16 开　页码：472 页

《新托福考试口语特训》

（另配光盘/磁带 4 盘）

Ji-Yeon Lee 著

◎ 大量真实练习语料，全面满足备考需求

◎ 提供多种练习方式，逐步掌握答题技巧

◎ 特设口语模拟试题，体验真实考试情景

定价：48 元　开本：16 开　页码：380页

《新托福考试听力特训》（第二版）

（含光盘 1 张）　　Ji-Yeon Lee 著

◎ 59 篇精选听力练习语料，题材广泛，全面满足备考需求

◎ 提供多种练习方式，逐步掌握答题技巧

◎ 特设听力模拟试题，体验真实考试情景

定价：58 元　开本：16 开　页码：452 页

《新托福考试写作特训》（第二版）

（含光盘 1 张）　　Ji-Yeon Lee 著

◎ 三个章节精练详解，两种题型各个击破

◎ 提供多种练习方式，逐步掌握写作技巧

◎ 特设仿真写作测试，体验真实考试情境

定价：46 元　开本：16 开　页码：304 页

《TOEFL iBT 口语满分模板》

邱政政　Gilbert Swann 编著

◎ 全面透析 TOEFL 考生口语弊端，帮助考生突破 TOEFL 口语瓶颈

◎ 首度构筑 TOEFL 口试题型的满分模板，方便考生高效备考

◎ 系统纠正考生口语表达的典型错误，精确提升考生的语音语调节奏，全力助推 TOEFL 口语的完美演绎

定价：25 元　开本：32 开　页码：312 页

《TOEFL iBT 听力新思维》

（含光盘 1 张）　　邱政政 编著

◎ "新""旧"TOEFL 的通用法则

◎ "M7"理论与实践的水乳交融

◎ 新 TOEFL 听力各种语音现象详析

◎ 列举新 TOEFL 听力必考场景、话题的特色词汇

定价：28 元　开本：32 开　页码：432 页

《TOEFL词汇词根 + 联想记忆法：45 天突破版》

（含光盘 1 张）　　俞敏洪 编著

◎ "词根 + 联想记忆法"实用有趣，有效提升词汇量

◎ 甄选重点词汇，紧跟 TOEFL 考试趋势

◎ 增加单词返记菜单，有助于复习和自测

◎ 再现真题例句，直击 TOEFL 考试要点

定价：45 元　开本：32 开　页码：528 页

《TOEFL iBT 词汇10000》(含光盘1张)
张洪伟　戴云　编著

◎ 源于真题目——收录托福真题的必备词汇与经典例句
◎ 奉献真经典——凝结托福名师的教学感悟与智慧结晶

定价：45元　开本：16开　页码：444页

《TOEFL iBT 听力词汇小伴侣》
邱政政　戴懿德　编著

定价：18元　开本：32开　页码：388页

《TOEFL iBT 口语词汇小伴侣》
张洪伟　翟少成　编著

定价：15元　开本：32开　页码：280页

《TOEFL iBT 阅读词汇小伴侣》
张洪伟　蔡青　编著

定价：15元　开本：32开　页码：204页

《托福写作词汇小伴侣》
张洪伟　戴云　编著

定价：16元　开本：32开　页码：332页

◎ 紧跟 TOEFL 考试趋势，权威指点
◎ 精选常考核心词汇，针对性强
◎ 分类词汇专业全面，重点突出
◎ 精选 TOEFL 常用短语与习惯搭配，实用性佳

《词以类记——TOEFL iBT 词汇》
(含光盘1张)　　张红岩　编著

◎ TOEFL iBT 最新词汇：覆盖听说读写
◎ 按学科和意群分类：细分至最小同义词区间
◎ 特配精美图片：辅助视觉联想

定价：35元　开本：32开　页码：424页

《TOEFL 核心词汇 21 天突破》
李笑来　编著

◎ 21 天不长——如果不背单词的话一如既往，21 天会很快过去——无所事事的日子总是轻松愉快
◎ 21 天不短——如果去背单词的话然而最终，21 天还是会很快过去——不同的是你已经脱胎换骨

定价：29元　开本：32开　页码：544页

《TOEFL 词汇精选》
张红岩　编著

◎ 词根词缀法促进高效记忆
◎ 最新更新词库，选词精确
◎ 融最近词汇测试重点对策

定价：23元　开本：32开　页码：448页

《TOEFL 词汇》
王玉梅　编著

◎ 紧跟 TOEFL 考试新趋势，收录词汇词频最新统计
◎ 科学选词，精确释义，同义词、派生词扫除记忆障碍

定价：30元　开本：32开　页码：456页

《TOEFL 词组》
王玉梅　包凡一　编著

◎ 紧跟 TOEFL 考试新趋势，常考词组一网打尽
◎ 释义精准，例句时新，配合热身练习，事半功倍

定价：28元　开本：32开　页码：392页

《TOEFL iBT 听力习语必备》
许杨　编著

◎ 习语来源生活，实用地道
◎ 例句囊括考点，详尽精妙
◎ 标准美语录音，字字清晰

定价：24元　开本：32开　页码：272页

《TOEFL iBT 语法精要》
戴云　编著

◎ 托福语法，逐一精解，涵盖全面
◎ 实考例句，详尽丰富，针对性强
◎ 名师指导，全面解析，轻松应试

定价：20元　开本：32开　页码：280页

《TOEFL iBT 高分作文》（含光盘 1 张）

李笑来　Johnson Weber　编著

◎ 中美英语言专家精心打造
◎ 把握新托福作文高分思维
◎ 185 真题范文全面覆盖最新题库

定价：48 元　开本：16 开　页码：432 页

《挑战 TOEFL iBT 作文满分》

许轶　编著

◎ 全面、系统地引进美国名校一流写作训练方法
◎ 适用于各个层次的考生，提供针对不同水平的因材施教的完全解决方案

定价：30 元　开本：16 开　页码：260 页

《10 天搞定 TOEFL 作文》

张红岩　编著

◎ 凝聚名师多年教学精华
◎ 经数十万学生实战检验
◎ 应对新一代 TOEFL 作文考试
◎ 演练 10 日，收获高分

定价：10 元　开本：32 开　页码：160 页

《新托福考试专项进阶——初级听力》

（附 MP3 光盘）

定价：42 元　开本：16 开　页码：288 页

《新托福考试专项进阶——中级听力》

（附 MP3 光盘）

定价：45 元　开本：16 开　页码：340 页

《新托福考试专项进阶——高级听力》

（附 MP3 光盘）

定价：45 元　开本：16 开　页码：348 页

《新托福考试专项进阶——初级口语》

（附 MP3 光盘）

定价：42 元　开本：16 开　页码：296 页

《新托福考试专项进阶——中级口语》

（附 MP3 光盘）

定价：38 元　开本：16 开　页码：244 页

《新托福考试专项进阶——高级口语》

（附 MP3 光盘）

定价：42 元　开本：16 开　页码：288 页

《新托福考试专项进阶——初级阅读》

定价：35 元　开本：16 开　页码：308 页

《新托福考试专项进阶——中级阅读》

定价：38 元　开本：16 开　页码：344 页

《新托福考试专项进阶——高级阅读》

定价：40 元　开本：16 开　页码：368 页

《新托福考试专项进阶——初级写作》

（附 MP3 光盘）

定价：40 元　开本：16 开　页码：268 页

《新托福考试专项进阶——中级写作》

（附 MP3 光盘）

定价：38 元　开本：16 开　页码：248 页

《新托福考试专项进阶——高级写作》

（附 MP3 光盘）

定价：42 元　开本：16 开　页码：304 页

《新托福考试专项进阶——阅读模拟试题(上)》

定价：36 元　开本：16 开　页码：252 页

《新托福考试专项进阶——阅读模拟试题(下)》

定价：36 元　开本：16 开　页码：252 页

《新托福考试专项进阶——听力模拟试题(上)》（附 MP3 光盘）

定价：40 元　开本：16 开　页码：256 页

《新托福考试专项进阶——听力模拟试题(下)》（附 MP3 光盘）

定价：36 元　开本：16 开　页码：220 页

◎ 《新托福考试专项进阶》系列丛书从托福考试所考查的听、说、读、写四项技能入手，为考生提供了详尽的考试指导，并将各技能分为初、中、高三级，通过独特的"进阶训练"方式，再辅以大量练习，让考生逐步掌握托福实考的技巧，同时切实提高英语实际运用能力，从而在短期内轻松取得托福高分。本丛书内容编排由易到难，循序渐进，实战性强，是不可多得的托福备考资料。

◎ 本丛书引进自韩国多乐园出版社。该社成立于 1977 年，在韩国英语教育出版领域始终处于领军地位。本丛书被韩国众多学校和培训机构指定为课堂教材，在托福考生中享有较高声誉。

《译艺：英汉双向笔译》

陈文伯 编著

结合翻译文本讲翻译理论，通俗易懂；既讲英译汉，又讲汉译英，双管齐下；外交学院教授陈文伯老师长期致力于英汉翻译的教学与研究之结晶；译法要点讲解精辟而细致，全面提升翻译水平；所选文本或趣味横生，或极富哲理，学习翻译方法的同时获得美的阅读体验。

定价：32 元　开本：32开　页码：392 页

《英语论文成功写作》

孙钰 （美）Sheryl Holt 编著

本书着重介绍专业英语论文的写作。其宗旨是帮助中国科研人员、研究生和留学生提高专业英语论文写作质量，促进与国际同行间的交流，增加论文发表的几率。

定价：25 元　开本：32开　页码：242 页

《16 天英语入门》

张隽 卓佳 编著

◎ 针对成人英语零起点学习编写
◎ 纠正英语发音，掌握语音知识
◎ 口腔、口形图利于读者模仿发音要领
◎ 语法讲解深入浅出，易于初学者掌握

定价：16 元　开本：32开　页码：156 页

《美国名校毕业演说集萃》

许轶 编著

本书收录了美国著名大学的毕业演说。这些站在美国顶级名校毕业典礼讲台上的演说者们，来自政界、商界、学术界、娱乐界……他们在这里"齐聚一堂"，侃侃而谈，以他们的视角、经历和感悟来传道、授业、解惑。

定价：20 元　开本：32开　页码：224 页

《生命如一泓清水》　　俞敏洪 著

全书分为四部分：生命如一泓清水、家的感觉、新东方的日子、在路上——新东方梦想之旅日记。除了畅谈生活、工作中的深彻感悟，全书首次记录了作者家庭成员之间、以及与父母、妻儿间的真挚感情。此外，本书第四部分以日记的形式详尽地记录了新东方梦想之旅的全过程。

定价：22 元　开本：16 开　页码：336 页

《我的哈佛日记》　　张杨 著

一个出生在 80 年代的年轻人，带着梦想独立地自我规划，走进了中国和世界上的顶级学府。这本书既沉淀了他生活中最真实的感受，也记录了他通过激烈的考验和出国申请的竞争，靠自己的努力蜕变成一个年轻的"国际中国人"的独特历程。

定价：25 元　开本：32 开　页码：304 页

《我的美利坚本科岁月》马俏 著

本书记述了作者从高考前的抉择到美国一流名校的留学生涯，从充实、和谐的美国社区见闻到充满冒险及人文关怀的异国游记，从单纯、快乐的校园生活到险象环生的求职之路，全方位展现了一位优秀的 80 后留学生的奋斗路程。同时，通过作者对生活的细腻观察，从一个女留学生的视角展示了现代美国及美洲国家的生活风貌。

定价：25 元　开本：32 开　页码：304 页

《带你去耶鲁》

曹蕴 马征 著

总统的摇篮——美国常青藤名校耶鲁大学。这里，是美国第一所具有授予博士学位资格的大学；这里，拥有全美大学中最早的博物馆、最古老的艺术馆和全世界规模第二大的大学图书馆；这里，走出了普林斯顿、康奈尔等著名大学的创始人，被誉为"美国学院之母"；这就是缔造了 300 多年传奇历史，以"光明与真知"为校训的学术圣殿——耶鲁大学。让我们一起走进耶鲁，揭开她神秘的面纱……

定价：22 元　开本：32 开　页码：252 页

《永不言败》　　俞敏洪 著

这本书里的俞敏洪，不仅是一位站在中国民办教育行业前沿的领军人物，也不仅是新东方团队的领导者和新东方神话的缔造者，他更是一位睿智的长者、一位辛勤的教师、一位慈祥的父亲、一位千百万学子心中可敬可爱的朋友。他会为你指出《生命的北斗星》，引导你突破《局限》，避开《习惯的陷阱》，最终走出人生的沙漠……

定价：18 元　开本：16 开　页码：200 页

读者反馈表

尊敬的读者：

您好！非常感谢您对**新东方大愚图书**的信赖与支持，希望您抽出宝贵的时间填写这份反馈表，以便帮助我们改进工作，今后能为您提供更优秀的图书。谢谢！

为了答谢您对我们的支持，我们将对反馈的信息进行随机抽奖活动，当月将有 20 位幸运读者可获赠**《新东方英语》**期刊一份。我们将定期在新东方大愚图书网站 www.dogwood.com.cn 公布获奖者名单并及时寄出奖品，敬请关注。

来信请寄： 北京市海淀区海淀东三街 2 号欧美汇大厦 19 层 北京新东方大愚文化传播有限公司
图书部收

邮编：100080 　　　　　　　　　　　　　　　　　　E-mail: bj62605588@163.com

姓名：_____ 　年龄：_____ 　职业：_____ 　教育背景：_____ 　邮编：_____

通讯地址：_____ 　　联系电话：_____

E-mail: _____ 　　您所购买的书籍的名称是：_____

---

1. 您是通过何种渠道得知本书的（可多选）：
   □书店 □新东方网站 □大愚网站 □朋友推荐 □老师推荐 □@新东方大愚图书(http://weibo.com/dogwood)
   □其他_____

2. 您是从何处购买到此书的？　□书店 □新东方大愚淘宝网 □其他网上书店 □其他_____

3. 您购买此书的原因（可多选）：
   □封面设计 □书评广告 □正文内容 □图书价格 □新东方品牌 □新东方名师 □其他_____

4. 您对本书的封面设计满意程度：□很满意 □比较满意 □一般 □不满意 □改进建议_____

5. 您认为本书的内文在哪些方面还需改进？□结构编排 □难易程度 □内容丰富性 □内文版式 □其他_____

6. 本书最令您满意的地方：□内文 □封面 □价格 □纸张

7. 您对本书的推荐率：□没有 □1人 □1-3人 □3-5人 □5人以上

8. 您更希望我们为您提供哪些方面的英语类图书？
   □少儿英语类 □初高中英语类 □四六级类 □考研类 □IELTS 类 □TOEFL 类 □GRE、GMAT 类 □SAT、SSAT 类
   □留学申请类 □BEC、TOEIC 类 □实用英语类 □商务英语类 □休闲欣赏类 □英语读物类 □其他_____
   您目前最希望我们为您出版的图书是：_____

9. 您在学习英语过程中最需要哪些方面的帮助？（可多选）
   □词汇 □听力 □口语 □阅读 □写作 □翻译 □语法 □其他_____

10. 您最喜欢的英语图书品牌：_____
    理由是(可多选)：□版式漂亮 □内容实用 □难度适宜 □价格适中 □对考试有帮助 □其他_____

11. 您对新东方图书品牌的评价：_____

12. 您对本书(或其他新东方图书)的意见和建议：_____
    _____
    _____

13. 填表时间：_____ 年 _____ 月 ___ 日